General Ulysses S. Grant

———•★•———

General Ulysses S. Grant

The Soldier and the Man

★ ★ ★

EDWARD G. LONGACRE

DA CAPO PRESS
A Member of the Perseus Books Group

Designed by Trish Wilkinson
Set in 10.5-point Fairfield Light by the Perseus Books Group

Library of Congress Cataloging-in-Publication Data

Longacre, Edward G., 1946–
    General Ulysses S. Grant : the soldier and the man / Edward G. Longacre. — 1st Da Capo Press ed.
        p. cm.
    Includes bibliographical references and index.
    ISBN-13: 978-0-306-81269-9 (hardcover : alk. paper)
    ISBN-10: 0-306-81269-X (hardcover : alk. paper) 1. Grant, Ulysses S. (Ulysses Simpson), 1822–1885. 2. Generals—United States—Biography. 3. United States. Army—Biography. 4. United States—History—Civil War, 1861–1865—Biography. I. Title.
E672.L86 2006
973.7'3092—dc22
[B]   2006009848

First Da Capo Press edition 2006

Maps by Paul Dangel

Published by Da Capo Press
A Member of the Perseus Books Group
http://www.dacapopress.com

Da Capo Press books are available at special discounts for bulk purchases in the U.S. by corporations, institutions, and other organizations. For more information, please contact the Special Markets Department at the Perseus Books Group, 11 Cambridge Center, Cambridge, MA 02142, or call (800) 255-1514 or (617) 252-5298, or e-mail special.markets@perseusbooks.com

1 2 3 4 5 6 7 8 9 — 09 08 07 06

For my mother's "only daughter," Joanne Dixon

CONTENTS

LIST OF MAPS

PREFACE

THIS BOOK DOES NOT PURPORT TO BE THE DEFINITIVE BIOGRAPHY OF ULYSSES S. Grant. One reason is that it covers his life only from birth through the end of the Civil War; any examination of Grant's presidential administration is best left to political historians. Furthermore, the present study, which highlights those events that materially influenced the development of Grant as a soldier and a man, is too brief to satisfy readers seeking a micro history of his military career. Recent biographies, including William S. McFeely's award-winning *Grant* (1981), Geoffrey Perret's readable *Ulysses S. Grant, Soldier & President* (1997), Brooks D. Simpson's incisive *Ulysses S. Grant: Triumph over Adversity* (2000), and Jean Edward Smith's magisterial *Grant* (2001), offer deeper, broader, and more detailed coverage of their subject's military operations.

In place of broad scope and heavy detail, *Ulysses S. Grant: The Soldier and the Man* concentrates on topics and issues that appear to have received insufficient attention or which, in the hands of other biographers, have generated more heat than light. These include Grant's boyhood and early married life, especially his years in Missouri and Illinois following his 1854 resignation from the army; his moral, ethical, and religious views; his conflicting attitudes toward the profession he had adopted; his relationships with his parents, his in-laws, and his wartime superiors and subordinates; and, especially, his weakness for alcohol, which, although exaggerated and misrepresented by many chroniclers, exerted a major influence on his military and civilian careers.

Although sensitive to the controversial nature of the subject and aware of the clamor it continues to provoke among Grant's more vociferous advocates, I am convinced that the general was, under criteria established by present-day medical specialists, an alcoholic. Grant was neither a constant drinker nor—except on a few well-publicized occasions—a falling-down drunk. At times, he appears to have drunk moderately and without noticeable effect. When he did imbibe to excess, he often made himself ill, which should have served as a deterrent to repeat occurrences. On few occasions did his consumption of alcohol cloud his faculties or impair his motor skills, and no one who wrote of Grant's personal habits contended that his drinking prevented him from discharging his ordained duties. Many of the anecdotes on which his reputation as a drunkard were built are exaggerations or fabrications, the fruit of army gossip that prized sensationalism over truth. That said, Grant became inebriated on too many occasions, and too often proved unable to stop drinking short of fortuitous or designed intervention, to be absolved of the charge of alcoholism. Quarreling over whether or not he had a drinking problem is less important to an appreciation of his strivings and accomplishments than determining how the habit affected him throughout the Civil War, which is what the present study hopes to accomplish.

In a very real sense, this book originated with my April 1982 participation in a panel session devoted to the subject of Grant's drinking problems presented during the annual meeting of the Organization of American Historians. Fellow panelists included Professor John Y. Simon of Southern Illinois University, the president of the Ulysses S. Grant Association and editor of the Grant Papers project; and Professor McFeely, whose portrait of Grant would soon be awarded the Pulitzer Prize for biography. The session involved the critiquing of a paper prepared by Professor Lyle W. Dorsett, then a member of the faculty of the University of Denver. Professor Dorsett's paper, a serious treatment of Grant's tendency to alcoholism later published in a scholarly journal, helped to shape, and in many ways to reorient, my thinking on the subject. More than two decades later, his observations continue to resonate with me. Although some of my opinions on the subject differ slightly from his, his groundbreaking research has materially influenced the thinking that went into this book.

It seems necessary—at least advisable—to state that in presenting my view of Grant's life and career I intend neither to condemn nor to vilify, but to illuminate and explain. At bottom, I hope to show why a habit that has compromised, crippled, and killed millions of souls since the dawn of time failed to prevent Ulysses Grant from gaining the confidence of his soldiers, his president, and the people of the North, and from attaining the highest honors an American soldier can aspire to.

★ ★ ★

In addition to Professor Dorsett (now a member of the faculty of the Beeson Divinity School at Samford University), numerous persons lent support and encouragement during the planning and researching of this book. Among others, I thank my editor, Robert Pigeon; my cartographer, Paul Dangel; my pictorial specialist, Bill Godfrey; my colleagues in the Air Force History Program, especially Bob Oliver; and my research assistant (who is also my wife), Melody Ann Longacre. Further, I acknowledge my indebtedness to the U. S. Grant Association, Carbondale, Ill., and to the staffs of the National Archives, the Library of Congress (especially the Manuscript Division), the New York Public Library, the United States Military Academy's Archives and Special Collections, the Historical Society of Delaware, the Doheny Library of the University of Southern California, the New York Public Library, the Gilder Lehrman Collection, the Historical Society of Pennsylvania, the College of William and Mary's Swem Library, and the interlibrary loan desks at the Bateman Library, Langley Air Force Base, Virginia, and the Virgil I. Grissom Library, Newport News, Virginia. I thank those who guided, accompanied, or assisted me during my trips to the various battlefields on which I traced Grant's steps, scrutinized his decisions, and attempted to discern his intentions. Finally, I thank those physicians and health officials who helped me attain a deeper understanding of alcoholism, especially in the context of nineteenth-century American society.

★ *Chapter 1* ★

"THAT BOY WILL MAKE A GENERAL!"

Eɴ ʀᴏᴜᴛᴇ ꜰʀᴏᴍ Nᴇᴡ Yᴏʀᴋ Sᴛᴀᴛᴇ ᴛᴏ ʜɪꜱ ɴᴇᴡ ᴅᴜᴛʏ ꜱᴛᴀᴛɪᴏɴ ᴀᴛ Fᴏʀᴛ Leavenworth, Kansas, Major James Longstreet of the U.S. Army Paymaster Department stopped over in St. Louis in the late summer of 1858. He spent a few days in the company of comrades he had not seen in years, some not since their days together at the United States Military Academy. One rainy afternoon, two of these officers called at Longstreet's rooms in the Planters House hotel. Hours of lively conversation followed: The trio exchanged war stories, matched recollections of shared events, and inquired after mutual friends. Choice cigars and alcoholic beverages added to the spirit of conviviality.

As the afternoon wore on, someone suggested a four-handed game of poker known as "brag." The idea found immediate favor, but where to find a fourth on short notice? Captain E. B. Holloway of the 8th U.S. Infantry offered to scare up someone who would fill the bill. Leaving the hotel, Holloway scanned the street outside for a likely prospect. Almost at once his eye fell upon a bearded, slightly stooped civilian in his late thirties or early forties, clad in a well-worn suit of clothes. An astonished Holloway recognized the man as a fellow member of the West Point class of 1843: Ulysses Grant, formerly a captain in the 4th Infantry who had resigned his commission a few years earlier under something of a cloud. The classmates exchanged warm greetings, after which Grant followed the captain into the hotel and up the stairs to Longstreet's room. Their coming ushered in a new round of hand-shaking and shoulder-clapping, for the South Carolina–born Longstreet, although one class ahead of Grant at the Academy, had been one of his closest friends in the cadet corps.

When the first wave of camaraderie subsided, Grant joined the officers at the card table. Throughout the game that followed, Longstreet snatched

1

covert glances at his old friend, noting his gnarly beard and rumpled dress. Grant appeared "a little stouter" than he had when Longstreet last saw him, "a little grayer perhaps, but [otherwise] quite the same as ever." What troubled Longstreet was the impression Grant gave of someone "looking for something to do." He had heard that the erstwhile captain was living a few miles from St. Louis, where he was farming, hauling wood, and doing "whatever he could otherwise to make a living." Longstreet, who a decade earlier had attended Grant's wedding here in St. Louis, knew that he had a newborn son as well as three older children—too many mouths to feed, Longstreet suspected, for a breadwinner of his caliber.[1]

These thoughts distressed Longstreet, but he tried to keep from showing his concern. Nor did he make reference to Grant's return to civil life. As he later told the biographer and essayist Hamlin Garland, Grant's old colleagues "knew of his retirement from the army, and we had heard more or less of the gossip concerning this event, but everyone knew Grant to be an honorable man and we knew he could not have done anything disreputable. . . . Nothing was said of his retirement; he did not mention it and, of course, we did not." Even so, because the abuse of alcohol had much to do with the unhappy event, Longstreet may have hesitated, if only briefly, when passing the bottle to his friend.[2]

Once the game began, Grant was mostly silent, as if he had nothing of importance to offer. He gave short answers to the few questions directed his way—the health of his wife and children, the local weather, the price of wheat and corn. Longstreet noted that Grant grew animated only when the conversation turned to their shared experiences in the Mexican War. He appeared to have fond memories of those days; after all, his life had been more settled and defined then, less dependent on the vicissitudes of the civilian economy.

When the game broke up and Grant took his leave, Longstreet, who believed the man "really in needy circumstances," was saddened to see him go. If he could have done so without embarrassing them both, he would have offered Grant some money. Instead, it was Longstreet who left with a fattened pocketbook. The following day, as the major stood on the street outside the hotel, Grant reappeared. Without preamble, he pressed into Longstreet's hand a five-dollar gold piece, which, Longstreet noted, "he insisted that I should take . . . in payment of a debt of honor over 15 years old." The older man tried to refuse the money, suggesting, as discreetly as possible, that Grant "was out of the service and more in need of it" than he was. But his friend would not hear of it. "I cannot live with anything in my possession which is not mine," he explained. Longstreet had no rejoinder: "Seeing the determination in the man's face, and in order to save him mortification, I took the money, and shaking hands we parted."[3]

As Grant shambled off, Longstreet must have reflected upon what a terrible mistake his friend had made, wasting his finished education, throwing away an honorable career. More depressing still was the likely prospect that Longstreet would never see or hear from him again.

★ ★ ★

Rivers would play a major role in Ulysses Grant's rise to success and celebrity. The first of these of any importance was the wide and swift-moving Ohio—in the early nineteenth century a major conduit of transportation and commerce between the East and the Old Northwest—which flowed barely a hundred yards from the door of the one-story wooden house in the hamlet of Point Pleasant, where Grant was born on April 27, 1822. He was the eldest child of Jesse Root Grant and Hannah Simpson Grant, who would rear five other children, three girls and two boys.

Grant's siblings were born in Georgetown, twenty-five miles from Point Pleasant, where the family relocated when their firstborn was eighteen months old. In moving from well-established Clermont County to newly settled Brown County, the Grants did not stray more than seven miles from the river that brought them and their neighbors prosperity, or, at least, the hope of prosperity. The banks of White Oak Creek, an Ohio confluent, abounded in the oak and ash that would furnish the tanning bark critical to Jesse Grant's trade. The tanyard he established there proved so profitable that within a year he had accumulated the funds he needed to erect a sturdy two-story brick house on Cross Street, just off the center square of the rough-hewn village that would soon become a county seat.[4]

Ulysses' father had led a hard life, but he had persevered to become a man of means and civic standing. A native of Westmoreland County, Pennsylvania, Jesse Grant was proud to trace his lineage to a Puritan couple who had departed England's West Country for Massachusetts Bay in 1630 and, five years later, for the wilds of the Connecticut River Valley. In 1799, when Jesse was five, his parents rafted down the Monongahela River to Fawcettstown, in the newly opened Northwest Territory. In that fertile corner of what would become the state of Ohio, Jesse's well-educated father, who had served as an officer in the Revolutionary War, seemed likely to prosper. But during the war, Noah Grant had acquired a fondness for liquor, and the hold it exerted on him not only drained away the profits he had accumulated from farming and cobbling but also gobbled up a considerable inheritance. Appalled by the degree of his father's dissipation and shaken by its effects on the family, at an early age Noah's eldest son shunned his example, taking a vow of sobriety, industry, and prosperity.

When Jesse's mother (Noah's second wife) died in 1805, the family suffered an irreparable fracture. Soon afterward, the wayward inebriate relocated once again, this time to Maysville, Kentucky, where his eldest son, Peter, had gone to establish a tanning operation. Only the younger children accompanied Noah to the Bluegrass State; their older siblings, including Jesse, were left behind to make their own way in the world. Jesse found work as an itinerant farmhand in and near Fawcettstown and then, from fourteen to sixteen, in the employ of one of his relatives, Judge George Tod of the Ohio Supreme Court. Exposure to the judge's Youngstown-area home taught the uneducated youngster the joys of learning and instilled in him an appreciation of life's finer things—thoroughbred stock, damask curtains, and dishware made not of rough-hewn pewter but of fine china. Jesse determined that he, too, would rise to such a state, not as a farmer but as an artisan in a field that promised material wealth as well as an opportunity to raise one's standing in the community.[5]

When he was sixteen, he followed the lead of his older brother by learning the business of tanning, a trade much in demand in young America. The work was hard and dirty—the long hours left its operatives weary and aching as well as reeking of tanning acid and the blood of slaughtered animals—but it was a job that Jesse found equal to his abilities, though not to his liking. He moved to Maysville, where for five years he apprenticed himself to Peter Grant, learning not only the basics of the profession but the nuances that would enable him to produce finer goods than the average tanner. At the end of his apprenticeship, he returned to Ohio to work for another tannery operator, the abolitionist Owen Brown. Jesse appreciated Brown's enterprise and industry; he also shared his employer's view of America's "peculiar institution" (he was fond of declaring: "I would not own slaves, and I would not live where there were slaves"). Yet Jesse eschewed the extremist position of Brown's son, John, an increasingly fervid antislaveryite who, forty-four years later, would help usher in a long and extremely bloody war.[6]

By 1817, Jesse had become a partner in a tannery in Ravenna, Ohio. The business was so profitable that in less than two years he had amassed fifteen hundred dollars—no fortune but enough to make him one of the wealthiest residents of his village. Then he watched his nest egg dwindle to nothing. An outbreak of ague, a debilitating disease akin to malaria, laid him low for many months and took not only his savings but his share in the local business. Upon recovering, an undeterred Jesse started over, hiring himself out once again, this time as a tanner's assistant in Point Pleasant.

As he slowly regained his lost wealth, Jesse, who judged a high percentage of his neighbors to be plodders and ne'er-do-wells in the mold of his father, accumulated a vast store of pride and self-esteem. His strong opinions, which he voiced just as strongly, and his tendency to contentiousness embroiled him in frequent disputes with his neighbors and involved him in more than a few lawsuits. These contretemps failed to alter his view of himself as a man of vision and talent. Although lacking a formal education, he had, in addition to strong hands and a robust work ethic, an inquisitive mind and a thirst for knowledge. In young adulthood, he developed a passion for national politics that found an outlet in his fervent support of Andrew Jackson's presidential campaigns. Jesse was bitterly disappointed by the failure of "Old Hickory" to gain the White House in 1824, but he was elated by his champion's successful effort four years later.[7]

To be accepted as a reputable member of his community, a man needed to marry well and raise a family in whom he could take pride. With the same single-mindedness he had demonstrated in his work, in his twenty-fifth year Jesse Grant began to seek an acceptable mate. In the summer of 1820, following several aborted courtships and one broken engagement, he made the acquaintance of an eligible young woman, Hannah Simpson, the daughter of a well-respected farmer whose father had emigrated from the north of Ireland in the middle of the previous century. Hannah, who was twenty-two when she met Jesse Grant, was born in Montgomery County, Pennsylvania, from which place her family had moved to southwestern Ohio. In the hamlet of Bantam, ten miles from Point Pleasant, her father began a successful husbandry; by 1820, his once-meager homestead had expanded to six hundred acres.[8]

Although sometimes characterized as a "handsome" woman, Hannah was no beauty; even Jesse would describe her as "a plain unpretending country girl," although one "remarkable for good sense, attention to her domestic duties, and serious Christian character, blended with easy manners." These were qualities appealing to an up-and-coming young man not yet established in business. For her part, Hannah, who by the standards of the time was hovering on the edge of old maidenhood, was willing to overlook Jesse's sharply drawn features, loudly voiced views, and overweening ambition. She persuaded her mother to approve his suit, and Mrs. Simpson brought her reluctant husband to the same point of view. On June 24, 1821, the couple was joined in wedlock in the Simpson family home.[9]

It may not have been a love match in the strictest sense, but the marriage was a success, primarily because it benefited both parties. Hannah found Jesse outwardly gruff but essentially the kindhearted and loving husband she had believed he would become. Jesse improved through constant exposure to Hannah's quiet, amiable nature. Hannah softened some of his rougher edges, although not always to a degree noticeable to those neighbors with whom he continued to feud. Even more remarkably, she enabled the family to retain the good opinion of those Jesse alienated by boasting of his material wealth or declaiming against federalism and slavery.

Hannah Simpson Grant helped her spouse in material ways as well. Better educated than he, she taught him grammar and syntax, skills that enabled him to hone his ability to orate in local debating societies and improve the quality of the letters he fired off to editors on a variety of political issues. Coming as she did from a pious family of Pennsylvania Presbyterians and, later, Ohio Methodists, she induced Jesse to profess his Christianity openly and to attend church regularly. In time, he became a respected member of the Methodist Church, whose teachings had a broad appeal to middle-class Americans, especially artisans equally committed to the salvation of their souls and the improvement of their social status.

More than anything else, Hannah helped Jesse prepare himself for fatherhood. Lacking as he did a model whose parental skills were worthy of adoption and convinced that his wife possessed an intuitive ability to nurture, Jesse turned to her for advice and support in rearing the children who were born of their union. His faith in his wife's parenting skills was unshakable, but in some respects it may also have been misplaced.[10]

★ ★ ★

Some of his biographers, especially those who wrote while their subject was alive, claimed that Ulysses Simpson Grant was a privileged son who enjoyed an idyllic upbringing. Yet he provided little evidence to support this contention. His published memoirs run to more than 250,000 words, but his parents are mentioned in only a few paragraphs. He explains only that he never endured "any scolding or punishing by [his] parents; no objection to rational enjoyments, such as fishing, going to the creek a mile away to swim in summer, taking a horse and visiting [his] grandparents in the adjoining county, fifteen miles off." In fact, he appears to have suffered none of the restraints imposed upon his brothers, Samuel Simpson (known in the family by his middle name) and Orvil, and his sisters, Clara, Virginia ("Nellie"), and

Mary Frances. The younger children were regularly disciplined, initiated into the Methodist faith, and compelled to attend the local meeting-house. Ulysses was never forced to do any chores other than those he performed with the aid of horsepower. These he enjoyed, for from childhood he displayed a love of horses, an understanding of their habits, and an appreciation of their benefits to man. Nor was he baptized or forced to attend church.[11]

Although later in life he evinced a commitment to the teachings of Methodism, the absence of prodding ensured that he never made regular appearances in church. Some chroniclers attempt to explain this lapse on the part of his devout parents by claiming that they were sensitive to his deep aversion to music, be it in the form of hymns, songs, or orchestral works. Throughout his life, Ulysses Grant would claim to be profoundly tone-deaf. Moreover, he would complain of the ill effects of music on his physical health, suggesting that it provoked, or at least intensified, the migraine headaches from which he continually suffered.[12]

Citing tonal distress as a reason for his parents' lack of interest in Grant's religious upbringing strains credulity. It is more plausible to suggest that their behavior indicates a studied neglect of their firstborn, a neglect that did not extend to their other children. This behavior appears to have been the norm from the boy's earliest days. An oft-told story relates that when he was an infant, Ulysses crawled into the back yard, where he frolicked among tethered horses with well-shod hooves. When concerned neighbors alerted Hannah to the danger, she explained that she was too busy to tend to him just then but insisted that the child's way with animals would protect him until she could tear herself away.[13]

Hannah's apparent indifference to her son may also explain why he went for several weeks without a given name. It took a gathering of family members at the Grant home in Point Pleasant to redress the oversight. Hannah and one of her sisters proposed as a first name Albert, in honor of Albert Gallatin, the Swiss-born statesman, diplomat, and financier who had left an indelible mark on his adopted Pennsylvania, and, in fact, on the entire nation, during the first quarter of the century. Someone else suggested Theodore, but eventually Hiram, the choice of the boy's father, won out. The child's step-grandmother, a lover of literature and history, supplied a middle name—Ulysses, the hero of Homer's immortal epic.

The boy's first name was a favorite with the menfolk of the family, but neither its bearer nor his mother admired it. Hannah would call her son "Ulysses," a name often shortened to "Ulys." When he grew old enough to appreciate how his first and middle names might be misused, the boy developed an aversion to the embarrassing acronym "HUG." Moreover, Ulysses was easily corruptible to "Useless," as indeed it was in the mouths of neighboring children given to teasing him. Over time, however, he adopted his mother's preference for his middle name, as did everyone else in his family.[14]

Jesse Grant's original preference for Hiram—which is of Jewish origin and means "The Exalted One"—is understandable. From the boy's earliest days, his father exalted him in word and deed, praising his gifts—real and imagined—to anyone who would listen. Jesse boasted about each of his children, but Ulysses was his favorite, mainly because he would attempt to do whatever his father asked of him. When the child was no more than two, Jesse was showing him off to his neighbors when someone happened by with a loaded pistol. Intrigued about how his son would stand the fire, Jesse borrowed the weapon and curled Ulysses' tiny finger around the trigger. Instead of reacting fearfully to the report, the child cried out in delight, begging for a chance to "fick it again!" While the proud father beamed, an amazed bystander is supposed to have exclaimed: "That boy will make a general!"[15]

A few years later, an itinerant phrenologist, when examining the contours of the boy's cranium during a public exhibition of his skills, supposedly uttered an even more momentous prophecy, pronouncing Ulysses a future president of the United States. The "professor" was wont to make the same prediction in the presence of other men of means who appeared inordinately proud of their offspring. Even so, it was observed that a visibly pleased Jesse Grant rewarded the man handsomely for his prediction.[16]

In later youth, Ulysses gave further indication of precociousness. When he was eleven, a traveling circus came to Georgetown, its leading attraction being a "mischievous pony, trained to go round the ring like lightning," throwing any boy who attempted to ride him bareback. To please his father, Ulysses volunteered to try his equestrian skills. Clinging tightly to the pony's sides and mane in the manner of an experienced jockey, he stuck to its back no matter how fast it galloped, how tightly it turned, or how wildly the audience reacted. Hoping to distract the boy and break his concentration, the ringmaster induced a trained monkey to leap onto Ulysses' head and shoulders, where he perched for the balance of the exhibition. The added burden failed to dismount the rider. After a few more rounds, the ringmaster called a halt and the crowd exploded into applause.[17]

Ulysses' feat had been made possible by his uncanny skill at handling horses, a skill that came to him so early that it made him appear born to the saddle. As he frequently asserted: "If I can mount a horse, I can ride him." Throughout Brown County he was widely known for his ability to calm the most fractious animals and break to the saddle even the wildest of mustangs. One of Grant's earliest biographers, Albert D. Richardson, claimed that by the time his subject was ten,

> horse-jockeys who had steeds suffering from a distemper, which was relieved by riding them so fast as to heat them, used to bring the animals to Georgetown, for the tanner's son to try them for a few miles at the breakneck gallop, in which his heart delighted. Neighboring farmers also brought refractory horses for him to train and subdue. More than once the little fellow was seen racing around the public square upon a kicking, rearing, pitching beast, to which, with arms clasped about its neck and fat bare feet pressed against its flanks, the lad was clinging with the same tenacity which he manifested later in life.[18]

Jesse Grant saw that he could get a great deal of hard work out of his oldest son so long as a horse was involved in the project. By the time he was eleven, Ulysses was doing the major share of the plowing on the Grant farmstead while sawing and hauling firewood not only for his home but also for the family tannery. Some biographers have suggested that the heavy workload had a physical effect, rendering him almost permanently stoop-shouldered. At about the same age, the boy added to the family's finances by driving travelers to Cincinnati, fifty miles from Point Pleasant. His youth notwithstanding, he was trusted to check into a city hotel, spend the night alone, and the next morning seek out those who required conveyance to Brown County.[19]

Ulysses was capable of melding physical strength with brainpower. When he was twelve, his ambitious father landed a contract to construct a jail for the county. The contract, which took several months to fulfill, entailed felling trees and hauling logs to the work site. Jesse entrusted the job to his son, who worked alongside adult laborers. One day, after he had brought a large supply of logs in from the woods, the boy informed his father that there was no point in his making another trip because the workforce was short-handed and no one was available to load the wagon. If this were so, Jesse asked, how had he managed to haul logs so heavy that grown men would have had trouble loading them? His son explained, quite matter-of-factly, that he had used his horse to pull the logs, one at a time, up an incline formed by a fallen tree, the end of which rested upon a stump. When each log had been raised sufficiently high, he had backed the wagon under it, chocked the wheels, and directed the horse to lower it into the conveyance. Jessie, surprised and pleased, beamed with pride at his son's ingenuity.[20]

Jesse Grant's frequent boasting of his son's skills and accomplishments (one neighbor called him "the greatest brag I ever met with") appears to have sprung from parental pride. Even so, the father was sufficiently egotistical that, one suspects, in singing Ulysses' praises he trumpeted his own as well. It is generally accepted that no apple falls far from the tree, and Jesse Grant thought of himself as a mighty oak indeed.[21]

★ ★ ★

Hannah Grant's disdain was in sharp contrast to her husband's obnoxious boastfulness; indeed, Mrs. Grant was never known to praise anyone, especially her children. Even in adulthood, their accomplishments went unheralded, and apparently unnoticed. When General Ulysses Grant visited the family homestead shortly after forcing Robert E. Lee to surrender his army at Appomattox, his mother welcomed him back without a smile and virtually without comment. Before turning back to her chores, she said only: "Well, Ulysses, you've become a great man, haven't you?" Three years later, when her son gained the presidency, every surviving member of his family attended the inaugural except Hannah, who was physically capable of making the journey east. During the Grant administration, father, siblings, and other relatives visited the White House more than a few times, but not once did Hannah accompany them. It was as if she feared that her presence would be construed as an act of homage.[22]

Even around her closest relatives, Hannah Grant was an inordinately private person. She seemed to regard a show of emotion as a symptom of weakness. Looking back in later life, her son could not recall hearing his mother laugh or cry. Whatever hopes, dreams, fears, or enthusiasms she might have entertained, she kept to herself.

Those who knew Hannah claimed for her a sweet nature, hidden as it was beneath a stoic exterior. Undoubtedly she loved her children, but she doted on none and never came close to coddling them. As when baby Ulysses frolicked among the family's horses, she could appear complacent over their health and well-being. When they fell ill, she did not fuss over them or shower them with exaggerated concern. As Hamlin Garland puts it, she "was not one of those mothers whose maternal love casts a correspondingly deep shadow of agonizing fear." She put them to bed, forced castor oil down their throats, and trusted to the Lord and their own constitutions.[23]

Hannah was so withdrawn that at least one historian suggests she may have been mildly retarded. Another observes that "she acted like a woman who is nourishing within herself a life-long secret." A more credible explanation is that she was the victim of an extraordinary set of inhibitions acquired in childhood, perhaps rooted in her Calvinistic upbringing. At some point during her religious education, she had come to believe it sinful to show a glimpse of her inner self to anyone but God.[24]

Some of her more notable traits communicated themselves to her first son. As a boy, Ulysses was widely described as well-behaved and amiable, but unusually quiet and reserved, reluctant to draw attention to himself, and ill at ease around strangers. Harsher observers regarded him as backward, simple-minded, or dense. Some of these critics were probably motivated by jealousy over the boy's celebrated skills as a horse master; others were reacting to the loud boasting of the father.

Claims that the boy lacked intelligence or shrewdness made the rounds of Georgetown. One that received especial attention centered around a horse trade the twelve-year-old Ulysses made with a Mr. Ralston, who owned a colt the boy greatly desired. The older Grant offered twenty dollars for the horse, but Ralston wanted twenty-five. At his son's pleading, Jesse agreed to pay the higher amount if necessary, but instructed Ulysses to haggle with the owner. When he went to see Ralston, however, the boy blurted out: "Papa says I may offer you twenty dollars for the colt, but if you won't take that, I am to offer twenty-two and a half, and if you won't take that, to give you twenty-five." Not surprisingly, he paid top dollar. As he recalled years later: "The story got out among the boys of the village, and it was a long time before I heard the last of it." He added philosophically: "Boys enjoy the misery of their companions, at least village boys in that day did, and in later life I have found that all adults are not free from the peculiarity."[25]

Townspeople who observed the boy in repose and were ignorant of his impressive capacity for physical labor considered him lazy. In fact, although Ulysses had an active curiosity, he was easily bored. As one of his early biographers points out, when his mind was not challenged and hard work was not demanded of him, "he was of sluggish habit all his days." Grant himself claimed that the older he grew, the more he tended to indolence—an exaggeration, perhaps, but in the minds of those who made no effort to understand him, not far from the mark.[26]

Reticence and self-restraint followed Ulysses Grant from youth into adulthood. He rarely revealed his feelings, even in the company of those considered to be his intimate friends. One of his wartime staff officers claimed that "he always avoided talking upon any subject which was personal to himself." A civilian telegrapher at his headquarters, who got to know

General Grant as well as anyone outside his family, called him "one of the most reserved men" he had ever known: "The faculty of restraint both in speech and in expression of the feelings was pronounced." Nevertheless, this man decried the all-too-common "impression among those who met him that he was cold and untutored in the ways of the sociable world." From personal observation he knew the general to be a sensitive, caring person, and he did not consider Grant's manner in any degree assumed. Even so, he regretted his inability to draw his chief into an expression of his private thoughts. Whenever the conversation got too personal, Grant would change the subject or simply clam up.[27]

Another inheritance from his parents was a set of moral and religious values that Grant adhered to, more or less, throughout his life. He seldom spoke on religious matters, and although he never joined the Methodist Church or any other sect, he was not an atheist as some observers have suggested, nor was he irreligious. He believed in a divine Creator, looked forward to an afterlife, and, whenever possible, observed the Sabbath. As one recent historian observed, Grant was a "committed" Christian: "His faith was simple yet sturdy. . . . Intimate acquaintances often reported that he had a deep and abiding respect for the spiritual. Furthermore, Grant's own writing exhibits a strong belief in an overruling Providence affecting not only his life but the affairs of the world. On many occasions, Grant was known to have attributed his life's success to God's benevolence."[28]

Other moral and religious principles Grant inherited from his parents included prohibitions against swearing, dancing, gambling, and corporal punishment. Witnesses testified that his language was free of obscenity and profanity; when provoked to wrathful utterance, the harshest epithets he resorted to were "Confound it!" and "Doggone it!" Such self-control was remarkable considering the highly stressful environment in which he lived throughout the Civil War. His telegrapher believed that "a man never lived, with possibly the exception of Job, who had more provocation to resort to profanity than Grant himself." For the better part of the conflict, John A. Rawlins of Galena, Illinois, a man given to fits of temper and colorful language, served as Grant's chief of staff. Grant would claim that Rawlins fulfilled an indispensable requirement: "He does all my cussing for me." Nor was Grant known to appreciate coarse jokes or stories. A friend recalled: "I have seen him freeze a man up instantly with a look when a vulgar story was started in his presence."[29]

Although a lover of wholesome entertainment, Grant never took a dance floor in his life, even after marrying a woman who loved to dance. The reason was not two left feet; his religious training deterred him from an activity he considered frivolous and sometimes indecorous. Nor did he gamble except in penny-ante games while in the army; and when he became a father, Grant steadfastly refused to take his hand to his children. His youngest son recalled having been spanked only once and only after excessive provocation. He reported his father as being so shaken by his action that he never repeated it.[30]

Only in a few instances did the religious teachings of his parents fail to impress themselves upon him. Although both Jesse and Hannah Grant were staunch antislaveryites, their son's attitudes toward the institution were more complex and slow to evolve. Although he never approved of slavery and never felt entirely comfortable in its presence, for the first forty years of his life he was no abolitionist. His Ohio boyhood was spent among pro-slavery people who had emigrated from Kentucky and Virginia, and after leaving the army in 1854 he resided in a slave state, Missouri. Thus it is hardly surprising that he considered it neither proper nor politic to condemn slave owners or to agitate for the liberation of their chattels. His attitude toward slavery began to change only after April 1861, when the issue became inextricably embroiled in the fate of the American Republic and he himself became the instrument of a government policy to stamp out the institution.

Another parental influence that seemed to have no effect on the boy was the abhorrence of alcohol. Although neither of his parents imbibed—Hannah from devotion to Methodism, Jesse from a studied rejection of Noah Grant's lifestyle—when they were at church, their son would steal down to the storm cellar, sometimes in company with friends. There he would drink from a large cask of blackberry cordial that his father had purchased for its supposed value in combating cholera, a disease that could reach epidemic proportions in the community. One of his companions later recalled of these clandestine sprees: "I don't know whether we took it right or not, but certain it is that we did not take the cholera." A latter-day historian asserts that, although the practice seems harmless enough, "it is important in a larger context. Ulysses Grant would slip off to take a pull on many a bottle after those early excursions to the cellar."[31]

★ ★ ★

The same biographers who credit Grant with a happy childhood claim that his youth and adolescence were lonely and unhappy times, made especially so by a tendency to a mild but chronic depression in the form of dysthymia. More recent chroniclers, including Bruce Catton, reject this casting of

Grant as "a sensitive child driven in on himself, forced in self-defense to cultivate an impassive stolidity to protect a bruised ego and a crippled, tormented psyche. . . . On the contrary, every recollection is of a singularly happy boyhood." To be sure, there were always those who teased and taunted him for one reason or another, but he had many friends, including those to whom, upon occasion, he could speak candidly of his fears, hopes, and aspirations. He joined these companions in various childhood pastimes. In addition to riding, he enjoyed ice skating, fishing, and swimming. He was especially proficient at skating, but he also considered himself an accomplished swimmer. At least once, however, he found himself in over his head—literally. When he was seven, he barely avoided drowning after falling from a fishing perch into the swift waters of a Brown County lake. His nine-year-old companion, Daniel Ammen (later a high-ranking officer in the United States Navy) came to the rescue, grabbing the collar of his jacket as the helpless boy swept past.[32]

One popular avocation that had no charms for him was hunting. Ever averse to killing animals, he refused to stalk birds, rabbits, or squirrels. Despite his pleasurable introduction to firearms as an infant, he never used them for amusement. The closest he came to engaging in the sport was when, as a young subaltern stationed in Texas shortly before the Mexican War, he accompanied another officer on a turkey hunt. His colleague flushed the game, but Lieutenant Grant "stood watching the turkeys to see where they flew—with my gun on my shoulder, and never once thought of leveling it at the birds. When I had time to reflect upon the matter, I came to the conclusion that as a sportsman I was a failure." He made no effort to overcome this supposed deficiency.[33]

Ulysses did not spend his boyhood solely at play or hard labor. Even a backwoods youth of his era could expect to spend time in the schoolroom, even if only for a only few weeks following the harvest season. The wealth he had amassed from his tanyard and livery business enabled Jesse Grant to provide his son with an education that was better than most families in Georgetown could give their children. Ulysses' educational experience began when he was sent at the age of five to the local "subscription schools" of Georgetown. During the winter terms of 1836–1837 and 1838–1839 he attended private boarding schools, first in Maysville, Kentucky, where he came under the eye of his aunt, the widow of Peter Grant; and then in Ripley, Ohio, ten miles from his home. Looking back near the close of his life, he denied having been anything like an accomplished pupil: "I was not studious in habit, and probably did not make progress enough for the outlay for board and tuition."[34]

The Georgetown schools were less like bastions of learning than holding pens for truants controllable only through the switch, and the private academies were not much better. "Both winters were spent," he wrote, "in going over the same old arithmetic which I knew every word of before, and repeating: 'A noun is the name of a thing,' which I had also heard my Georgetown teachers repeat, until I had come to believe it."[35]

Despite the unchallenging curriculum, he did not fault his teachers—even those who ran the subscription schools—for his failure to excel. Other pupils, more receptive to the prevailing teaching methods, absorbed enough knowledge to embark on challenging and rewarding professional careers. Two of his fellow students even became members of Congress. Ulysses would outstrip both, however, in the extent of his formal schooling, which, as Richardson noted, was supplemented by attendance at "evening spelling-schools." During this time, perhaps encouraged by his father, he also joined a juvenile debating club, "at which, however, he never spoke."[36]

Ulysses' orderly, methodical mind enabled him to excel in the mathematics courses offered at Maysville and Ripley even though he never opened an algebra text until attending West Point. Because they appealed to none of his tastes, he did less well in the other subjects, notably grammar and composition. If a lesson caught and held his interest, he made respectable grades, but he was easily bored, especially when asked to absorb knowledge he considered inapplicable to those career fields that appealed to him.

When Ulysses was in his early teens, his father asked him what profession he might like to enter: "I want you to work at whatever you like and intend to follow," he explained. His son expressed three very different interests: obtaining a college education, possibly with a view to teaching; farming; and trading on the Father of Waters, the Mississippi. He was not sure which occupation would prove most satisfying or for which he had the greatest aptitude, but he was certain of one thing—he was not going to follow Jesse into the tanning business. "I detested the trade," he recalled, "preferring almost any other labor." He had worked in the family tanyard occasionally since his early teens, and he vividly remembered the bone-numbing labor it demanded, the stench of the caustic chemicals it required for its operation, and, above all, the suffering of the trapped, terrified animals about to be slaughtered for their hides.[37]

If Jesse's dreams of a bright future for his son were to come true, Ulysses had to finish his education. Yet, despite the father's growing prosperity, when the time came for the boy to start college, Jesse decided that he lacked the necessary funds. Instead, aware that West Point charged no tuition, he decided to seek an Academy appointment for his son. As Jesse remembered, before he did so he broached the idea to Ulysses and gained his approval. His son, however, would claim that he had no inkling of what was in store for him. When in the winter of 1838 he learned that Jesse had taken the steps to apply for an appointment, it was news to him.

But it was not good news. Ulysses had never considered a military career, and the idea appealed to him not at all. "I won't go," he recalled telling his father. But Jesse Grant thought otherwise and would brook no argument in the matter. The incident marked one of the few times that Ulysses' father had ordered him to do something he found disagreeable. By the time he wrote his memoirs, Grant's recollection had somewhat changed: "I really had no objection to going to West Point, except that I had a very exalted idea of the acquirements necessary to get through. I did not believe I possessed them, and could not bear the idea of failing." But his father's purpose remained fixed, and Ulysses acquiesced in it out of simple necessity.[38]

Jesse's timing was fortuitous. Congressman Thomas Hamer of Ohio had the prerogative of filling a vacancy in the Corps of Cadets created by the recent dismissal of a local appointee, the son of the Grant family's physician. Hamer had been a close friend and debating opponent of Jesse Grant's before diverging political views came between them. Once a loyal Democrat, as Hamer continued to be, Jesse had transformed himself into an avowed capitalist and ardent nationalist. Jesse had left the party of Andrew Jackson after Old Hickory refused to extend the life of the Second Bank of the United States, an institution his party considered inimical to states' rights but which Jesse saw as integral to national prosperity. Over time, the erstwhile friends had come to regret their estrangement, but neither was willing to make the first move toward burying the hatchet. Jesse's application for his son furnished Hamer with an opportunity to heal the rift. After the appointment went to Ulysses, the Democratic congressman and the convert to the new Whig Party let bygones be bygones. Their renewed friendship would endure until Hamer's death, as a general officer of volunteer troops, during the Mexican War.[39]

By appointing Jesse's son to the Military Academy, Congressman Hamer was responsible not only for the name Ulysses Grant would make as a soldier but also for the name by which he would be known to generations of Americans. Originally, Jesse believed that Senator Thomas H. Morris controlled the state's Academy appointments; thus he failed to contact Hamer until the 1838–1839 congressional term had almost expired. Given only one day to process the application, Hamer had no time to gather basic information on Jesse's son. In his haste, he made out the appointment in the name of "Ulysses Simpson Grant." Upon his matriculation, Ulysses pointed out the error, only to find Academy officials unwilling to tackle the paperwork required to make the change. When his name first appeared on the cadet rolls as "U. S. Grant," it induced fellow cadets to bestow on him a nickname that would cling to him throughout his years in the army. Originally rendered as "United States Grant," in time the moniker became "Uncle Sam Grant," until finally shortened to "Sam."[40]

★ ★ ★

Although at seventeen Ulysses was already a seasoned traveler ("I had been east to Wheeling, Virginia, and north to the Western Reserve, in Ohio, west to Louisville, and south to Bourbon County, Kentucky"), the youngster dreaded the trip he made in the latter part of May 1839 from Bethel, Ohio, to his new home in the Hudson highlands. "A military life had no charms for me," he insisted, "and I had not the faintest idea of staying in the army even if I should be graduated, which I did not expect." Thus the journey east by steamer, canal boat, and railroad—the latter at the fantastic clip of almost twenty miles per hour—was too short for him. He delayed his arrival by spending several days sightseeing in Philadelphia and Manhattan (the side-trips would bring a sharp reprimand from home). As a result, he did not reach the august institution in upstate New York until May 29.[41]

From the first, he felt out of place in the rigorous, restrictive, and conformity-driven environment of the nation's premier soldier school. He tolerated his first summer encampment, which he found "wearisome and uninteresting"; but when the camp was broken up and the cadets ("plebes," as the fourth-year men were called) moved into barracks, he appeared resigned to the situation: "I felt as though I had been at West Point always, and that if I staid to graduation, I would have to remain always." The prospect horrified him, but unwilling to return home without cause and believing he would soon flunk out, he steeled himself against the ordeal to follow. Even so, for a time he clung to the hope (never realized) that Congress might act favorably on a proposed piece of legislation to abolish the Academy altogether. Should his schooling end in that manner, it would spare him the humiliation of failing.[42]

To his amazement, he passed his initial examinations without difficulty, just as he had the perfunctory entrance exam that had preceded the encampment. His proficiency in mathematics stood him in good stead—that subject, after all, formed the foundation of the engineering curriculum to which the institution owed its prestige—and his fair-to-middling performance in the few other disciplines to which he was exposed in his first two years proved to be no worse than that of most of his fellow cadets.

Life at West Point was made bearable by the personal associations he formed. He was not one to collect friends, but he found himself on close, even intimate, terms with a few classmates, especially those with whom he roomed, Frederick T. Dent of Missouri and Rufus Ingalls of Maine being among them. He made enough friends—Dent, Ingalls, Simon Bolivar Buckner of Kentucky, and eight others—to help form a secret fraternal society, the Twelve in One. Some of these attachments would last a lifetime, and even casual acquaintances provided contacts helpful to his future career.

He might have been more popular had he been more talkative and self-promotive, or sufficiently gifted to excel in the rudimentary athletic activities offered by the school. Throughout his West Point career he remained as quiet, and almost as shy, as he had been at home, and he did not possess the stature, the skill, or the desire to compete successfully in field sports. Upon entering the academy he affected an almost childlike appearance—smooth of face, barely five feet, one inch tall, and weighing no more than 117 pounds. Over the next four years, he added six inches to his height and several pounds to his girth.[43]

During his first class year, he contracted "Tyler's Grippe," a debilitating illness alarmingly suggestive of consumption—a disease that would kill his brother Simpson and his sister Clara—which reduced his weight to its pre–Academy level. Even at the peak of his growth, however, he was not athletic material. He made an attempt to master only one sport, soccer, but as James Longstreet recalled, he "was not heavy enough to be good in the rush. He usually hung on the outskirts of the crowd and was ready for the kick when it came his way."[44]

In the classroom, his grades were average. He performed capably enough in the higher mathematics courses that he came to believe he might secure a position on the faculty as an assistant professor in the discipline. Yet even the math courses did not come easily to him. As he wrote to one of his cousins during the earliest days of his cadetship, "we have tremendous long and hard lessons to get in both French and Algebra. I study hard and hope to get along so as to pass the examination in January. This examination is a hard one they say, but I am not frightened *yet*." In this letter, he went to some lengths to deprecate his appearance, which he considered anything but soldier-like: "If I were to come home now with my uniform on . . . you would laugh. . . . My pants sit as tight to my skin as the bark to a tree and if I do not walk *military*, that is if I bend over quickly or run, they are very apt to crack with a report as loud as a pistol. . . . If you were to see me at a distance, the first question you would ask would be, 'is that a Fish or an animal?'."[45]

Although he passed the fearsome January exam, his claim of diligent study is open to question. He appeared to work hard, but no more than necessary to remain in good standing on the roll of general merit. "I did not take hold of my studies with avidity, in fact I rarely ever read over a lesson the second time during my entire cadetship," he admitted in his memoirs. He gave as a reason that old bugaboo, his susceptibility to boredom: "I could not sit in my room doing nothing."[46]

His grades reflected his faulty approach to his studies. At the close of his first year at the Academy, out of his sixty-member class he ranked sixteenth in mathematics but only forty-ninth in French. He improved somewhat during his third-class year, at the end of which, in his pared-down class of fifty-three, he stood tenth in math and forty-fourth in French. In his added courses, he ranked only twenty-third in military drawing and forty-sixth in ethics.

His almost imperceptible improvement continued the following year, when he stood fifteenth of forty-one cadets in the general science course known as natural philosophy, nineteenth in drawing, and twenty-second in chemistry. In his final year, his standing slipped a notch; mediocre grades in engineering and ethics matched those he received in the tactical courses offered during a cadet's senior session. Among the thirty-nine other members of his class who managed to graduate, he ranked twenty-fifth in artillery tactics and twenty-eighth in the tactics of the arm to which he was fated to be posted, the infantry. His final ranking on the roll of general merit was twenty-first, just below the class median. It was a record of determined mediocrity, one that neither exalted nor condemned its bearer.[47]

Presumably, he would have improved his grades in tactics had he studied the many military texts that reposed in the Academy's "fine library," but he rarely if ever did so. In place of instructional manuals he spent his free time reading novels—"not those of a trashy sort," he was quick to point out, but the works of esteemed authors such as James Fenimore Cooper, Washington Irving, and Sir Walter Scott. Perhaps it was this predilection that won Grant, during his senior year, the presidency of the Academy's only literary society. One might suppose that his avoidance of heavier reading would cause him difficulties when called to shoulder the duties of his profession. Yet in the absence of theoretical knowledge, he would make do very nicely with practical application and common sense, weapons not every officer had in his arsenal.[48]

Class standing was a function not only of classroom performance but also of "general merit." Because the latter was heavily affected by receipt of those demerits that a cadet's superiors handed out for a bewildering array of offenses, some of them quite trivial, many cadets who did well enough in their studies saw their general standing decline, sometimes precipitously, under the weight of these black marks. This was not the case with Cadet Grant, who during his academic career amassed, respectively, fifty-nine, sixty-seven, ninety-eight, and sixty-six demerits—none close to the fatal number of two hundred per annum that constituted grounds for instant dismissal.[49]

His infractions were common ones: lateness to class and, once there, inattention; failure to take proper care of his uniform, arms, and accoutrements; flawed performances on the drill field, where his stooped frame and nonchalant air kept him from looking soldierly. His missteps were not always his fault: On one occasion, a husky cadet given to bullying smaller classmates deliberately crowded Grant out of the ranks, so provoking the slow-to-anger cadet that he tore into his tormentor and thrashed him soundly. In fact, Grant, whose slight frame and quiet manner made him an inviting target, had numerous physical encounters with fellow cadets, not all of whom he easily conquered. Reportedly, it took four bouts with one muscular antagonist, who repeatedly drew Grant into violent confrontations, before the persevering Ohioan emerged victorious.[50]

If Grant drew more than a few demerits for engaging in fisticuffs, he was never gigged for violating one notorious prohibition—a clandestine journey to Benny Havens's tavern, in neighboring Highland Falls, which catered to thirsty, entertainment-starved, and risk-taking cadets. James Longstreet would claim that Grant never visited the watering hole during his cadetship, although another source has him going once—at the urging of his roommate, Ingalls—and barely escaping detection and punishment. It cannot be determined that he drank while on Academy grounds, but supposedly he swore off liquor after observing a fellow cadet in a drunken stupor. The story suggests that up to that time he imbibed at least occasionally. Apparently he did indulge in smoking, a vice often linked with alcohol consumption. He began using tobacco at the Academy—sometimes in a pipe, more often in the form of a cigar—mainly, it would appear, from the thrill of partaking of a forbidden pleasure. Tobacco addiction would become for him a more destructive habit than alcohol—one day it would kill him.[51]

Whether the source was drinking, smoking, or some other prohibited activity, the upsurge of demerits that marked Grant's second class year cost him the only honor the academy bestowed upon him. At the outset of that term, shortly after returning from the two-month furlough granted every cadet at that point in his scholastic career—an all-too-brief period he spent among family and friends in Ohio—he found, much to his surprise, that he had been appointed a cadet sergeant. He did not consider himself entitled to the promotion either by classroom or drill-field performance, and thus he was not shattered when the promotion was revoked later in the year. In his memoirs he reduced the matter to a simple statement: "I was dropped, and served the fourth year as a private."[52]

Despite the deficiencies in his education, Grant emerged from the Academy highly esteemed by his fellow cadets. Typical of their impressions of him were these: "A clear thinker and steady worker"; "not a prominent man in the corps, but respected by all"; "a very much liked sort of youth"; "no bad habits whatever"; "never said an untruthful word even in jest"; "taking to his military duties in a very business-like manner"; and "much respected as a man of firmness." Yet another classmate, looking back thirty years later, spoke for many who knew him: "I had a warm admiration for Grant, though none of us were wise enough to predict his brilliant future. I am astonished that we did not, for the Grant of to-day was the Grant of West Point."[53]

The observer ought not to have chided himself for failing to recognize his classmate's potential—Grant himself did not. When he left West Point on the day of his graduation, June 30, 1843, he considered himself, as he had upon entering the institution four years before, officer material of the poorest sort, and he could foresee no likelihood of improvement. Perhaps his self-view was in keeping with the low opinion he continued to entertain of army officers as a group.

He could count only a couple of exceptions to this belief. In addition to a few of his closest friends in the cadet corps, he highly admired Captain Charles Ferguson Smith of the 2nd United States Artillery, the impeccably attired, ramrod-erect, and scrupulously fair Commandant of Cadets; and Winfield Scott, the fifty-three-year-old future commanding general of the United States Army, who visited the Academy and reviewed the cadet corps during Grant's first summer encampment. Scott, in fact, became his *beau ideal* of military manhood. His first impression of Scott was one of physical splendor: "With his commanding figure, his quite colossal size and showy uniform, I thought him the finest specimen of manhood my eyes had ever beheld, and the most to be envied." So musing, he recalled a strange thought that had entered his mind upon beholding Scott for the first time: "I could never resemble him in appearance, but I believe I did have a presentiment for a moment that some day I should occupy his place on review—although I had no inclination then of remaining in the army."[54]

No one in his right mind would have predicted that before thirty years were out, Charles F. Smith would become one of Ulysses Grant's most faithful subordinates; and that Winfield Scott, then approaching his eightieth year and well into retirement, would present Grant with a copy of his memoirs that bore the inscription: "From the Oldest to the Greatest General."[55]

★ *Chapter 2* ★

"A Most Remarkable
and Valuable Young Soldier"

Wᴴᴇɴ ʜᴇ ʟᴇꜰᴛ Wᴇꜱᴛ Pᴏɪɴᴛ, Gʀᴀɴᴛ ʜᴀᴅ ɴᴏ ɪᴅᴇᴀ ᴡʜᴀᴛ ʜɪꜱ ꜰɪʀꜱᴛ ᴀᴄᴛɪᴠᴇ-duty assignment would be. Upon passing the final examination, the members of the class of 1843 were instructed to list their preferences for units and arms of the service. Grant's first choice was the only mounted regiment in the army, the 1st United States Dragoons, a hybrid organization dating to 1833; members of the regiment were armed, equipped, and trained to fight mounted and afoot as conditions warranted (a second dragoon outfit had been formed three years later, but a penurious Congress had converted it to infantry a few months before Grant graduated).[1]

Grant's preference for a dragoon berth is hardly surprising. His uncanny ability to understand and control horses remained one of his most remarkable attributes. Whenever an obstreperous mount had been added to the Military Academy's stables, he was chosen to gentle it. His prowess in the saddle had been demonstrated time and again during his four years as a cadet. He had displayed it with especial verve when, in the last weeks of its schooling, his class was put through its paces before a blue-ribbon audience that included General Winfield Scott and the Academy's board of visitors. The crowning event of the review was a high-jumping exhibition performed by Grant aboard a long-legged, powerfully built sorrel named York, a horse that few other cadets dared ride. A member of Grant's class had advised him against the stunt: "Sam, that horse will kill you some day." The rider's reply was matter-of-fact: "Well, I can die but once."[2]

On the day of the review, the school's riding-master, H. R. Herschberger, set the leaping bar to a height of six feet, five inches, then called out: "Cadet Grant!" One of the younger onlookers, James B. Fry of Illinois, an applicant for a place in the incoming class, noted that the audience collectively held its breath as the "clean-faced, slender, blue-eyed [actually, grey-eyed] young fellow" in the saddle readied himself and his steed for the Herculean feat. Fry watched intently as Grant dashed forward to the end of the riding hall: "As he turned at the farther end and came into the stretch across which the bar was placed, the horse increased his pace, and, measuring his strides for the great leap before him, bounded into the air and cleared the bar, carrying his rider as if man and beast had been welded together. The spectators were breathless. 'Very well done, sir!' growled old Herschberger." When the applause of the crowd finally died away, Fry said, "the class was dismissed and disappeared; but 'Cadet Grant' remained a living image in my memory."[3]

Although it could not ignore Grant's aptitude for mounted service, the Academy in its dubious wisdom turned down his application for a dragoon commission. Instead, he was posted to his second choice, the 4th U.S. Infantry. He would join the regiment, then on station at Jefferson Barracks, Missouri, as a brevet second lieutenant. The brevet was an at-large commission rather than one accorded to a specific regiment. Grant would not formally be entered on the rolls of the 4th Infantry, which already had a full complement of officers, until a vacancy occurred in its ranks. Because the small army of the time (seventy-five hundred officers and men) allocated a specified quota of commissions to each of its units but lacked a pension system, officers remained on active duty long after age or physical disability should have returned them to civilian life. Vacancies, therefore, were caused only by resignations, transfers, and deaths.

When he departed West Point, Grant's assignment had yet to be announced; in fact, he waited several weeks to learn where he would report for duty. He spent those weeks visiting his family, which during his schooling had moved back to Claremont County, settling in Bethel, ten miles west of its former home. There Jesse Grant had built a comfortable house of brick while establishing a new and larger tannery, funded by the sale of the older one. Ulysses soon discovered that his father had made much the same impression on his new neighbors as he had on the good folk of Georgetown. One of Bethel's more broadminded natives, however, would claim that Jesse's unpopularity redounded "entirely to his credit, as his enemies were almost entirely composed of his political opponents and small minded neighbors who were filled with jealousy and envy on account of his material prosperity."[4]

Jesse's eldest had visited the new home once before, during the furlough that followed his third class year. On that occasion, startled by the physical transformation her son had undergone at West Point, Hannah Grant had welcomed him with an exclamation: "Ulysses, you have grown much straighter." Her son agreed, explaining: "That was the first thing they taught me." Presumably, his posture had not deteriorated since.[5]

West Point also taught him to take pride in his hard-won education and his status as a commissioned officer. His disappointment at failing to gain his unit preference was diluted by the eventual arrival of his shiny blue uniform, its shoulders topped by twin insignia straps of gold braid. He had been waiting anxiously to suit up: "I was impatient to get on my uniform and see how it looked, and probably wanted my old school mates, particularly the girls, to see me in it."[6]

The reference to female admirers suggests a side to Grant's personality that few biographers have explored. If Hamlin Garland is correct, however, in his youth the lieutenant had at least one sweetheart, Mary King, with whom he corresponded while at the Academy and to whom he presented one of the illustrations (some of which were quite accomplished) he rendered while studying military drawing. Hamlin admits that "of her little can be learned save that she had accepted another wooer." He adds that "it is not remembered that Ulysses grew wan with grief."[7]

Clad in the attention-getting garb of his new profession, the self-absorbed youngster spent part of his furlough visiting relatives and friends in Georgetown and elsewhere in southern Ohio. The pleasurable interlude came to an abrupt halt in Cincinnati, where, as the result of a disagreeable encounter with a street urchin, "the conceit was knocked out of me." A ragged, barefooted boy, observing Grant trotting down a busy street, began to shout out the lyrics of a popular, antimilitary ditty:

"Soldier, will you work? No-siree—I'll sell my shirt first!"[8]

The boy's chanting not only ravaged Grant's self-esteem but triggered memories of past humiliations: "The horse trade and its dire consequences were recalled to mind." He returned to Bethel with the boy's taunts echoing in his ears, only to find his ordeal not yet over. As he neared the livery attached to the tavern that sat opposite the Grant home, he observed the stable-hand—a young man of dissolute habits but possessed of a certain sense of humor—parading up and down the street in a pair of sky-blue trousers crudely altered to resemble those of an army officer, complete with "a strip of white cotton sheeting sewed down the outside seams in imitation of mine." Looking back on these incidents, Grant cited them as the reason he acquired "a distaste for military uniform that [he] never recovered from."[9]

★ ★ ★

On the last day of September, two months to the day since leaving West Point, Brevet Second Lieutenant Grant reported to the headquarters of his regiment at Jefferson Barracks, on the outskirts of St. Louis. The post, the largest in the army, was home station to the majority of the companies that comprised the 3rd and 4th Infantry. The newcomer quickly settled into the routine of garrison life and made or renewed acquaintances with his fellow officers, most of whom shared his alma mater, including his old friend "Pete" Longstreet. He quickly developed an admiration for many of his seniors, especially the post commander, Colonel Stephen Watts Kearny of the 3rd, who, although a strict disciplinarian, was no martinet. "Every drill and roll-call had to be attended," Grant remembered, "but in the intervals officers were permitted to enjoy themselves, leaving the garrison, and going where they pleased, without making written application." Another object of his admiration was the leader of his regiment, Colonel Josiah H. Vose, "a most estimable man, of exemplary habits" who preferred to confine himself to administrative duties while his subordinates exercised direct command of the outfit.[10]

He was less taken with some of the junior officers, including Captain Robert Christie Buchanan of Maryland, a stickler for regulations and detail who appeared to enjoy punishing his subordinates for any lapse in conduct, no matter how petty. From the first, Buchanan and Grant clashed, especially after the captain, the president of the officers' mess, began to levy fines on the newcomer, in the form of compulsory contributions to the regimental fund, whenever Grant was late—even by a few minutes—for mess call. The animosity that grew between them peaked when Grant, having been docked several times, refused to accept an especially exorbitant penalty. The consequences of this act of defiance would prove not only long-lasting but detrimental to his career.[11]

To escape the dull routine of the post and his superior's displeasure, Grant took long rides through the countryside during off-duty hours. On several occasions, he dined as a guest, sometimes in company with fellow officers, in the homes of families disposed to be hospitable to their neighbors in the army. One of the first of these excursions was to White Haven, a well-appointed farm along Gravois Creek five miles west of the post, the home of the Dents, the family of Grant's favorite roommate at the Military Academy.

His first trip was a payback for a visit Fred had made to the Grant home in Ohio, but he failed to connect with his classmate. One day earlier Fred, himself a newly minted brevet second lieutenant, had left home to join his regiment, the 6th Infantry, on the western frontier. Yet he had paved the way for his friend by informing his oldest sister that Sam Grant was the "finest boy he had ever known . . . he is pure gold."[12]

As it turned out, neither was seventeen-year-old Julia Dent at home when the lieutenant paid his first call at White Haven—she was spending that season as a guest of a prominent family in St. Louis—but he was welcomed by the majority of her family, including her mother, her two brothers, and two sisters. Grant found the Dents a typical Missouri family of the period, proud of their Southern roots and the trappings of prosperity that included a work force of nineteen slaves. The Dents were also outspokenly opposed to a national government they considered increasingly antagonistic to their region's political, social, and economic institutions.

Lieutenant Grant had grown up among people with similar beliefs, and at West Point he had studiously avoided being drawn into the debates about sectional issues that were beginning to divide Northern- and Southern-born members of the cadet corps. Thus he felt comfortable among the Dents and responsive to the genial, old-world style of hospitality they practiced. Even so, neither then nor afterwards did he forge a warm relationship with the family patriarch, Frederick Dent, Sr. The crotchety and argumentative "colonel" (a title he had bestowed upon himself), scion of a cultured family from Maryland, saw the young visitor—although well-behaved and evidently sincere in his desire to please—as an undesirable. It was obvious that Grant's origins were humbler than the colonel's own. What was infinitely worse, he came from a family that neither kept slaves nor favored slavery. For all he knew, the Grants were wild-eyed abolitionists, a species the colonel despised and feared.[13]

If Grant did not hit it off with Dent, Sr., he had no difficulty warming up to his eldest daughter, whom he met upon Julia's return from the city the following February. "After that," he recalled, "I do not know but my visits became more frequent; they certainly did become more enjoyable." In fact, he appears to have been smitten at their first meeting, or very soon after. It must have been love in the truest sense, for it seems unlikely he was swept away by Julia's looks. One recent biographer has noted that "she was, to anyone who wanted to be critical, dumpy, cross-eyed, and plain. But appearances aside, she was full of life, voluble, strong-willed and optimistic."[14]

Having been the apple of her father's eye from birth, Julia was also more than a little spoiled. Grant, however, recognized none of these potential drawbacks as impediments to his attraction to her. He concentrated on her more appealing characteristics, especially her openness, her lack of guile, and her ability to put him at ease, evident from the moment they met. He was also thrilled to find that she loved horses and was an accomplished equestrienne. Her interests and abilities enabled them to share each other's company apart from the circle of her close-knit family. "We would often take walks," he wrote, "or go on horseback to visit the neighbors, until I became quite well acquainted in that vicinity."[15]

Without some external force to prompt him, Lieutenant Grant was too shy to openly express his growing affection for Julia. It took a far-reaching series of military, political, and diplomatic events to induce him to unburden himself in her presence. The initial act was a controversial proposal to grant statehood to the Republic of Texas, which had received its independence from Mexico only seven years earlier. At that time, Texas officials had sought annexation to the United States, but antislavery interests in Congress had prevented the measure from being adopted. By late in 1843, however, President John Tyler, fearing that foreign powers, especially Great Britain, had designs on the republic, proposed annexation. Even as Ulysses Grant was accompanying Julia Dent on horseback outings, the Congress was again agitating the Texas issue. In June of that year, the United States Senate would reject Tyler's proposal. Still, it was by no means certain that annexation was a dead letter. In fact, it would become a major issue in the next presidential campaign.

Mexican sensibilities having been inflamed by Tyler's obvious intentions, the War Department thought it politic to station troops close to the disputed region should violence, and perhaps war, break out there. On April 20, 1844, the 3rd Infantry was ordered from Jefferson Barracks to Fort Jesup, twenty miles east of the Texas border, the soon-to-be-designated headquarters of Brevet Brigadier General (later Major General) Zachary Taylor's "Corps of Observation." Rumor had it that Grant's regiment would soon join its sister outfit at that frontier outpost. From there, perhaps, it would move even closer to the Texas line.[16]

The sudden prospect of being sent far from Julia Dent rocked Grant's peace of mind. He had just obtained a twenty-day leave of absence to visit his family in Ohio. Before he left, he returned to White Haven to bid his beloved goodbye. On this occasion he screwed up enough courage to ask her to wear his West Point ring. The gesture took Julia aback; she recalled his telling her that should he ever offer that trinket to a lady it would be in the form of an engagement ring. She declined, telling him, "Mamma would not approve of my accepting a gift from a gentleman." "Rather put out" by her refusal, Grant soon took his leave. Before going, however, he asked whether she would think of him while he was away. She said she would, but "never for a moment" did she think of him as a prospective lover. "I was very happy when he was near, but that was all." Yet no sooner had he ridden off than she realized how lonely she felt in his absence.[17]

Just after Grant left Jefferson Barracks for the steamboat journey to Ohio, rumor became fact, the 4th Infantry being ordered to pack up and head south. A messenger with an order canceling Grant's leave failed to catch him. Not until he reached Bethel did he learn of his regiment's movement, and then only via a letter from a fellow officer—he never received official word of the transfer. At his comrade's suggestion, Grant did not cut short his furlough; but at the end of twenty days, he reported back at Jefferson Barracks. The post adjutant, Lieutenant Richard Stoddert Ewell, a "much esteemed" member of the 1st Dragoons who years later became a prominent Confederate, prepared papers authorizing Grant to join his regiment in Louisiana. At the latter's request, Ewell agreed to withhold the order until Grant could complete another visit to White Haven. This appears to have been the real reason he had chosen to return to Missouri instead of going directly from Ohio to Louisiana.[18]

After procuring a horse, he started out for the Dent farmstead. En route he had to cross the bridgeless and rain-swollen Gravois Creek, which he encountered at one of its least fordable points. He could have turned back and scouted for a better crossing, but a life-long superstition prevented this. Over the years, whenever he had gotten lost en route to an unfamiliar destination, he refused to turn back but forced himself to keep going until he found his way from another direction. On the present occasion, therefore, he followed his usual method: "I struck into the stream, and in an instant the horse was swimming and I being carried down by the current." Perhaps memories of his near-drowning as a boy flashed through his mind. In this instance, his horse found its footing and carried its rider to the far bank, wet but safe.[19]

When he arrived at White Haven, the doorman ushered him inside. Minutes later, Julia hurried down from her bedroom to greet him. She was startled but not surprised to find him wearing a suit of her brother John's clothes in place of his creek-soaked attire. One of her sisters had already informed their visitor that Julia had dreamed he would return unannounced, clad in civilian attire, and speaking the same words he had just uttered. Unimpressed by Julia's presentiment but pleased to learn that he had worked his way into her unconsciousness, he spent several happy days at her home. On one, he accompanied her to St. Louis, where she served as bridesmaid at a schoolmate's wedding. Perhaps inspired by the happy occasion, on the way back to White Haven he made an unambiguous statement of his feelings for her, a declaration that life without her would be "insupportable." Again, Julia played coy: "I simply told him I thought it would be charming to be engaged, but to be married—no! I would rather be engaged."[20]

Again disappointed by a lukewarm response to a heartfelt gesture, Grant had to settle for presenting her with his class ring to formalize their courtship. They filled the rest of his time at White Haven with long rides and quiet walks, during which he tried to persuade her to commit herself to a life with him. Although she seemed to warm to the prospect, she begged him not to say anything to her father: "He consented to this simply on account of shyness, he acknowledged to me." Then, too soon, it was time for him to go, and the lovers parted, not to see each other for more than a year.[21]

★ ★ ★

Jesse Grant's passionate interest in national affairs notwithstanding, his oldest son was no political animal. Even so, during his years at the Military Academy Sam Grant had formed some fairly strong opinions about how and under what conditions his country's military should be engaged. He considered the army the backbone of national defense, but he had trouble accepting the notion that it should be used as an instrument of political policy, especially a policy that favored the interests of one class over another. Concerning Texas, he saw Tyler's efforts at annexation as a ploy by a native Southerner to extend the reach and power of slavery. An act such as this, if consummated, would upset a sectional balance wrought by delicate compromise.

A quarter-century before the annexation issue became a subject of warm debate, efforts to bring the territories of Maine and Missouri into the Union had produced a Senate proposal that effectively drew a line between North and South. The proposal would have prohibited slavery in that part of the Louisiana Purchase north of 36′30″ north latitude—that is, above the southern boundary of Missouri. The House of Representatives had rejected the legislation, but eventually a bargain had been sealed that enabled Missouri— much to the gratification of the Dents and their slaveholding neighbors—to enter the Union without prohibiting human property. But the proposal fixing slavery's boundary had acquired a degree of permanence, making it appear that pro-slaveryites had changed the rules of the game to suit their purposes. The apparent violation made opponents of the institution suspicious of efforts to extend slavery into those more westerly lands yet to be organized for statehood.[22]

Although Grant entertained few reservations about Missouri's sanctioning of slavery, he was uncomfortable with the thought that Texas, being below 36'30", might serve as a new breeding ground for the institution and a seat of power for the "slaveocracy." He was even more troubled by the possibility that his regiment would be forced to serve as a tool for furthering this expansion. And he was especially upset by the prospect that the unit's presence so near a hotly disputed territory would bring on a morally indefensible war between a young and mighty America and an aged and feeble Mexico.

For months after he joined his regiment at "Camp Salubrity," three miles from Nachitoches, Louisiana, nothing occurred to make armed conflict appear imminent. By the time of his arrival, the 4th Infantry had settled into the same static routine that had characterized its life at Jefferson Barracks. A few patrols were dispatched toward the Texas border in response to reports that civilians bent on stirring up trouble had invaded the Rio Grande country. For the most part, however, the regiment, in common with the units that preceded and followed it to Louisiana, played a waiting game that was not expected to end until the results of the coming presidential canvass became known.

It was a listless, enervating period for everyone involved. Pete Longstreet, who had preceded Grant to the Louisiana-Texas border, later recalled that his friend, who had never gambled at Jefferson Barracks, began to play poker at Camp Salubrity (a recently established outpost of Fort Jesup) solely as a means of combating boredom. "As a matter of fact," the South Carolinian wrote, "we had nothing to do down there in camp, except to watch for the mail and when it rained, time was excessively heavy. We used to play all day at penny-ante."[23]

Poker may have helped Grant kill time, but watching the mail became his primary interest. Within a day of reaching Nachitoches he was writing to family, friends, and the teenager he loved. On June 4, he informed Julia of his safe arrival at his new post, a journey made bearable by "the most pleasing recollections of the short leave of absence" he had spent at White Haven. He gave a detailed account of the trip; described the primitive country, which he found surrounded by forests and infested with "Ticks, Red bugs, and a little creeping thing looking like a Lizard" that he didn't know the name of; and expressed his regret at having to leave St. Louis so suddenly: "I was just learning how to enjoy the place and the *Society*, at least a part of it." He closed by inserting several blank lines, explaining that if his correspondent interpreted them correctly, "they will express more than words."[24]

During the next ten months, while the 4th Infantry whiled away the seasons at Camp Salubrity, he wrote several times to Miss Dent, and was happy to receive letters in return—hers were always fewer than his, which made their receipt a true occasion. Over time, their expressions of regard for each other grew more ardent, Julia admitting that she dreamed more frequently than ever of her absent lieutenant, Grant expressing an ever more desperate longing to see her again. By January 1845, enough terms of endearment had been exchanged that he could write: "Why should I use to you here the language of flattery, Julia, when we have spoken so much more plainly of our feeling for each other?"[25]

Soon after he wrote, agitation in Washington and Mexico City rose to new heights over the Texas question, although it did not immediately affect the situation along the Texas border. At the end of February 1845, Congress reversed its former course by heeding the mandate given Tyler's recently elected but yet-to-be-inaugurated successor, James K. Polk, to annex the contentious republic. On March 3, two days after the House supported the Senate's actions, Tyler signed a resolution granting Texas statehood. Polk, almost as soon as he occupied the Executive Mansion, took steps to have the legislation put into effect, then turned his attention to the equally daunting task of acquiring for his nation the provinces of California and New Mexico.

Not unnaturally, the Mexican government considered the actions of Tyler, Polk, and the Congress as acts of aggression. On June 4, President Jose Joaquin de Herrera repeated his country's oft-expressed intention to keep Texas from joining the American Union by all means possible. The Polk administration refused to be cowed; on June 29, General Taylor was ordered to occupy northwestern Texas with his three thousand troops. Taylor prepared to move to his initial destination, Corpus Christi, by sending his infantry in transports from New Orleans and his cavalry via overland march from Fort Jesup.[26]

Lieutenant Grant was on hand to make the movement with his regiment, but just barely—an interlude up north almost cost him the opportunity. On April 1, he obtained five weeks' leave of absence and made a mad dash for St. Louis, White Haven, and the girl he had pined for over the past ten months. He arrived at the Dent household only one day before Colonel Dent set out for his native Maryland, there to settle some legal business involving the family. When Julia spied her favorite lieutenant galloping up to the front gate on a dapple gray horse, she tore herself away from the neighbors and friends who had gathered to bid her father Godspeed. She expected her beau to kiss her warmly; after briefly touching her hand, the shy visitor "passed on to greet the company, many of whom he knew." When at last they were alone, Ulysses informed her that the following morning he intended to accompany Mr. Dent to his point of departure in St. Louis and there ask him a "most important question." Julia, who had become happily reconciled to their marriage, was thrilled to hear that he had finally found the courage to ask her father's consent.[27]

In his memoirs, Grant recalled that on this trip he "secured the desired approval." Julia, however, insisted that when Grant broached the subject of their betrothal and marriage, her father raised objections, chief among them "the roving life [she] would have to lead as a soldier's wife," for which he considered his daughter "entirely unfitted." In fact, Colonel Dent had no intention of loosening his paternal bonds on Julia, especially by entrusting her to a lowly officer of Northern birth and sensibilities.[28]

According to Julia, Grant suggested to her father the possibility of his leaving the army to become a college instructor. This seems unlikely, for no such position was then available, and he had no firm intention of teaching anywhere except his alma mater. Even that prospect appeared remote. Although his mathematics instructor at the Academy had promised to recommend him for an assistant's position, the effort had been derailed by his posting to Louisiana. If indeed he made such a proposal to Julia's father, it did not soften the old man's position. He advised the lieutenant "to stick to his profession"; and although he professed to have no personal objection to Grant, he repeated his desire that his daughter not experience a knockabout, transient life with a husband lacking fair prospect of promotion and decent pay. The only sop the colonel gave Julia's suitor was permission to continue his correspondence with his beloved.[29]

Grant had to be content with this meager gesture. He was consoled by his awareness that the colonel's wife considered him capable of great things and therefore favored his suit. Like her daughter, Mrs. Dent awoke to portentous dreams. In one of these, Grant appeared in the guise of a great man—a president or potentate of some sort—before whom everyone bowed and offered obeisance. Perhaps Julia's mother, fortified by this powerful vision, could duplicate the success of Grant's maternal grandmother, who had persuaded Hannah Simpson's father to accept as a son-in-law a man he considered unworthy of his daughter's hand.[30]

★ ★ ★

Grant returned to Camp Salubrity during the first week of May 1845. At once he wrote to Julia asking whether her father had commented on their recent heart-to-heart and calling his visit to White Haven "the most pleasant part" of his life: "In fact it seems more like a pleasant dream than reality." He expected soon to be moving down the Mississippi to New Orleans, but the transfer was delayed by the deliberate manner in which Texas officials responded to the offer of statehood made by Congress. Not until early July did a convention of elected delegates officially accept annexation and reject the Mexican government's counterproposal of full independence for Texas. In October, the convention's action would be ratified by popular vote, and two days before year's end Texas would enter the Union as the twenty-eighth state.[31]

It was July 3 before the 4th Infantry departed Grand Ecore, Louisiana, for New Orleans, where it arrived two days later. The outfit was posted to the local military installation; there it "again waited weeks," as Grant recalled, "for still further orders." Ordinarily, regimental personnel would have spent much of the time sightseeing in the nation's most cosmopolitan city, but because the feared *vomito*—yellow fever—was making its annual visit to the area, the 4th was confined to New Orleans Barracks for the greater part of its stay. Even at a distance, the soldiers took in the sights and sounds of the local culture, some of which jarred the sensibilities. One morning, Grant came awake on his barracks cot to the sound of small arms' fire. Peering out the window, he observed a group of civilians but could not tell what they were up to. Upon inquiring, he was told that the gunfire was indicative of "nothing; only a couple of gentlemen deciding a difference of opinion with rifles, at twenty paces."[32]

Grant and his comrades spent two months in New Orleans. By the time its men piled into ships for the run down the Gulf Coast to Corpus Christi Bay, his regiment was commanded by its executive officer, Lieutenant Colonel John Garland. Soon after reaching New Orleans, Colonel Vose, suspecting that field campaigning was imminent, had quit his desk for the drill field, where he attempted, for the first time in many months, to put the companies and battalions of the 4th through their paces. The "old gentleman" managed to complete only a couple of evolutions before suffering a stroke. He turned back toward his headquarters, stopped, clutched his heart, and fell over dead. His sudden demise, coming as it did on the verge of the regiment's invasion of disputed territory, appeared a bad omen. Although he was soon replaced by Colonel William Whistler, the new commander was sixty-five and reported to be a tippler. Grant undoubtedly considered Lieutenant Colonel Garland better qualified, physically and intellectually, to take charge of the outfit.[33]

The channel at the mouth of Corpus Christi Bay being extremely shallow, the men of Grant's outfit were carried to shore aboard steam launches by way of Shell Island, almost twenty miles out in the Gulf. For several days Grant did duty on that rugged spit of land before accompanying a large detachment of his regiment ashore. At the mouth of the Nueces River, his company encamped near a fishing village that sported an American-run trading post dealing primarily in leaf tobacco and cotton goods. In this venue, the lieutenant obtained a close-up view of the people whose military forces he expected to meet in battle before long. Although he found most of the natives to be hardworking, law-abiding, and deeply religious, he believed the Mexican people had been robbed of enterprise and initiative through centuries of Spanish oppression. They had, he wrote, "been brought up ignorant of how to regulate or how to rule." What seemed worse, after winning their independence in hard-fought battle, the people had adopted many of the same stultifying laws with which their European overlords had perpetuated their rule.[34]

Grant's regiment spent the next six months at Corpus Christi as General Taylor slowly massed and organized his four-thousand-man "Army of Occupation." Although capable of giving a good account of itself in battle, the force was not sizable enough, and did not occupy a critical enough position, to provoke the Mexican forces of Major General Pedro de Ampudia, commander of the Division of the North, into commencing hostilities. Grant was convinced that such provocation was requisite to the war aims of the Polk administration. An attempt by Ampudia to challenge Taylor's occupation would furnish a pretext for aggressive action by the Americans under the fiction of self-defense.

For this state of affairs, Lieutenant Grant did not blame Taylor, whom he considered a pawn in the hands of his civilian superiors. As an avowed Whig, Taylor was considered a political rival of Polk's; and if rumors were true, the general was suspicious of the motives that had sent him to the Texas coast. In time, Grant come to admire "Old Rough and Ready," not only for his tacit opposition to the expansionist policies of Washington but also for his brand of leadership. In contrast to colleagues and superiors, including Winfield Scott, Taylor was a modest, unostentatious soldier who preferred nonmilitary or semi-military attire to gilt-spangled uniforms and avoided enslavement to military custom and detail. His behavior was in keeping with Grant's attitudes toward dress and deportment. Then, too, he applauded Taylor's ability to keep his head in a crisis: "No soldier could face either danger or responsibility more calmly than he. These are qualities more rarely found than genius or physical courage."[35]

Later, when he came under the command of General Scott, Grant was able to appreciate his professional gifts as well. He came to consider Scott a greater strategist than Taylor, and just as accomplished a tactician. He also trusted Scott, another declared Whig, not to allow himself to be manipulated for political purposes by the Democrats in power. In comparing the two commanders, however, Grant made a distinction that in his memoirs he reduced to a single sentence: "Both were pleasant to serve under—Taylor was pleasant to serve with."[36]

★ ★ ★

While waiting for further orders, Taylor's army passed the long, sweltering months at Corpus Christi "engaged in all the duties pertaining to the officer and the soldier." Such duties Grant now performed as a full-rank second lieutenant, but one assigned to the 7th Infantry. Despite the loss of his regimental commander, and his friction-laden relationship with Captain Buchanan, Grant desired to remain in the ranks of the 4th. He saw a means of returning to his desired posting when he learned that a recently promoted second lieutenant in the 7th, Franklin Gardner (later a Confederate general despite his New York roots), had been assigned—to his chagrin—to the 4th. In short order, Grant and Gardner made application to swap assignments, and within a few weeks their petitions were granted.[37]

While at Corpus Christi, Grant spent his duty hours engaged in company, battalion, and regimental drill, and his off-duty hours writing to the woman he addressed as "Dearest Julia." Over the next two years, while the lovers remained far apart, he would send her at least forty-one letters—almost two a week—from the theater of operations in Texas and Mexico. Each would give Julia as much of the war news as Grant thought fit to tell her (although some letters included graphic details of battle and gory descriptions of comrades' wounds). Increasingly, the correspondence abounded in expressions of love for Miss Dent and of the suffering their estrangement was causing him. For the first time in his life, the emotionally repressed Grant had found someone to whom he could bare his heart, and even his soul. Should something occur to prevent their marriage, he doubted that he would find another with whom he could share his most private thoughts and his most poignant feelings.

Whenever opportunity arose, the lieutenant sought detached assignments that would hold at bay his loneliness and ease the discomforts of camp life in a desert-like environment. In December. he accompanied a wagon train on a month-long journey to and from San Antonio, where the Alamo's defenders had made history a decade earlier, and Austin, the new state's capital. It was on this trip that Grant revealed himself a poor hunter of wild turkeys—as well as a poor estimator of the number of wolves in a pack. The clamorous beasts following the wagons for a large portion of the journey howled up such a storm that Grant surmised it came from the throats of at least twenty of them. When he finally gained a close-up view, he discovered that only two wolves were responsible for the unearthly racket. Looking back after a long political career, he reflected that he had been reminded of this incident several times over the years when he "heard the noise of a few disappointed politicians who had deserted their associates. There are always more of them before they are counted."[38]

Returning safely to the Rio Grande, Grant found a novel way to escape dull routine, if only briefly. Forced to provide their own entertainment, the officers of Grant's regiment formed an acting troupe, which they persuaded Grant to join. They planned a series of performances in an eight-hundred-seat amphitheater constructed during off-duty hours under the supervision of Captain John Bankhead Magruder of the 1st U.S. Artillery. The theater opened on January 8, 1846, with a production of the *Moor of Venice,* an adaptation of *Othello.*

In keeping with the practices of Shakespeare's time, the lithe, smooth-faced Grant was cast in the role of the vivacious but worrisome daughter of Senator Brabanito. How well he might have met the demands of the part will never be known, for his improbable casting was objected to by Lieutenant Theodoric Porter, who had the title role. The dissatisfied Porter sent all the way to New Orleans for a professional actress, whom he persuaded to come south and replace Grant. Presumably, she filled the bill, for *The Moor of Venice* played to packed audiences throughout its run, which ended early in March with the army's departure from Corpus Christi. Six weeks later, the play's leading man was dead, the victim of Mexican irregulars prowling the banks of the Rio Grande.[39]

The orders that caused General Taylor's command to quit its long-occupied position on the Nueces sent it one hundred and fifty miles to the south. It was to take up a position on the Rio Grande near Brownsville, directly across from the city of Matamoras. Grant believed he knew why the army wanted a more forward post: "It was desirable to occupy a position near the largest centre of population possible to reach, without absolutely invading territory to which we set up no claim whatever."[40]

Taylor's advance, which his enemy could hardly ignore, was made in four columns, each one day's march from the next, an arrangement that tempted the Mexicans to intervene. Still, no opposition materialized. Just north of Brownsville, the columns closed up to cross the Arroyo Colorado, then descended upon the Rio Grande, which they reached on March 28. Taylor fortified his position against the approach of enemy troops, who finally appeared to be seeking a confrontation.

It took another six weeks for the two armies to come into contact at full strength. On April 24, Major General Mariano Arista, General Ampudia's recently installed successor, reached Matamoras and assumed command of the more than five thousand troops in the vicinity. While he organized them for battle, Arista informed Taylor under flag of truce that hostilities between the United States and Mexico had begun (even though the U.S. Congress would not pass a formal declaration of war until May 13). Immediately afterward, the Mexican commander advanced a portion of his force across the river below Taylor's position, and on April 30 he followed with his main body. Taylor responded by falling back to the coast at Port Isabel, where he gathered supplies and assimilated reinforcements from New Orleans. Then he returned south to rescue a garrison across from Matamoras that Arista had begun to besiege.[41]

Apprised of Taylor's approach, Arista moved to bar the Americans' path; when an opportunity for more decisive action arose, he attacked. The result was the first pitched battle of the conflict, Palo Alto (May 8), followed by equally heavy fighting the following day at Resaca de la Palma. Both were tactical victories for Taylor. The first was won through the effective use of artillery; the second turned on dramatic achievements by dragoon and foot units. Grant saw no action in the first engagement, but in the second, after his immediate superior, Captain George A. McCall, was sent off on a scouting mission, he led his company in a belated charge that resulted in the capture of some Mexicans, including a wounded colonel. The significance of the feat, which occurred after the battle had turned, Grant downplayed ("the battle of Resaca de la Palma would have been won, just as it was, if I had not been there"). Still, he had performed coolly and effectively under fire even as officers and men all around him were struck down, some blown apart by shot and shell. This fact should have quieted at least some of the doubts he continued to harbor about his aptitude for soldiering.[42]

Following their twin defeats, Arista's forces fell back across the river to Matamoras, some so hastily that they drowned in the raging stream. With the cooperation of Commodore David Conner's naval squadron, Taylor made preparations to force a crossing and pursue toward Mexico City. On May 18, his advance echelon occupied recently abandoned Matamoras, thus transforming itself into the "Army of Invasion." There his ranks were swollen by an influx of volunteer units including an Ohio regiment whose major, Thomas Hamer, had appointed Grant to the Military Academy. Grant was glad to see him; he considered the politician-turned-soldier "one of the ablest men Ohio ever produced." Hamer would win promotion to brigadier general only to contract a virulent disease that took his life at forty-five. In a letter of sympathy to his benefactor's widow, Grant observed that "he died within the sound of battle, and that was a pleasure to him as a brave soldier."[43]

Grant believed that had he survived the war, Hamer would have risen all the way to the White House. Hamer evidently thought just as highly of Grant, in the military sense. Shortly before his death, he informed a friend that he had found Lieutenant Grant "a most remarkable and valuable young soldier." He added, "I anticipate for him a brilliant future, if he should have an opportunity to display his powers when they mature. . . . Lieutenant Grant is too young for command, but his capacity for future military usefulness is undoubted."[44]

★ ★ ★

Because of the extended supply line he was compelled to maintain, Zachary Taylor counseled his civilian superiors against an advance directly against Mexico City from the Rio Grande. He recommended a campaign against Monterrey, a move that would isolate Mexico's northwestern provinces from the rest of the country. His advice was accepted, but the War Department pursued a parallel plan to invade the Mexican interior by way of the Gulf Coast, starting from either Tampico or Vera Cruz.

By early June, while Lieutenant Grant was writing to his beloved in hopes that her father had consented to their marrying, Taylor was directing his attention, and his army's movements, toward Monterrey. The general believed that once he was in position to attack the city, its garrison would evacuate. In fact, the newly reinstalled commander in chief of Mexico's forces, General Antonio Lopez de Santa Anna, advised against defending Monterrey; but the local commander, Ampudia, believed the abandonment or surrender of the city would reflect badly on himself and his troops. His sense of honor decreed that there would be a battle for control of the main population center of northeastern Mexico.

Not until late September, after a month of advancing across a sun-scorched desert, mainly on night marches, was the Army of Invasion, now nearly twenty thousand strong, in position to assault the well-fortified city. When he attacked on September 21, Taylor ordered Lieutenant Colonel Garland, temporarily commanding a division, to make a diversionary attack on the east side of the city. If Garland's feint succeeded, another division under Brevet Major General William Jenkins Worth would assault the western side of Monterrey.

Garland made a valiant effort, but Grant would fault him for attacking head-on against forts that he could have bypassed, thereby incurring heavy losses. Garland's assault eventually bogged down, whereupon Taylor sent in a second wave, including the 4th Infantry, which seized a fortified tannery on the city's northeastern outskirts and attacked nearby "Fort Diablo," a strategically located position whose defenders took a heavy toll of the *americanos*.[45]

This day, Lieutenant Grant was assigned to an inactive sector in his role as acting quartermaster of his regiment (he would not formally be assigned to the position until the following spring). He began the battle with the supply train in rear of the column northeast of the city, but he found he could not resist the pull of combat. Without permission, he rode to the scene of the fighting, met his regiment on the outskirts of the city, and, still in the saddle, joined its assault on the tannery and Fort Diablo. When the position proved too formidable to take, the 4th fell back, regrouped, and advanced against other, less formidable works farther to the east. In this movement, Grant participated aboard a second steed—he had loaned his horse to the foot-weary adjutant of the 4th, who was killed in the fight. Grant was immediately detailed to fill the fallen man's position. Thus, wrote William S. McFeely, "Grant had shed the grocery-clerk guise of the quartermaster and forced his way into a position of small authority in a battle."[46]

His regiment's second attack carried Grant through the fire-swept streets of the city, where he dodged bullets by riding half in, half out of the saddle. When dwindling ammunition brought the 4th to a halt short of its objective, the central plaza, the newly appointed adjutant volunteered to fetch more. One foot in the stirrups, the other astride the saddle, his body shielded by the horse's sides, he again ran a gauntlet of fire. "It was only at street crossings that my horse was under fire," he recalled, "but these I crossed at such a flying rate that generally I was past and under cover of the next block of houses before the enemy fired. I got out safely without a scratch."[47]

Gathering up the promised ammunition, he turned to ride back to his regiment. Before he could start out, the regiment joined him on the city outskirts, having retreated in a body at the order of its brigadier commander. The 4th Infantry's, and Lieutenant Grant's, role in the battle was effectively over.

Two days later, the long-delayed main effort finally went forward. Supported by simultaneous advances in diverse sectors, Worth's men overran fortifications along the west side of the city and fought their way to the plaza. Their penetration, and the enemy's inability to dislodge it as it had Garland's earlier advance, persuaded General Ampudia to cease firing and seek an armistice. After much deliberation, Taylor accepted his surrender but, hopeful of "conquering a peace" through accommodation, he granted Ampudia's request that his troops march out carrying their personal arms.[48]

★ ★ ★

Following the September 26–28 withdrawal of Monterrey's defenders, the Army of Invasion enjoyed what Grant termed "a quiet camp life until midwinter." In actuality, it was November 13 when Taylor, at the behest of his superiors in Washington, informed Santa Anna that the armistice established two months earlier had been terminated and active operations had recommenced. Subsequently, Taylor moved southwestward toward Saltillo and Buena Vista, but with only a portion of the army that had captured Monterrey. Most of his regulars, including the 4th Infantry, had been taken from him to reinforce the column preparing to move on Mexico City from the Gulf Coast.

This force had been entrusted to General Scott, another move that Grant perceived to have political overtones. Taylor had won so many highly publicized victories that Whig politicians and editors were clamoring to nominate him for the presidency, a move the Polk administration wished to thwart, or at least forestall. Polk intended to do so by denying Old Rough and Ready a force large enough to win another major battle. The "excess" troops thus went to Scott, another Whig, but one whose political influence was considered less potent than his colleague's. As Grant saw it: "It was no doubt supposed that Scott's ambition would lead him to slaughter Taylor or destroy his chances for the Presidency, and yet it was hoped that he would not make sufficient capital himself to secure the prize."[49]

If Grant's view of the military-political situation was accurate, Polk and his advisors achieved only one of their objectives. Although stripped of his regulars, Taylor would defy the odds to defeat a larger Mexican force at Buena Vista the following February. The triumph would help sweep him into the White House in November 1848. Scott's campaign against Mexico City would prove even more successful, gaining him the Whig Party's presidential nomination in 1852, but he would go down to defeat at the hands of one of his own brigadiers, the Democrat Franklin Pierce.

When Scott reached the mouth of the Rio Grande in December 1846, he at once began to carve up Taylor's army. Most of the nearly five thousand troops that he took from his subordinate (to whom Scott added perhaps seven thousand more) reached him by way of the port of Tampico. The rest, under General Worth, including Grant's regiment, joined the coastal column after a return march to the Rio Grande.

Grant was surprised when Worth moved north with a rapidity bordering on the frantic, for as soon as his troops reached the river they went into camp for several weeks to await transportation. On March 6, 1847, Scott's army finally began its passage down the coast toward its initial objective.

Three days later, the troops came ashore at Vera Cruz and began to lay siege to the walled city. Confined to his quartermaster's duties this day, Lieutenant Grant observed the progress of the investment from afar as Scott pounded the garrison with his heavy batteries. By March 26, doubtful that he could hold out much longer, the city's commander opened a correspondence with his opponent. Three days later, he surrendered his five thousand troops.[50]

Survival instincts—Vera Cruz, which had been built upon the coastal plain, was susceptible to the annual onslaught of the *vomito*—prompted Scott early in April to depart the captured citadel and take the road to Mexico City, two hundred and fifty miles away. On April 17 and 18, elements of his command successfully engaged the enemy at Cerro Gordo, and, three weeks later, occupied the city of Puebla. There the commanding general awaited reinforcements, including ten newly formed regiments of regulars. Delays in assimilating these units and readying them for field campaigning consumed four months.[51]

Although Grant considered the Puebla vicinity a healthy and picturesque venue, he was quite willing to leave it by the time Scott finally resumed his march through the Valley of Mexico. By now Grant reposed utmost confidence in the expeditionary commander. As when he had beheld Scott for the first time at West Point, he viewed the erect and towering Virginian as a paragon of military élan. Ever togged out in the full panoply of military finery (his nickname, after all, was "Old Fuss and Feathers"), Scott went nowhere without an entourage of staff officers and escort troops; and he was insistent that a soldier, when in his presence, should observe every regulation and honor every custom of military culture. Yet there was more to the man than splendid uniforms and attention to minutiae. Scott was articulate, even eloquent, in expressing his battle plans and reporting his army's operations. He was an expert in the theory and practice of warfare. He exuded cool-headedness and grace under fire. And despite his airs and pretensions, he was personable enough to connect on a human level with the lowliest private in the ranks. All in all, he seemed just the man to lead the way into the fabled Hall of the Montezumas.[52]

Validating Grant's trust, Scott engineered a campaign so masterly in its tactical and strategic applications that no less a critic than the Duke of Wellington would pronounce it "unsurpassed in military annals." On August 7, he advanced the army, four divisions strong, toward Mexico City by deftly circumventing an extensive *pedregal* (lava bed) and some of the most mountainous terrain in the country. The route was replete with obstacles, but because of the difficulties they posed, Santa Anna had not expected Scott to come that way; thus he failed to defend it adequately. Scott's ability to evade or sur-mount the hazards facing him was largely due to daring reconnaissance per-formed by members of his staff, notably his favorite aide, Virginia-born Captain Robert E. Lee of the Corps of Engineers, an officer whom Grant came to know, though only slightly, in the aftermath of this campaign.[53]

Despite the roadblocks, the army advanced with remarkable speed, the result of Scott's decision to cut loose from his supply lines, a move whose advantages were not lost on Quartermaster Grant. But in stripping his col-umn for speed, Scott did not sacrifice hitting power. He first encountered the enemy in strength at Contreras, just outside the capital, on August 19–20, where he won an overwhelming victory. At Churubusco, five miles closer to Mexico City, he struck Santa Anna again on August 20, suffering approximately one thousand casualties while inflicting six times as many on his opponent.

From Churubusco, Scott advanced to the suburb of Tacubaya, where he halted under the terms of an arranged armistice while officials of the warring nations attempted to work out a peace agreement that would result in the acquisition not only of Texas but also California and the New Mexico Terri-tory for the United States. Santa Anna, now serving as his country's presi-dent as well as its military commander, had no intention of granting these demands; he exploited the armistice to perfect his defense of Mexico City. By early September, negotiations had stalled, the armistice was lifted, and fighting resumed. Scott's next victory came at Molino del Rey on September 7 and 8, after which he made his final approach to the walled and gated capital. Throughout September 12, he subjected the city to a massive bom-bardment, and the next day sent his divisions against its many and intricate defenses.[54]

During the long advance against the enemy capital, Grant had seen com-bat only at Molino del Rey. There he captured some demoralized defenders and encountered a disabled colleague—none other than his old friend (and, he hoped, his future brother-in-law), Fred Dent. He placed the young lieu-tenant, who had taken an ugly wound in the thigh, in a position that shel-tered him from flying missiles, and he saw to it that Fred received medical aid before his wound turned critical.[55]

Thus far, Grant's participation in combat had been limited to a backwater of the fighting, and his services had made no impact on the outcome. On September 13, he again laid aside his staff duties, but this time to play a ma-jor role in the storming of the Garita de San Cosme, the northeastern portal to Mexico City. Simultaneous with that effort, other troops attempted to enter the Garita de Belen, a little more than a thousand yards to the south, and several columns of troops assaulted the fortified castle of Chapultepec, on the city's southwestern outskirts.

While advancing with his regiment toward that gate under a torrent of musketry and cannon fire, Grant spied a mountain howitzer that had become detached from its parent unit. With commendable initiative, he had the little cannon broken down to its several parts. Then, over the protests of a local priest, he helped its crew manhandle the piece up the steps of a church situated on the south side of the road leading to the gate. When they reached the belfry, the crew reassembled the howitzer. With Grant acting as spotter, the men were soon delivering a plunging fire on the gate's nearest defenders.

Grant's daring and foresight had the desired effect: The fire kept the Mexicans far enough from the gate to permit Worth's troops to batter their way through to the center of the city. Attackers elsewhere were similarly successful in gaining entrance, and by late in the day Santa Anna again had been forced to flee at the head of a demoralized army. In abandoning his capital, he conceded final defeat.

Grant's exploit with the howitzer attracted the notice of General Worth and two of his subordinates—all mentioned him prominently in their after-action reports. Worth was so pleased by the effect of the shelling that he sent Grant a second howitzer, unaware that the belfry was too small to accommodate it. Grant briefly considered telling Worth as much when one of the latter's staff officers, Lieutenant John C. Pemberton, escorted him to the general's side, where he delivered a brief report of his operations. After giving the matter thought, however, Grant decided to keep his mouth shut. He had begun to suspect that September 13, 1847, would prove to be a red-letter day in his military career, and he decided not to ruin it by contradicting a major general to his face.[56]

★ Chapter 3 ★

Union and Separation

Short days after the capture and occupation of Mexico City, Grant wrote to Julia: "Since my last letter to you four of the hardest fought battles that the world ever witnessed have taken place, and the most astonishing victories have crowned the American arms. But dearly they have paid for it! The loss of officers and men killed and wounded is frightful."[1]

The carnage may have been excessive, but victory has a way of sponging up the blood as well as making the careers of those who caused it to be spilled. Those at the top of the chain of command—Taylor, Scott, Pierce, and several of their subordinates—would reap renown from the outcome of this campaign. Lesser-ranking officers such as Sam Grant, however, would have little to show for their participation in the conquest of America's elderly neighbor. Looking back on this, his first wartime service, he would offer this reflection: "I had gone into the battle of Palo Alto in May, 1846, a second lieutenant, and I entered the city of Mexico sixteen months later with the same rank, after having been in all the engagements possible for any one man and in a regiment that lost more officers during the war than it ever had present at any one engagement."[2]

Still, he had profited only to the extent of having his name inserted in the reports of three superiors and having gained a couple of hollow-sounding honors. He would be awarded two brevets—that of first lieutenant for his prosaic involvement in the fighting at Molino del Rey, and that of captain for his heroics at the San Cosme gate. Although regulations permitted him to wear the insignia of the highest brevet rank, he remained a very junior officer. In the peacetime army, it took the average lieutenant a decade or more to advance to the full grade of captain, and even longer to attain field rank. At that pace, even should he remain in the service for twenty years, Grant

45

might never attain battalion command, let alone command of a regiment such as the 4th.

These considerations would have depressed any ambitious, self-respecting officer; but with the din of battle fading, Grant also faced a return to the uninspiring routine of the supply service. As peace negotiations and occupation duty dragged on into the winter months, he briefly found himself "somewhat busy" at Tacubaya, the village southwest of Mexico City to which his regiment had been transferred following Santa Anna's retreat. Here his most time-consuming chore was to provide his increasingly tattered comrades with clothing that would enable them to survive the cold-weather season. For some reason, General Scott had been unable to procure an adequate supply from the United States, the result being that, although the army hired local tailors to remove the deficiency, clothing continued to be "so much needed that it was seized as fast as made up."[3]

Grant's duties increased considerably when his superiors conferred on him the additional responsibility of regimental commissary officer (he had relinquished the adjutancy he had temporarily accepted on September 13). Supplying his outfit with sufficient rations while subsisting on what was available in an enemy's country required the greatest enterprise. So, too, did the concomitant necessity of building up the regimental fund that furnished the musicians of the 4th with a portion of their pay. Grant met the challenge by renting a bakery in Tacubaya, hiring local bakers, buying fuel and other supplies as frugally as possible, and producing enough bread to feed not only his own outfit but much of the rest of the army as well. The bread contract he secured with the army's chief quartermaster returned enough profits to keep the 4th's bandsmen thumping and tootling away, even if their tin-eared benefactor could not appreciate the joyous sounds they produced.[4]

★ ★ ★

The spring of 1848 found Sam Grant and his comrades still on occupation duty outside the Mexican capital. By now, at least, the long-extended peace negotiations had produced the Treaty of Guadalupe Hidalgo. Approved by the Senate on March 10 and ratified by the Mexican congress two months later, the pact ceded California and New Mexico to the United States at a cost of fifteen million dollars and recognized U.S. sovereignty over all of Texas north of the Rio Grande.

With a treaty completed, it was supposed that the 4th Infantry would quit the conquered land and return to the United States. When these orders, too, were slow in coming—and until they did, no leaves of absence could be granted—Brevet Captain Grant became frustrated and downhearted. For too long, his thoughts had been riveted on Missouri, White Haven, and Dearest Julia. The letters he received from her—never as many as those he sent out—he read and reread again and again before ceremoniously retiring them to his trunk. In replying to her, he expressed "great anxiety" over the prospect that their estrangement would never end. Months ago, he had wailed: "The idea of staying longer in this country is to me insupportable. Just think of the three long years that have passed since we met." Now, he was "nearly crazy to get away." So desperate was he to see his soul mate that he considered the wildly impractical scheme of paying her way to Tacubaya ("if you were here I should never wish to leave Mexico").[5]

His homesickness only intensified, and soon his longing for Ohio, Missouri, and Julia was no longer susceptible of distraction. The army's supply demands had diminished with the return of warm weather, and he had relinquished his commissary duties. He was no longer busy enough to forget his wretched situation, even for a few hours. Perhaps not surprisingly, he sought release from his troubles in alcohol. Some of his comrades, seeking to protect the heroic reputation Grant later achieved, would claim that he never drank while in Mexico. Others maintained that he did imbibe, but not to excess. Some could understand the temptation he was exposed to as a custodian not only of arms, equipment, and clothing but also of medical supplies, including stockpiles of whiskey and wine. Looking back years later, the drum major of the 4th insisted that, although he never saw Grant in a drunken state, "he did drink a little." After all, "that was pretty good whisky he had [access to]."[6]

Others who knew Grant at Tacubaya reported that he drank heavily enough to show the effects. Early in May 1848, Captain John W. Lowe of the 2nd Ohio Volunteers, an acquaintance of Grant's from their Georgetown days, was surprised by the quartermaster's "altered" appearance. In a letter to his wife, Lowe wrote that Grant, whom he had always known to be clean-shaven, had grown a scraggly beard that stretched almost to his waist and made him look rather like a vagrant. More shockingly, "I fear he drinks too much but don't you say a word on that subject." Another colleague was more nonchalant in portraying Grant's stint of occupation duty: "He went about a good deal with horse-farriers, took his drinks, smoked his pipe," and employed every weapon at his disposal against the listless, and seemingly endless, routine.[7]

He went to great lengths to take his mind off Julia, his poor prospects for advancement, and the dullness of his existence. One Sunday, he even forced himself to attend a bullfight, although convinced that he would not enjoy it. "The sight to me was sickening," he recalled. "I could not see how human beings could enjoy the sufferings of beasts, and often of men, as they seemed to do on these occasions." In May, he joined a party of fellow officers that included several future commanders of Confederate forces, including Captains Henry Hopkins Sibley and George Crittenden and Lieutenant Richard H. Anderson, in climbing Popocatepetl, "the highest mountain in North America," and traversing the Valley of Cuernavaca to explore Mexico's mammoth caves. These expeditions may have provided release from his suffering, but not surcease.[8]

His ordeal finally neared closure in June, when the occupation forces began to pack up in preparation for their return to the United States. The brigade to which Grant's outfit was attached massed at Jalapa, two miles from Vera Cruz, where it awaited transportation north. The move to Jalapa, which was situated "above the *vomito*," had ostensibly been made for health reasons. Even so, several regiments, including the 4th, were held in camp for a week while yellow fever ravaged not-distant parts of the country. Grant's health had been good throughout his service in Mexico, but he feared, as he told Julia, that "exposure to weather and a Tropical Sun had added ten years" to his age. "At this rate I will soon be old"—even if the calendar said otherwise.[9]

Even if he had aged beyond his years, he stepped sprightly enough when on July 11 he boarded the transport that would carry his regiment up the Rio Grande. The journey was slow and much-delayed, and for a time progress was almost imperceptible; but on July 23 he was finally deposited at East Pascagoula, Mississippi, the site of Camp Jefferson Davis, namesake of a local colonel who had led a bayonet charge that helped turn the tide at Buena Vista. No sooner did Grant set foot in camp than he obtained a sixty-day leave of absence that included a proviso for a two-month extension. After turning over his supply duties to Lieutenant Henry Wallen, he bade farewell to his comrades and, accompanied by their good wishes, headed north by steamer and train for Bethel, Ohio.[10]

En route he sent the last two letters he would address to Julia for months to come. Before this, he had not written to her for several weeks. Troubled by his silence, Julia was made happy again when—in fulfillment of another prediction that had come to her in a dream—she learned of the missives' arrival in St. Louis through the "advertised letters" section of the newspaper. They had failed to find her at White Haven because during that summer her family had resided in a townhouse in the city that Colonel Dent originally rented so that Julia and her sister Nell "might more conveniently enjoy the gay society of St. Louis." When Julia claimed the letters, she learned that her fiancé wanted her to set a date for their wedding. It turned out that a date could not be decided until he reached her side in the last days of July. He boarded at the Planters' House hotel, for he intended the trip to be brief; from St. Louis he planned to visit his family in Ohio. Because he would not return to the city until mid-August, the couple settled on August 22 for their gala day.[11]

By this time, all obstacles to their union had been surmounted. Through patient but determined effort, Mrs. Dent and Julia's siblings had reconciled Colonel Dent to a situation he lacked the power to control. Grant's prominent mention in battlefield dispatches had also played a role in overcoming Dent's less-than-lofty opinion of the young officer. So, too, had Grant's ministrations to the colonel's wounded son, which may have saved Fred's life.

If the Dents were accepting of (or resigned to) the marriage, Grant's family seems to have known little or nothing about their son's plans until his visit to Bethel. One of Grant's earliest biographers claims that on this occasion Hannah Grant made her only comment on her son's decision to take a wife: "A wise thing, Ulysses." Apparently, no member of the family accompanied him to St. Louis for the wedding, although he assured them that he would soon return in the company of his blushing bride.[12]

The nuptials were celebrated at the Dent house on the corner of Seventh and Gerre Streets. Although some accounts describe the event as an elaborate affair attended by dozens of the bride and groom's friends and relatives, Julia recalled that her wedding was simple: "The season was unfavorable for a large gathering, and our temporary home in St. Louis was small." She wore "a magnificent, rich, soft, white, watered silk" gown with a fringed veil of white tulle, a present from the matriarch of the O'Fallon family, in whose home she had been a favorite guest. The groom was attired in his dress uniform, which included an unfamiliar accessory, a sheathed saber. One guest recalled, "There were some good-natured criticisms about his bearing at the wedding. He wore his regimentals and some people thought it would have been better had he dressed in civilian's clothes. They said he seemed very awkward and embarrassed and his long sword nearly tripped him up several times."[13]

That evening, Julia's family hosted a reception attended by all their "*old friends in the city*" as well as a few of Grant's comrades, Pete Longstreet among them. A table set up in the rear parlor provided the guests with fruits, iced drinks, "and all that papa's hospitality and good taste could suggest for the occasion." The latter included a wedding cake that Julia considered "a marvel of beauty." If the refreshments included wine or punch spiked with alcohol, the groom either abstained or partook moderately—at any rate, there were no embarrassing incidents other than those caused by that unruly sword.[14]

There were also musicians. Julia recalled, "Two of my gay bridesmaids took a turn around the room, saying they could not resist waltzing just a round or two." Sam Grant, who had never overcome his aversion to dancing, did resist the lure of the waltz. Bride and groom took no turn on the dance floor, although it may be supposed that at some point Julia whirled about in the arms of a father still resentful about having to give her up to a man he did not believe would make her happy.[15]

The bridal couple began their honeymoon by traveling up the Mississippi to the homes of the groom's relatives and friends. It was an especially memorable journey for Julia, who had not ventured far from St. Louis and had never traveled on a steamboat. They stopped first at Louisville, where they visited some of Grant's cousins, one of whom, Elizabeth Thornton Grant, the wife of Jesse Grant's nephew Solomon, accompanied them to Ohio. Julia enjoyed being a guest of her husband's Louisville relations; some were prosperous, and they entertained the newlyweds lavishly.

Understandably, Julia was somewhat nervous upon meeting the members of Grant's immediate family; and, in fact, she encountered a slightly cooler reception in Bethel than she had in Kentucky. Ulysses' grandmother (Hannah Grant's stepmother), who had come from the farm at Bantam to greet the bride, was "sweet and lovely" to her. Jesse Grant "met me cordially, I might say affectionately." But although she later extolled her mother-in-law as "the sweetest, kindest woman" she had ever met, it appears that Hannah failed to greet her son's wife as warmly as might have been expected. Some of Julia's relatives believed Hannah viewed her as the pampered daughter of a family with unjustified claims to gentility. Mrs. Harry Boggs, the niece of Colonel Dent, explained to Hamlin Garland that "old Mrs. Grant was a woman who did her own house work, and she couldn't think well of a daughter-in-law who employed slaves." Unwilling to embarrass Julia, Hannah never brought up the subject of the Dent "servants" in conversation with her. Still, it was a sore spot in their relationship, one that never entirely healed.[16]

Julia took an immediate liking to Ulysses' brothers and sisters—she would claim a special bond with Clara and Jennie Grant. It would appear, however, at least at first, that both girls regarded their new sister-in-law as spoiled and flighty, and occasionally condescending, although also warm-hearted and kind and deeply in love with their brother. Julia was positively enchanted by the youngest Grant, eight-year-old Mary, who, being less judgmental than her siblings, was wholly accepting of Ulysses' bride. She enjoyed showing off for Julia, who was especially impressed by the child's outsize vocabulary: "She never by any chance used any but the most elegant words to express her childlike thoughts." All in all, she was "well satisfied with [her] dear husband's family."[17]

They spent several days among Grant's relatives, friends, and neighbors. While Julia and the womenfolk talked of children, cooking, and domestic matters, Ulysses swapped recollections with old friends and regaled them with tales of military life, including "graphic accounts of his experiences during the Mexican War." Grant's conviction that political machinations had dictated the course of the conflict found its way into his conversation, one listener noting that he described the invasion of Mexico as "unjust and unholy."[18]

When the time came to leave Bethel, the bride and groom returned to the river, which carried them to towns and cities—Georgetown, Maysville, Cincinnati—where other Grant relations lived. Julia recalled, "We saw these places through magic glasses. . . . Some of the homes we visited were humble, some were not. All were charmingly hospitable and pleasant. Mr. Grant was much pleased that I liked his family and his Ohio friends."[19]

It was mid-October—shortly before his orders required him to report to his next duty station, Detroit Barracks—before the couple returned to White Haven. They spent the last six weeks of the extended leave in the Dent fold. When it was time to depart, the prospect of a lengthy separation from home and loved ones drove Julia to tears. Consoled by parents and husband, she choked off her sobs; soon she and Ulys were again on the river heading north. En route, they made a final, brief visit to Bethel, where they picked up Grant's sister Clara, who had given in to Julia's entreaties that she accompany them to Detroit, there to spend the winter with them.

Several days out of Ohio, they reached Detroit Barracks, which fronted Lake Michigan, where they joined a portion of Grant's regiment. Companies C and E of the 4th Infantry, accompanied by Colonel William Whistler, had arrived from Mississippi on November 17. Detachments were about to depart to garrison Detroit-area installations, including Forts Graciot and Mackinack, but Whistler had decided to establish regimental headquarters at Detroit Barracks (also known as Fort Brady).

Grant, having recently returned to his duties as regimental quartermaster, expected to remain at the post for the duration of his duty tour. Only days after reporting, however, he learned differently. Apparently, Whistler preferred the services of Grant's temporary successor, Lieutenant Wallen, who wished to remain at Detroit. Flouting seniority, the colonel ordered Grant to report, instead, to Brevet Colonel Francis Lee, who commanded another element of the regiment at Madison Barracks, Sackets Harbor, New York.

Grant had no desire to quit one Great Lakes instillation for another (Madison Barracks sat on the shore of Lake Ontario). He preferred to be stationed closer to his home, especially for his sister's sake. Then, too, as one of his biographers notes, Detroit "was supposed to have attractions in a social way, although a frontier post." Grant protested that as regimental quartermaster his place was at the headquarters, but Colonel Whistler was adamant that he should go and Wallen stay. Grant obeyed, although he warned his commander that he would file a protest with the War Department.[20]

The trip east, made at a most inopportune time of the year, was, as Julia described it, "long, fatiguing, and expensive." She noted, "Navigation [on the lakes] was closed and we had to hire any conveyance we could to reach this far-off and out-of-the-way place." The hazards of travel deterred Clara Grant, who returned to Bethel rather than accompany them. When, at the end of the extended journey, Brevet Captain and Mrs. Grant reached their new residence—the first they would share as husband and wife—they strove to make the best of their situation. They moved into a unit in the married officers' quarters, set up a household, and kept the fireplace stoked against the frigid winds that blew off the lake. Julia, although unused to housekeeping, struggled to keep the place warm, cheery, and spotless. Apparently she succeeded, for whenever they entertained her husband's bachelor comrades they would exclaim, "Grant, you look so happy, so comfortable here, that we are all almost tempted to get married ourselves."[21]

Quartermaster Grant managed to keep himself happily busy on duty and off. The regimental drum major, who had gotten to know him well during the war in Mexico, was happy to renew his acquaintance at Sackets Harbor: "He was very sociable, always talked to a man freely and without putting on the airs of a superior officer." The man recalled some of the ways the newly chean-shaven Grant strove to keep himself physically fit:

> He used to ride and drive a great deal. . . . He used to practice with clubs. Some said he punched a sand-bag. I never saw him do that, but he was a strong little man, and could take care of himself. He and Mrs. Grant used to go to little dancing parties, but I don't think he ever danced. He lived very modestly—he couldn't afford to do anything else on his pay. His only dissipation was in owning a fast horse; he always liked to have a fine nag, and he paid high prices to get one.[22]

Despite the irregularities involved in their posting, Mr. and Mrs. Grant would entertain fond memories of Madison Barracks, especially of the personal attachments they formed there. But "just as we had concluded that it would be very pleasant at Sackets Harbor for the winter," Washington upheld Grant's protest and ordered him back to Detroit. By then, however, the lake had frozen over and local travel had all but ceased; he was forced to remain on station until navigation reopened. But the turn of events did not upset Julia: "We had a lovely winter, made many friends, and when we left for Detroit by the first boat in the spring [of 1849], I really shed tears at parting with them."[23]

Once back at Detroit Barracks, Grant regained the position and authority that had been taken from him so irregularly. He and his young wife started housekeeping anew, this time in a one-story frame house on Fort Street along the periphery of the installation. The snug little cottage enjoyed ample grounds as well as a stable that housed Grant's fleet little mare, Nellie Bly. By now the couple had a household staff of two—a "house girl" whom a local friend had engaged for them, and Ulys's young valet, Gregorio. Lieutenant Grant had found the boy, homeless and penniless, in Mexico. He had arranged to have him brought north with his regiment; when they were back in the United States, Grant paid for the boy to receive an elementary education.

Happy to have servants at her beck and call once again, Julia thoroughly enjoyed keeping house for her officer husband. She especially cherished the "culinary experiments" she performed in the kitchen with the assistance of the house girl. Thus she was bitterly disappointed to find her support staff halved by Gregorio's defection, after less than a year in service to them, as the result of "some meddlesome person" having suggested that he might do better as his own master. Julia never understood why anyone in her employ, whether slave or servant, would trade her happy home for an uncertain, unsettled existence in the outside world.[24]

In the late summer of 1849, Julia became pregnant with their first child. It was agreed that she should return to White Haven for her confinement and delivery. Thus Grant was alone during much of his second stint in Detroit. Although the evidence is sketchy and far from conclusive, it appears that at this point, probably for the first time since leaving Mexico, he began to drink. Below the Rio Grande he had turned to alcohol as a means of combating boredom and homesickness; now he used it to fend off recurring bouts of loneliness. While his wife was by his side, he rarely imbibed, but when they were apart only liquor seemed to dull the pain.

While Grant was stationed at Detroit, Zachariah Chandler, a local merchant of some prominence, was making his initial foray into political life as a candidate for mayor of the city. Then a Whig, Chandler would later join the fledgling Republican Party; through its ranks he would rise to become one of the most powerful members of the United States Congress during the latter half of the nineteenth century. In his memoirs, Grant mentions Chandler's political bid, but gives no hint of having had a run-in with the man. In fact, in January 1851, Grant swore out a complaint against the future mayor for failing to clear the snow and ice from the sidewalk in front of his Jefferson Avenue home. One night while going to or from the post, the quartermaster had slipped on the walk and severely sprained his leg. Other officers had barely avoided the same fate; they may have urged Grant to take action against the negligent merchant.

When Grant's complaint was taken up, Chandler demanded a jury trial and defended himself in court. The heart of his defense was that Grant had been sent sprawling not by the icy snow but by his drunkenness on the night in question. Unwilling, perhaps, to antagonize the military, the court found for the complainant. But the fine it levied upon Chandler—a grand total of six cents—suggests that the jury believed his version of events.[25]

Grant was not present at White Haven when on May 30, 1850, Frederick Dent Grant—"a fine, great boy," his proud mother pronounced him—came into the world. As soon as she and the baby were able to travel, the new father took leave to bring them back to Detroit, where for the next eleven months they shared the little house on Fort Street. During this period, nothing suggests that Grant drank to excess. With his growing family by his side, his world was complete and secure; he no longer sought release from it.[26]

He may have fallen back on old habits, however, after leaving Detroit and returning to Sackets Harbor—to which Colonel Whistler had decided to transfer regimental headquarters—in April 1851. This time, Grant traveled alone, Julia having gone to White Haven to show her family "how [the] boy had grown and to see [her] loved ones again." How long Grant expected to be apart from wife and child is not known, but probably less than the five months it amounted to. By September, he was frantically writing to Julia and asking her to join him at Madison Barracks—he could not bear their separation any longer. She consented to return, which she did soon afterward, although not without difficulty; she failed to meet him in Detroit as arranged, the result of an errant telegram informing him that she had left White Haven for Michigan.[27]

It may be surmised that during their most recent estrangement, Grant had been intemperate, perhaps egregiously so. Furthermore, he appears to have discovered—or had it brought to his attention—that his habits had begun to affect his performance as quartermaster. Possibly other officers who imbibed irresponsibly had come to the same realization, and Grant saw in their shared experience a basis for banding together to fight the common enemy. When Julia joined him at Sackets Harbor, she learned that he had formed a chapter of the national organization known as the Sons of Temperance. It seems unlikely that he would have done this unless in her absence he had drunk heavily enough to warrant a dramatic effort at self-reform.[28]

Although dedicated to eradicating a serious social problem, the Sons of Temperance (forerunner of today's Alcoholics Anonymous) had some of the elements of a fraternal organization, which helped it attract members. A close acquaintance of Grant at Sackets Harbor recalled that the officer made public and ritualistic show of his affiliation, marching in temperance processions "and wearing the regalia of the lodge. . . . It took courage in those days to wear the white apron of the Sons of Temperance, but Lieutenant Grant was prepared to show his character."[29]

This man, who appears to have accompanied Grant to events where alcohol flowed freely, was surprised that his companion had taken such a drastic step, and asked him why. The officer replied by paraphrasing a temperance spokesman whose lecture he had attended: "There is no safety from ruin by drink except from abstaining from liquor altogether." His commitment to abstinence may have made him feel worthy of God's grace, for after Julia and Fred joined him he accompanied them to the local Methodist meeting, which he had not attended in their absence.[30]

The settled existence Grant led following his family's return lasted nine months. In June 1852, Colonel Whistler announced that regimental headquarters was to be moved to the Pacific Coast. Four and a half years earlier, gold had been discovered in California; ever since, fortune-seekers had been making their way there to pan for the precious metal. An increased military presence was deemed necessary to maintain order among the wide-open gold towns that had sprung up across the erstwhile Mexican province and to subdue the dwindling number of Native Americans disposed to challenge the tide of white settlement.

To reach its new posting, the 4th Infantry would travel by ship to Panama, thence by steam train, canoe, and muleback across the vegetation-choked, insect-infested, and disease-ridden isthmus. Upon reaching Panama's Pacific coast, they would board a steamer for the run to San Francisco. Not perceiving the hazards involved, Julia, although almost eight months pregnant with their second child, looked forward to an exciting passage through Central America. At the last minute, however, her husband persuaded her to return to White Haven with Fred and remain there until he had settled in at his new post. At that time he would come to Missouri and escort Julia and both children to California.[31]

After seeing wife and child off for Missouri, Grant accompanied his regiment to its pre-departure station, Fort Columbus in New York harbor. The 4th spent only ten days in Manhattan; then, on July 5, Lieutenant Colonel Benjamin L. E. Bonneville, commanding in place of the aged Whistler, placed the regiment aboard a fleet of transports for the run down the Atlantic Coast.

Almost from the start, the trip proved a horrid ordeal, one that drained the physical and mental resources of the 651 officers and men of the 4th and the fifty dependents who accompanied them. The voyage took an especially heavy toll on Grant. Forced to endure the rigors of the passage while shouldering the many burdens incumbent on a quartermaster, the Son of Temperance again turned to alcohol. In quick time his drinking assumed a fixed pattern. The officer in command of the overcrowded ship that carried the regiment through rough and heavy seas recalled that Grant's duties did not permit him to turn in until three or four in the morning. Until that hour, he would pace the deck of the *Ohio*, trying to unwind so that he might sleep. The sympathetic captain, who retired at midnight, gave Grant permission to use the liquor cabinet in his cabin: "Every night after I turned in, I would hear him once or twice, sometimes more, open the door quietly and walk softly over the floor, as not to disturb me; then I would hear the clink of the glass and a gurgle, and he would walk softly back."[32]

The transports reached Aspinwall in Limon Bay on July 16; but when the passengers disembarked, they found their troubles had only begun. The port town was ankle-deep in water and mud, courtesy of the local rainy season. "At intervals," Grant observed, "the rain would pour down in streams, followed in not many minutes by a blazing, tropical summer's sun. These alternate changes, from rain to sunshine, were continuous in the afternoons. I wondered how any person could live many months in Aspinwall, and wondered still more why any one tried."[33]

After numerous delays, the travelers boarded a train that bore them across marshlands submerged in rank vegetation and alive with sand-flies, mosquitoes, snakes, and venomous insects. The half-finished railroad (it would not reach the Pacific coast for another two and a half years) stopped on the north bank of a stream later immortalized in verse and song:

> *Beyond the Chagres River*
> *Are paths that lead to death,*
> *To the river's deadly breezes,*
> *To malaria's poisonous breath.*[34]

Soldiers not accompanied by wives and children and not detailed to guard the outfit's camp and garrison equipage boarded "bungos"—dugout canoes poled downriver by native boatmen "not inconveniently burdened with clothing" as far as Gorgona. From that village they would cover the twenty-mile stretch to the coast at Panama City aboard mules. At Panama, the well-appointed steamer *Golden Gate* would be waiting to transport them to their ultimate destination.

While the main body of the 4th—comprised of seven companies, Lieutenant Colonel Bonneville, and the headquarters staff—moved off, Grant remained behind with the regimental property and the rest of the travelers. The latter included a few nondependent civilians, notably some Catholic nuns on missionary service. Grant escorted the diverse group down the Chagres to Cruces, five miles above Gorgona. Additional overland transportation was supposed to be available at Cruces, but Grant discovered that the "impecunious American" who had been hired by the Pacific Mail Steamship Company to move the 4th's baggage to Panama City had leased all his pack animals. The result was a week-long layover that turned deadly when a fast-spreading outbreak of cholera ravaged the area. This virulent gastrointestinal disease killed with diabolical speed; before long, as Grant observed, "men were dying every hour."[35]

In an effort to prevent additional fatalities, Grant—whose own health, providentially, never faltered—located enough mules to send the baggage and the soldiers detailed to guard it on ahead to the coast. "He took great interest in us," an enlisted man reported, adding that the quartermaster carefully instructed the party how to dress in that forbidding clime (stripped to pantaloons and undershirts) and what to drink (anything but the local water). Grant even provided money of his own to purchase supplies and medicines as needed. These precautions proved only partially effective, for, after reaching Panama City, several members of the unit came down with the cholera.[36]

While the supply company forged ahead, Grant remained at Cruces with the soldiers who were already ill and their dependents until he could contract with a native (at double the going rate) for the remainder of the required transportation. By the time his party got off—the men aboard mules and the women and children in hammocks slung over the shoulders of native porters—about one-third had succumbed to cholera or to one of the many other diseases endemic to the area, principally smallpox and dysentery. Still others died en route to the coast; they included twenty children the same age as Fred or younger. Grant would credit his foresight for saving the lives of his wife and their two children (Julia had given birth to Ulysses, Jr., at White Haven on July 22).[37]

That so many survived the hellish journey was testimony to Grant's care and concern. The wife of one soldier declared that "he was like a ministering angel" to them all. This being so, it is especially regrettable that while the *Golden Gate* was en route to San Francisco, Panama's leading newspaper should have published allegations that on the trip from the Chagres to the coast the enlisted men of the 4th had virtually been abandoned by their officers. The *Panama Herald* report, the source of which was never identified, specifically charged Quartermaster Grant with abdicating his responsibilities to the regiment in his haste to reach Panama City, where he checked himself into a hotel. According to the report, while Grant enjoyed every creature comfort, dozens of less fortunate travelers, wholly exposed to the elements, suffered and died. Adding insult to insult, the paper charged Grant with sneaking aboard the *Golden Gate* without paying his hotel bill. When the 4th reached California, outraged fellow officers defended Grant in print against the *Herald*'s "scandalous and malicious falsehood." Grant himself never published, or caused to be published, a word in his own defense. He advised Julia and his parents to ignore stories critical of his conduct while crossing the isthmus.[38]

When Grant and those in his charge finally straggled into Panama City, the steamer waiting for them refused to sail until the ship was thoroughly fumigated and the local health authorities could declare the cholera outbreak contained. Not till the close of August was the quarantine lifted and the steamer permitted to put to sea. As Grant noted nonchalantly enough: "The disease did not break out again on the way to California, and we reached San Francisco early in September." By then, eighty-five soldiers—13 percent of the number that had sailed for New York on July 7—lay buried on the isthmus or on Flamenco Island, south of Panama City.[39]

★ ★ ★

Though he survived the nightmare of the Panamanian crossing, in a very real sense Grant did not survive the ordeal that began when he reached his new duty station. He found his somewhat ramshackle port of entry, San Francisco, alive not only with gold-rush fever but with a spirit of industry and initiative that boded well for its future. Yet he could not say the same of the installations to which he was posted over the next two years: Benicia Barracks, outside San Francisco; Fort Vancouver, Oregon Territory; and Fort Humboldt, California. Daily life at the first two was tolerable despite the high prices that goods of all kinds commanded locally (at Benicia, flour sold at the outlandish price of twenty-five cents per pound, one potato went for an equally exorbitant sixteen cents, cabbage was six cents a head, "and other articles in proportion"). At least the Indian troubles, which until recently had threatened the security of all military installations along the coast, had simmered down, though Native Americans maintained a notable presence throughout California, the Oregon Territory, and the newly established Washington Territory.[40]

From the time he set foot on the coast, Grant developed an abiding interest in the peaceful tribes he was exposed to, whose folkways he studied at some length. He admired many of their customs and attitudes, and he applauded their adoption of peaceful ways. As for their conversion to the culture of the white man, he was discouraged to find that "they had generally acquired some of the vices of civilization, but none of the virtues, except in individual cases."[41]

Grant's outfit spent only a few weeks at Benicia Barracks before being transferred to Fort Vancouver. Thanks to the temporary diminution of the Indian wars, life in Oregon proved to be as slow and unchallenging as it had at Detroit and Sackets Harbor. To fill his off-duty hours while also making the local economy work on his behalf, he joined with other officers in leasing property along the Columbia River; buying and selling horses, farm implements, and seed; and planting potatoes, corn, onions, and carrots. When they learned that ice was scarce in San Francisco, during the winter he and his partners paid to have one hundred tons of ice cut out of the river and shipped south along with hogs, chickens, and other livestock. During a trip to San Francisco, Grant and his fellows rented space in a hotel and furnished it as a men's social club, complete with a billiard room.

Although these and other commercial ventures promised hefty profits, for one reason or another all failed. The Columbia flooded its banks and destroyed the crops Grant had so diligently planted; the horses and farm tools sold slowly; an unexpected glut of imports from Alaska ruined the ice-shipping venture; most of the pigs and chickens died en route to market; and the agent he had hired to manage the social club absconded with the proceeds. Grant would leave the Pacific as poor as he had been upon arriving.[42]

His business reverses served to deepen the gloom he felt at being once again far apart from Julia and the children, one of whom he had never seen. He tried desperately to find a way for his family to join him, but the failure of his several ventures denied him the needed funds. Even keeping in touch with them was difficult and sometimes nigh-impossible: Mail service between his posts and the States was irregular and much-interrupted. As usual, he wrote more letters to Julia than he received from her. When she did write, her news tended to depress him even more. No wonder that the 4th's drum major described him as "always sad" while at Fort Vancouver. One of his sergeants recalled that Grant showed him a letter on which Julia had traced the hand of baby Ulysses: "He put the letter back without a word, [but] his eyes were wet." On another occasion, Julia sent him locks of her hair and those of the children. Grant braided them into a single strand, which he knotted about his neck. He would wear the keepsakes daily for the rest of his life.[43]

If he had a difficult time in Oregon, his life became unbearable when in August 1853 he was transferred to Fort Humboldt at Bucksport, two hundred miles north of San Francisco. Situated on a bluff overlooking Humboldt Bay, the newly established installation was so remote that it made Grant's earlier posts look like the garden spots of the universe. In fact, Humboldt has been described as the most dreary and isolated billet in the nineteenth-century army, a singular distinction indeed. "You do not know how forsaken I feel here!" he told Julia the following February.[44]

Almost from the day he arrived at Humboldt, Grant was beset by physical as well as psychological distress. His old malady, the migraine, bedeviled him, and at other times he was laid up with the "chills," a recurrent, malaria-related malady he had contracted in Mexico. When in February 1854 he had a tooth extracted, he lay in bed for almost two weeks, most of the time in excruciating pain, his face so swollen it was "round as an apple." Being laid up, of course, made his sense of isolation, of being cut off from contact with home and family, more acute. It did not help that mail service at Humboldt was even worse than it had been at Vancouver. The entire time he was in California, he received only one letter from his wife. "I think I have been [separated] from my family quite long enough," he told Julia early in February, "and sometimes I feel as though I could almost go home 'nolens volens.'"[45]

He did not have to resort to such an extreme. The previous September, Grant had learned of his promotion to the full grade of captain, to take effect the following April. The advancement ended his service as regimental quartermaster and conferred on him the duties of a company commander of infantry. The promotion also resulted in his subordination to his old nemesis, Brevet Lieutenant Colonel Robert Buchanan, under whose supervision Fort Humboldt had been established. Past animosities were soon rekindled, and Grant found himself in Buchanan's doghouse with demoralizing frequency.

At Fort Vancouver, Grant, his temperance society connections long forgotten, had engaged in some serious drinking, but apparently not continuously. In California, he settled into the pattern of a binge drinker, one who drinks more or less heavily, often under the influence of stress or depression, but at irregular intervals often triggered by threats to peace of mind, self-image, or physical health. Although people showing these tendencies are alcoholics in the true sense of the term, they may function more or less effectively in their daily lives. If able to hide their affliction, they can hope to escape detection and avoid any consequences.

Apparently Grant, while in Oregon, succeeded in disguising his weakness for liquor. Following his transfer to California, however, his misery became overwhelming and he no longer bothered to drink on the sly. Henry Heth, then an officer in the United States infantry and later a Confederate general, quoted a close friend of Grant's at Fort Humboldt, Lewis Cass Hunt (a future Union general) to the effect that "Grant . . . got to drinking on the Coast very hard; used to go on long sprees till his whole nature would rebel and then he would be sick."[46]

Later Grant himself, in attempting to quash rumors that he drank too much in the prewar army, asserted that he could not have done so because heavy consumption sickened him. This argument fails to prove his claim, however, for alcoholics have been known to continue drinking even when aware of the physical consequences. The desire to keep imbibing under such circumstances merely emphasizes the severity of their addiction.

Over time, in fact, Grant dropped his claim that he could not tolerate heavy drinking. Early in the Civil War he informed one of his subordinates, Captain (later General) Augustus L. Chetlain, of his predilection: "I have a natural craving for drink. When I was on the coast I got in a depressed condition and got to drinking." Chetlain discerned a pattern in Grant's behavior that persisted throughout their association: "Whenever he was idle and depressed this appetite came upon him," although when he recovered from his funk "he was all right."[47]

According to Lewis Hunt, Grant's drinking became an increasing source of contention between him and his superior. More than once Buchanan warned him of the penalties his actions might trigger and the effect they would have on his career. Evidence suggests that Grant promised to reform, but he could not muster the physical and psychological strength to do so. One day during a post function he appeared before his company in a drunken state; Buchanan had him arrested and restricted to quarters. Previously, as an incentive for Grant to moderate his behavior, Buchanan had ordered him to compose an undated and unsigned letter of resignation from the army. Following this latest and most flagrant delinquency, he presented the letter to Grant and asked him whether he ought not to sign it. Grant agreed, and quietly affixed his signature. He told Hunt afterwards, with a burst of bravado, "I'll be the greatest cit [i.e., citizen] in the nation," and one of the most successful farmers in Missouri.[48]

Many historians question the circumstances of Grant's resignation, and more than a few contend that it had nothing to do with his personal habits or his superior's displeasure with them. And yet, although some details of the above account are open to dispute, a preponderance of evidence gives it weight. Grant's self-defeating behavior at Forts Vancouver and Humboldt came to the attention of too many credible witnesses to permit the story to be dismissed out of hand; then, too, Buchanan's attitude toward officers who drank, and his preference for levying harsh punishments, are well-established. Although he forwarded his subordinate's resignation to the War Department without appending a reason for it, the omission does not sustain the claim of Grant's defenders that Grant left the army only because he could not bear his estrangement from home and family. His loneliness contributed heavily to the chain of events that caused his downfall, but the proximate cause was his weakness for liquor combined with his inability to control his urges even when confronting the gravest of consequences.[49]

★ ★ ★

Grant's resignation took effect on July 31, 1854. Authorized an extended leave and having made his farewells, he left Fort Humboldt by ship on May 7. His recent recovery from another lengthy illness permitted him to file his final reports as company commander. He reached San Francisco on May 8, where he called upon a banker friend, T. H. Stevens, with whom he had deposited seventeen hundred fifty dollars at 2 percent interest. Stevens put him off, promising to have Grant's money for him if he returned at the end of the month. Grant reluctantly remained over in San Francisco, where he visited Julia's eldest brother, Louis, who was running a boat service at Knight's Ferry on the Stanislaus River. When he returned to Stevens's bank on the appointed day, however, he learned that his friend had left town on undisclosed business.[50]

Disheartened, Grant repaired to the quartermaster's office in the city, where he presented a voucher to collect forty dollars in per diem pay. Although steamship lines transported army officers, even when on nonofficial travel, without charge, Grant needed the money to pay for meals during the passage. He left San Francisco on the steamer *Sierra Nevada* on June 1 for the run down the coast to Nicaragua. Enabled to avoid disease-ridden Panama, he encountered few delays on his journey to New York, which he reached aboard the *Prometheus* on June 25. By now his pay had been spent; to secure the means to continue on to Missouri he made a quick visit to Sackets Harbor, whose sutler—with whom Grant had gone into partnership in several business ventures on the West Coast—owed him eight hundred dollars. Unwisely, he notified the debtor in advance of his arrival. Like Grant's banker friend, the man was not on hand when the ex-officer came calling. Grant returned to Manhattan empty-handed and virtually penniless.[51]

Reduced to begging, he paid a call to the army post on Governors Island, New York Harbor, where he found Captain Simon Buckner of the 6th Infantry, a fellow member of the One in Twelve Society at West Point. Buckner agreed to accompany his old classmate to the Astor House, where Grant was staying, to discuss his overdue account. The hotel's proprietor was well known to Buckner, who offered to vouch for Grant until money could be obtained to pay the bill. Apparently Buckner also lent his old classmate a small amount of cash, part of which Grant used to telegraph his family—which now resided in Covington, Kentucky, across the Ohio River from Cincinnati—for travel funds. He would have an opportunity to repay Buckner's generosity eight years hence, under radically different circumstances.[52]

After being contacted by his son, Jesse Grant sent the necessary money, although reluctantly, and perhaps even spitefully. Whether or not aware of the reasons behind it, Jesse was greatly displeased by his son's resignation. Believing that the military offered the only viable career for Ulysses, he had sent a letter to Jefferson Davis—now the secretary of war—in which he called his son's action an error in judgment and asked that his resignation be set aside. When Davis's office replied that it was too late to undo the deed, Jesse turned his anger on the son whose potential for greatness he had so loudly trumpeted to everyone within earshot. Seemingly forgetful that it was he who had directed Ulysses to West Point, Jesse was soon complaining to all about him that the Military Academy had "spoiled" his son for a career—any career—in the civilian world.[53]

In August, former Captain Sam Grant reached White Haven to reclaim the life he had left behind when embarking for Central America so very long ago. With tears of joy in his eyes, he returned to the bosom of his family—to the wife whose image he had taken to bed with him every night of his lonely duty in Oregon and California, to the apple-cheeked little boy he had not seen for more than two years, and to the infant he had not yet come to know. For Julia, the homecoming was a Godsend, marking as it did the start of a new life for them all. "How very happy this reunion was!" she exclaimed. "One great boy by his knee, one curly-headed, blue-eyed Cupid on his lap, and his happy, proud wife nestled by his side. We cared for no other happiness."[54]

Yet not even she, the fount of optimism and good cheer, could say how long that happiness would endure.

Chapter 4

HARDSCRABBLE YEARS

JULIA'S FATHER WAS LESS THAN ENTHUSIASTIC ABOUT GRANT'S RETURN TO Missouri. He was not pleased by the prospect of having to help support a second family, one headed by a son-in-law whose irregular habits and questionable decisionmaking seemed to validate the Colonel's low opinion of his skills and prospects. Still, there seemed no help for it, and so he tried to make the best of the unhappy situation in which Grant's resignation had placed the Dent family.

When Grant, accompanied by Julia and the boys, made a several-week visit to his parents' new home in Kentucky, he was given a mixed reception. Hannah Grant, who had never approved of her son's profession, was pleased that he had left it. Her husband, however, continued to fume over Ulysses' resignation and to fret that his failure might attach itself to the entire family. When he learned that his son intended to start farming, Jesse, fearing that Ulysses lacked the ability to succeed at such an arduous and chancy occupation, tried to dissuade him. He offered his son a position in the leather goods store he had established some years before in Galena, Illinois, now run by Simpson and Orvil. Ulysses, unhappy at the prospect of living off his father's grudging charity and offended by his stipulation that Julia and the children should live with him and Hannah while their husband and father worked in Illinois, rejected the proposition out of hand. Instead, he asked for a loan—only enough to set him up in his husbandry. Accounts as to whether Jesse agreed to assist his son conflict, but it is likely that, urged to it by his wife, he contributed something—how much remains unknown.[1]

To make a go of his new occupation, Grant was even more heavily dependent on the generosity of his father-in-law. This was slow to activate, but eventually Ulysses was made a grant of one hundred acres of unplowed land along the road to Gravois Creek on the northern periphery of the White Haven estate. Colonel Dent made certain that his son-in-law knew that the gift was being made not in his name but in Julia's. He also agreed to transfer four slaves from the family's workforce to Julia's service. Julia, her husband, and her children were given permission to occupy the "stately" house of stone known as "Wish-ton-Wish" (the title of a James Fenimore Cooper novel—supposedly the Native American word for "whippoorwill") that Louis Dent had built on a wooded hill a mile and a half from White Haven before business interests called him to California. From these vantage points, Dent, Sr., could oversee the welfare of his daughter and his grandsons—at least he could save them from starvation, which he feared would be their lot absent his watchful care.[2]

According to Julia, her husband surprised everyone who doubted his ability to make a living with his hands. That winter, the family lived in the Dents' townhouse in St. Louis; but the following spring, they moved onto the land that had been presented to Julia. Having purchased or borrowed the requisite resources—horses and mules, farm implements, and seeds—Ulysses rolled up his sleeves and set to work to coax a living from the semifertile soil. As he toiled, Julia looked on approvingly and offered encouragement. "His crops yielded well—that is, much better than papa's, but not as much as anticipated from his calculations on paper—and I was a splendid farmer's wife," she recalled. "Ulys brought me all the new breeds of chickens. . . . The two little boys and I used to greatly enjoy throwing handfuls of wheat and other grain to this beautiful feathery portion of our family." Although less enjoyable for her husband, farming appealed to his desire to make his own living. A friend who one day followed Grant to the fields found him "in shirt-sleeves, leading the mowers, and covered with the sweat of honest industry." It was said that "being really fond of his new occupation, he devoted himself to it with a will."[3]

To succeed fully in his new venture, he sometimes required the assistance of others. He was not comfortable, however, with ordering about the slaves Julia had inherited, and he was loath to punish them. "He was no hand to manage negroes," Mrs. Boggs observed years later. "He couldn't force them to do anything. Mrs. Grant would say 'aren't you going to whip Jule for doing that?' And he would only smile and say, 'No, I guess not.' He was just so gentle and good tempered." In place of slave labor, he hired men to help him clear the land on which he planted cash crops—chiefly wheat, corn, and garden vegetables, "driving one team in person, while his little son drove another, thus saving the expenses of two extra hands. He ploughed and planted in the spring, and when the summer had ripened his crops he was the foremost hand in the harvest-field."[4]

When the harvesting was done, he went into the timberland that fringed his property, felled trees, and hauled firewood to St. Louis for sale. The four dollars per cord he charged did not make him wealthy, but the enterprise did supplement the family's income through the winter. While pounding the streets of the city, he occasionally encountered army friends such as Major Longstreet and Captain Holloway. According to Hamlin Garland, his former colleagues found him an incongruous sight, "dressed in farmer fashion, with his trousers tucked into his old military books." To a man, they did not believe he could be happy in his new incarnation; indeed, they viewed him as "a man with an all-pervading air of hard luck and vain regrets."[5]

Yet if he had regrets, they were few and ephemeral. Years later, reminiscing about this time in his life, he asked a former neighbor: "Do you recollect when I used to supply your husband with wood, and pile it myself, and measure it too, and go to his office for my pay? Mrs. Blow, those were happy days; for I was doing the best I could to support my family." Most important, he was free of the daily misery of living half a continent away from the place he thought of as home. Then, too, he was able to make a living in the great outdoors surrounded by the wonders of nature, not cooped up in some stuffy office. Of no small significance, he was busy enough, and contented enough, that he felt no urge to drink.[6]

One day in 1857 he ran into William T. Sherman, a member of the West Point class of 1840, whom Grant had known briefly at the Military Academy. Sherman, who had resigned from the army four years earlier for an unsatisfying career as a banker and a militia officer in San Francisco, had come to consider himself "a dead cock in a pit." Of their chance meeting, Sherman recalled only that it gave him the opportunity to comment on their shared failures in life. As he told Grant, "West Point and the Regular Army were not good schools for farmers, bankers, merchants, and mechanics." Grant, however, did not share his schoolmate's view that they were something of a disgrace to their alma mater. The two would meet again a few years hence, at which time they would compare notes and reconsider Sherman's observation.[7]

For a time Grant, despite his lack of experience at farming, appeared destined for prosperity. His first harvest yielded an abundant crop of wheat and grain as well as two hundred pounds of potatoes to the acre, "which then commanded a high price." With the proceeds of his toil, he was able to make improvements to his wife's property, eventually including a sturdy house wrought by his own hands. Uncomfortable at living under his brother-in-law's roof and desiring a home more adaptable to his growing brood (his daughter Nellie had been born in July 1855), during the summer of 1856 he began building a two-story "dogtrot house" of hewn logs, which, in ironic contrast to the lofty titles the Dents gave their homes, he christened "Hardscrabble." The labor that went into the house, which was completed the following September, gave its builder great satisfaction, but his family inhabited it for only one season. In January 1857, Julia's mother—she who had envisioned great things for her son-in-law—passed away. Her death left Colonel Dent so lonely that Julia answered his plea to return with her family to White Haven.[8]

For the next several months, Grant worked his own farm while tending the Colonel's lands as well. It was a daunting regimen and it took its toll, as did the baleful effects of the Panic of 1857, which ruined his hopes for a third consecutive bountiful harvest. The nationwide depression caused farm prices to sink ruinously, but Grant labored on in hopes of working his way out of the debts he continued to accumulate. By August, however, he faced the reality of a poor wheat crop (seventy-five bushels instead of the four to five hundred he had expected), and he nearly conceded defeat. He spent more and more time on the streets of St. Louis selling at cut-rate prices the firewood he had chopped and transported to market through great physical exertion. That Christmas he was forced to pawn his pocket watch and gold chain to buy presents for the family.[9]

Hope sprang anew the following year, but 1858 produced another disappointing harvest as well as a family-wide epidemic of sickness. Typhoid and bilious fever struck each of the children—which included newborn Jesse, the fourth and last child to grace the Grant home—and it nearly carried off eight-year-old Fred. Their parents were stricken by chills and fever. Julia recovered in time to nurse the children, but Grant was attacked by a more virulent strain of the disease, malaria-like in its symptoms and reminiscent of the "fever and ague" that had afflicted him severely in childhood. This time he was laid up for more than a year, weakened to the point of "not being able to even attend to [his] hands, much less work [him]self."[10]

The illness finished off Grant's dreams of a successful husbandry, forced his once-settled life onto some tortuous paths, and immersed him in gloom. Julia claimed that while he lay abed, wracked by pain and debility, Jesse Grant came up from Kentucky in hopes of persuading his son to leave the land and help him operate yet another tannery. It was a job that as a boy Ulysses had sworn never to stoop to. Now, according to his wife, he was so desperate to feed his family that he accepted his father's offer and made plans, as soon as he was well, to move his family to Covington.

That fall, he recovered sufficiently to put his farm implements, stock, and crops up for auction. At about the same time he sold Hardscrabble to a neighbor, taking part payment in cash and the rest in the form of a mortgage that, as it turned out, the tenant could not keep up. Then, for some reason, the arrangement between father and son fell through. Julia, who was opposed to it from the start, maintained that it was scuttled "through the interference of Captain Grant's sisters." She was delighted by the turn of events, but she never explained why or how it came about.[11]

★ ★ ★

Left with a small sum from the sale of the farm and house, but with debts to pay off and no prospect of employment, Grant was forced to consider a career for which he had neither the interest nor the aptitude. At the intercession of Colonel Dent, it was arranged that he should join one of Julia's cousins in the real estate business in St. Louis. From a first-floor office at No. 35 Pine Street, Harry Boggs not only bought and sold land but collected rents and negotiated loans secured with real property. The well-established business—St. Louis was growing by leaps and bounds—promised Grant a steady income. Undoubtedly with the assistance of his father-in-law, Grant paid a considerable fee to go into partnership with the proprietor.[12]

Although not completely recovered from his illness—recurrent attacks of ague and rheumatism weakened him for months after he rose from his sick bed—on the first day of 1859 Grant left Julia and the children at White Haven and traveled alone to St. Louis. For several weeks before he found a house to rent in "not altogether a pleasant neighborhood" down by the river, he boarded with the Boggs. In their townhouse fourteen blocks from the office, he occupied a single room furnished with a bedstead, a chair, and a wash-bowl. On Saturdays he would leave the city, usually on foot, to spend the weekends with his family. That summer, when his tenant evacuated Hardscrabble, Grant traded the log house to an employee of the local court for a frame cottage "with a high roof and pleasant overhanging shade-trees" on the outskirts of St. Louis. He moved his family there in July.[13]

Before Julia and the children joined him—perhaps afterwards as well—he would at times flee Boggs's office and wander through the city as if in a stupor. Mrs. Boggs did not attribute his amblings or his forlorn appearance to a physical cause: "I don't recall that he was ill when he came to live with us, but he seemed to be much depressed. . . . I never heard him laugh out loud. He would smile, and he was not a gloomy man, but he was a sad man."

When she met him on the street, he struck her as being "the most obscure man in St. Louis. Nobody took any notice of him." He could have been one of those unfortunates—a beggar, a derelict—who, because they are an implied reproach to society, are studiously avoided when they cannot be altogether ignored.[14]

Early on, Grant realized that he did not measure up to the demands of his new profession. Mrs. Boggs observed that although "the Captain" could perform clerical work "and wrote [in] a good clear hand," he was of little help to her husband, who, being in delicate health, had hoped that his partner would relieve him of some of his administrative burdens. That did not happen. "His intentions were good," Mrs. Boggs admitted, "but he hadn't the faculty for keeping affairs in order." On one occasion, her husband went east on business, "leaving the Captain in charge, and when he returned found everything upside down. The books were in confusion, the wrong people had been let into the houses and the owners were much concerned."[15]

Not only was the new man incapable of producing a proper balance sheet but he would lease properties to indigents and undesirables—at least one tenant turned out to be a prostitute. Even worse in the eyes of his partner was Grant's ineptitude at collecting overdue accounts. His naive faith in the sacredness of a man's word impelled him to accept at face value every tale of woe, however contrived or outlandish. Moreover, he lacked the hard heart and the ability to persuade, cajole, or threaten a delinquent into paying up.[16]

In September, by mutual agreement, Boggs and Grant dissolved their partnership. In his memoirs, Grant gives as a reason a general lack of business (the work amounted to "no more than one person could attend to, and not enough to support two families"). In reality, his inaptitude for the job made their association impractical.[17]

If Grant had even a modicum of luck, he would not be unemployed for long. A few weeks before he left Boggs's employ he learned that the position of St. Louis County Engineer was about to be filled; it came with an annual salary of almost two thousand dollars. He applied for it, citing his technical education and military experience and enclosing endorsements from no fewer than thirty-six residents of the county, including Lieutenant J. J. Reynolds, his engineering instructor at West Point, now a professor of mechanics and engineering at one of St. Louis's most revered institutions of higher learning, Washington University. Once before, Reynolds had gone to bat for Grant, who had sought an instructorship at the same school, but the man's support had counted for naught, just as it would on the present occasion.[18]

Grant learned, to his dismay, that local politics rather than professional qualifications ruled the selection process. Despite his Whig tendencies, his ties to the Dents marked him as a Democrat. As he informed his father, he was being mislabeled: "I never voted an out and out Democratic ticket in my life." Three years earlier, he had cast his only presidential ballot for James Buchanan. He made this choice not because "Old Buck" was the Democratic candidate but because Grant feared that the election of the radical John C. Frémont, the first presidential standard-bearer of the Republican Party, would precipitate disunion, which in turn would bring on a war between the sections. Grant stressed that in every other election he had voted for "the candidates that, in [his] estimation, were the best fitted for the different offices."[19]

A majority of the five-man commission that had the power of appointment were supporters of the Free Soil Party, a liberal-leaning political organization that would later affiliate with the Republicans. These men threw their support to Grant's chief rival—a man he later misidentified as an immigrant—who secured the appointment. Grant must have wondered whether the outcome would have been different had the Free Soilers known that six months earlier he had emancipated the only slave he had ever owned. It appears that, even though he was virtually penniless, he had bought William Jones from his father-in-law for the express purpose of setting him free. This was a powerful statement of Grant's attitude toward slavery; he could have made fifteen hundred dollars or more had he sold William to another master.[20]

Grant's run of ill luck continued to dog him, even when things seemed to be looking up. Through the assistance of friends—perhaps some of those who had endorsed his bid for county engineer—in early November he secured a position in the local customs house, which paid twelve hundred dollars a year. Within a month of starting the job, he was again on the pavement. The superintendent who had hired him had died suddenly, and his successor swept the house of prior appointments.[21]

Farmer, real estate agent, federal employee—Grant had failed at all three. The depression these job losses must have visited upon him might have driven him to the bottle had his family not been on hand to comfort and console him—and had he not lacked the money to buy whiskey regularly. No evidence exists to prove that he drank to excess during this time of sampling life on society's lower rungs.

His plight was pathetic enough to evoke even the sympathy of his father. Jesse Grant recalled that when Ulysses came to him, hat in hand, in the spring of 1860, "for advice and assistance," he had been unemployed for almost six months. Concerned—though rather belatedly—for the welfare of his grandchildren and sensitive to the effect his son's pauper-like status might have on the Grant name, Jesse renewed his offer of steady employment within the family fold.[22]

This time, he attached no stipulations, no caveats. Ulysses would not have to work in the tannery at Covington, nor would he have to leave his wife and children in the care of his parents. He and his family would move to Galena, where he would work in Jesse's leather store, not with a view to permanent employment but until something better turned up. He would effectively be subordinated to his younger brothers, who had been running the business in distant partnership with their father for the past several years. He would receive a niggling salary—eight hundred dollars—for which he would keep the company's ledgers, wait on customers, and perform unspecified "heavy" work.

The job smacked of menial labor; worse, it incorporated elements of the work Ulysses had failed to handle successfully in Harry Boggs's office. And yet it appeared to offer an opportunity for advancement, even if it came at a price to his family. Because Simpson Grant, the designated proprietor of the store, was in declining health—he would succumb to tuberculosis in September 1861—at some point Ulysses might find himself assuming a larger, more significant share of the business. If Jesse's offer constituted an act of charity, at least it promised to take many burdens off his son's back.[23]

Ulysses saw that he had little choice but to accept. Not entirely through his own fault, but due to circumstances he had helped bring about, he had hit bottom, imperiling his family's well-being. He hated his inability to provide for his wife and children as he wished to. His wife was used to finer things than their present situation provided for her, and his children deserved a decent schooling outside the home. The only way up and out was to rely, once again, on the largesse of a father who considered him a disgrace to generations of acquisitive, successful Grants. In May 1860, he swallowed what little pride remained to him and moved his family by steamboat up the Mississippi to Galena, there to start over for what must have seemed the thousandth time in his life.[24]

* * *

The family's new home was "a charming, bustling town, nestled in the rich ore-laden hills of northern Illinois," recalled Julia Grant, who, when looking back, always found something cheery and reassuring in every twist and turn her life took: "The atmosphere was so cool and dry, the sun shone so brightly, that it gave us the impression of a smiling welcome." Following a brief stay in his brother's home, her husband found a seven-room brick house to rent for little more than a hundred dollars per year. Julia would claim that it sat "high up the hill on the west side of the town, in the best neighborhood and with a lovely view." In actuality, the house was rambling and rundown, and it perched so high up the bluff that to reach it one had to climb a two-hundred-foot-high set of steps. It was the best the family could afford.[25]

By contrast, J. R. Grant Company, which did an annual business of one hundred thousand dollars, was an impressive concern that occupied a four-story building in the heart of the town. Albert Richardson enumerated its high-quality and high-priced line of goods as "shoe-findings, saddlery hardware, French calf, fancy linings, and morocco, all bought in the East, and in domestic leather tanned in the chestnut oak-woods of Ohio, from hides purchased in Galena." The store's newest employee had never handled such pricey items, and when he waited on customers he sometimes charged too little for them. His shortcomings incurred the wrath of his brothers and called into question not only his value as a salesman but also his native intelligence.[26]

Although hired as a clerk, he spent much of his time as a hauler and a laborer. He weighed leather for distant customers, then packed their purchases and delivered them by wagon or sleigh, covering many miles in all kinds of weather. As he recalled, the store "had customers in all the little towns in south-west Wisconsin, south-east Minnesota, and north-east Iowa." Jesse Grant owned leather stores in some of those locations, and his son visited them regularly, usually to deliver stock.[27]

His deceptively powerful body enabled him to manhandle loads heavy enough and bulky enough to stagger a man twice his size. One young fellow who visited the Galena store in the winter of 1861 hoping to meet the new clerk did not at once recognize him:

A farmer drove up with a lot of hides on his sleigh, and went inside to dicker, and presently a stoop-shouldered brownish-bearded fellow, low, with a slouch hat pulled down over his eyes, who had been sitting whittling at the stove when I was inside, came out, pulling on an old light-blue soldier's overcoat. He flung open the doors leading down into the cellar, laid hold of the top hide, frozen stiff it was, tugged it loose, towed it over and slung it down the chute. Then one by one, all by himself, he heaved off the rest of them, a ten-minutes' tough job in that weather; until he had got the last of them down the cellar, then slouched back into the store again, shed the blue coat, got some hot water off the stove and went and washed his hands, using a cake of brown soap, then came back and went to whittling again, and all without a word to anybody.[28]

Equally impressive was the honesty and forthrightness Grant displayed in his dealings with customers. Because he was not adept at haggling, he was sometimes taken advantage of, which greatly upset his brothers as it would have the father to whom they had to answer even though he never set foot in Galena. Richardson wrote: "So, whenever a difficult or an important customer was to be dealt with, Orvil, Simpson, or one of the clerks took him in charge."[29]

From the first, Grant felt out of place in the mercantile trade, and he did not consider the work he put in worth the salary paid him. Still, he was buoyed by his happy home life. He looked forward every evening to leaving the hustle and bustle of the store for the warmth and cheer of his rented cottage on the riverbank. Julia was happily busy in the kitchen and boastful that their cuisine was "most excellent." The children were attending school, generally doing well in their studies, although the oldest seemed to get into more than his share of schoolground fights (his mother observed that at least half an hour every night was devoted to "listening to Fred's stories of his prowess and sometimes of his defeats, the latter always accompanied with the express determination . . . of getting even"). Grant's youngest, Jesse, now approaching four, was also of a pugnacious demeanor; invariably, he would greet his father's evening return with a challenge to wrestle. The response he elicited only whetted his appetite for combat: "I do not feel like fighting, Jess, but I can't stand being hectored in this manner by a man of your size." And they would tussle gleefully for several minutes, sometimes joined by Fred, Ulysses, Jr. (known in the family as "Buck"), and Nellie, a tomboy by virtue of growing up among so many brothers.[30]

Grant's life in Galena may have been only a marginal improvement over the one he had led in Missouri, but it was enough to sustain him in his difficult transition from independent yeoman to hired hand in his family's employ. There was much in his present situation to trouble him, to fill him with unease and anxiety, yet it had been several months since he felt the urge to upend a bottle. He had no intention of returning to the habits that not only had cost him a career suited to his abilities but also had forced him into occupations less in keeping with his tastes and skills. That, at least, was something Ulysses Grant could feel good about.[31]

★ ★ ★

During his travels on behalf of the family concern, Grant had frequent occasion to converse with customers, draymen, stable hands, loungers in the local country store, and the miscellaneous gentry of the distant towns he visited. Especially given the divisive state of the nation, he found himself more and more drawn into a discussion of politics, something that did not come naturally to an ex-soldier whose profession had taught him to be basically apolitical.

In his memoirs, he claimed that by 1861 he, like many another of his countrymen, had developed the conviction that war between the sections was inevitable and unavoidable but that it would be brief—no more than a few sobering, bloody months. Grant had become convinced that Southern-ers believed the people of the North were not in earnest when declaring they would fight if necessary to keep the Republic intact. For decades, Southern politicians had "denounced the Northerners as cowards, pol-troons, Negro-worshippers; claimed that one Southern man was equal to five Northern men in battle; that if the South would stand up for its rights the North would back down." Yet he was certain that the North would not back down. He believed that when the South became convinced that the other section meant business, the war would cease and union and amity would be restored—on what basis he could not say; but he fervently hoped that a new social order would rise in the South, one in which white planters did not control poor whites and oppress African Americans and honest labor was not degraded and ridiculed.[32]

During the watershed presidential election of 1860, Grant, who had veered from Whiggery to the Democratic Party after partisan politics cost him the engineer's job, supported the candidate of the party's Northern wing, Stephen A. Douglas. The senator from Illinois had many notable accom-plishments on his record, not the least of which was his authorship of the "popular sovereignty" doctrine under which settlers could determine whether a new state would permit slavery or outlaw it, regardless of legal en-actments and accepted practice. Grant did not support his man at the polls—as a new resident of Illinois he could not vote. Still, his sympathies were well enough known that Galena's Democratic faithful elected him president of their political club. But he refused to serve. "I am not a voter," he protested. "I never voted but once in my life; and besides, I desire to at-tend to my business and not dabble in politics."[33]

In fact, even before the presidential canvass was underway he had begun to reassess his political convictions. As small businessmen with antislavery views, Simpson and Orvil Grant were staunch Republicans, and they tried to convert him to their faith. They appeared to enjoy some success, for their brother had come to despise the man he had helped put in office with his only presidential vote. By publicly declaring that the Southern states had no con-stitutional right to secede but that the federal government had no effective means of forcing them to remain in the Union, James Buchanan had become the quintessential impotent executive.

Although still harboring reservations about the radical tinge of the Republican Party, Grant had begun to wonder whether the party's standard bearer, the former congressman Abraham Lincoln, also of Illinois, might not prove a stronger leader in time of crisis than the man who three years earlier had defeated him for a Senate seat. Douglas appeared to spread his integrity quite thinly when he tried to placate his Northern supporters without alienating the Southerners whose votes were crucial to his success. At least Grant knew, or believed he knew, where Lincoln stood. Lincoln would fight to sustain the preeminence of the federal government over the whims and petty prerogatives of the several states. Most likely, his election would mean war; but maybe a war was the only way to close the sectional divide once and for all. For this reason, perhaps, Grant lent material support to the local chapter of the "Wide Awakes," those Republicans given to public demonstrations in support of Lincoln's candidacy. "I did not parade with either party," he explained, "but occasionally met with the 'wide awakes' . . . in their rooms, and superintended their drill."[34]

When the results of the November election became known locally, the Wide-Awakes celebrated and serenaded Lincoln's victory. That victory, which had come to pass despite Lincoln's receipt of almost two million fewer popular votes than the combined total of his three challengers (Douglas; John C. Breckinridge of Kentucky, the Southern Democratic candidate; and John Bell of the Whig-oriented Constitutional Union Party), gave rise to a "jollification" at the J. R. Grant Company store. Richardson noted that "the captain assisted his brothers to play the host, dispensing oysters and liquors, of which all except him partook. He seemed as much gratified as any one at the result, and from that time was regarded by his friends as a moderate Republican."[35]

Numerous Southern politicians, especially those radical secessionists known as "fire-eaters," had long predicted that Lincoln's election would cause the Union to fracture. Six weeks after the votes had been tallied, South Carolina precipitated the breach. On December 20, 1860, a convention in session in Charleston publicly declared that the state's action in ratifying the United States Constitution had been repealed "and that the union [then] subsisting between South Carolina and other states, under the name of 'The United States of America'" was dissolved. For his part, Ulysses Grant had anticipated the action; still, he was shaken by the news. "It is hard to realize," he wrote, "that a State or States should commit so suicidal an act . . . though from all reports I have no doubt but five of them will do it." In fact, over the next five months, ten other states joined South Carolina in secession, most of them through the vote of a convention, three of them (Texas, Virginia, and Tennessee) by referendum.[36]

By February 1861, Grant had no doubt that war was imminent. When one of his Galena friends suggested that most Southerners lacked the fortitude to back their inflammatory rhetoric with weaponry, Grant told him he was sadly mistaken: "If they ever get at it they will make a strong fight. . . . Each side underestimates the other and overestimates itself." Thus he was not amazed when on April 12 the spark was applied to the powder keg in the form of South Carolina's bombardment of the United States garrison inside Fort Sumter, in Charleston Harbor. A week later, following the call of the newly inaugurated Lincoln for seventy-five thousand volunteers to enter federal service for ninety days (the total of troops he was authorized to call for under existing statutes), Grant wrote to his slaveholding father-in-law: "Now is the time, particularly in the border Slave states, for men to prove their love of country. I know it is hard for men to apparently work with the Republican party but now all party distinction should be lost sight of and every true patriot be for maintaining the integrity of the glorious old *Stars & Stripes,* the Constitution and the Union." He added that unless the South quickly ended its experiment in disunion, blood would be spilled promiscuously and slavery would be doomed.[37]

He might have saved his breath, for Colonel Dent was in no mood to reconcile with a government he blamed for decades of hostility toward the South. Mrs. Boggs, who kept close tabs on the Dents from her St. Louis home, claimed that when he learned that Grant had sided with the national government in the impending crisis, the Colonel "swore with a big oath that if his worthless son-in-law ever came on his land he would shoot him as he would a rabbit."[38]

As volunteers North and South began to flock to recruiting stations, Grant saw his own course with intensifying clarity. "Having been educated for such an emergency, at the expense of the Government," he informed his father, "I feel that it has upon me superior claims, such claims as no ordinary motives of self-interest can surmount." Although he had made no commitment to the local or state authorities, he offered his services in organizing and drilling a company-size force of volunteers from Galena and its environs. He promised the would-be soldiers that, if they desired, he would accompany them to the capital, Springfield. Once there, if he could "be of service to the Governor [Richard Yates] in organizing his state troops," he would do so. He closed with a burst of patriotic fervor: "There are but two parties now, Traitors & Patriots and I want hereafter to be ranked with the latter, and I trust, the stronger party."[39]

Much pleased with his son's declaration, Jesse Grant, who never hesitated to pull strings when he deemed it appropriate, wrote on Ulysses' behalf to Attorney General Edward Bates, promoting his son for high command. Jesse gave the cabinet member from Missouri a thumbnail sketch of his son's military service, but avoided any reference to why he had left the army. It is not known whether Bates responded to this letter from a correspondent unknown to him—one suspects that he did not.[40]

Five days before he wrote to his father, Grant attended the first of several public meetings called to gauge and galvanize local sentiment in the wake of Fort Sumter's surrender. Like the majority of those in the audience, he was disappointed by the opening remarks of Galena's mayor, who, to a chorus of boos and cat-calls, advocated a policy of moderation and conciliation. He was followed by more militant speakers, chief among them Elihu B. Washburne, a U.S. congressman, and John Aaron Rawlins, a Galena lawyer. Both men—the former a Republican, the latter a long-time Democrat—urged that military action be taken against the South. The swarthy, black-eyed Rawlins, a passionate and eloquent speaker, was especially impressive. He hammered his theme home for forty-five minutes: "The time for compromise had passed," he said. "We must appeal to the God of Battles to vindicate our flag."[41]

The exhortations of the speakers affected Grant personally, perhaps because he knew both men, though only slightly. At first he had regarded Washburne as an "ultra extremist," especially on the issue of slavery. To be sure, the congressman was a staunch abolitionist. Grant, although opposed to slavery in principle and desirous of barring its spread to the western territories, did not believe in interfering with it where sanctioned by law. One month before Lincoln's election, however, Grant, during a visit at the offices of the *Galena Gazette,* had been introduced to Washburne, with whom he had a lengthy discussion about politics local and national. He had come away "very much pleased" by the man's sentiments, which Grant was surprised to find "so nearly in accord with his own."[42]

He had only a slightly deeper acquaintance with Rawlins, who for a time had served as legal counsel to the J. R. Grant Company. Before the public gathering, all Grant knew of the man's politics was that Rawlins had been a candidate for presidential elector on the Douglas ticket and, in a series of debates with his Republican opponent, had done his candidate proud. After hearing him speak on April 16, Grant was greatly impressed by Rawlins's nonpartisan patriotism and his unhesitating support of the national government in its time of trial. Thus he took to heart Rawlins's message that the hour to stand up and be counted had arrived. Walking home from the meeting with his brother Orvil, Grant mused out loud: "I think I ought to go into the service." His brother agreed that he should; in Ulysses' absence, he would "stay at home and attend to the store."[43]

As a West Pointer and former officer of infantry, his first impulse was to seek a berth in the regular establishment. Not until May 24, however, did he address a letter to the adjutant general of the army, in which he tendered his services "until the close of the war, in such capacity as may be offered." He added: "In view of my present age and length of service, I feel myself competent to command a regiment, if the President, in his judgment, should see fit to intrust one to me." In his memoirs, Grant explains that he "felt some hesitation in suggesting rank as high as the colonelcy of a regiment"; by this time, however, he had gained confidence in his abilities: "I had seen nearly every colonel who had been mustered in from the state of Illinois, and some from Indiana, and felt that if they could command a regiment properly, and with credit, I could also."[44]

He never received a response. This did not suggest that the government considered the former captain unequal to the demands of the position he had sought. The adjutant general's office simply pigeonholed the application along with hundreds of others it had received from old soldiers seeking reinstatement and a position of authority and responsibility.

Although undoubtedly disappointed by the lack of courtesy shown him by an institution he had served faithfully for fifteen years, Grant had other, pressing responsibilities to attend to, these on the state and local level. Two days after the meeting at which Washburne and Rawlins orated, a second public gathering was held in the Joe Daviess County Courthouse for the purpose of forming a local military unit to be offered to Governor Yates. Grant recalled: "Although a comparative stranger I was called upon to preside; the sole reason, possibly, was that I had been in the army and had seen service." Another motive was his established identity as a Douglas Democrat (his in-progress conversion to Republicanism was not local news). Its organizers deemed it important that the meeting have a bipartisan coloration.[45]

With "much embarrassment and some prompting," Grant took charge of the event. After he gaveled the audience into silence, several speakers—some of whom had declaimed two nights earlier, some of whom had not previously been heard—tried by words and gestures to induce local men of military age to fill up the ranks of the company Galena would raise. Their arguments must have been persuasive, for almost two dozen stepped forward that night and signed the enlistment roll, and another twenty did so the following day. One day after that, forty youths from the surrounding countryside declared their intent to enlist.[46]

At first in mufti, then in blue frock coats and gray breeches sewn by the ladies of Galena and based on a pattern provided by Captain Grant, the Jo Daviess Guards began to organize, drill, and elect officers. Several volunteers petitioned Grant to accept the post of captain, but he turned them down, believing himself more valuable as a drill instructor—believing himself, too, worthy of the higher rank he had sought in his letter to the adjutant general. Because he refused to command the Guards, the position went to Augustus Chetlain. A popular merchant with no military experience, Chetlain requested that Grant continue to instruct the men in the manual of arms while helping him learn how to lead. Grant agreed to devote all his time to the task of making the men into something resembling soldiers. He would never set foot inside the family store again.[47]

By the evening of April 26, he had accompanied the Galena company to its training rendezvous on the outskirts of Springfield, known, fittingly enough, as Camp Yates. The encampment had been in operation for some weeks; even before the Jo Daviess Guards arrived, it was overflowing with men, animals, and supplies. Confusion was rampant, and chaos was imminent. One of Yates's military aides would claim that the governor, horrified by the state of affairs, asked whether he knew of a soldier or ex-soldier with the ability to restore order. When the aide recommended Grant, Yates asked him by wire to take charge of the camp. Grant was flattered but refused the offer because he had not finished drilling the Galena company.[48]

In fact, that job was nearly done, and he intended to return to Galena. Before he could depart, however, both the governor and Congressman Washburne (the latter was in Springfield to confer with Yates even though the two men were not personally close) prevailed upon the drillmaster to stay over until the legislature completed action on a bill to authorize the acceptances of more than the six regiments of infantry that had been apportioned to the state under Lincoln's call for ninety-day men. So many Illinoisans had volunteered for the war that ten additional regiments, one from each congressional district, had to be formed to accommodate them.[49]

By remaining in Springfield, Grant was brought face-to-face with the governor, who asked his help in determining how well Illinois was prepared for war. Grant agreed to inspect the state armory and report on the condition of the weapons stored there. On April 29, he informed Yates that the building held 905 muskets and rifles, most of which appeared to be in working order but all of which needed cleaning. This chore completed, Grant made himself available for additional service as needed. A grateful Yates took him up on the offer, assigning him to the task of assisting the state's adjutant general in organizing volunteers into companies, battalions, regiments, and batteries for field service.[50]

Grant tackled the work with enthusiasm, but quickly found himself reduced to a mere clerk. The important paperwork was handled by another civilian employee with whom he shared the "small poorly furnished room" to which he had been assigned. The man did enough work for both of them, making Grant feel superfluous. One day, Augustus Chetlain stopped by and asked how he was doing. Grant looked up "with an expression of weariness and disgust on his face and said, 'I am copying orders and I am going to quit and go home. Any enlisted man could do this as well as I, or better.'"[51]

But he did not go home, perhaps because it appeared that Yates was about to make him a drill instructor at the camp to which the Jo Daviess Guards had reported. The governor changed his mind, however, and asked Grant to help muster into federal service the several additional regiments. Here at least was a job with obvious military utility, so he took it on. Subordinates assigned to him by Yates handled most of the new outfits, but Grant mustered in three regiments that had gone into camp in the southern part of the state.

The first hailed from Belleville, eighteen miles east of St. Louis. Upon arriving in that town, however, Grant found the regiment several days shy of completing its formation. He spent the interim in the city across the Mississippi. He found not only St. Louis but much of Missouri—at least the Unionist element thereof—in an uproar over the perceived intent of their Southern-sympathizing governor, Claiborne Jackson, to use the state militia ("the Missouri State Guard") to seize the city's United States arsenal, then manned by two companies of Regulars under Captain Nathaniel Lyon. At the eleventh hour, however, Jackson's plans were ruined by Francis Preston Blair, a Republican congressman and a prominent citizen of the city, who formed a company of volunteers loyal to the federal government and led it to Lyon's assistance. Looking back, Grant had little doubt that, without Blair's intervention, St. Louis "would have gone into rebel hands, and with it the arsenal with all its arms and ammunition." Later that spring, Grant applied to Blair and Lyon (the latter having been promoted to brigadier general of volunteers) for a commission in their ranks, but to no avail. He also made application to fill a reported vacancy in an Indiana regiment, only to be informed by Governor Oliver Morton that his state's quota of officers was full.[52]

The Federal forces in St. Louis were not content to remain on the defensive. Grant was in the city on May 10 when Lyon, urged on by Blair, led a force of several thousand Regulars and volunteers, many of the latter being members of St. Louis's pro-Union German-American community, in an advance against Camp Jackson, the local rendezvous of the State Guard. The fewer than one thousand troops gathered there under Brigadier General Daniel M. Frost, a New York-born Southern sympathizer, intended to resist arrest, but Lyon's precipitate action caught them by surprise and persuaded them to surrender without a fight. The militiamen were marched back to the arsenal, where they were disarmed and paroled, a move applauded by Captain Grant, a spectator to the early stages of the confrontation.

En route to the arsenal to witness the denouement, Grant engaged in a low-key argument with a fellow streetcar passenger, "a dapper little fellow" of pronounced Southern sympathies. Indignant at Lyon's occupation of Camp Jackson and his hauling down of its secessionist banner, the man loudly proclaimed that "when a free people can't choose their own flag" things had reached a pretty pass: "Where I come from if a man dares to say a word in favor of the Union we hang him to a limb of the first tree we come to." Grant blandly replied that the man was maligning St. Louis: "I had not seen a single rebel hung yet, nor heard of one; [but] there were plenty of them who ought to be." The quiet rejoinder effectively silenced the young dude, who, Grant said, was "crestfallen."[53]

Other Southern sympathizers were not so easily subdued. When Lyon's men marched the captured militia through the streets to the arsenal that afternoon, unruly crowds gathered along the route; they shouted threats and curses at the soldiers, threw bricks and stones, and brandished firearms. One bystander opened fire. The column came to a sudden stop and soldiers returned the fire, causing the crowd to disperse in panic. The shooting went on for several minutes; when it stopped, nearly thirty civilians lay dead in the streets. Although Grant appears not to have witnessed the "Battle of St. Louis," his West Point classmate William T. Sherman had scurried for cover along with his seven-year-old son, Willie.[54]

For days after order was restored, St. Louis remained tense and agitated, Unionists and secessionists roaming the streets and threatening one another with violence. Grant did not linger to witness the aftermath. In response to new orders, he boarded an eastbound train to Mattoon, Illinois, where he was to muster in the so-called 7th Congressional District Regiment. He did so on May 15. He supervised the men as they signed the muster rolls and then, during a brief but impressive ceremony, swore them as a body into federal service.

While in Mattoon, waiting for another local regiment to complete its organization and present itself for enlistment, Grant took the time to acquaint himself with the recruits he had transformed into Federal soldiers. He liked the looks of the enlisted men, and some of the "shoulder-straps" appeared to be promising material. He was not impressed, however, with their colonel, Simon S. Goode of Decatur. The Kentucky-born Goode was tall and handsome, and he affected the image of the warrior with his high boots, jaunty headgear, and fierce-looking Bowie knife. But it did not take long for Grant to perceive that, although Goode had served in Mexico as well as on the celebrated filibustering expedition that tried to seize Nicaragua for the United States in 1857, the man did not know the first thing about how to command a regiment or how to instill discipline. Grant feared that, under his command, the 7th would quickly dissolve into chaos.[55]

Many of the junior officers felt as he did. A few days after he returned to Springfield, one of them, Lieutenant Joseph W. Vance, came up from Mattoon to enlist his help in getting rid of Goode, who, in addition to being a military novice, was a bully, a tyrant, and a drunkard. Grant listened patiently to the man's litany of woes but pleaded an inability to help. A disappointed Vance returned to the outfit, but not before assuring Grant that the regiment as a whole had formed a most favorable impression of him. Officers and enlisted men alike had expressed a hope that he might be persuaded to oust and replace Goode. The men had even voted to name their muddy stubble-field of a camp in his honor.[56]

Grant had had no desire to interfere with the internal workings of the 7th, but the thought of taking charge and straightening out things had a certain appeal. A few days after meeting with Vance, he returned to Mattoon at the urging of another of Goode's subordinates, Captain Ed Harland. Harland corroborated Vance's statement of the 7th's contrasting attitudes toward the man who purported to command it and the man who had mustered it in. Still Grant refused to commit himself to deposing Goode. His hesitation was rooted in his oft-displayed refusal to resort to the wire-pulling by which many politicians in uniform—most of them totally unfit for command—had secured high rank in the volunteer army.[57]

After May 22, when his mustering work ended, Grant obtained leave to visit Julia and the children in Galena. Returning to Springfield several days later, he found himself without pressing duties. Frustrated that his application to the adjutant general had brought no response, he applied for and received a week's leave, ostensibly to visit his parents in Covington. While in

Kentucky, however, he crossed the Ohio to Cincinnati, headquarters of George B. McClellan.

Until his resignation in 1858 to pursue a lucrative engineering career, McClellan had been one of the most promising young officers in the army. Working in Ohio when the war began, he had quickly made himself indispensable to Governor William Dennison and was now a major general in that state's volunteer force. Recently, he had garnered much favorable publicity by advancing through the mountains of western Virginia to rout a smaller enemy force near the village of Philippi. Grant had known the man briefly at West Point, McClellan having entered the Academy during his final year there, and he knew of McClellan's service in Mexico as a valued member of General Scott's staff. Now he hoped to gain a command under "Little Mac."

He could have saved himself a trip. Although he was warmly received at McClellan's headquarters by other West Pointers, including Brevet Major Seth Williams (Class of 1842), Grant failed to obtain an audience with the commander. He cooled his heels in an anteroom for two days—McClellan did not even acknowledge his presence. The snub rankled, especially considering Grant's implied claim to seniority: "I was older, had ranked him in the army, and could not hang around his headquarters" any longer without forfeiting a large amount of self-respect. Buttoning up his dejection, he left and returned to Springfield.[58]

★ ★ ★

During his absence from Illinois, significant events had taken place on the national and local scenes. In Virginia, troops loyal to the newly established Confederate States of America had begun to assemble in the northern and central reaches of the state, skirmishing with blue-coated soldiers almost within rifle-shot of the federal capital. Other Virginians built defenses along the Virginia Peninsula to block an advance from Union-held Fort Monroe. On June 10, a few thousand Federals who had massed near the latter installation blundered into a fight with a smaller but more organized force of Confederates near Big Bethel Church. The first major land battle of the war ended in Union defeat and retreat.

One day later—and nine hundred miles westward—Nathaniel Lyon and Frank Blair met with Governor Jackson and the new commander of the Missouri State Guard, Major General Sterling Price, at the Planters House hotel in St. Louis. Perhaps in the same rooms where Grant had played poker with James Longstreet, the four officers tried to agree on terms of a state-wide truce but failed to reach a consensus. Afterwards, Jackson and Price hastened back to the state capital at Jefferson City while Lyon began to develop plans for an advance against that place. The following day, Jackson called for fifty thousand volunteers to take back Missouri from Yankees, German Americans, and other undesirables. East and west, the young war was heating up.[59]

Of more personal interest to Ulysses S. Grant, while he was failing to gain a command under McClellan, a delegation of officers from the regiment he had mustered in at Mattoon had gone to Springfield to talk Governor Yates into firing Colonel Goode and replacing him with a more experienced and less tyrannical officer. Captain Harland presented the officers' case in explicit terms, stating "all that [he] knew about his [Goode's] drunkenness, his threats, idiotic commands, etc.," and reciting a laundry list of disciplinary problems inside the regiment. Harland feared that if Goode continued in command the regiment would not agree to reenlist for three years, as now required of every volunteer outfit.[60]

Yates heard the captain out, then, troubled by what he had heard, sent for the rest of the officers. A few days later, every member of the field and staff except Goode assembled in the governor's office, where Yates sounded them out on the possibility of replacing their commander. Of the entire group, including Lieutenant Colonel John W. Alexander, only one officer—a junior lieutenant—attempted to defend the colonel, and his arguments carried little weight.

Yates pondered the matter for some minutes, then asked: "Gentlemen, have you ever canvassed the availability of Capt. Grant, the officer who mustered you in?" Almost at once, ears perked up and faces brightened. The positive response settled the question in Yates's mind. While Grant was still on leave in Kentucky, the governor notified him by telegram that he had been appointed colonel of the regiment now known as the 21st Illinois Volunteer Infantry.[61]

The cable failed to reach Grant at Covington, which he had left for Springfield and another stopover in St. Louis on the way. Not until he returned to the state capital did he learn that his long and demoralizing hunt for a position of some authority and responsibility in the armed forces of the Union had borne fruit. His gratification knew no bounds, but it matched Yates's measure for measure, if only in retrospect. Years later, looking back on June 16, 1861, the day he made out Grant's commission, the governor called it "the most glorious day" of his life.[62]

★ *Chapter 5* ★

TRIAL AND ERROR

ON JUNE 7, GRANT'S REGIMENT, ALMOST ONE THOUSAND STRONG, HAD BEEN transferred from Mattoon to Camp Yates. Nine days later, the newly minted colonel took a streetcar to the campground and assumed command. He found his job very much cut out for him. The regiment had acquired a nickname—"Yates's Hellions"—that perfectly captured the corporate behavior that had made it the scourge of Mattoon. There it had torn down civilians' fences, raided farmers' chicken coops and spring-houses, and threatened passers-by with bodily harm. Simon Goode had done nothing to curb his men's obnoxious and sometimes violent ways; they had come to believe they could do whatever they pleased throughout the day and then carouse through the night as long as they returned to camp in time for reveille.[1]

Grant intended to force the men to act like soldiers instead of hooligans, but to those who eyed him closely during his first hours in camp he appeared to lack the physical strength and mental toughness to command. For one thing, he looked nothing like a colonel, or for that matter like a soldier. John E. Smith, a friend from Galena—former leader of the local Wide-Awakes—accompanied Grant to camp on that morning of June 16, 1861. In memorable prose he described the impression Colonel Goode's successor made on his new charges:

> Grant was dressed in citizen's clothes, an old coat worn out at the elbows, and a badly damaged hat. His men, though ragged and barefooted themselves, had formed a high estimate of what a colonel should be, and when Grant walked in among them, they began making fun of him. They cried in derision, "What a colonel!" "Damned such a colonel," and made all sorts of fun of him. And one of them, to show off to the others, got behind his

back and commenced sparring at him, and while he was doing this another gave him such a push that he hit Grant between the shoulders.[2]

Grant reacted by bending over, retrieving the hat that had hit the ground, dusting it off, and replacing it on his head. Without uttering a word, he turned and stared hard at his assailant, who quickly took a step back and began to search his comrades' faces as if seeking guidance. Finally, in a low but firm voice, Grant ordered everyone on the parade ground to form ranks. After a slight hesitation and with audible grumbling, the men shuffled into a ragged line and stood still, awaiting another command.

Grant walked down the line, looking every man in the face but saying nothing. His uncommunicativeness threw everyone off his guard. They had expected a former officer in the Regular Army to take umbrage at such treatment as he had received, to display his outrage in a profanity-laden but wholly impotent tirade. The lingering silence, which suggested a self-confidence that did not need to be verbalized, confused them. In that instant, everyone on the parade ground began to form a second opinion of this little stoop-shouldered man in the shabby suit. Minutes before, they had sized him up as someone who could not "pound dry sand in a straight hole." Now they began to see him as "a singed cat," somewhat the worse for wear physically, but "more alive than he look[ed]."[3]

Over the next couple of days, the newcomer whom the regiment had come to refer to as "the quiet man" proved he meant business. On June 18 he published an address in which he stated his intentions: "In accepting this command, your Commander will require the cooperation of all the commissioned and noncommissioned officers in instructing the command and in maintaining discipline, and hopes to receive also the heavy support of every enlisted man." Left unsaid was what he might do if he failed to receive such cooperation and support, but even the densest private must have suspected that things would go hard on anyone who violated the regulations Grant laid down for the regiment.[4]

The first of these, promulgated on June 19, forbade anyone, officer or enlisted man, to be out of camp after sundown without the consent of Colonel Grant. Soldiers would be permitted to leave camp during the day without a pass, but they had to be back in their tents before evening retreat was sounded. Anyone returning after retreat would be arrested and punished. Furthermore, when off the camp grounds, they were to be on their best behavior: "All men when out of Camp should reflect that they are gentlemen—in camp soldiers, and the Commanding Officer hopes that all of his command will sustain these two characters with fidelity."[5]

The moderation and restraint inherent in these orders were characteristic of their author. Neither at this time nor ever after did Grant attempt to impose the ultrastrict discipline of the regular service on the citizen-soldiers over whom he exercised authority. Whenever possible, he would explain to these men what he expected of them and would appeal to, rather than demand, their cooperation. If the humane approach did not work, he would come down on them heavily, simply because he had to. But the choice was theirs—and he never failed to extend it to them.[6]

His patience, however, was not infinite, and he found he needed to punish in a public way some of the more flagrant malefactors. The night after he assumed command, a drunken Simon Goode showed up at regimental headquarters and demanded to be mustered in—if not at his old grade, then as a first sergeant. Grant, perceiving an attempt to incite opposition to his rule, peremptorily ordered the man out of camp and advised him never to return—if he did not go of his own volition, Grant would throw him out. Spluttering with rage, Goode went, never to be seen again in the ranks of the regiment he had once "commanded."[7]

Over the next two days, two inebriated enlisted men resisted arrest and attempted to defy Grant's authority to levy punishment. The first laughed contemptuously when Grant told other men to lock him in the guardhouse. When the others hesitated to obey, Grant seized the offender by the collar and "gave him a quick jerk, which made him spin like a top," according to Hamlin Garland. "Before he had gathered his faculties together he was hustled to the gate and kicked into the road."[8]

The second man, a tall, burly troublemaker known as "Mexico," appeared to present a tougher problem. He offered no resistance when Grant sent him to the guardhouse, but told the colonel, in earshot of the entire regiment, that for every minute he spent there, he would exact a price: "I'll have an ounce of your blood." Grant had the man tied, gagged, and tethered to a post in the midst of camp as a warning to any others who thought of threatening their commander.[9]

After some hours, and with the eyes of the camp on him, Grant personally untied Mexico's gag, let him loose, and stood motionless, arms folded across his chest. A few of Mexico's comrades urged him to lash out at Grant. Instead, he quietly slunk away to his company, in whose ranks he disappeared, to offer no further trouble. "This ended all question of Grant's power to command both himself and his men," Garland observed. "Recalcitrants still read books of military regulations, and denied his right to do this or that; but the great majority of the regiment, being excellent men and good soldiers, welcomed a colonel who knew his duties and the limits of his command."[10]

Within a fortnight of Grant's coming, the regiment began to demonstrate not only a semblance of order and discipline but some small amount of proficiency on the drill field. Whenever he was gone from camp, which was often, Grant entrusted the tactical instruction to Lieutenant Colonel Alexander. Grant was called away on a variety of errands, not the least important of which was to visit his family in Galena; while there, he procured a colonel's uniform and all the accoutrements, including a saber and a brace of pistols, a war horse, a saddle, and tack—all funded by a loan of three hundred dollars from E. A. Collins, a local merchant who had been one of Jesse Grant's many business partners.[11]

Grant was back at Camp Yates on June 28 to preside over the ceremony in which the regiment would be transformed from a ninety-days' outfit into one enlisted for three years' service "unless sooner discharged," the 21st Illinois Volunteer Infantry. Earlier, he had sensed an undercurrent of sentiment in the ranks to oppose the transition, and he worried that a few malcontents would sully their comrades' growing image as stalwart defenders of the Union. Thus he had accepted—albeit with some misgivings—the offer of two visiting congressmen to address the regiment prior to the swearing-in, ostensibly to fire the men's enthusiasm for extending their commitment.

The rub was that both men—John Alexander McClernand and John Alexander Logan—were Illinois Democrats, not members of the party administering the war effort; and Logan, who hailed from a district populated by numerous emigrants from Dixie, was regarded in some circles as a Southern sympathizer. Grant was vastly relieved when both men strongly advocated a gloves-off policy toward the enemies of the Union. He was especially taken with Logan's speech, which "breathed a loyalty and devotion to the Union" that inspired his men "to such a point that they would have volunteered to remain in the army as long as an enemy of the country continued to bear arms against it." Captivated by the impassioned rhetoric, the regiment "almost to a man" signed on for three years. In the not-distant future Grant would again have occasion to tap the talents of both speakers, this time in their capacity as general officers in the volunteer service.[12]

When the polished orators had finished, the newly sworn-in recruits called upon their commander to make his first speech to the regiment. Grant surprised and disappointed them; to the cries of "Speech! Speech!" he responded: "Men, go to your quarters!" For a minute or two his audience milled about in stunned silence, then quietly dispersed.[13]

Grant's rejoinder was "not a jest, it was an act of moral courage," wrote J.F.C. Fuller, the distinguished British soldier-historian.

There was no humbug about this man, and a vast amount of common sense. How many others would have exclaimed: "Go to your quarters"? How many another would not have been surprised by the sudden call for a speech, and being unbalanced would have said something pleasant and jocular. Grant saw before him a *canaille* and not a regiment, and when they shouted he saw a still greater *canaille,* and he treated his undisciplined rabble as such.[14]

It was his job to turn that gaggle of pea-green youngsters into mature, experienced fighting men. Words alone would not accomplish that, so he would not waste his time uttering them.

★ ★ ★

The 21st Illinois remained at Camp Yates, pounding the drill plain and learning the routine of soldier life, until July 3, when their colonel moved them, on orders, to the Mississippi River village of Quincy, almost one hundred miles west of Springfield. They might have gone by railroad, as another regiment had at a cost to the government of seven hundred dollars. Grant decided that his men would go on foot. Not only would this save Governor Yates the cost of transportation, it would introduce the men to the rigors of field campaigning.[15]

The lesson he taught them was a hard one, but it was one they needed to learn—and he administered it in such a way that they would not forget it. The first day out, the regiment made five miles, but when the march was resumed at 6:00 a.m. the next day, no one was ready. Grant waited for them to wake up, get breakfast, and hit the road. On the third morning, with many of his men still asleep at marching time, he started without them. Half-dressed recruits, most of whom had not eaten, raced frantically to catch up with their more punctual comrades. After a while, Grant halted the column so that the laggards could close up and complete their toilet. On the fourth morning, everyone was ready on time. The rest of the journey was made with a minimum of straggling.[16]

"My men behaved admirably," Grant wrote to his father, "and the lesson has been a good one for them. They can now go into camp after a day's march with as much promptness as veteran troops; they can strike their tents and be on the march with equal celerity." They had also learned to slake their thirst on a long, hot march with nothing stronger than water. On the first day of the journey, some of the men broke ranks to avail themselves of alcoholic refreshment at a roadside tavern, then rejoined the column in a state of intoxication. From personal experience Grant knew the disastrous effects of liquor on soldierly deportment and discipline. When Grant discovered the source of the trouble, "he went to the house in person [where] he found a churn full of whisky," Ed Harland recalled. "He picked it up, and with his own hands emptied the whisky upon the ground."[17]

The journey ended prematurely in a flurry of conflicting orders. Near Naples on the Illinois River, Grant was overtaken by a communiqué from the headquarters of the local military department ordering his regiment to Ironton, Missouri, southwest of St. Louis. A steamboat was to transport the men and their equipage; but when she was delayed by an accident, Grant put his men into camp and waited. The delay was vexing, but it provided him with a fine war horse. One day, a local farmer brought into camp a "clay-bank" (i.e., cream-colored) stallion named Jack, which Grant immediately appropriated for his own. The horse would serve him faithfully for the next two years.[18]

Finally came orders to move to Quincy, then to cross the Mississippi and hasten to Monroe City on the Hannibal & St. Joseph Railroad. Near Monroe City an Illinois regiment needed help; it was reportedly surrounded by a much larger body of Confederates. This latest turn of events left Grant anticipating his first battle action since that day, fourteen years ago, when he had trained his little howitzer on the defenders of Mexico City. The prospect bothered him greatly, not because he feared his courage would falter but because for the first time in his life he was shouldering the burden of command ("if some one else had been colonel and I had been lieutenant-colonel I do not think I would have felt any trepidation"). Before he could test his mettle, however, the beleaguered Illinoisans straggled into Quincy, having slipped the trap set for them.[19]

The regiment's reprieve was relatively short-lived. No longer needed at Monroe City, Grant ferried his outfit across the river, then led it down to the village of Palmyra, where it remained for a few days before advancing farther south to guard a bridge over Salt River. That service consumed two weeks, at the end of which new orders directed Grant to locate and assault a force of indeterminate size under Colonel Tom Harris, the guerrilla leader who had failed to bag that Illinois regiment at Monroe City. Harris's men were thought to be encamped about twenty-five miles southwest of Grant's present position, outside the hamlet of Florida. That nondescript collection of clapboard dwellings had a claim to distinction—although one yet unknown—as the birthplace of one Samuel Langhorne Clemens, currently a private soldier in the Missouri State Guard, soon to desert to the Nevada silver fields and then to California. In both venues he would gather material for the classic works of literature he would write under the nom de plume of Mark Twain.[20]

It took a few days to collect the regiment's baggage and equipment for the march south. The delay was vexing, but this was the easy part of the operation. "While preparations for the move were going on I felt quite comfortable; but when we got on the road and found every house deserted I was anything but easy," Grant admitted. "In the twenty-five miles we had to march we did not see a person, old or young, male or female, except two horsemen who . . . decamped as fast as their horses could carry them."[21]

On the second day of the march, the column neared Harris's camp, which, scouts reported, was situated in a creek bottom at the foot of a hill perhaps one hundred feet high. Grant cautiously led the way forward. He described vividly what went through his mind as he covered the last mile or so to his objective:

> As we approached the brow of the hill from which it was expected we could see Harris' camp, and possibly find his men ready formed to meet us, my heart kept getting higher and higher until it felt to me as though it was in my throat. I would have given any thing then to have been back in Illinois, but I had not the moral courage to halt and consider what to do; I kept right on. When we reached a point from which the valley below was in full view I halted. The place where Harris had been encamped a few days before was still there and the marks of a recent encampment were plainly visible, but the troops were gone. My heart resumed its place. It occurred to me at once that Harris had been as much afraid of me as I had been of him. This was a view of the question I had never taken before; but it was one I never forgot afterwards. From that event to the close of the war, I never experienced trepidation upon confronting an enemy, though I always felt more or less anxiety. I never forgot that he had as much reason to fear my forces as I had his.[22]

Discovering that Harris had put forty miles between his command and Grant's, the colonel countermarched his regiment to the Salt River bridge. His next assignment was to occupy the village of Mexico, thirty-five miles to the south, where Grant was to assume command of a subsidiary of

Brigadier General John Pope's District of Northern Missouri. Pope was a senior subordinate of Major General John C. Frémont, the politician-general whom Grant had voted against in the presidential election of 1856. From his headquarters in St. Louis, Frémont—a Mexican War hero, an explorer (known far and wide as the "Pathfinder of the West"), and the son-in-law of Missouri's most powerful solon, Senator Thomas Hart Benton—reigned over the Western Department, a vast fiefdom that encompassed Missouri, Illinois, and all territory as far west as the Rocky Mountains.[23]

If Frémont had influential political patrons, so did Ulysses S. Grant—though he was unaware of the fact. On July 31, two days after being assigned to the post at Mexico, Grant's name made the list of officers recommended to the Senate for promotion to brigadier general of volunteers. His appointment had been strongly urged by several Illinois politicians, foremost of whom was Elihu Washburne. Another supporter was Lyman Trumbull, the Republican senator, whom Grant may have met when, on May 11, he mustered in a regiment at Trumbull's hometown of Belleville. Presumably as a result of the clout these lawmakers wielded, the appointment received quick confirmation by the Senate. Of even greater advantage, when Grant received his appointment he found that it had been backdated, for purposes of seniority, to May 17.

He was equally surprised and pleased by the promotion, which he considered "very complimentary," and particularly so because he had "never asked a friend to intercede on [his] behalf." It pleased him, too, to have additional pay to send home to his family, with whom he kept in touch by mail as often as his increasing duties permitted. On the other hand, he regretted his pending separation from the officers and men of the 21st Illinois; he had only begun to instruct them in battalion drill, working from a manual of arms he had never read up to that time. He considered his association with the regiment "highly satisfactory." With justifiable pride, he noted: "I took it in a very disorganized, demoralized and insubordinate condition, and have worked it up to a reputation equal to the best, and, I believe, with the good will of all the officers and all the men."[24]

Almost immediately, he began to build the basis of his generalship. His first concern was to form a staff of aides-de-camp. Believing that one should be selected from the regiment he had turned over to Lieutenant Colonel Alexander, he selected Lieutenant Clark B. Lagow. He also chose Lieutenant William S. Hillyer, who as a civilian lawyer in St. Louis had shared No. 35 Pine Street with Boggs & Grant, Real Estate Agents. Lagow and Hillyer, both in their early thirties, were of a class known to a later generation as "good old boys." Neither was a soldier in the truest sense; they were amiable and easygoing, addicted to good food, strong drink, and endless games of poker. Their personal habits would complicate Grant's ability to keep his own under control.[25]

Grant wished to choose a third staff officer from among his close acquaintances in Galena. The man he selected, whose abilities and tastes differed radically from those of Lagow and Hillyer, would not join him until mid-September, delayed by the sad duty of attending to his tubercular wife, who lay dying at her family's home in upstate New York. This was John Rawlins, whose passionate call to defend the Union by all necessary force regardless of political affiliation had so impressed Grant. Rawlins's name had been linked to the formation of at least two Illinois regiments, in either of which he might have secured field rank. But as soon as he received Grant's offer of an aide-de-camp's position—"a compliment unexpected," as he called it—he replied: "Gladly and with pleasure I accept it."[26]

Rawlins would prove a valuable counterweight to the baleful influence of the other aides. He was conscientious, hardworking, a stickler for detail, and a zealous advocate of temperance. He had his faults—a volatile temper, an impatience with any effort that did not produce immediate results, a tendency to curse and swear when angry or frustrated—but from the day he joined Grant's military family he would devote himself to promoting the career of the officer he considered the preeminent weapon in the military arsenal of the Union.

Grant's first assignment at his new rank sent him to Frémont's headquarters at St. Louis. The Pathfinder immediately ordered him to Ironton to take charge of the troops assembling in the southeastern corner of Missouri. Grant intended to comply with proper haste, but he delayed his visit to St. Louis long enough to look in on some old friends and acquaintances, one of whom had since become an enemy. He paid a brief visit to Jefferson Barracks, his first duty station as an army officer, where he lit up the few familiar faces still on duty there. Then he called on Harry Boggs, who refused his outstretched hand and behaved as if he wished to spit in Grant's face.

Although Grant remained in civilian garb—he had given away his colonel's uniform and had yet to procure a brigadier's—his former partner sized him up as the Yankee general he had become. The sudden and unexpected transition stoked Boggs's ire. "He cursed and went on like a Madman," Grant explained in a letter to Julia. "Told me that I would never be welcom[e] in his hous[e]; that the people of Illinois were a poor miserable set of Black Republicans, Abolition paupers that had to invade their state to get something to eat." Another man might have taken umbrage, but not one who had risen so high in the world that his critics looked tiny and impotent: "Harry is such a pitiful insignificant fellow that I could not get mad at him and told him so." Grant's rejoinder only triggered another burst of Boggsian profanity.[27]

At first Grant considered extending his visit long enough to make a quick foray to Galena, but he decided he could not afford to. Accompanied by the 21st Illinois, he took a steamer down to Ironton. Arriving at that isolated and vulnerable post adjacent to a landmark eminence, Pilot Knob, he acquainted himself with the elements of his enlarged command, strengthened the local defenses, and reconnoitered the countryside. His scouts picked up a rumor that several thousand Rebels under Brigadier General William J. Hardee—the prewar tactician whose manual of arms Grant had used to instruct the 21st in battalion drill—was moving to attack Ironton. Within days, however, the threat began to dissipate; in a letter to his sister on August 12, Grant wrote: "Hardee's force seems to have [been] reduced, and his distance from here to have increased."[28]

Enemy movements elsewhere in the state were not so easily dismissed. By August 12, Grant had learned that the forces of Lyon and Blair, which in mid-June had chased Governor Jackson and his state troops out of Jefferson City and into the southwestern corner of Missouri, had been soundly defeated, and Lyon killed, in battle at Wilson's Creek, near Springfield. The news came as a shock to Grant, but more so to his departmental commander. Frémont, perhaps for the first time, saw his domain as vulnerable and his troops as fighting on the defensive.

Frémont's was not the only enclave threatened by determined and energetic Confederates. On July 16, a small army of would-be soldiers under Brigadier General Irvin McDowell (Winfield Scott's favorite aide now that Robert Lee had gone over to the other side) had left Washington in response to the "On to Richmond" urgings of Northern editors, politicians, and citizens. McDowell's path to the newly established Confederate capital ended eighty miles short of his objective. On July 21, along a creek called Bull Run and near a railroad station known as Manassas Junction, McDowell's so-called army clashed with a smaller force of equally untried recruits under Brigadier General Pierre G. T. Beauregard, the assailant of Fort Sumter, and General Joseph E. Johnston, until recently commanding in the Shenandoah Valley. The defenders held their ground stubbornly, blunting every Union attack and, near the end of the day, propelling McDowell's invaders back across the Potomac.[29]

These sudden major changes in the war situation caused Grant to reconsider his view of the future. In his letter of August 12, he admitted to his sister: "I don't know what to think. That the rebels will be so badly whipped by April next that they cannot make a stand anywhere, I don't doubt. But they are so dogged that there is no telling when they may be subdued."[30]

A little more than a week after reaching Ironton, Grant prepared to launch a strike on an enemy force reported to be at Greenville, thirty-five miles south of his headquarters. He started toward his objective in two columns; but on the morning of August 17, before the movement was far advanced, a train brought to Ironton Brigadier General Benjamin Prentiss with orders placing him in command of Grant's district. Although believing that his promotion had made him senior to the new arrival, Grant turned the expedition over to Prentiss and departed for St. Louis, where he planned to place the matter before General Frémont.[31]

Instead of adjudicating Grant's seniority, Frémont directed him to assume command of troops in and around the state capital. Uncertain whether the new assignment was an advancement or a demotion, the brigadier proceeded at once to Jefferson City, where he found "a great deficiency in everything for the comfort and efficiency of an army. Most of the troops," he told Frémont, "are without clothing, camp and garrison equipage." Moreover, ammunition was in short supply and available artillery was insufficient to hold the place. He did the best he could to rectify the deficiencies, but he was not on the ground long enough to accomplish anything of lasting value. By August 28, barely a week after reaching the capital, he was on a train heading back to St. Louis, where "important special instructions" awaited him at Frémont's headquarters.[32]

The back-and-forth shuttling showed no signs of ceasing. The Pathfinder sent him south yet again, this time to Cape Girardeau on the west bank of the Mississippi, provisional headquarters of the District of Southeast Missouri, whose territory also included lower Illinois. He had been recommended for the important post by some of Frémont's subordinates, one of them being General Pope, who described Grant to his superior as "a Soldier by education & experience & a discreet prudent man." Grant suspected that the duties he took on at Cape Girardeau would take up his "entire attention." As always, he did not mind hard work so long as he could keep busy at it: "All I fear, is that too much may be expected of me." This was, after all, his largest command to date.[33]

The first thing expected of him was to take charge of an expedition to overawe a few thousand guerrillas under Brigadier General M. Jeff Thompson, a bold and colorful partisan leader who had once been mayor of St. Joseph,

Missouri. Troops involved in the operation were to be drawn not only from the Cape Girardeau vicinity but also from Ironton and Cairo, Illinois, at the juncture of the Mississippi and Ohio Rivers. Grant planned a carefully coordinated pincers operation, which he looked forward to applying to Thompson—only to have it thwarted by General Prentiss, who, because he continued to believe himself Grant's senior, resisted taking orders from him. When Prentiss left the field in a huff to report his grievance at St. Louis, the project was shelved. "Little harm was done, as Jeff Thompson moved light and had no fixed place for even nominal headquarters," Grant later reflected. "He was as much at home in Arkansas as he was in Missouri, and would keep out of the way of a superior force."[34]

The guerrilla hunt having ended before substantially begun, Grant moved his headquarters across the Mississippi to Cairo. The river village was surrounded by leaky levies, infested with rats, and buried in mud, but it was also one of the most strategic points in the embattled Union—in Bruce Catton's words, "a gateway to and from practically everywhere, north, south, east and west." From this pivotal position, a Union column might penetrate the enemy's country, striking toward Confederate Tennessee or formally neutral but largely hostile Kentucky. This was possible only, however, if southeastern Missouri could be cleared of the enemy's presence.[35]

The Confederacy had no intention of abandoning the west bank of the river; in fact, it intended to increase its presence on both sides of the Mississippi. On September 3, the day Grant wrote a letter thanking his congressional patron Elihu Washburne "for the part [he had] taken in giving [Grant his] present position," Major General Leonidas Polk, a West Pointer who had become a bishop in the Episcopal Church only to trade his clerical robes for a Confederate uniform, violated Kentucky's neutrality by occupying Columbus, across the river from Belmont, Missouri. Ostensibly, Polk had done so in response to the Union buildup at Cairo. Fearing their state would soon be overrun by Rebels, Kentucky loyalists invited Union intervention, and Grant heeded their call.[36]

He was prompted to act by reports that Polk intended to occupy Paducah, which sat by the mouth of the Tennessee River almost fifty miles east of Cairo. The rapidity and determination Grant exhibited in reacting to the threat would become hallmarks of his generalship. On the evening of September 5, without waiting to receive Frémont's approval (which was eventually given), he loaded two infantry regiments and a battery aboard transports, steamed up the Ohio River, and next morning occupied Paducah, with its large Southern-sympathizing population, without opposition. "The citizens

were taken by surprise," he recalled. "I never saw such consternation de-
picted on the faces of the people." Similarly shocked were the four thousand
Confederate troops Grant learned had been en route to the place but who,
finding Paducah occupied by an unknown number of Yankees, had returned
to Columbus.[37]

After placing troops in strategic positions around the town, filling the
riverfront with a cooperating force of gunboats, and throwing up protective
works, Grant prepared to return to Cairo. Before he did, however, he composed the only proclamation to local civilians he would issue during the war.
The document assured the people "of our peaceful intentions, that we had
come among them to protect them against the enemies of our country, and
that all who chose could continue their usual avocations with assurance of
the protection of the government." His claim of a purely defensive movement, although rejected by diehard secessionists, resonated with a majority
of the locals, as did his disinclination to interfere with private property, including slaves.[38]

Grant's edict also received favorable publicity in the North. Even Lincoln, who objected to his generals' addressing occupied Southerners, was reported to have approved of its content and tone. The president realized that
to win the hearts and minds of his fellow Kentuckians, the government
would have to respect property rights and defer to local sensibilities. Grant's
action was a happy contrast to the radical, ham-fisted policies that John Frémont had adopted. The departmental commander had declared martial law
throughout his domain, had authorized the confiscation of land belonging to
those in rebellion against the federal government, and had announced that
the slaves owned by these people would be freed. These and other inflammatory acts would impel Lincoln to revoke Frémont's emancipation decree
and then, in early November, relieve the Pathfinder of his command.[39]

Grant's movement against Paducah not only brought him—probably for
the first time—to the president's attention but garnered him his first flurry of
news coverage, although it was largely confined to Kentucky, Missouri, and
Illinois newspapers. The publicity, and the general satisfaction his policies
received among Southern sympathizers as well as supporters of the Union,
highly gratified him. Perhaps as a result, he looked forward to additional opportunities to take action against enemy forces in the Bluegrass. By late September, back at his headquarters at Cairo, he was informing his sister Mary
that he had extended his lines almost half way to Polk's bailiwick at Columbus. Ordinarily, such a move would have heralded an early advance, but his
forces had been much reduced: "It would be imprudent to make an attack

now until I am reinforced," he wrote. Still, "I hope some day, if I am allowed to retain this command, to give a good account of ourselves."[40]

★ ★ ★

In his memoirs, Grant observed: "From the occupation of Paducah up to the early part of November nothing important occurred with the troops under my command." During the interim, however, he had been substantially reinforced: He now had twenty thousand troops at his disposal, although they were spread across a wide front and many of them were green recruits who needed to be "drilled and disciplined preparatory for the service which was sure to come." The material might be too raw to rely on in a fight, but the knowledge that he had under his control as many soldiers as Taylor and Scott led in Mexico was gratifying as well as daunting.[41]

Grant returned to active operations early in November, about the time of Frémont's relief. Late in September Frémont had finally departed his desk in St. Louis to conduct a field campaign against Sterling Price and his State Guard. Though the campaign would end indecisively, to support it Grant and other subordinates were ordered to prevent the Confederates in Kentucky from interfering with the Pathfinder's plans. By November 5, rumors reached Grant's headquarters at Cairo that General Polk was ferrying troops across the river to Belmont and from there into the interior of Missouri to reinforce Price. It was Grant's job to prevent Polk from detaching additional forces by way of a demonstration against Columbus. The Union force that held Paducah—now commanded by Brigadier General Charles F. Smith, Grant's model of soldierly deportment during his cadet days at West Point— was also to advance on Columbus, making Polk believe he was the object of a pincers movement.[42]

Although in his memoirs Grant goes to some lengths to deny it, a dispatch he sent to Smith on the fifth suggests that he intended to do more than feint against the Rebels in Kentucky: Attacking the Rebel encampment at Belmont "would enable [him] to drive those they [had] there out of Missouri." He had a ready-made pretext for exceeding his orders in this manner. Three days earlier, in response to another directive, he had sent one of his newly formed brigades, Colonel Richard J. Oglesby's, down the Missouri side of the river to catch Jeff Thompson's irregulars, who were attacking Union outposts and looting supply depots. When, early on November 7, another of Grant's subordinates, Colonel W.H.L. Wallace, informed him that Confederates were crossing from Columbus to Belmont with the apparent intent of cutting off Oglesby, Grant had all the ammunition he needed to do what he had intended to do anyway—attack and rout the Rebels gathering at Belmont.[43]

By the time he got Wallace's message, Grant had already moved downriver from Cairo at the head of approximately three thousand Illinois and Iowa infantrymen and two companies of cavalry. The expeditionary force was divided into two brigades, one under Grant's senior subordinate, John McClernand, whose oratory had helped persuade the men of the 21st Illinois to reenlist for three years' service. The Democratic congressman's support of the war (and his friendship with Abraham Lincoln) had brought him a brigadier generalship, which should enable him to fulfill long-held dreams of martial glory. The troops were conveyed downriver by transports escorted by two gunboats in charge of Lieutenant Henry Walke. The operation marked the outset of an increasingly contentious relationship between Grant and McClernand, but also the beginning of Grant's long and productive association with the United States Navy.

On the night of November 6, the expedition halted about six miles above Columbus. Next morning at daybreak, Grant landed the troops a couple miles farther south, beyond range of Confederate batteries on the opposite bank. With commendable speed he put ashore his entire force and led it inland—all but five companies of Illinoisans, whom he left on the river to guard the transports. For a mile or more, his advance attracted only scattered and ineffective artillery fire. When his men finally encountered the enemy, they drove him, as Grant recounted, "foot by foot, and from tree to tree, back to his encampment on the river bank, a distance of over 2 miles." Because at this stage of the fight they outnumbered their opponents three-to-one, Grant's men had little trouble evicting the Rebels from their position and occupying the camp they abandoned. Grant's first effort in tactical command appeared a smashing success.[44]

The Union leader was so intent on pressing his attack and so fearful of disrupting its momentum that when his horse (a bay, not his claybank steed Jack) stopped a rifle ball and threw him hard to the ground he bobbed up, brushed himself off, mounted a borrowed steed, and regained his place at the head of the column. In his eagerness to pursue the routed foe, however, he neglected to deploy a reserve force to cover his rear. Nor did he detect the approach of several regiments of Confederates that Polk's ranking lieutenant, Brigadier General Gideon J. Pillow, was ferrying across from Columbus to contain Grant's penetration. The reinforcements circled upstream to mass between the attackers and their transports, sealing off their route of withdrawal.

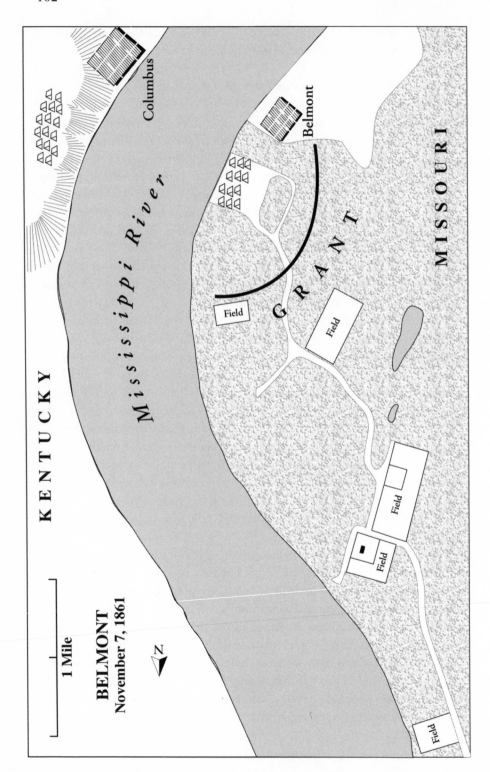

KENTUCKY

Columbus

Mississippi River

Belmont

GRANT

MISSOURI

Field

Field

Field

Field

Field

1 Mile

N

BELMONT
November 7, 1861

Compounding his errors, Grant lost control of many of his soldiers at the height of their success. Given his relatively brief acquaintance with volunteers, he had not expected them, once they took the enemy camp, to stop and loot it. Adding his voice to the shouted commands of his brigade and regimental leaders, Grant tried to get them moving again. The Rebels they had displaced were huddling at the foot of a bluff within easy striking distance, willing to surrender to any coherent force that advanced on them. But none advanced, and the opportunity to bag hundreds of prisoners went by the board. Then, almost too late, Grant detected the approach of Pillow's troopships. He tried to turn against them the six cannons his men had seized, but to little avail.

The frustrated expeditionary leader, who had no wagons in which to carry off captured equipage, erred yet again by ordering his men to set fire to it. The column of smoke that ascended into the sky told Polk that the Yankees held the camp; thus he could pound it with his artillery without fear of endangering his own soldiers. Within minutes, Grant's men found themselves hammered in front by shot and shell and laced by small-arms' fire in rear. Believing themselves surrounded, some of the officers suggested that Grant surrender to avoid further bloodshed. Their commander would not consider it: "We had cut our way in and we would cut our way out." In his postaction report, he omitted mention of his subordinates' entreaties: "Our troops were not in the least discouraged," he claimed.[45]

At his command, the men turned toward the rear and started back to the steamers at the walk, then at the double-quick. All semblance of formation was lost as they ran a gauntlet of fire that accounted for a majority of the nearly five hundred casualties that Grant's force suffered this day. More than 200 of these men were cut off and captured during the race to the river. Another 125 were wounded men whom Grant had been unable to evacuate. The latter included Colonel Henry Dougherty, commander of Grant's second brigade, who had been shot three times.[46]

Through a combination of hard fighting and good fortune, the Federals broke through the gray cordon and reached the transports, which quickly put out into the river. While they scrambled aboard, Grant remained behind to conduct a lone reconnaissance. He had been informed that a column under Pillow was advancing to cut off the rear of the departing force. The solitary scouting mission took Grant through a field of harvested corn opposite the steamboat landing. Riding forward through the stubble, he suddenly found himself staring into the faces of gray-clad troops advancing along the opposite side of the field, less than fifty feet away. Hoping the enemy would mistake him for one of their own, but for all that expecting to take a bullet—more likely, numerous bullets—in the back, the brigadier instinctively turned and trotted back to the river.

For some inexplicable reason, no one fired on him. Once he was out of rifle range, he put spurs to his horse and galloped unhurt to the landing. But as soon as his horse slid down the bluff to the landing and he boarded the last waiting troopship, a minié ball passed through a wall of the pilot's cabin and struck the spot he had been occupying less than a minute earlier.[47]

Soon the vessel was underway, relieving Grant's pent-up anxiety. Although peppered at long range by Rebels along both banks of the river, the ship sustained no serious damage. Grant's first battle as a field commander was history. It had been marred by mistakes and miscalculations, and his men's escape had been a near thing. But they and their commander had survived to fight another day—presumably with greater skill, heightened vigilance, and a deeper appreciation of the capabilities of their foe.

★ ★ ★

Although his soldiers had occupied and torched the camp at Belmont and dispersed its occupants, Grant had not deterred Polk from shuttling troops to Missouri. Even so, impressed by the stout fighting his men had done on both the offensive and the defensive, he chose to regard the engagement as a victory—although he later had his initial after-action report rewritten to reflect a changed perspective on what he had intended to accomplish that day. In an address disseminated among the command, he claimed that although he had taken part in many sanguinary engagements in Mexico, he "never saw one more hotly contested or where troops behaved with more gallantry" than that of November 7, 1861.[48]

Other observers were less complimentary. Although the War Department did not press him for his reasoning in attacking Belmont, Northern editors, perhaps influenced by soldiers' tales of being surrounded, cut off, and forced to run for their lives, criticized Grant's handling of the battle and questioned why it had been fought. Grant's newly installed departmental commander, the officious and condescending Major General Henry W. Halleck (known in the army as "Old Brains" for his supposed erudition, he having written extensively on strategy and tactics) failed to support Grant against his critics or give him a vote of confidence.

Halleck, in fact, might have accepted as truth, or at least half-truth, some of the outlandish charges that followed Grant for a time after Belmont— many coined not by soldiers but by disgruntled contractors and speculators whose efforts to gain a monopoly on army business at Cairo Grant had thwarted. The most sensational of these was the wholly unsubstantiated allegation that he had been drinking heavily at Cairo before the fight, and perhaps even on the field of battle. Lurid accounts of Grant's tippling in the Old Army began to circulate, and the details of his 1854 resignation were dredged up and given new scrutiny.[49]

Charges of mismanaging a battle could be passed over with a shrug, but claims of drunkenness on duty were too serious, too potentially devastating to Grant's career, to be ignored. In December, Congressman Washburne, Grant's primary political sponsor in Washington, wrote to his Galena friend John Rawlins, who had joined Grant's staff at Cairo two months earlier, and asked for a candid assessment of Grant's personal behavior. The cold-water zealot from Galena—now filling the official position of Grant's adjutant general and the self-appointed role of guardian of his reputation—replied that there was no substance to the charges: "When I came to Cairo, General Grant was, as he is today, a strictly total abstinence man, and I have been informed by those who knew him well, that such has been his habit for the last five or six years. . . . If you could look into General Grant's countenance at this moment you would want no other assurance of his sobriety. He is in perfect health, and his eyes and intellect are as clear and active as can be." In concluding his defense, Rawlins felt compelled to add: "I say to you frankly, and I pledge you my word for it, that should General Grant at any time become an intemperate man or an habitual drunkard, I will notify you immediately, will ask to be removed from duty on his staff (kind as he has been to me), or resign my commission."[50]

Rawlins realized that Washburne, who had linked his interests and aspirations with Grant's, would serve as a powerful defender of the general's good name. Yet the adjutant was aware of how difficult that job might become. A thin line appeared to separate the healthy, contented, and abstemious Grant from the bored, frustrated, nervous Grant who might be tempted by circumstance, association, or nature to drown his discontent in alcohol. For this reason, Rawlins was already working hard, though behind the scenes, to rid the staff of Lagow and Hillyer and men like them, and replace them with professional soldiers who would regard their position as that of coadjutor, not as buddy to the general commanding.

If Grant was in danger from falling off the wagon either through boredom (for several weeks after Belmont his command was relegated to static operations) or depression (brought on by his merciless pounding in the press), he was rescued not only by Rawlins's zealous protectionism but also by a visit from his family. At his earnest entreaty, a few days after the battle, Julia, accompanied by all four of the children, came to stay with him at Cairo. She told him of a vision she had had of him—on horseback as if in battle—on the day she packed for the trip. Upon his inquiry, she fixed the exact time of the experience. He informed her that at that very hour he had been riding away from the enemy-infested cornfield with, as he feared, hundreds of rifles trained on him. In that moment of peril, "I thought of you and the children, and what would become of you if I were lost." The shared psychic experience made their union all the more emotional, and he cherished the days she and the children spent with him in the bank building he had transformed into the headquarters of his recently renamed District of Cairo. The almost constant coming and going of officers, men, and civilians prompted Julia to liken the place to a "great barracks."[51]

She and the children made the most of their visit. They rode about in a medical wagon outfitted as a coach and escorted by a cavalry troop; they accompanied the local flag-of-truce boat as it churned down the river toward enemy lines; they visited and shopped in occupied Paducah; and they attended reviews and parades at which General Grant presided. Julia recalled, "How proud I was sitting there in our ambulance with my friend Mrs. Hillyer [wife of the general's aide] and our little ones witnessing the reviews and hearing the bands play 'Hail to the Chief' as *my* General rode down the columns inspecting!" Desirous that her husband look his absolute best on these occasions, she gently nagged him into trimming the gnarly thicket that had adorned his face since the war's commencement into a rather elegant beard, one he never again let grow out of control.[52]

The only undesirable feature of the visit was the mysterious illness that befell nine-year-old Buck, who became "delirious with pain and fever." His parents' concern was alleviated only after the general, returning from a brief trip to St. Louis, brought with him medicine prescribed by one of the city's leading physicians. When administered to the boy, the tonic restored him to health with almost mystical rapidity. Days later Buck accompanied his mother and siblings to Covington, where they would reside with Grant's parents, as the general desired. Julia carried with her a large roll of greenbacks, which her husband had pressed into her hand shortly before her departure. "Take care of it," he told her, "you will need it. It may be some time before I can give you any more, as I expect to be on active duty from this [time] on."[53]

* * *

Julia and the children left because their husband and father had been called into the field. He had received orders from Washington, relayed by Halleck, to launch an offensive south of his present location. The operation was designed as a diversion in favor of Brigadier General Don Carlos Buell, a West Point acquaintance of Grant's who in mid-November had assumed command of the Department of the Ohio, headquartered at Louisville. By early January 1862, President Lincoln as well as George B. McClellan—who two months before, strictly on the basis of his potential for greatness, had replaced Winfield Scott as commanding general of the army—and the new secretary of war, Edwin McMasters Stanton, were urging Buell to operate against those Confederates holding Bowling Green, Kentucky, prior to invading East Tennessee to relieve the region's many Unionists from Rebel occupation. The Union's ruling triumvirate believed that Halleck should support this ambitious agenda by menacing the Columbus-area Rebels. Halleck had complied by ordering Grant to invade Kentucky.[54]

Although foreseeing rigorous campaigning, Grant formed two columns. The first, under McClernand, six thousand strong, he sent into the western part of the Bluegrass. The other, led by C. F. Smith, went up the west bank of the Tennessee River. Grant moved with McClernand's command, which left Cairo on January 10. There followed an arduous, eleven-day journey through a bleak countryside in falling temperatures. "The weather was very bad; snow and rain fell; the roads, never good in that section, were intolerable," Grant recalled. "We were out more than a week splashing through the mud, snow and rain, the men suffering very much."[55]

In the end, their exertions appeared to go for naught, for logistical deficiencies and other factors combined to scuttle Buell's move into East Tennessee. The diversion did, however, prevent reinforcements from being sent to Mill Springs, in eastern Kentucky, where on January 19 four thousand Federals under Brigadier General George H. Thomas defeated a force of equal size under Brigadier General Felix Zollicoffer, who was killed in the fight. Zollicoffer's defeat meant that the right flank of the main Confederate defensive line in the west had been broken, dashing the hopes and skewing the plans of the ranking officer in that theater, General Albert Sidney Johnston. By retreating, the Confederates effectively abandoned Kentucky to enemy control and created the possibility of a Union advance into Tennessee.[56]

In addition to aiding Thomas, Grant's expedition stimulated his interest in advancing into strategic Middle Tennessee. It would be a simple matter of transporting troops, convoyed by the navy, down the Tennessee and/or Cumberland Rivers. En route to objectives farther south, the army could operate against, and probably seize, two fortified points on the Tennessee, Forts Heiman and Henry, as well as Fort Donelson on the Cumberland, twelve miles farther east.

Shortly after returning from Kentucky, Grant secured permission to travel to St. Louis and lay before General Halleck a plan to descend the Tennessee. He expected a cordial greeting from his new superior; instead, the portly, goggle-eyed Halleck received him coldly: "Perhaps I stated the object of my visit with less clearness than I might have done, and I had not uttered many sentences before I was cut short as if my plan was preposterous. I returned to Cairo very much crestfallen."[57]

Grant did not, however, give up on the project. His faith in it was bolstered by General Smith, who on the recent diversionary operation had reconnoitered Forts Heiman and Henry and found them vulnerable to attack from either water or land. Then, too, Grant received the support of Flag Officer Andrew Hull Foote, who commanded the gunboat fleet along that stretch of the Mississippi within Grant's domain. On January 28, Grant resubmitted the project to Halleck, this time with Foote's strong endorsement, and four days later permission to move against the Tennessee River forts reached Cairo.[58]

Preparations for the operation got underway at Paducah on February 2. Grant initially proposed to take no fewer than seventeen thousand troops, but a shortage of transport forced him to leave almost half that many behind until the fleet could land, disgorge its cargo, and return to Cairo. Escorted by Foote and seven of his gunboats, the expedition proceeded downriver in two detachments, McClernand in command of the first, Grant personally directing the second, farther to the rear.

The first leg of the journey was made without incident, which disclosed that Fort Heiman had been evacuated. When within sight of the projected landing site, Grant boarded one of Foote's gunboats for a personal reconnaissance of Fort Henry, which was defended by approximately one thousand troops and seventeen cannons. At first, Grant and his party attracted poorly aimed and badly undershot projectiles, but then Henry's longer-range guns started in and nearly blew the little vessel out of the water. The scouting mission came to an abrupt end.[59]

By 10:00 A.M. on February 3, McClernand's transports had bumped to a landing at Bailey's Ferry, four miles below the fort. Five hours later, his entire command was on Tennessee soil. When the last man debarked, Grant accompanied the empty transports to Paducah, where he picked up the balance of his force. He was back at the landing early on February 5.

Although he had intended to move inland as quickly as possible, he felt constrained to await the last troopship in the flotilla, which had not appeared as of that evening. Expecting it to be on hand by daylight, he issued orders for an advance on Henry at 11:00 A.M. on February 6. The plan called for a simultaneous assault by land troops and seamen. The army would invest the garrison while the navy assaulted it at close quarters. But Grant failed to ensure that the infantry moved out on time, and en route to its objective he dispersed it greatly. The upshot was that the infantry had yet to reach the fort at 11:00 A.M. The considerate Foote waited another ninety minutes. Then, fearing to delay his attack any longer, he went ahead with his part of the program.[60]

For some hours, his boats engaged Henry's water batteries. The attackers took numerous hits; one shell exploded a gunboat's boiler, making casualties of fifty of her crew, but the fleet remained on station against increasingly ineffective gunnery. Foote eventually realized that the enemy cannoneers were the only troops remaining in the fort. Its commander, Brigadier General Lloyd Tilghman, believing an effective defense impossible, had evacuated the main portion of the garrison along the muddy road to Fort Donelson. Most of his men reached the larger work in time to add their weight to its defense, but Tilghman was overtaken en route and made prisoner along with almost one hundred of his soldiers. It was a matter of time before the Confederates working the guns at Fort Henry surrendered to the navy.

The outcome dismayed Grant, who felt cheated of his right to claim a share of the day's success. Yet he realized that he himself was primarily responsible for the missed opportunity; he did not attempt to shift the blame to McClernand or any other subordinate. Nor did he begrudge the navy its success. The first thing he did after riding Jack into the fort was to board Foote's flagship and congratulate the flag officer on his dramatic victory. Then he sent a dispatch to Halleck, explaining the foul-up in coordinating operations but playing up the happy denouement and adding, with an uncharacteristic touch of bravado: "I shall take and destroy Fort Donelson on the 8th and return to Fort Henry with the forces employed."[61]

★ *Chapter 6* ★

A HERO IN DISGRACE

Grant had promised more than he could deliver. Intermittent rain turned the eastward-leading roads into soup, hindering the passage of men, horses, wagons, and cannons. Additionally, Flag Officer Foote required time to take his gunboats back up the Tennessee and then down the Cumberland to assist the overland effort. On February 7, accompanied by Rawlins and other staff officers and escorted by a detachment of horse soldiers, Grant reconnoitered to within a mile of the fort, which was garrisoned by a larger force than had held Fort Henry; how much larger, Grant could not determine at the time, but in the days ahead he estimated the garrison as more than twenty thousand. The Confederacy could not afford to lose so many fighting men, but they were too few to withstand an attack by a determined commander such as Ulysses Grant.

Fort Donelson was commanded by a triumvirate of general officers, only one of whom was worthy of his rank. The man at the top was Major General John B. Floyd, another politician in uniform, secretary of war in the Buchanan administration. He was a notorious figure to Northerners, who, given the high office Floyd had vacated and the public trust he had violated, considered him a special breed of traitor. Next in line was Gideon Pillow, who had provided much of the opposition to Grant at Belmont. Pillow had long military experience, having served as a major general in the Mexican War. That appointment, however, owed less to Pillow's ability than to his friendship with President Polk, his former law partner. Pillow's service in Mexico was chiefly notable for his falling out with Winfield Scott, who had him arrested for planting newspaper stories lauding himself and criticizing his superior. At the time, Grant, a strong supporter of Old Fuss and Feathers, considered Pillow a malcontent and a fraud; his opinion had not changed

111

over the years: "I . . . judged that with any force, no matter how small, I could march up to within gunshot of any intrenchments he was given to hold." To Grant's mind, the only worthy opponent inside Donelson was his West Point classmate Simon Buckner, who had vouched for Grant when he was stranded in New York City, penniless and forlorn, in the summer of 1854.[1]

The reconnaissance of February 7 convinced Grant that, unless the garrison left the fort to attack him en route, he could position his forces in a semicircle nearly enclosing the fort on its land side. By crossing Indian Creek on Donelson's south side and Hickman Creek on the north, he could anchor both of his flanks close to the river. At first he had worried that his force was too small to maintain a strong line above and below the fort, but his concerns had been allayed when major reinforcements ordered by Halleck began to reach him within days after Fort Henry's surrender. The additions included troops from Kansas supplied by Major General David Hunter and, from Buell's army, a large division under Brigadier General William Nelson, followed by a separate brigade led by Colonel John M. Thayer. Many of these forces had been shuttled to Grant by C. F. Smith's successor at Paducah, Brigadier General William T. Sherman, who, although senior to Grant, toiled selflessly to assist him in the present venture. Sherman's zeal and cooperative spirit—embodied in a dispatch of February 15 in which he invited Grant to command him "in any way"—gratified the expeditionary leader and began a long and close relationship between the two.[2]

The newcomers would give Grant a force of 17,500. When he moved against Donelson, he would leave twenty-five hundred of these men, under Brigadier General Lew Wallace, at and near Fort Henry to guard the spoils captured there. Thus Grant planned to attack Donelson with—as he thought—five thousand fewer soldiers than his opposition.[3]

★ ★ ★

Grant, confident that the defenders of Donelson would not contest his advance and seemingly unconcerned that much larger forces under General Johnston might oppose him by advancing from Nashville, moved east on two roads that paralleled each other for much of the distance to the Cumberland. These paths had been carefully reconnoitered by Grant's chief engineer officer, Lieutenant Colonel James Birdseye McPherson, an energetic and talented young Regular who was becoming an indispensable member of the brigade staff. The advancing troops encountered no opposition worthy of the name, and by 10:00 A.M. on February 13, Grant's dispositions were complete. Smith's division, less Wallace's brigade, held the Union left, or west,

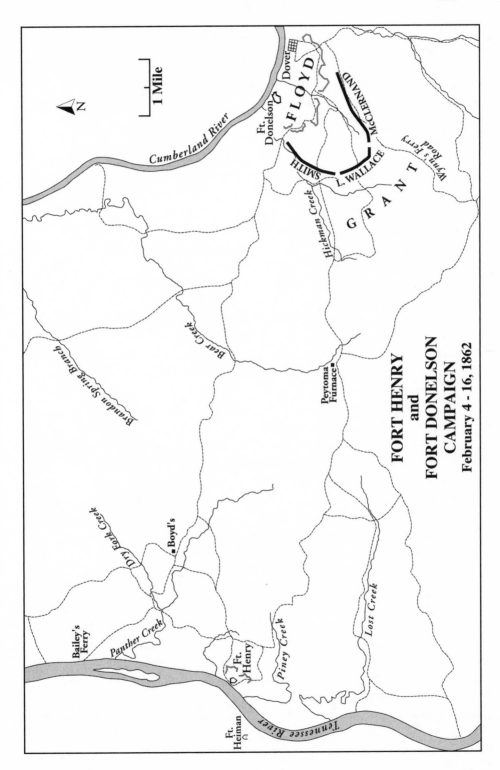

FORT HENRY
and
FORT DONELSON
CAMPAIGN
February 4 - 16, 1862

1 Mile

N

Cumberland River

Dover

Ft. Donelson

FLOYD

McCLERNAND

SMITH

L. WALLACE

Wynn's Ferry Road

GRANT

Hickman Creek

Bear Creek

Brandon Spring Branch

Peytona Furnace

Boyd's

Dry Fork Creek

Bailey's Ferry

Panther Creek

Ft. Henry

Piney Creek

Lost Creek

Ft. Heiman

Tennessee River

flank along a line that extended to Hickman Creek. McClernand, on the opposite flank, covered the roads leading to the village of Dover, three-quarters
of a mile southwest of the fort, where General Floyd had his headquarters.
Grant noted that "the troops were not entrenched, but the nature of the
ground was such that they were just as well protected from the fire of the
enemy as if rifle-pits had been thrown up." His artillery was sheltered from
counterbattery fire by being sunk into the mud-coated earth. The Federals'
only vulnerability was their exposure to the raw weather—alternately rainy
and snowy—against which they had no protection.[4]

When he wrote his memoirs, Grant recalled that the only action to occur on
February 13 began when McClernand made a limited attack in hopes of capturing a battery opposite him that was delivering a galling fire on his position.
Grant harshly criticized the failed assault and faulted McClernand for launching it against his express orders. By the time Grant wrote, he was living with bitter memories of repeated personal and professional disputes with McClernand,
which he permitted to color his retrospective evaluation of his subordinate.

In fact, February 13 witnessed three separate battles of note, each of
which consumed several hours. The first occurred in Smith's sector, where
three brigades moved close to the enemy lines southwest of Donelson, drew
heavy fire, and pulled back to a ridge beyond rifle-range. Then the navy got
into action as the gunboat *Carondelet,* directed by the recently promoted
Commander Walke, exchanged fire with the fort's water batteries for two
hours or more before drawing off to resume shelling around a bend in the
river. McClernand's engagement was brought on by his attempt to emulate
Smith's partial success in moving closer to Donelson's outworks, thus tighten-
ing the fort's encirclement. Only when a Rebel battery threatened his progress did the division leader order an assault; but effective defenses, accurate
enemy fire, difficult terrain, and the inexperience and lack of discipline on
the part of the attackers caused the effort to collapse short of its objective. All
three actions violated Grant's stated prohibition against bringing on a full-
scale engagement. He concentrated his censure against McClernand; either
he forgot Smith's and Walke's actions or he overlooked them.[5]

During the night of February 13, Flag Officer Foote arrived above the fort
with three ironclads and two wooden gunboats. With him came transports
carrying Thayer's brigade, which had originally reported to Grant at Fort
Henry. The six infantry regiments under Thayer disembarked the next morning. At about the same time, Wallace's brigade, which Grant had called from
Henry to Donelson, also joined him.

With his entire force now in hand, Grant settled down to a semi-investment
of the fort, which consisted of a series of shallow earthen entrenchments en-

circling several artillery positions; part of the line was shielded in front by an abatis of felled and sharpened logs. Grant's original strategy called for his troops to hold the defenders inside their trenches while Foote's vessels squared off against Donelson's water batteries. He was hopeful that the navy could run past the fort into a more advantageous position for an attack. Yet when Foote moved down to give battle on the afternoon of February 14 the fort's heavy guns had their way with the four boats he had committed to the fight, each of which was disabled or seriously damaged. Foote's flagship, the *St. Louis,* was struck no fewer than forty-nine times. The battered vessels—one of which had lost its pilot-wheel, another its tiller-ropes—were forced out of action along with their commander, who had been painfully but not dangerously wounded.[6]

On the morning of February 15, Foote sought a conference with Grant. Hobbled by his injury, the seaman entertained the army leader aboard the *St. Louis,* anchored north of the fort. In Grant's absence, Captain Rawlins again notified the division commanders to maintain their positions and refrain from precipitating an engagement. This time, McClernand and Smith obeyed, but the enemy felt bound by no such restraint. Grant had just concluded his meeting with Foote when Captain Hillyer, anxious and breathless, galloped up with word that the Confederates had launched a sortie along the Wynn's Ferry Road, south of Dover. The unexpected assault had caught the Federals off guard. McClernand's line had been broken; many of his troops had run to the rear in panic and disorder.

Galloping to the scene aboard his claybank charger, Grant must have feared disaster; but when he passed those sectors held by the troops of Smith and Wallace (the latter, who had been given charge of most of the recent reinforcements, held the Union center due west of Donelson), he noticed that their lines remained intact. Only when he reached McClernand's position did he witness defeat and demoralization, although by now most of the fugitives had stopped running. He found the routed men "standing in knots talking in the most excited manner," a situation that disturbed him. "No officer seemed to be giving any directions. The soldiers had their muskets, but no ammunition, while there were tons of it close at hand. I heard some of the men say that the enemy had come out with knapsacks, and haversacks filled with rations." That told him the Rebels were attempting not a sortie but a breakout in the direction of Nashville. If it could be contained, he could force the garrison's surrender.[7]

Grant was no genius, but he recognized opportunity when it beckoned. Turning to his chief of staff, Colonel J. D. Webster, he shouted above the roar of artillery and the staccato crack of rifle fire: "Some of our men are pretty badly demoralized, but the enemy must be more so. . . . The one who attacks first now will be victorious and the enemy will have to be in a hurry to get ahead of me." The rub was that counterattack appeared to be the last thing General McClernand had in mind.[8]

When he reached McClernand's field headquarters south of the Wynn's Ferry Road shortly before 2:00 P.M., Grant found his senior subordinate huddling with Lew Wallace. The two officers were trying to decide how to regain the offensive, but Grant was furious to find them inactive when every minute might mean the difference between victory and defeat. Wallace recorded the upshot in characteristically vivid prose (in later years he would write *Ben-Hur* and other historical novels): "Grant's face, already congested with cold, reddened perceptibly and his lower jaw set upon the other. Without a word he looked at McClernand." The general began a long-winded description of the crisis that had enveloped his division. Grant cut him off with a gruff command. Jabbing a gloved fist at the Wynn's Ferry Road, he shouted: "Gentlemen, that road must be recovered before night." Out of frustration, or perhaps to dramatize his impatience, he crushed in his hand a sheaf of papers he had been carrying, then announced, "I will go to Smith now. At the sound of your fire, he will support you with an attack on his side." Then he turned Jack about and rode off to put his plan in motion.[9]

As Grant started west, accompanied by Colonel Webster, both men called out to the troops they passed, who appeared to have retreated only because they had exhausted their ammunition: "Fill your cartridge boxes, quick, and get into line; the enemy is trying to escape and he must not be permitted to do so." Most of those who heard the injunction dutifully obeyed. As soon as they resupplied, they returned to the fight, slowly but steadily pressing back the Confederates who had struck them only to fall back as if suddenly intent on holding the ground they had seized. In fact, the defenders were attempting to respond to conflicting orders from the befuddled and irresolute Floyd and Pillow, who seemed to want them to defend and attack at the same time. One result was that many Rebels returned to their entrenchments just as the breakout seemed certain to succeed. This was the price the Confederacy had to pay for entrusting troops to two officers who, added together, failed to equal one soldier.[10]

Although the reloaded units under McClernand and Wallace would play important roles in Grant's counterthrust, his hopes of a successful containment rested on the mental and physical abilities of Charles F. Smith. He placed his confidence in the right man. As soon as he reached Smith's side and explained what he wanted done, the division commander pulled himself up to his full height of six feet, saluted smartly, and exclaimed: "I will do it!"[11]

"The general was off," Grant recalled, "in an incredibly short time," riding at the forefront of his troops. As Grant had predicted, once his men had negotiated a path around the fort's abatis, they quickly surmounted the rifle pits beyond. To those few men who hung back, Smith was heard to shout: "No flinching now, my lads! Here—this is the way! Come on!" His resolute words and calm demeanor had the desired effect. "I was nearly scared to death," one of his raw recruits later recalled, "but I saw the old man's white mustache over his shoulder, and went on."[12]

When darkness fell, Smith's division was occupying the position its opponents had held through the previous two days. Grant was exultant: "There was now no doubt but that the Confederates must surrender or be captured the next day." His ranking opponents agreed, but only after proposing and then rejecting a half-baked plan to extricate their troops under cover of night by way of the narrow, muddy roads that snaked along the riverbank south and east of Dover. When Floyd and Pillow finally acknowledged the necessity of surrendering, one of their most combative subordinates, Colonel Nathan Bedford Forrest, refused to be a party to it. Cloaked in darkness, he led his cavalry command, accompanied by a few hundred infantry comrades, to safety along some of those back-door routes. It was determined that the rest of the garrison would be handed over to Grant in hopes of being quickly paroled, exchanged, and permitted to return to the field.[13]

Buckner would take charge of the surrender arrangements, for neither of his superiors was willing to submit to captivity. When he was secretary of war, the Virginia-born Floyd had been accused of transferring arms and ammunition from Northern to Southern arsenals in anticipation of an intersectional war. Now he feared that if he fell into Union hands he would be executed. Accompanied by the infantry brigade he had brought with him from his native state, Floyd decamped aboard a steamboat that arrived from the east side of the river shortly before dawn on February 16.

Pillow, meanwhile, was ferried across the river on a flatboat, a move dictated by an exaggerated perception of his own importance and of the propaganda value of his capture. When Grant, after receiving Buckner's surrender, asked his old friend why Pillow had abandoned his post, Buckner replied: "Well, he thought you would rather have hold of him than any other man in the Confederacy." According to Buckner, Grant quickly replied, "Oh, no, if I had got him I'd let him go again; he will do us more good commanding you fellows."[14]

Such good-natured banter occurred only after an exchange of messages early on February 16 that produced resentment and ruffled feathers. Hoping to gain the best possible terms for his troops, Buckner sent Grant a proposal to appoint representatives to work out a surrender agreement. Expecting leniency and consideration from the colleague whose financial distress he once had relieved, Buckner was surprised and angered by Grant's reply: "Yours of this date, proposing armistice and appointment of commissioners to settle terms of capitulation, is just received. No terms except unconditional and immediate surrender can be accepted. I propose to move immediately upon your works." Buckner stewed over the communiqué for a time, then sent Grant a message praising "the brilliant success of the Confederate arms" and criticizing the "ungenerous and unchivalrous terms" Grant had proposed, which he nevertheless accepted.[15]

Later in the morning, with white flags fluttering from the Rebel lines and Union troops in the process of disarming the defenders and occupying their positions, Grant rode out to Dover to greet Buckner. Their recent contentiousness seemingly forgotten, the old friends exchanged not only jokes about Buckner's superiors but also stories of their West Point days and accounts of their lives since their last meeting. At some point, Grant, recalling Buckner's generosity during that down-and-out period, announced: "My purse is at your disposal." Buckner declined the offer, but thanked his opponent for extending it. Soon afterwards, he accompanied his soldiers aboard the transports that would deliver them into captivity in the North.[16]

By then, Grant had dashed off word of Donelson's fall to his departmental commander. Later that day, he penned a detailed account of the operation, which began: "I am pleased to announce to you the unconditional surrender this morning of Fort Donelson, with twelve to fifteen thousand prisoners, at least forty pieces of Artillery, and a large amount of stores, horses, mules, and other public property."[17]

★ ★ ★

"Unconditional surrender" was a new term in the American lexicon, a phrase unfamiliar to the Northern public. It was, however, pleasing to the tongue and it seemed to bear repeating out loud. Unionists had thus far savored few victories, and, as a result, celebrated few heroes. The "Young Napoleon," George McClellan, had been considered the best bet to win and wear the hero's mantle, but his successes in western Virginia had been few and low key; by early 1862, they were distant memories. Since then, he had precious little to show for the power and authority that had been conferred upon him. Instead of taking the field to chastise the enemies of the Union, Little Mac was still locked inside Washington, where he continued to organize, drill, and discipline the Army of the Potomac, command of which had devolved upon him following the disaster at Bull Run.

In the West, neither of the ranking commanders had a major victory to his credit. Halleck had done nothing but squat at a desk, Buell little more than plan, maneuver, and beg Washington for more troops. The venerable but decrepit Winfield Scott had been shelved; Nathaniel Lyon was dead, killed on the brink of defeat; and George H. Thomas was too far down the chain of command—besides, he had been born in the South and was rumored to have considered an appointment in the Confederate ranks.

Thus, U. S. ("Unconditional Surrender") Grant had no competition for the honor of first major military hero of the Union. His fame spread across the nation overnight, the time it took the telegraph to click out the news of Fort Donelson's surrender. Within days, reporters were swarming over Grant's headquarters in the rear and clamoring for passes to join his army in the field. Military colleagues and civilian superiors wired their congratulations, sincere and feigned. And private citizens deluged him with boxes of cigars in response to reports that he had passed through the recent fight with his teeth clamped around an unlit cheroot. Fortunately, rumors that the general had other appetites did not produce a flow of gift bottles of whiskey.[18]

Because he was humble and self-effacing by nature, and because he regarded Donelson's capture as a means rather than an end—a stepping-stone to greater triumphs, occupying large sections of Tennessee, pushing ever deeper into the western Confederacy—Grant did not wallow in his success, nor did he savor it for long. He did, however, form a sense of the magnitude of the victory: He wrote to Julia that "this is the largest capture I believe ever made on the continent . . . it followed one of the most desperate affairs fought during the war." Five days later, he responded to a congratulatory letter from Elihu Washburne: "On the 13th, 14th, and 15th our volunteers fought a battle that would figure well with many of those fought in Europe, where large standing armies are maintained." Characteristically, he added this: "I feel very grateful to you for having placed me in the position to have had the honor of commanding such an army and at such a time. I only trust that I have not nor will not disappoint you." He closed by stressing that he considered his work only begun: "The road to Nashville is now clear, but whether my destination will be there or farther west can't yet be told. I want to move early, and no doubt will."[19]

One of those in position to give Grant due credit for his accomplishment, Henry Halleck, failed to do so. Perhaps this should have come as no surprise; after all, the departmental commander, although reinforcing Grant for the movement down the river from Cairo, had never wholly embraced the project, and, in fact, had tried to scuttle it. Even so, the extent to which he neglected his subordinate's accomplishments was, and remains, shocking. Most historians attribute his unconscionable behavior to his jealousy over Grant's vast and sudden celebrity. Halleck's attitude may also have derived from a suspicion that after Donelson Grant (recently installed as the commander of the District of West Tennessee) believed he had won the right to act independently, or at least without the close supervision of higher authority.

Halleck revealed his frame of mind by telegraphing Washington that Fort Donelson's fall was the work of General Smith, whose promotion to two-star rank was richly deserved ("honor him for this victory and the whole country will applaud"). Halleck, as the ranking general in the West, also claimed a portion of the credit for himself. Three days after Donelson's capitulation, he finally issued an order thanking Grant, Flag Officer Foote, and their forces for contributing to the victory. He did not single out Grant for promotion but lumped him in with Pope and Buell, neither of whom had played a role in the outcome. His recommendation was quickly acted upon; Grant's promotion to major general of volunteers was backdated, fittingly, to February 16.[20]

Although never quick to take offense at personal slights, when writing his memoirs Grant recalled with some bitterness: "I received no other recognition whatever from General Halleck." That such neglect constituted a personal rather than an official slight was indicated by Grant's subsequent receipt of a "warm congratulatory letter" from Halleck's chief of staff, Brigadier General George W. Cullum, then at Cairo. Halleck had dispatched Cullum to that point because it was the terminus of the military telegraph. From Cairo, the staff officer could receive and forward to St. Louis all communications from Grant. This, at least, was the theory behind Cullum's presence there, but subsequent events would challenge that theory.[21]

Halleck's unwillingness to extend congratulations was not the extent of his spiteful treatment of Grant. Immediately after receiving Buckner's surrender, Grant reported to department headquarters that unless he received orders prohibiting it he would extend his operations to Confederate-occupied Clarksville, twenty-five miles upriver from Dover, and from there to Nashville. He expected to occupy those places by February 21 and March 1, respectively. Hearing nothing from headquarters to deter him, Grant dispatched General Smith and his division to Clarksville. Smith found the place deserted and, on February 19, took undisputed possession. Reports said that Nashville was also being emptied of Rebel troops; thus Grant sent William Nelson and his men to Nashville, toward which, it turned out, Buell's army was also moving via overland march from Bowling Green. On February 25, Nelson arrived at

Nashville to find the enemy gone and the city as ripe for occupation as Clarksville had been.[22]

Ignorant of Buell's imminent occupation of the city, Grant notified Halleck's headquarters that he was moving to Nashville. On the way, he stopped at Clarksville to confer with Smith. The old general handed him a communiqué from Buell, whose advance echelon had reached the Cumberland opposite Nashville. The message—in effect a complaint that troops from Halleck's department had crossed into the Department of the Ohio—conveyed Buell's concern that his force on hand was not large enough to dislodge the enemy, whom he believed still held Nashville. Thus he ordered Smith to reinforce him with "all the available force under [his] command."[23]

Grant and Smith both thought such a precaution unnecessary, but agreed that the order should be obeyed. As Smith prepared to do so, Grant went on ahead to Buell's headquarters. There he had an acrimonious meeting with his colleague, who insisted that Nashville was in danger of being retaken by the enemy; if this happened, Nelson's small division might be annihilated. Grant argued otherwise, opining that the sounds of fighting coming from across the river did not mean Nelson was in danger, only that his advance was sparring with the enemy's rear guard as it withdrew from Nashville. Grant proved to be right, and presently Buell rescinded his order that Smith join him in the city.[24]

Grant's invasion of Buell's jurisdiction and the generals' low-key but nevertheless contentious exchange came to Halleck's attention. He blamed Grant for both occurrences. Of greater significance, he held Grant culpable for not responding to communications from departmental headquarters. Grant had been in regular touch with General Cullum at Cairo by mail packet, but messages from Halleck to Grant were received by a telegraph operator who was responsible for sending them on to Grant. Unknown to anyone in command, the telegrapher was an enemy saboteur; he made certain the dispatches never reached their intended recipient. Thus Grant was kept ignorant of his superior's intentions, desires, and needs.

The upshot of this disruption of communication was a message that somehow got through to Grant on March 4. This was one day after Halleck sent it to Fort Henry, where he believed Grant lingered. Grant was ordered to turn his command over to General Smith and confine himself to Fort Henry and its environs. The message ended with the ominous query: "Why do you not obey my orders to report strength and positions of your command?"[25]

This was the first indication Grant had received that Halleck needed such information. Four days later, another terse message from his superior castigated him for going to Nashville without authorization. Grant's action was "a matter of very serious complaint at Washington," Halleck wrote; indeed, it was so grievous that he had been advised to arrest Grant on his return. Grant had no idea that the Tennessee capital was off bounds to him, for the only official description of his command failed to define its limits. The content and tenor of Halleck's dispatches gave Grant the unhappy impression that his superior was laying for him.[26]

In fact, Halleck would have been pleased to shove Grant out of the command picture in Tennessee. In his operations against Henry and Donelson and then down the Cumberland to Clarksville, the brigadier had moved very fast—too fast, and without sufficient regard for the dangers involved, to suit Halleck's cautious, conservative nature. Especially when moving against Fort Donelson, Grant could have been attacked and destroyed had Sidney Johnston marched north from Nashville to challenge him.

Halleck preferred subordinates who took orders—and acknowledged orders—and he had no patience with those who operated without restraint or guidance. Even before Grant advanced on Donelson, Halleck had proposed to Secretary Stanton the establishment of a single geographic command for the western theater. It would comprise three departments: Buell's Department of the Ohio, a Department of the Missouri under David Hunter, and a Department of the Mississippi to be commanded by Halleck's aged friend Major General Ethan Allen Hitchcock—or, should Hitchcock demur, by William T. Sherman, one subordinate whom Halleck regarded highly. In this command structure (which was never adopted) there was no place for Ulysses Grant.[27]

By March 1, when he addressed his harshly worded dispatch to Grant at Fort Henry, Halleck had decided that if he must keep his wandering subordinate in the field he would attach him to a short leash. Having failed to place Buell under his command, Halleck relinquished his effort to control operations on the Cumberland. Now he wanted Grant to move up the Tennessee and raid Rebel positions south and west of Nashville as he went. Grant was to target railroad facilities in West Tennessee and northern Mississippi, including the transportation hub of Corinth.

Thanks to the saboteur, this order did not reach Grant; when he failed to respond to it, Halleck assumed he was being insubordinate, something Old Brains could not, and would not, tolerate. On March 3, he informed McClellan—who had been harassing Halleck with inquiries about troop strength and positions, inquiries that Halleck had forwarded to Grant without reply—that Grant was being criminally uncommunicative as well as insubordinate, as his unauthorized visit to Nashville testified. Grant, said

Halleck, was also to blame for reports that the troops he had left on the upper Cumberland were running amuck, looting the homes and property of local civilians. "It is hard to censure a successful general immediately after a victory," Halleck admitted, "but I think he richly deserves it. I can get no returns, no reports, no information of any kind from him. Satisfied with his victory, he sits down and enjoys it without any regard to the future. I am worn out and tired with this neglect and inefficiency." Hinting that a command change was in order, he added: "C. F. Smith is almost the only officer equal to the emergency."[28]

McClellan replied to Halleck's tirade in a letter that carried Secretary Stanton's endorsement. Halleck had their full support in resolving an obviously troubling personnel problem. "The future success of our cause," McClellan explained, "demands that proceedings such as Grant's should at once be checked. Generals must observe discipline as well as private soldiers. Do not hesitate to arrest him at once if the good of the service requires it, and place C. F. Smith in command."[29]

What Halleck had written thus far could be regarded as excusable given the circumstances of the case as he understood them, but on March 4 he acted reprehensibly by forwarding to McClellan an ugly and untrue rumor: "Grant has resumed his former bad habits. If so, it will account for his neglect of my often-repeated orders. I do not deem it advisable to arrest him at present, but have placed General Smith in command of the expedition up the Tennessee. I think Smith will restore order and discipline." As Grant ruefully observed: "Thus in less than two weeks after the victory at Donelson, the two leading generals in the army were in correspondence as to what disposition should be made of me, and in less than three weeks I was virtually in arrest and without a command."[30]

Here Grant exaggerated—no order for his arrest was ever issued, and although he temporarily lost control of many of the troops who had captured Donelson, even after Smith replaced him he retained command of the latter's division. But it was true that Halleck's actions, and McClellan's sanctioning of them, had placed Grant under a cloud of suspicion, one that could ruin his career. At first incredulous over his sudden fall from grace, Grant eventually became so downcast and depressed that on March 7, "believing sincerely that [he] must have enemies . . . trying to impair [his] usefulness," he asked to be relieved from duty under Halleck. Two days later, he repeated the request.[31]

Halleck turned down his petition and denied that enemies had come between them, but the response failed to ease Grant's mind. A few days later, he traveled down to Smith's new headquarters near Savannah, Tennessee, the jumping-off point for the expedition toward Corinth that Smith was now to command. There, he appeared to be "in great depression of spirits," according to Colonel Thayer:

> He referred to his humiliating position and drew from his pocket a dispatch which he handed to me to read. It was a curt message from Halleck which said: "Why don't you report?" As I handed the dispatch back, I raised my eyes and saw the tears coursing down his face, as he uttered these sorrowful words: "I don't know what they intend to do with me. I have sent in my reports daily," and then he added: "But what command have I now?"

General Smith, who himself had been the object of a campaign to demote or remove him by editors and politicians who considered him too lenient on Southern sympathizers, commiserated with Grant but could do nothing to help him.[32]

In letters to his wife, the deposed commander merely explained the misunderstanding that had developed between him and his superior as the result of circumstances beyond the control of either, and expressed the fervent hope that things would speedily be resolved. Aware that his relief had made the newspapers, he wrote to Julia to reassure her: "All the slanders you have seen against me originated away from where I was." He did not accuse Halleck of any malicious intent in taking action against him, for he had no knowledge of his superior's slanderous comments to Washington. He believed he retained the good will of his superior: "I know, though I do not like to speak of myself, that General Halleck would regard this army badly off if I was relieved."[33]

Already he had tried, with minimal success, to explain and defend himself to his superior. As yet unaware of the telegrapher's role in his plight, he emphasized to Halleck that he had maintained regular contact with General Cullum at Cairo. If some of his dispatches had failed to reach St. Louis, "it may be that many of them were not thought of sufficient importance to forward more than a telegraphic synopsis." He had not knowingly disobeyed Halleck in visiting Nashville. In fact, he went to great lengths to explain his subsequent actions, including his failure to obey Halleck's recent order to assume command of Fort Henry. This, he noted, would be impossible: "The Tennessee is now so high . . . [that] the water is about six feet deep inside the fort." His efforts to exonerate himself were cleverly framed. If Halleck's chief of staff had been lax in relaying Grant's messages to headquarters, that was hardly Grant's fault. And if Halleck was so out of touch with conditions in his own department that he did not know Fort Henry was under water, how could he be certain that Grant was responsible for the offenses he was accused of?[34]

The day after Grant wrote, Halleck hit him with the allegation that he was to blame for "the want of order & discipline, and the numerous irregularities in [his] command since the capture of Fort Donelson." These had "attracted the serious attention of the authorities at Washington," he claimed. "Unless these things are immediately corrected, I am directed to relieve you from the command." Here Halleck was implying that the War Department had learned of the "irregularities" from outside sources (presumably, directly from the complainants), not from him, and that the threat of Grant's relief had originated with McClellan and Stanton. It would appear that Halleck's duplicitousness knew no bounds.[35]

Grant felt blindsided as well as stigmatized by this latest allegation, to which he replied with some heat. He sternly denied that any action of his had contributed to looting or the destruction of citizens' property. He even enclosed orders forbidding such activity and setting penalties for it, which he had issued to his troops after Donelson's capture. Then he let Halleck know that he would no longer submit to unfair criticism: "There is such a disposition to find fault with me that I again ask to be relieved from further duty until I can be placed right in the estimation of those higher in authority."[36]

In these words he threw the gauntlet at Halleck's feet. If he could not make his superior see his side of the issue, he would demand a formal investigation into his conduct by higher-ups. Grant's threat proved highly effective. Halleck realized that a court of inquiry would disclose his behind-the-back effort to malign and discredit a talented and successful subordinate. He had another reason for moderating his behavior toward Grant. On March 10, the adjutant general of the army had informed him that Lincoln had gotten wind of the controversy surrounding Grant. By the president's direction, Halleck was to report whether his subordinate had left his command without proper authority, had failed to submit troop returns as required, and had acted insubordinately in any instance. If the answer to any of those questions was yes, Halleck must provide all relevant details. Lincoln, it appears, had formed a favorable impression of Grant and a suspicion that Halleck was persecuting him. Old Brains must put up or shut up.[37]

A fortuitous improvement in his own fortunes made it easier for Halleck to backtrack and end his campaign to discredit and depose Grant. On March 11 he realized his greatest ambition when Lincoln granted him authority over all

Union forces west of the Allegheny Mountains in the capacity of commander of the newly formed Department of the Mississippi. (The reorganization also resulted in McClellan's being relieved of his responsibilities as commanding general and restricted to leadership of the Army of the Potomac, then on the verge of advancing on Richmond via the Virginia Peninsula). Whether or not Halleck acknowledged it, the honor thus conferred on him was largely a result of the glory that Grant's recent victories had reflected upon him. He had also benefited from the favorable publicity accorded another recent success in his domain, the March 7–8 victory of the Union Army of the Southwest, led by Brigadier General Samuel Ryan Curtis, over a larger Confederate force under Major General Earl Van Dorn at Pea Ridge (Elkhorn Tavern), Arkansas.[38]

Within hours of receiving Grant's third request to be relieved, Halleck finally told him the truth—that there was "no good reason for it." Intimating that he was speaking for the powers in Washington, he asked only that Grant enforce discipline throughout his command. He added, "Instead of relieving you, I wish you as soon as your new army is in the field to assume the immediate command and lead it on to new victories."[39]

The tone of his letter was conciliatory, sympathetic, and amicable—qualities noticeably been missing from his correspondence with Grant over the past several weeks. The gravest crisis in Grant's military career was over.

On March 16, Grant, mightily relieved by his reinstatement, hastened back to Savannah by steamboat to take command of the troops that had been assembling there under General Smith. The original complement had been intermittently but substantially increased; the expeditionary force now numbered almost forty-five thousand troops, the most ever assigned to a commander in the western theater. Halleck believed that even more would be needed for the campaign of destruction he had mapped out for Eastport and Corinth, Mississippi, and Jackson and Humboldt, Tennessee. At Savannah, on the east bank of the Tennessee River, sixteen miles above Corinth, Grant's troops would make contact with Buell's fifty-thousand-man Army of the Ohio, then on the march south from Nashville.

For weeks, Halleck had been attempting, without success, to enlist Buell's participation in his expedition. The latter, who disliked playing a supporting role in any operation, had been reluctant to commit himself to a campaign on the Tennessee. Now, at last, Halleck had the authority to compel his cooperation. The addition of Buell's command would allow Grant, in overall command of the coming operation, to bring overwhelming strength to bear on the nearest enemy force, then congregating in and around Corinth. This was the Army of the Mississippi, led by Albert Sidney Johnston with General Pierre Beauregard as second-in-command. It numbered slightly less than forty thousand troops of all arms.

By March 17, when he reached Savannah, Grant's army consisted of five divisions commanded by Major Generals Smith, McClernand, and Lew Wallace and Brigadier Generals Stephen A. Hurlbut and William T. Sherman. The last-named had relinquished his post at Cairo to serve gladly under a man he had outranked by seniority when both were brigadiers. With the exception of Hurlbut, who was more of a desk general than a field commander, each of these officers had combat experience (Sherman's baptism of battle had come at Bull Run; he had been transferred to the West shortly afterwards).

Grant was generally pleased with the quality of his subordinates, although greatly disappointed to learn, only days after reaching Savannah, that he would have to do without the services of Smith, who had cut his right leg when jumping from land into a yawl on the Tennessee. The injury became infected, and the infection spread to other parts of the body. Before April was out, he would be dead, a tremendous loss to the Union war effort, and to Grant personally. When Smith went on the disabled list, Grant replaced him with a highly competent citizen-soldier who had done well in brigade command at Fort Donelson, Colonel William H. L. Wallace (no kin to Lew Wallace), who was speedily promoted to brigadier general. As reinforcements continued to pour in, Grant formed a sixth division, which he entrusted to the brigadier with whom he had twice argued over seniority issues, Benjamin Prentiss.[40]

Soon after arriving on the scene, Grant transferred the army, with the exception of Lew Wallace's division, to Pittsburg Landing on the west bank of the Tennessee, about six miles downriver from Savannah. This put the bulk of Grant's troops in the proper position for an advance on Corinth. Wallace's men he left where he found them, also on the west bank but only a mile below Savannah, at Crump's Landing. The positioning would prove to be a mistake, for the distance between Wallace and his colleagues was considerable and the roads that connected the two locations were few and poor.

Reports had General Johnston fortifying at Corinth as if awaiting attack. Grant believed them and therefore saw no reason to entrench his army as Halleck wished; nor did any of his subordinates, including Sherman, who had an especially sharp eye for terrain and the defensive possibilities it presented.

Grant would claim that he had considered digging rifle pits and erecting field works and that he had ordered Colonel McPherson to lay out a defensive perimeter. McPherson, however, reported that the only practicable line would run in rear of the army's encampment. Grant, who expected to move out as soon as Buell reached him, would not consider relocating thousands of tents and countless items of equipment.[41]

As he had demonstrated when advancing on Forts Henry and Donelson, Grant felt little concern about what his enemy might do to him; he concentrated on what he could and should do to the enemy. As the plain-speaking Sherman later observed, there was one aspect of generalship at which Grant had no peer: "He don't care a damn for what the enemy does out of his sight, but it scares hell out of me." On the present occasion, Grant appeared not to have the faintest notion that Johnston would take the offensive while he himself remained stationary. He ought to have considered the possibility if only because Buell's advance from the Cumberland to the Tennessee was an open secret. It made sense that the Army of the Mississippi would not wait until two opponents could combine against it, geometrically increasing the odds of a Union success.[42]

As April came in and warm breezes—the first hints of spring—began to waft across the Tennessee River country, Grant's pickets exchanged jabs with Confederate cavalry in advance of Johnston's main body. On April 4, the Rebel horsemen snatched up a several-man outpost five miles south of Pittsburg Landing. A pursuit by a portion of one of Sherman's brigades failed to overtake the attackers or to free their prisoners. The small coup was a harbinger of things to come, for two days earlier Johnston had put his men on the road to Pittsburg Landing. Still, Grant was not worried; he was more concerned with recovering from the ankle injury he had suffered when his second warhorse, Fox, a powerful gelding, slipped and fell on him. At the same time, Grant's irritation over Buell's slow approach was somewhat relieved when the advance echelon of the Army of the Ohio, Nelson's division, reached Savannah. At once Grant made plans to ferry Nelson over to Crump's Landing. The main body of Buell's command was not far behind; it reached the Savannah vicinity near sundown on April 5.

The following morning, which began as a quiet Sunday, Grant, who had been confined to crutches since his accident, was at breakfast on his headquarters steamer off Savannah preparatory to riding out to meet and greet Buell. He never had the chance to do so, nor did he finish his meal, cut short as it was by the rising sounds of musketry from the direction of Pittsburg Landing. At first, Grant was uncertain whether the shooting indicated a pitched battle; or, if it did, where the fighting was centered. To cover all bases, he sent a staff officer to inform Buell of the change in plans; meanwhile, he personally directed Lew Wallace to place his command under arms, ready to move wherever needed on short notice. He would see neither officer for the rest of the day. Most of Buell's troops would not cross the river until evening. Wallace, although subsequently and peremptorily ordered to Pittsburg Landing, did not reach there until after dark, the result of taking westward-leading roads and then countermarching in response to repeated calls from Grant. As he galloped south, Grant also ordered Nelson to move down the east side of the river to a point opposite Pittsburg Landing; from there, he was to cross the river as quickly as possible.[43]

At about 9:30 A.M., when Grant reached the scene of the action near Pittsburg, he found a major battle in progress and part of his line—the right flank, anchored by Sherman's division of largely untried troops, which stretched eastward from a tributary of Snake Creek to a log chapel known as Shiloh Church—overrun and broken. The opening assault, conducted by William Hardee's division, had been launched at about 5:00 A.M., but it took three hours of thrust and parry before the Confederates broke through and sent Sherman's recruits scrambling to the rear. Grant found, to his relief, that McClernand's veteran division, in Sherman's left rear, held firm; but the next division eastward, Prentiss's, was overwhelmed and routed even though it had given a strong account of itself.[44]

Though forced to fall back, Prentiss and his subordinates managed to rally many of their troops after they had fled two miles or so to the north. They formed a new position around a tree-fringed stretch of ground along a sunken road later dubbed the "Hornet's Nest" for the savage fighting that took place there over the next six hours. By holding on so long, Prentiss may have saved Grant's army from destruction, but by remaining in his vulnerable position after Sherman, and then McClernand, fell back to the line held by the reserve divisions of Hurlbut and W.H.L. Wallace, Prentiss ensured that his command would not survive. In his memoirs, Grant implicitly censured the brigadier for attempting a stand at the Hornet's Nest, where his troops repulsed eight attacks during the afternoon. It is true that Prentiss's action smacked of the suicidal. At about 4:00 P.M., with his men and their ammunition all but exhausted and Hurlbut's and Wallace's troops on his flank and rear giving way (Wallace falling mortally wounded while leading his men to safety), the brigadier surrendered what remained of his force, about twenty-two hundred men. Yet there is strong reason to believe that Prentiss spoke truthfully when he claimed in his after-action report that Grant had ordered

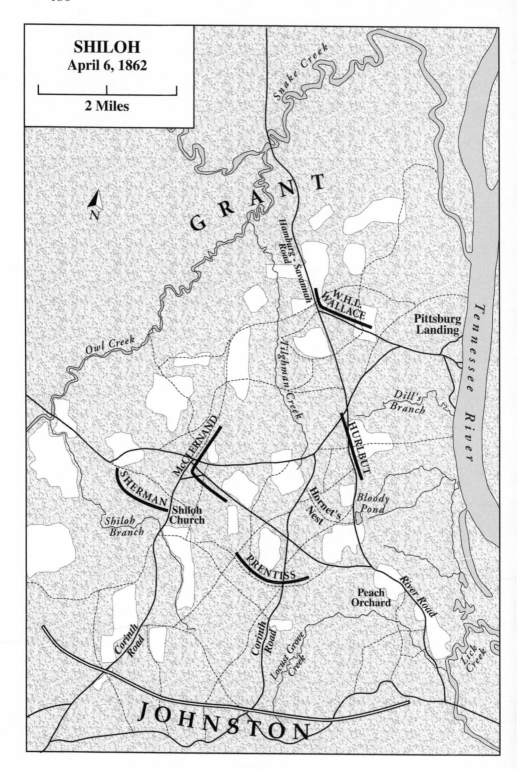

SHILOH
April 6, 1862

2 Miles

N

Snake Creek

G R A N T

Hamburg - Savannah Road

Tilghman Creek

W.H.L. WALLACE

Pittsburg Landing

Owl Creek

Dill's Branch

Tennessee River

McCLERNAND

HURLBUT

SHERMAN

Shiloh Church

Hornet's Nest

Bloody Pond

Shiloh Branch

PRENTISS

Peach Orchard

River Road

Corinth Road

Corinth Road

Locust Grove Creek

Lick Creek

J O H N S T O N

him, soon after the first attack on the Hornet's Nest, to hold his position for as long as possible.[45]

Grant maintained that, with the exception of Prentiss's salient, "a continuous and unbroken line was maintained all day from Snake Creek or its tributaries on the right to Lick Creek or the Tennessee on the left above Pittsburg." He reduced the fighting to "Southern dash against Northern pluck and endurance." He went on:

> Three of the five divisions engaged on Sunday were entirely raw, and many of the men had only received their arms on the way from their States to the field. Many of them had arrived but a day or two before and were hardly able to load their muskets according to the manual. Their officers were equally ignorant of their duties. Under these circumstances it is not astounding that many of the regiments broke at the first fire. . . . Better troops never went upon a battle-field than many of these, officers and men, afterwards proved themselves to be, who fled panic-stricken at the first whistle of bullets and shell at Shiloh.[46]

Various factors saved the Army of the Tennessee from annihilation and permitted the fighting to be renewed and decided the following day. Following their initial, successful attacks, the equally untried Confederates lost all semblance of formation and organization, making it difficult to coordinate and sustain their offensive. After falling back to more defensible positions, most of Grant's troops dug in and held their ground stubbornly; when forced to give it up, they withdrew in tolerably good order. Sherman was especially effective in persuading his green troops, once they had recovered from the initial shock of combat, to fight as if they were veterans—and in the process he won Grant's eternal gratitude. Even so, by late afternoon the entire army had been forced back against the west bank of the Tennessee; there, it formed a battered, dented line enclosing Pittsburg Landing.

An event especially fortuitous to Grant's army was the death in midafternoon of its leading antagonist. Having called up additional troops to enable his assault to sweep inexorably toward the Tennessee, Sidney Johnston was sitting his horse in a little hollow when his right leg stopped a rifle ball. The wound appeared minor, but an artery had been lacerated; within an hour, the senior Confederate officer in the West was dead of blood loss. Beauregard, a more cautious tactician, assumed command but exercised it tentatively. Doubtful that enough daylight remained to enable Johnston's offensive to reach its conclusion, and concerned by the destructive fire of twenty or more long-range cannons that Colonel Webster, Grant's chief of staff and an experienced artilleryman, had positioned on high ground at Pittsburg Landing, Beauregard ordered his troops to break contact and fall back.

Thus he withheld an attack that might have shoved the Yankees off the battlefield and into the Tennessee. Believing that Buell's troops would not be on the field until late the following day, the Rebel leader determined to land the decisive blow at dawn. His decision would prove to be the salvation of Ulysses Grant's army, career, and reputation.[47]

★ *Chapter 7* ★

"I Can't Spare This Man"

By nightfall, April 6, the Army of the Tennessee had been mauled to the tune of seven thousand casualties, but it continued to hang onto the battlefield by its collective fingertips. The cannons that Colonel Webster had placed atop a hill that overlooked the landing effectively anchored the army's left flank. Extending westward were the divisions of Hurlbut (largely intact, having seen less action than its comrades and intermingled with the remnants of W.H.L. Wallace's command), McClernand, and Sherman, the latter's right flank reaching almost to the bank of Snake Creek. Prentiss's division had been taken off the board, its men either dead, run off, or under guard in the Confederate rear. Grant would refer to each of the remaining divisions as "complete in its organization and ready . . . for any service it might be called upon to render." He admitted, however, that each had been "more or less shattered and depleted in numbers from the terrible battle of the day."[1]

Whether, in this condition, Grant's army by itself could have assumed the offensive is unlikely. Fortunately, it would not have to: Shortly after the guns fell silent that evening, Buell's army began crossing the Tennessee. By early the next morning, the division of Brigadier General Thomas L. Crittenden and one brigade of Brigadier General Alexander M. McCook's division had reached the west bank. There they joined Nelson's troops, some of whom had crossed in time to shore up Grant's left before the first day's fight ended; the remainder had completed the crossing during the night. After the firing died down, Lew Wallace's errant command also reached the field. A relieved Grant placed Buell's army on the far left, between Hurlbut and a wide and deep ravine that emptied into the Tennessee. Grant stationed Wallace's five thousand effectives on the opposite flank, extending across Snake Creek.[2]

With Buell and Lew Wallace on the ground, Grant became convinced that he could snatch victory from defeat by going over to the offensive. Before dawn on Monday, April 7, he visited each of his division leaders, explaining in detail his role in the fast-developing strategy. He spent an especially long time with Sherman, whose steady performance under extreme stress had helped secure the critical right flank of the army. Grant had begun to see the red-haired Ohioan as a strong right arm on whom he might lean in times of crisis.

During his rounds, Grant directed each of his division leaders, as soon as it was light, to send out skirmishers to locate the enemy, then move forward and engage him. The emphasis on taking the offensive was communicated to the rank-and-file during the night. The news, added to the well-publicized arrival of reinforcements, helped take the men's minds off the miserable weather—a cold, heavy rain fell throughout the night. Both armies suffered, but Beauregard's probably more so than Grant's. Although Buell's and Wallace's arrival remained unknown to the Confederates, their morale had been damaged by the prevailing suspicion that they had squandered their best chance for a victory on this field.

Having thoroughly briefed his subordinates on what he expected of them the next day, Grant spent the rest of the night shouldering the same hardships as his officers and men. He camped out under a tree a few hundred yards from the riverbank, but could get no sleep—less a fault of the rain than of his still-painful swollen ankle. Shortly after midnight, he transferred his headquarters to a log house near Pittsburg Landing. He had believed the place unoccupied, but found it serving as a field hospital where amputations were being performed. The sights and sounds—the piles of amputated limbs, the pools of blood, the screams and moans of the patients—proved too much for Grant, who described the scene as "more unendurable than encountering the enemy's fire." He quickly exited and returned to his waterlogged perch under the tree. His reaction to that tableau of human misery gives the lie to the stereotype of Grant as insensitive to his soldiers' suffering and thus ever willing to sacrifice them on the altar of victory.[3]

At 7:30 A.M. on April 7, Grant, sleepless but reinvigorated, attacked his enemy all along the line. He found that the Confederates had fallen back half a mile or more from their most advanced positions of the previous day, possibly to gain the shelter of the encampments they had overrun early on April 6. Spearheaded by fresh troops on each flank, under a persistent drizzle the Federals pushed the Confederates even farther to the south, slowly regaining the ground they had relinquished the previous day. Late in the morning, however, resistance stiffened, and the Federals were forced back in turn. Many rallied in and around a peach orchard about two miles east of Shiloh Church and a mile and a half south of the shot-riddled trees that enclosed the Hornet's Nest. Supports from the rear not only secured this position but enabled Grant's men to attack out of it.[4]

By the middle of the afternoon, Beauregard's army had been uprooted from almost every point it had occupied early in the day; now it was squeezed into a compact position along the road from Pittsburg Landing to Corinth. Having learned that many Rebels were already using the road as a retreat route, Grant calculated that one last, determined effort would dislodge the rest. Thus he rode forward to the scene of action, where he gathered up a few regiments, "or parts of regiments," formed them into a battle line, and led them through a clearing toward the enemy's heavily wooded position. "After marching to within musket-range," he wrote, "I stopped and let the troops pass. The command, *Charge,* was given, and was executed with loud cheers, and with a run, when the last of the enemy broke." Later, he would learn that Beauregard, denied promised reinforcements from Arkansas under General Earl Van Dorn, had ordered the last of his troops to disengage and head south. Before sundown, the Confederates were in full retreat to Corinth.[5]

Grant's army had escaped disaster—but barely. So had the general himself, who had come under heavy artillery fire and had his scabbard dented by a minié ball. Now that defeat had become victory, a pursuit seemed in order, but Grant was not prepared to mount one. He considered the army too exhausted and disorganized to start south right away. Then, too, the rain had thoroughly saturated the roads leading toward Corinth. Grant felt justified in permitting the men to remain in place through the reminder of April 7. Once rested, they could begin the task of patching the holes in their ranks, tending to their wounded, and burying their dead, as well as those of the enemy.

Not until the morning of April 8 did a pursuit force—Sherman's division, some of Buell's troops, and a small body of cavalry—start out. Six miles from the battlefield, foot and horse soldiers were suddenly attacked by Bedford Forrest's cavalry, covering Beauregard's withdrawal. The Federals reeled, then halted, dug in, and repulsed a second assault, in the process wounding Forrest. At this, the Confederates drew off, but the blow they had dealt effectively quenched the pursuers' desire to advance unsupported toward the Rebel rear.[6]

★ ★ ★

When first accounts of the fighting near Shiloh and Pittsburg Landing hit the Northern newspapers, the battle was described as a complete and utter triumph. Grant and his ranking subordinates were lauded as heroes, their soldiers as equals of the finest, fiercest warriors of all time. Although not seduced by the hyperbole, Grant agreed with the general assessment that a hard-fought victory had been won. On April 8, he wrote to Julia:

> Another terrible battle has occured [sic] in which our arms have been victorious. For the number engaged and the tenacity with which both parties held on for two days, sharing an incessant fire of musketry and artillery, it has no equal on this continent. . . . The loss on both sides was heavy[,] probably not less than 20,000 killed and wounded altogether. The greatest loss was sustained by the enemy.

Later, more authoritative calculations placed the totals at 13,047 Union and 10,694 Confederate casualties, but Grant's belief that his enemy had suffered more heavily is understandable in the context of Beauregard's retreat.[7]

Within a week of the initial reports, the Northern press began to reassess the results of the contest. It had become clear that although the Confederates had relinquished the field, the two-day struggle had been a ghastly bloodbath. What was worse, at the outset, the Union troops had been taken unawares despite ample warning of an enemy advance, and hundreds had been driven from the field in disgraceful rout. Only last-minute reinforcements and Beauregard's irresolution had saved the army from a defeat of epic proportions. For this sorry state of affairs, the high command was obviously to blame. On April 16, Horace Greeley's *New York Tribune,* which echoed the sentiments of dozens of other Northern papers, thundered that "an investigation should be made of the utter inefficiency and incompetency, if not the downright treachery, of the generals."[8]

One general soon became the focus of editorial vituperation, and it mattered not that a few weeks earlier he had been hailed as a military demigod. Grant, it was alleged, had mismanaged the battle from start to finish. He had scattered his forces promiscuously along the Tennessee and had failed to provide them with ample means of defense, and had established his headquarters on a boat nine miles from the battlefield, a decision that prevented him from taking command during the critical early phase of the battle. Once he reached the field, he had exercised little or no control over the struggle, and at its end he had been caught flatfooted, unable to mount a pursuit worthy of the name.

Grant had not compiled an official report of the engagement, nor would he ever compile one. This was so, he explained, because Buell and his subordinates had issued their own reports directly to Halleck, denying Grant the information he needed to put the fighting he experienced into context. Even so, he had made some pronouncements of victory that had found their way into print. "Why does not General Grant tell the truth?" Greeley demanded. In a subsequent editorial he asserted that "there was no more preparation by General Grant for an attack than if he had been on a Fourth of July frolic."[9]

It did not take long for the press, as well as many of its readers, to circulate rumors that Grant had been drunk before or during the battle, or both. The reading public began to believe that his insobriety and unreliability had cost him the trust of his soldiers—that was why they had performed so poorly under him on April 6. Referring to Grant's army, a *Tribune* correspondent reported: "No respect is felt for him, and no confidence is felt in him, and his conduct was the one topic of discussion around campfires."[10]

Even as the press had its field day, some of Grant's supporters attempted to defend his generalship and his conduct during the battle. In a letter to his family, William Sherman wrote:

> The hue and cry against Grant about surprise is wrong. I was not surprised and I was in advance. Prentiss was not covered by me, and I don't believe he was surprised. . . . It is outrageous for the cowardly newsmongers thus to defame men whose lives are exposed. The real truth is, the private soldiers in battle leave their ranks, run away and then raise these false issues. The political leaders dare not lay the blame where it belongs.

A few days later, Sherman resumed his attack on the Fourth Estate: "We all knew we were assembling a vast army for an aggressive purpose. The President knew it. Halleck knew it, and the whole country knew it, and the attempt to throw blame on Grant is villainous."[11]

Grant's highest-ranking superior also defended him against newspaper criticism. Soon after the battle, Alexander K. McClure of the *Philadelphia Times* traveled to Washington to urge Abraham Lincoln to jettison Grant, whom McClure considered worse than a drunkard: a loser. The editor occupied a high place in Republican Party circles, but Lincoln was able to look him in the eye and explain: "I can't spare this man. He fights."[12]

Characteristically, Grant made little effort to defend himself, remaining, as one biographer put it, "as silent as Achilles in his tent." It was not that the allegations of personal and professional misconduct failed to bother him. As he informed his political patron, Washburne:

> To say that I have not been distressed at these attacks upon me would be false, for I have a father, mother, wife, and children who read them, and are distressed by them, and I necessarily share with them in it. Then, too, all subject to my orders read these charges, and it is calculated to weaken their confidence in me and weaken my ability to render efficient service in our present cause. . . . I would scorn being my own defender against such attacks except through the record which has been kept of all my official acts, and which can be examined at Washington at any time.[13]

Although he refused to defend himself, he did not want others, especially family members, to take on the job. He was embarrassed and upset when he learned that his prideful, thin-skinned father had arranged for the publication in newspapers of documents calculated to refute charges that Grant had been taken by surprise at Shiloh and had lost the confidence of his troops. The last thing Grant wanted was for Jesse to launch a letter-writing campaign in a misguided effort to salvage his son's reputation.[14]

One person from whom Grant did expect an expression of support failed to speak up for him either then or later. As though believing those critics who pronounced the victor at Shiloh incompetent to command, Henry Halleck determined for the first and only time in his career to take the field at the head of an army in active operations—Grant's army. On April 9, he wired his subordinate from St. Louis: "I leave immediately to join you with considerable reinforcements. Avoid another battle, if you can, till all arrive." Grant must have suspected that his superior, aware that the defeated enemy was in full retreat, saw an opportunity for favorable publicity by running Beauregard to earth.[15]

Soon after reaching Grant's headquarters on April 11, Halleck made plans for a southward advance. Before he started, however, he added to his field forces the small army under John Pope that had recently forced the surrender of the Confederate garrison on Island No. 10, a Mississippi River fortification a dozen miles south of New Madrid, Missouri. The addition of Pope's men to those of Grant and Buell gave Halleck almost 120,000 troops, more than twice the number available to Beauregard following Van Dorn's arrival at Corinth on May 1.

After massing this vast host, Halleck divided it into a right and left wing, a center element, and a reserve. He placed George Thomas, whose division had been a part of Buell's army, in charge on the right, gave Pope the left wing, assigned Buell to cover the center, and relegated McClernand, the only nonprofessional in the group, to the reserve. Although Grant was designated second-in-command of the entire force, from the beginning his was an anomalous position. Halleck's decision not to assign him a specific field force suggested that Grant was being penalized for the bad press Halleck's department had received after Shiloh. Grant expressed some of these beliefs in a letter to Halleck, dated May 11. "It is generally understood through this army," he wrote, "that my position differs but little from that of one in arrest." This impression was strengthened when orders to the various field elements nominally under Grant's command came directly from Halleck. Thus: "I deem it due to myself to ask either full restoration to duty, according to my rank, or to be relieved entirely from further duty."[16]

Halleck replied by feigning surprise that his subordinate had any reason to take offense: "You certainly will not suspect me of any intention to injure your feelings or reputation, or to do you any injustice." As proof of his good intentions, Halleck cited the many public attacks made on Grant over the past three months: "I have done everything in my power to ward [them] off. If you believe me your friend, you will not require explanation; if not, explanation on my part would be of little avail." Such legalistic reasoning (Halleck had practiced law in California after resigning his commission the same year that Grant had left the army) seems designed more to justify his personnel decisions than to explain them, but, temporarily at least, it appears to have silenced Grant's protests.[17]

Grant's discontent resurfaced when the advance on Corinth got under way. Despite his prohibitive advantage in manpower, Halleck moved at a glacial pace, as if expecting to be ambushed. Each day the army marched a few miles, then halted to erect heavy defenses. It took three weeks to cover the twenty miles between Pittsburg Landing and Beauregard's base of operations. When he finally drew near his objective, Halleck disregarded Grant's opinion that they would find the place evacuated; instead, he hunkered down, expecting to be attacked at any time. On May 30, the army, now within cannon-shot of Corinth, was drawn up in line of battle, ready for a finish fight, when its scouts probed the Rebel defenses and found them empty. His ranks reduced by illness, poor morale, and desertion, two days earlier Beauregard had evacuated in the direction of Tupelo.

During the latter stages of the advance, Grant had offered some suggestions about the order in which the army should approach Corinth. Years later, Grant's military secretary and biographer Adam Badeau claimed that "Halleck scouted [i.e., mocked] the idea, intimating that Grant's opinions need not be expressed until they were called for. In accordance with this intimation, Grant did not again obtrude them." Yet, according to Jesse Grant, who assisted another of the general's early biographers, his son responded to Halleck's cutting remark in language stronger "than he had *ever* used *before* to any one, and expected to be arrested and tried for it."[18]

He was not arrested, but his relations with Halleck continued to deteriorate, producing a most unhappy state of mind. His depression seems to have affected his physical health, which indirectly led to a drinking spree. One of Julia's cousins, William Wrenshall Smith, was visiting Grant at this time and traveling with his headquarters. At dinner one day, Grant suffered a severe attack of indigestion. Smith attributed it to the stress the general was under as well as to his sensitive stomach and "injudicious" eating habits. Upon being consulted, one of Grant's surgeons prescribed a quantity of brandy, which Smith, who knew how greatly Grant was affected by even a small dose of alcohol, considered the worst possible treatment. He claimed that soon after imbibing, Grant seemed to lose all reason. Calling for his horse, he was soon off on a cross-country jaunt, "over fallen logs and ditches," risking life and limb; Smith, greatly concerned, galloped off in fast pursuit. Grant eventually tired of the chase and permitted his in-law to lead him back to his tent, where "he was all right again" before long. Smith railed, "The Doctor was a fool to have given him such medicine as that."[19]

Soon after the army occupied Corinth, whose defenses the worry-wart Halleck immediately strengthened, Grant's sense of grievance peaked. He seriously considered resigning his commission. He told Julia how few his duties had become now that Halleck personally handled all army business and Rawlins ("one of the best men I ever knew") took most of the routine paperwork off his hands. Sadly rather than happily, he informed his wife that he would soon take leave to visit her and the children. Apparently he intended, once out of Halleck's department, never to return. He would either seek a position in some other command or, for the second time in his military career, submit his resignation and go home as a civilian.[20]

When he learned of Grant's intentions, William Sherman paid him a visit. The two men, who had already developed a deep admiration for each other, had become close friends, and Sherman thought highly enough of Grant that he tried to prevent him from making a fatal mistake. The previous year, when he led a force in Kentucky, Sherman himself had strongly considered leaving the service for good. Fatigue and stress had sapped him of energy and clouded his judgment, and he was smarting from newspaper criticism— derived from some mordant and pessimistic observations he had made on the future of the war effort—that he had lost his mental faculties.

Sherman had endured, however, until the important command tendered him before Shiloh propped up his morale and revived his self-respect. Although his division had been routed early on April 6, he had rallied it sufficiently to win kudos for his performance on the second day as well as promotion to major general. Now Sherman considered himself "in high feather." The same could happen to Grant if he stuck it out and bided his time. If he left, he "could not be quiet at home for a week when armies were moving."[21]

Grateful for Sherman's advice and struck by the logic behind it, Grant reversed himself and vowed to remain with the army. It was one of the wisest decisions he ever made.

★ ★ ★

Less than three weeks after occupying Corinth, Halleck restructured his army group, permitting Grant, Buell, and Pope to "resume the command of their separate army corps." The order also announced the swap of Thomas's and Sherman's divisions; the former was transferred to the Army of the Tennessee, the latter to Buell's command. A subsequent order relocated the headquarters of Grant's District of West Tennessee to Memphis, some seventy-five miles northwest of Corinth. The move had been made in response to a request from Grant himself. If he was resigned to remaining under Halleck's supervision, he could at least get out from under Halleck's thumb.[22]

Grant's service at Memphis, which began on June 21, enabled him to make a lasting and favorable impression on the local inhabitants, most of whom were avowed secessionists. He dined with several with whom he engaged in frank and thoughtful conversation about political and military matters that a less polite and broadminded commander would not have tolerated. On one occasion, a supposed Unionist resident called at his headquarters to request a pass through the lines so that he might join the Confederate army. Surprised but not upset, Grant launched into what his visitor called "a short but powerful argument" to prove "the impolity" of his stand. The man appreciated the points Grant raised, but remained firm in his intention, to which the general replied, "You have been very frank with me. I wish that all I have met in the South would be as candid as you have been." He then provided the required permission. Grant's low-key reaction surprised the visitor, who was also "very much moved by his kindness." Thereafter, Grant always "occupied . . . a high place" in the man's estimation.[23]

The general also made a favorable impression on the children of Southern-sympathizing families. One day, while hunting on a farm near their homes on the outskirts of Memphis, a group of boys was approached by a cavalcade of blue-coated horsemen. When the riders reined in by a house only a few feet away, the youngsters feared they were about to be taken into custody—rumor had it that the Yankees were not beyond squeezing information of military value out of children. When the rider in front, "a heavy set man with a reddish brown beard" and two stars on his shoulders, leaned down from the saddle, teenaged J. Preston Young—later a local historian of some note—whispered to his companions: "We are in for it!"

Young and his companions were as much surprised as they were relieved when the general dismounted, knocked at the door of the farm house, and politely asked for a glass of water. After drinking, he thanked the lady of the house for her kindness, then turned and engaged the boys in nonthreatening conversation—a talk such as a father would have with a son who had just received his first hunting rifle—before bowing in their direction, remounting, and leading his entourage up the road. Young recalled that the general "seemed a very kind, courteous gentleman." When Grant was out of sight, he turned to his friends and said, "If Yankees were all like that I kinder like 'em."[24]

Another who met Grant for the first time in Memphis and came away pleased was Charles A. Dana, the former assistant editor of Greeley's *New York Tribune,* now a War Department emissary (later he would become one of Edwin Stanton's assistant secretaries of war). In mid-June, Dana had arrived in Cairo as a member of a commission charged with examining local claims against the War Department. On July 4, he and the other Washingtonians journeyed down the Mississippi by steamboat to attend an Independence Day celebration in Memphis. That evening, he was a guest at a dinner gotten up in Grant's honor by some of the general's officers. The former newspaperman spent the meal seated between the guest of honor and his chief of staff.

Dana was impressed by both General Grant and Captain Rawlins, but especially by the former. In contrast to many of the political and military celebrities he had met over the years, Grant displayed no overt egotism or arrogance. He struck Dana as "a man of simple manners, straightforward, cordial, and unpretending." More to the point, he impressed Dana as a winner. Although he had been pilloried by the press for his decisions and actions on the first day at Shiloh, the battle had ended in victory, Grant's second battlefield success in two months. No other Union commander had made such a record.[25]

The need for victors seemed more acute than ever, now that the so-called Peninsula Campaign had ended in ignominious defeat for the Army of the Potomac. A little more than a month ago, General McClellan had led the primary Union fighting force in the East to the very doorstep of Richmond before turning tail and running from his new and intimidating opponent, Robert E. Lee. Now McClellan's army was huddling, under Lee's watchful eye, on the north bank of the James River, more than twenty miles from its objective. It seemed doubtful that the Young Napoleon would muster the nerve and energy to have another go at the Confederate capital. Dana must have wondered what McClellan's army might have accomplished under a firm and masterful hand such as Grant's.[26]

Grant had no way of knowing that his visitor was forming such a favorable image of him. Certainly he had no inkling that at critical times during the next three years his professional fortunes would depend on the solicitude of this dapper, erudite civilian who had the ear, and the confidence, of William Stanton.[27]

★ ★ ★

Grant's tenure at Memphis lasted only three weeks, and it ended on a high note thanks to fortuitous circumstance. Ever since relieving McClellan of the position, Abraham Lincoln had been acting as his own general in chief. The president never claimed to be qualified to direct military operations— he did so, as he saw it, out of sheer necessity, fearing that none of his commanders was equal to the responsibility. But in the wake of McClellan's failure on the Peninsula, Lincoln decided that his field generals needed a superior to turn to for direction and advice, one who was a professional soldier. On July 11, ten days after McClellan ended his retreat to the James, Lincoln called on Henry Halleck to fill the vacant post and ordered him to Washington.

In time, Halleck would come to feel that the job was that of "simply a military advisor of the Secretary of War and the President," one that required him to "obey and carry out what they decide[d] upon, whether [he concurred] in their decisions or not." At the time it was tendered to him, however, he considered it a high honor as well as the culmination of a long and distinguished career of faithful service. Thus he was overjoyed to relinquish the Department of the Mississippi. Six days after receiving notice of his appointment, he was on an eastbound train.[28]

But who would succeed him? As Halleck's senior subordinate, Grant expected the job would be his, as Halleck's message of July 11 calling Grant to department headquarters seemed to indicate. But Halleck provided no details; in fact, when Grant reached Corinth, he learned only that Old Brains was leaving for good and that Grant would take over his headquarters. But he was not appointed to the vacated position; he remained commander of the District of West Tennessee.

Halleck had not pressed his civilian superiors to appoint Grant in his stead. He had another man in mind for the position, and a strange choice it was, one that indicated the low opinion he continued to entertain of Grant. Halleck requested the chief quartermaster of his department, Robert Allen, an old friend and trusted subordinate, to fill the post. The offer floored Allen, who protested that he lacked the rank for the job (Halleck promised to fix that through wire-pulling) and that he was far too busy in his current capacity to take on duties and responsibilities so different from those he now shouldered.

Eventually Allen persuaded Halleck to drop the matter, but the latter still refused to hand the department to Grant. Instead, one day before he left for the East, Halleck signed an order that enlarged Grant's district to encompass two others, effectively giving him command of every military resource between the Tennessee and Mississippi Rivers to as far north as Cairo. Those resources included not only Grant's own Army of the Tennessee but the troops formerly led by John Pope, who had preceded Halleck to the eastern theater. Pope's small but well-publicized success against Island No. 10 had gained him command of a second Union army in Virginia, one assigned to cooperate with the Army of the Potomac in trapping and crushing Lee. Pope would soon have the chance to test his abilities against Lee's; the latter was on the verge of turning in Pope's direction and challenging him to battle between the Rappahannock and Rapidan Rivers.

Pope's old command, the Army of the Mississippi, was now entrusted to Major General William Starke Rosecrans, a talented strategist and tactician who had made a name for himself as McClellan's second-in-command in western Virginia before heading the District of Corinth under Halleck. As Grant would learn, the forty-three-year-old Ohioan was too headstrong, too slow-moving, and too independent-minded to make a model subordinate. At this stage of the war, however, Grant was impressed by the man's reputation and happy to have him on his team.[29]

When he replaced Halleck, Grant was distressed to learn how truncated and scattered the forces of the Department of the Mississippi had become. Almost immediately after chasing Beauregard out of Corinth and occupying the place, Halleck had dispatched Buell's Army of the Ohio toward Chattanooga with instructions to repair the torn-up track of the Memphis & Charleston Railroad as he went. Halleck had detached numerous other forces to repair and guard another critical supply conduit, the Mobile & Ohio. The rest of Halleck's once-mighty command had been spread thinly throughout the department, so much so that when Grant took over his expanded district he considered himself on the defensive "in a territory whose population was hostile to the Union." In fact, he was confronted by two major forces—Van Dorn's Confederate Army of West Tennessee, about fourteen thousand strong, positioned south and west of Corinth, and Price's corps-sized Army of the West, then occupying Grand Junction, Tennessee, and Holly Springs, Mississippi.[30]

The third major Confederate command in the theater, still known as the Army of the Mississippi but only a few months from being redesignated the Army of Tennessee, was now only an indirect threat to Grant's department. After its retreat to Tupelo in June, it had lost its commander, Beauregard, to poor health and a series of disputes with Jefferson Davis. The Confederate president had replaced the prickly Creole with Braxton Bragg, a subordinate in whom he reposed great confidence despite the man's miserable personality and mediocre record as a corps commander. Davis had helped to persuade Bragg to move his thirty thousand soldiers from Mississippi, via northern Georgia to Chattanooga, Tennessee, thus countering Buell's much-interrupted advance toward that point. The president believed that if Chattanooga fell to Buell, the all-important rail connection between the West and the Virginia theater would be severed; the city's loss would also open Georgia—especially Atlanta, the industrial center of the Deep South—to invasion.

From Chattanooga, Bragg would be in a position to cooperate with yet another Confederate army in the West, under Lieutenant General Edmund Kirby Smith, who supposedly intended to invade Middle Tennessee. Smith and Bragg would agree, instead, to invade Kentucky, whose people—especially young men of military age—were expected to rally to the Confederate banner once relieved of Yankee occupation. It became Buell's task to run these forces to earth and turn them back; the result would be the Perryville Campaign of August-October 1862.[31]

Even before Buell pursued Bragg into Kentucky, Grant was called on to reinforce him substantially. In July and August, he dispatched several divisions to his colleague's support; by early September, the departures had reduced Grant's force to fewer than fifty thousand, divided among his left wing (Rosecrans's army, in and near Corinth), his center (the command of Major General Edward O. C. Ord, whose lines extended from Bethel to Humboldt on the Mobile & Ohio), and his right wing (the Memphis-area troops of "Cump" Sherman). The manpower reductions he had undergone in the face of Van Dorn and Price's maneuvers within striking distance of Corinth made the late summer of 1862 "the most anxious period of the war" for Grant.[32]

Meanwhile, his administrative burdens continued to multiply. On August 2, he had been ordered by Halleck and Stanton to ration and forage his command off the hostile countryside, confiscating the property of avowed secessionists—part of a renewed effort to "handle rebels within [Union] lines without gloves." The implications of this policy bothered him, and he executed it only to a degree. For instance, he was enjoined to evict or imprison "active [Southern] sympathizers" from his district, especially those suspected of giving aid and comfort to the enemy. Looking back years later, however, he could not recall having arrested or confined any citizen at any time during the war, although many civilians had been imprisoned by officers who invoked his name as authority for their actions. In every instance brought to his attention, Grant had the person or persons released. "There were many citizens at home who deserved punishment because they were soldiers when an opportunity was afforded to inflict an injury to the National cause," he reasoned. "This class was not of the kind that were apt to get arrested, and I deemed it better that a few guilty men should escape than that a great many innocent ones should suffer."[33]

Grant had an especially difficult time enforcing that part of Washington's confiscation policy applicable to cotton brokers in the occupied South. He had no objection to capturing or confiscating cotton from Southern sympathizers or avowed secessionists because its sale would help defray the immense cost of carrying on the war. The conflict had all but completely stanched the flow of cotton from the South to the mills of New England and Europe; as a result, the cost of the commodity had soared to astronomical figures. But if the government benefited from the sale of cotton, so did the hordes of unscrupulous speculators, armed with trading permits issued by the Treasury Department, who descended on the regions the army had occupied and bought cotton from farmers for resale in the North at a tremendous markup.

It was bad enough that these traders—few or none of whom ever considered defending their nation in uniform—were able to turn the war to their profit. What was worse, when able to purchase cotton in no other way they would pay "loyal" sellers in gold or prohibited goods such as weapons and medicine, most of which quickly found their way inside Confederate lines. Grant objected to the orders that required him to provide protection to permit-carrying traders; often he helped them ship their purchases from government-run trading stations on the Mississippi River to northern ports aboard steamboats and railroads operating in Grant's domain. Grant's attitude was shared by a majority of his officers and men—those, at least, who could not be bribed to overlook or take part in the illicit trade. As he put it, "men who had enlisted to fight the battles of their country did not like to be engaged in protecting a traffic which went to the support of an enemy they had to fight, and the profits of which went to men who shared none of their dangers."[34]

Grant's birthplace, Point Pleasant, Ohio

Engraving of Hannah Simpson Grant and Jesse Root Grant

Grant upon graduation
from West Point, 1843

Julia Dent Grant

Brigadier General Zachary Taylor, U.S.A., Grant's commander during much of the Mexican War

"Hardscrabble," the homestead Grant built with his own hands

Engraving of Congressman
Elihu B. Washburne of Illinois,
Grant's political patron

Engraving of Brigadier
General (later Major
General) John A. Rawlins,
Grant's adjutant general
and chief of staff

Engraving of
Brigadier General
Ulysses S. Grant, 1861

Major General Henry W. Halleck,
U.S.A., commanding general
(1862–1864) and chief of staff
(1864–1865) of U.S. Forces

Drawing of Grant at Fort Donelson, February 15, 1862

Major General Simon Bolivar Buckner, C.S.A., defender of Fort Donelson

Grant as a major
general, 1863

Drawing of Grant (center) at the headquarters of Major General George H. Thomas's
Army of the Cumberland, Chattanooga, Tennessee, October 23, 1863

Major General William T.
Sherman, U.S.A.

Admiral Andrew Hull Foote,
U.S.N.

Major General John A.
McClernand, U.S.A.

Major General James B.
McPherson, U.S.A.

Drawing of Union attack at Vicksburg, Mississippi, May 22, 1863

Lieutenant General John C. Pemberton, C.S.A., defender of Vicksburg

President Abraham
Lincoln, 1865

Secretary of War
Edwin McMasters Stanton

Major General George Gordon Meade, U.S.A., commander of the Army of the Potomac, 1863–1865

General Robert E. Lee, C.S.A.

Grant (seated, far left) and his staff, 1864

Drawing of Union attack at Cold Harbor, June 3, 1864

Siege lines of Petersburg, Virginia

Major General Philip H. Sheridan, U.S.A.

Ulysses Grant, Julia Grant,
and their youngest son, Jesse,
at army headquarters, City
Point, Virginia, 1865

Grant as lieutenant general and commanding general of U.S. Forces, 1864–1865

He refused to issue trading licenses to buyers or agents suspected of trafficking in prohibited war goods. On at least two occasions, he withheld the warrants even though aware that the traders had been granted permits by Abraham Lincoln himself; on neither occasion did the president overturn Grant's ruling. Beginning in August 1862, however, Grant began to single out for prohibition Jewish traders, speculators, and agents, an action Lincoln would publicly disavow to the detriment of Grant's reputation as a humane and fair-minded administrator.[35]

★ ★ ★

On September 7, Grant learned that the forces of Van Dorn and Price had joined and were heading toward Corinth. Although he had taken steps to strengthen the defenses Beauregard had erected around the town, he was "much concerned" by the dual nature of his mission—not only to resist attack on an important transportation center but to prevent the enemy from detaching forces to assist Bragg in his apparently imminent showdown with Buell.[36]

The Union appeared to be facing a crisis of dire proportions. Not only were the forces of Bragg, Van Dorn, and Price in motion but Lee's Army of Northern Virginia, fresh from routing Pope's Federals in the Battle of Second Bull Run (Second Manassas), had begun to cross the upper Potomac into Maryland. George B. McClellan, who had assimilated Pope's beaten forces into his army, had yet to launch a vigorous pursuit, raising the possibility that Lee might be across the Mason-Dixon Line before seriously challenged. Little wonder that Grant considered this period one of supreme tension and anxiety.

In every instance, however, the fears he entertained for the survival of the Union effort went unrealized. In mid-September, McClellan turned back the tide of invasion in a day of horrific carnage near Sharpsburg, in western Maryland. Three weeks later, Buell overtook Bragg at Perryville, Kentucky, and, despite tactical errors and missed opportunities, managed a tactical draw to which Bragg responded by withdrawing into East Tennessee. Although generally given credit for a victory, Buell compounded his fumbling on that field by staging a lethargic and inept pursuit that cost him his command.[37]

Of more immediate interest to Grant, Van Dorn and Price failed to achieve any of their objectives in advancing against his lines. On September 13, Price's seventeen thousand men, a few days' march distant from Van Dorn's column farther south, occupied Iuka, a depot on the Memphis & Charleston twenty miles east of Corinth. Concerned that Price intended not to attack him but to slip away and join Bragg, Grant, who lacked enough troops at Corinth to challenge the Army of the West, called in Ord's forces from Bolivar and Jackson, Mississippi, and had them cooperate with Rosecrans in attacking the occupied village.

The combined force would have approximated the strength of Price's command, but the Federals never achieved cooperation. Miscues by Rosecrans enabled Price to isolate and attack his command on September 19. The Rebel leader enjoyed initial success; but when his thrust ran out of energy, Rosecrans counterattacked. Pushed back on his heels and discovering that Ord was threatening his flank, Price evacuated the town that night. Riding to the scene of minor triumph, Grant urged Rosecrans to make a vigorous pursuit. He was greatly disappointed by the slow, half-hearted, and unproductive result.[38]

In the weeks after Iuka, Van Dorn not only linked with Price but added other scattered forces to produce an army twenty-two thousand strong. By the end of September, Grant believed the Confederate commander intended to strike outposts on the Mississippi River, including Sherman's enclave at Memphis; but within a few days, it became clear Van Dorn was intent on attacking Corinth, which Rosecrans was holding with a slightly larger force. Coming in from the northwest, Van Dorn attacked the town late on the morning of October 3, driving in much of Rosecrans's command, which had yet to fully concentrate for defense. The uprooted Federals lost heavily before rallying behind interior lines of defense that Grant had added in recent weeks. By sundown, not only had the offensive been contained but Van Dorn's left rear was under threat by a flanking force ordered up by Rosecrans.

That night Grant, whose field headquarters were now at Jackson, almost sixty miles from the embattled stronghold, mobilized reinforcements from outlying points in his district. They included a provisional division under Brigadier General James B. McPherson, Grant's erstwhile chief engineer. McPherson's command was a reward for its leader's effective performance as the superintendent of military railroads in Grant's department. The thirty-three-year old Ohioan had succeeded in that job despite lacking experience in transportation, and he would make a success in his new capacity as field commander despite a background limited to staff duty. Although his delayed receipt of orders ensured that he would reach Corinth too late to take part in the second day's battle, McPherson made a contribution to victory. During the fight, his approach had become known to Van Dorn. The news had, as Grant thought, "a moral effect" on the Rebel leader's generalship. Perhaps as a result, the day ended with the decisive repulse of an attack on Battery Robinett, along Rosecrans's left flank, west of Corinth.[39]

As at Iuka, as soon as the enemy withdrew, Grant ordered Rosecrans to follow closely. Again, his subordinate failed to obey, even though Grant had "given specific orders in advance of the battle for him to pursue the moment the enemy was repelled." Rosecrans defended himself by pointing out that his command was exhausted after a hard-fought and sometimes desperate two-day battle, but Grant was unmoved.

"Old Rosy" attempted to make amends the following day. He started out on the wrong road and had to countermarch, but he made up the time and was soon on Van Dorn's heels. Just as he was about to overtake his quarry, Grant ordered him to cease and return to Corinth. Grant's reasoning was that it was too late to bag the Confederates without suffering heavy losses; had Rosecrans proceeded much farther, "he would have met a greater force than Van Dorn had at Corinth and behind intrenchments or on chosen ground and the probabilities are he would have lost his army."[40]

Rosecrans, who believed himself on the verge of administering a coup de grace, protested his recall and complied with the order grudgingly. The incident fostered a bitter hostility between him and his superior that was fated to last through the rest of the conflict. It persuaded Grant to consider relieving Rosecrans from duty in his army. In the end, the War Department saved him the trouble by ordering Rosecrans to replace Buell at the head of the Army of the Ohio (recently renamed the Army of the Cumberland). Grant was quite happy to see him go.[41]

Most historians fault Grant for compelling Rosecrans to break off his pursuit. From scouting reports Grant knew, or should have known, that no reinforcements were coming Van Dorn's way; had Rosecrans pressed his pursuit, he would have stood a good chance of bagging his opponent's tired and disorganized command, rather than vice versa. Some of these same historians theorize that the incident reflected a growing caution and conservatism in Grant's generalship. Having been abused by editors, politicians, and the citizenry of the North for taking chances at Shiloh, he had begun to act tentatively, reluctant to commit large elements of his command until virtually assured of success. Once supremely proactive, he now seemed content to react to events instead of determined to influence them.

If Grant had indeed become defensive-minded, he risked throwing away a great advantage he had enjoyed over other field commanders in the Union ranks. He had begun the war low on the totem pole of command and with a reputation that still suffered from his forced resignation from the regular service. In 1861, as another historian has observed,

Grant had no sterling military career to protect . . . no brilliant political future to enhance. . . . When generals who had high self-esteem proved overly cautious because they knew an erroneous move or devastating defeat could cripple their chances for promotion, glory, or political advancement, Grant the habitual loser could follow his usually correct assessments of the military scene. Because he did have keen instincts, because he was a natural leader of men in combat, and because he had absolutely nothing to lose, Grant could brush aside caution.

Now, perhaps, he believed he did have something to lose. Attempting to protect it by playing it safe might saddle him with a much greater loss in the long run.[42]

★ Chapter 8 ★

THE SWORD OF DAMOCLES

Even as fighting raged at Corinth, Sherman wrote to General Grant about the progress he was making in fortifying Memphis and its environs. He suggested that if Grant came up and observed the work being done he would agree that Memphis was the best jumping-off point for a campaign on the Mississippi. With this thought as a springboard, Sherman launched into a discussion of the river's strategic importance and the necessity of controlling it from source to mouth if only for its effect on the Rebel-sympathizing population. He observed spiritedly:

> I am daily more and more convinced that we should hold the river absolutely and leave the interior alone. Detachments inland can always be overcome or are at great hazard, and they do not convert the people. They cannot be made to love us, but may be made to fear us, and dread the passage of troops through their country. With the Mississippi safe we could land troops at any point, and by a quick march break the railroad, where we could make ourselves so busy that our descent would be dreaded the whole length of the river, and by the loss of negroes and other property [they] would in time discover that war is not the remedy for the political evils of which they complained.[1]

The points Sherman had raised made Grant wonder whether he was wasting too much of his army's strength in holding territory—towns, railroads, outposts—and defending it against repeated attacks by Confederate regulars and partisans. If he had not already done so—and, assuredly, he had done some thinking along these lines—he began to consider seriously leaving lower Tennessee and northern Mississippi behind and driving deep into the Magnolia State via the Mississippi Central Railroad. The logical objective of such a penetration would be well-fortified Vicksburg. The long-range cannons the Confederates had mounted on the bluffs above and below that river town commanded navigation on the Mississippi, preventing Grant and his colleagues in Tennessee from linking with the troops in and around the South's largest city, New Orleans, which had been in Union hands since the previous spring. A second fortified post on the river, at Port Hudson, Louisiana, 130 miles below Vicksburg, ensured that the Yankees at New Orleans could not move far upstream. Yet Port Hudson was a small concern and dependent for its existence on Vicksburg; should the latter fall, it, too, would go, albeit with a lesser crash.

Should the Federals gain control of the river below Vicksburg, they would not only cut the Confederacy in two, breaking the vital communications link between the western theater and the Trans-Mississippi but also command the Confederate interior for miles around. No railroad, supply depot, or troop rendezvous would be beyond striking range of a force that owned the Mississippi. Yet although the rewards were great, the labor involved was daunting. This past spring, the United States Navy had tried but failed to reduce Vicksburg on its own. Late in June, Admiral David G. Farragut had succeeded in running the fort's guns with a fleet of ironclads and mortar boats out of New Orleans. Although Farragut's feat looked spectacular, it accomplished nothing of strategic value—Vicksburg's fifteen-thousand-man garrison remained unmolested.[2]

On October 26, one day after he assumed command of the newly established Department of the Tennessee, encompassing Cairo, Forts Henry and Donelson, northern Mississippi, "and the portions of Kentucky and Tennessee west of the Tennessee River," Grant put his thoughts on the Mississippi River project before General in Chief Halleck. He wrote: "With small re-enforcements at Memphis I think I would be able to move down the Mississippi Central road and cause the evacuation of Vicksburg and to be able to capture or destroy all the boats in the Yazoo River." The Yazoo flowed into the Mississippi below Vicksburg and nearly met it again at Helena, Arkansas, 160 miles north of the stronghold; only a levee prevented the northern link-up. Lest Halleck think his goals too ambitious, Grant added: "I am ready, however, to do with all my might whatever you may direct, without criticism."[3]

Halleck directed nothing to Grant's attention, which suggested that the latter enjoyed a certain leeway in deciding how and where to use the resources at his disposal. Grant calculated that, apart from the troops he must assign to guard the major railroads in his department and to occupy such strategic points as Corinth, Memphis, and Jackson, he had about thirty thousand to maneuver with. Currently his command was arranged into a left wing under James McPherson, a centrally located force under Brigadier General Charles S. Hamilton, and a right wing at Memphis under Sherman. Grant believed that his forces equaled those available to Lieutenant General John C. Pemberton, commander of the Confederate Department of Mississippi and Eastern Louisiana, which included Vicksburg. Grant knew Pemberton from the Old Army—as a lieutenant on the staff of William J. Worth, he had escorted Grant to his commander's side during the climactic fighting in Mexico City—but although Grant respected him as a soldier, he did not consider the Pennsylvania-born Confederate a tactical or strategic genius. Nor did he believe that Vicksburg was an impregnable citadel. The trick was to find the proper way to approach it—admittedly, a dicey proposition.

Grant began his campaign against "the Gibraltar of the Confederacy" by taking baby steps. In the first days of November, he advanced toward Pemberton's most extended outposts. On November 8, he occupied Grand Junction, Tennessee, and Holly Springs, Mississippi—Pemberton having evacuated both places upon Grant's approach—then threw a force seven or eight miles farther south along the railroad.[4]

The following day, Grant's operation acquired a sense of urgency when, at his temporary headquarters at La Grange, Tennessee, he received a dispatch from General Hamilton. After giving a progress report on his division, the brigadier passed along a report from a correspondent in Wisconsin that every new regiment being recruited in that state was to be assigned to Major General John A. McClernand. Was Grant aware of this development? Was it true? What did it mean?[5]

In fact, the news caught Grant flat-footed, but it should not have. For weeks, rumors had been flying that his one-time subordinate, who had left the army in early August on an extended leave to visit Springfield, Illinois, and then Washington, D.C., was up to something spectacular, an action that would elevate John McClernand, the volunteer officer, above the professional soldiers who commanded in the West. Grant should have believed the man capable of such a coup—ever since the war began, McClernand had been a self-promoter of the first magnitude. After Belmont, he had sent his initial report of the battle not to Grant, his superior, but to General McClellan in Washington. And in his official account of Fort Donelson, McClernand had suggested that his division alone had compelled the garrison to surrender. In reporting his division's activities at Shiloh, McClernand outdid himself. In direct violation of Grant's order that official communications be passed up through the chain of command, he sent directly to the White House another self-congratulatory report ("my division, as usual, has borne or shared in bearing the brunt" of the action), in which he criticized the way Grant had conducted the battle.[6]

McClernand's boastful claims created tension between him and his superior, but several acrimonious encounters during the summer of 1862 brought their relationship almost to the breaking point. Twice in August, the generals exchanged charges that McClernand had failed to obey an order to fortify the rail depot at Bolivar, Tennessee, against a pending attack, and that Grant had ordered some of Ord's troops into McClernand's bailiwick without notifying McClernand beforehand. McClernand also incurred his superior's wrath by clashing with some of Grant's favorite subordinates, including James McPherson.

McClernand was determined to prevail in his struggle with Grant, whom he considered officious, plodding, and disrespectful toward volunteer officers. When he left the army for Washington, the Illinoisan gained an audience with his old friend Abraham Lincoln. To the president he pitched a plan for a massive operation—to be commanded by himself and to be conducted by regiments he would help raise and organize—to capture Vicksburg and Port Hudson and open the full extent of the Mississippi River to Northern shipping. An event such as this would not only assist the war effort but also provide a desperately needed outlet for western farmers and produce merchants who now had to pay exorbitant rates to ship their goods to market via the railroads and the Great Lakes. Already these disgruntled civilians had helped vote antiwar politicians into office. If they failed to gain some relief from their financial woes, they might elect more of this ilk, with baleful effects on Lincoln's efforts to preserve the Union.

At this point in the war, with several enemy invasions barely contained and no substantial victories to trumpet, Lincoln was desperate for a military breakthrough. The extent of his desperation was such that he not only listened attentively to McClernand's proposal—which, if all else failed, promised to bring additional volunteers into the army—but also appeared to approve it without reservation. McClernand would not only gain an independent command but also the cooperation of a naval force under Admiral David Dixon Porter, whose headquarters were on the Mississippi at Cairo. Porter's ships would convoy transports loaded with McClernand's soldiers toward Vicksburg by way of the Yazoo River, the movement to begin in late November or early December.[7]

McClernand believed he had won carte blanche from Lincoln, but things were not quite as they appeared. On October 20, when McClernand received his orders from Stanton, they contained caveats that the general either overlooked or ignored. He was authorized to raise volunteers in the Northwestern states, organize them into field forces, and ship them to Memphis, Cairo, or any other rendezvous that met General Halleck's approval. The catch was that McClernand could launch his expedition only when he had formed "a sufficient force not required by the operations of General Grant's command."[8]

In adding such fine print, Lincoln and Stanton were hedging their bets. They were aware that Grant had begun preliminary operations aimed at taking Vicksburg; they would not force him to desist so that McClernand could go ahead. In this way, the government could expect two efforts to be made against Vicksburg, and so the odds of ultimate success would be increased. And if Grant's operation got in the way of McClernand's, it would be McClernand's problem to solve.

Lincoln and his war secretary also hedged on the issue of McClernand's independence. His orders stipulated that whatever forces he organized would "remain subject to the designation of the general-in-chief, and be employed according to such exigencies as the service in his judgment [might] require." It is unlikely that the last restriction worried McClernand. Aware of Halleck's less than lofty regard for Grant, he probably doubted that Halleck would intervene on Grant's behalf should a conflict of authority threaten to hamper the Vicksburg operation.[9]

A jubilant McClernand left the capital. During the next few weeks, he visited the governors of Illinois, Indiana, and Ohio. To each he proposed using his substantial political influence to swell local recruiting. His words fell sweetly on his hosts' ears, for the governors were seeking ways to meet their state's quotas under Lincoln's recent call for three hundred thousand additional three-year enlistments.

Executive-level cooperation having been secured, McClernand set about raising the needed manpower. Thanks to the assistance of local recruiters and to the lure of enlistment bonuses offered by the states as well as many counties and municipalities, the results would meet McClernand's most sanguine expectations. Within two months, enough new outfits would complete their organization to provide him with the numbers he needed to open the Mississippi, win the war, and make John McClernand the next president of the United States.

All of which should have boded ill for Ulysses S. Grant. Indeed, what he could learn of McClernand's machinations from the newspapers (whose information was necessarily incomplete because not even the most enterprising editor knew the contents of McClernand's orders) suggested that the politician-general intended to move against Vicksburg with some of Grant's troops, including subordinates such as Sherman. The prospect of having to share a critical mission with a politically motivated rival worried the head of the Department of the Tennessee: "Two commanders on the same field," Grant observed, "are always one too many, and in this case I did not think the general selected had either the experience or the qualifications to fit him for so important a position. I feared for the safety of the troops intrusted to him, especially as he was to raise new levies, raw troops, to execute so important a trust."[10]

He determined to do what he could to thwart McClernand's designs. First, however, he required a working knowledge of the extent of the man's authority. On November 10, from his headquarters at La Grange, Tennessee, he sent a blunt inquiry to Halleck: "Am I to understand that I [should] lay still here while an Expedition is fitted out from Memphis or do you want me to push as far South as possible? Am I to have Sherman move subject to my order or is he & his forces reserved for some special service?" Halleck would recognize the reference to "special service" as meaning "service under McClernand." Grant must have waited anxiously for his superior's reply, which reached him on the morning of November 12. Halleck reassured him: "You have command of all troops sent to your Dept., and have permission to fight the enemy when you please."[11]

So Grant had a chance to beat McClernand to the punch. He would have to move fast, and he would need the help of many people, including the superior with whom he had been on the outs not so long ago. But he was determined to make the most of the opportunity. Two days after receiving Halleck's cable, he notified Sherman that he should be prepared to move from Memphis to Holly Springs, there to join with Grant in launching an overland drive against Vicksburg.

★ ★ ★

On November 8, one of those who would help Grant realize his hopes for outmaneuvering McClernand and gaining unchallenged command of the Vicksburg operation reported for duty at La Grange. This was twenty-five-year-old First Lieutenant James Harrison Wilson of the Corps of Topographical Engineers. Born in Shawneetown, Illinois, a graduate of West Point, Class of July 1860 (in which he ranked sixth among forty-one cadets), Wilson was energetic, brash, and headstrong. A devotee of the success ethic, he believed his talents had been undervalued and underused in the eastern theater, where he had reported after a brief stint of garrison service at Grant's old bailiwick, Fort Vancouver. He had served effectively as a staff officer on the fall 1861 expedition against Port Royal, South Carolina, and in the March-April 1862 investment of Fort Pulaski, Georgia, but he failed to gain the promotion and authority he craved.

Wilson's youth, inexperience, and lack of political support had stymied his quest to gain high rank in the volunteer service, although when he was in Washington he had received a conditional offer of a position under John McClernand, a back-home friend of Wilson's family. Wilson was wary of accepting a berth under a politician-general, but he was flattered by McClernand's offer; he might have accepted it except that the general had not received his orders from Stanton at the time Wilson's request for a transfer to Grant's department came through.[12]

Wilson was not certain of his reception at La Grange—for that matter he was uncertain of his future under Grant, who, although successful enough in the field, seemed to have his faults constantly publicized by the newspapers. Thus Wilson was pleased to be greeted warmly by John Rawlins, now a lieutenant colonel, who informed him that Grant was then at Memphis conferring with Sherman on the future offensive operations of the Army of the Tennessee.

Rawlins, who introduced himself as a friend of Wilson's grandfather, expressed a desire to make friends with the newcomer as well. Wilson provided differing accounts of what else Rawlins told him upon this first meeting. In his published memoirs, he quoted Grant's adjutant as desiring "to form an alliance, offensive and defensive," with Wilson. Rawlins solicited Wilson's help in protecting Grant's good name and position in the army by denying ammunition to spiteful critics, potential usurpers, and fault-finding journalists. However, in private conversation with Hamlin Garland fifteen years before his recollections were published, Wilson claimed that Rawlins's first words to him were laden with expletives and harsh characterizations: "I want you to know the kind of man we are serving under. He is a God damned drunkard, and he is surrounded by a set of God damned scalawags who pander to his weakness. Now for all that, he is a good man and a nice man; and I want you to help me [form] an offensive alliance and defend him against the God damned sons of bitches." Rawlins then produced a pledge signed by Grant not to imbibe while in the field. "That has been broken," the staff officer explained disgustedly. "It isn't the first of such pledges and it will be broken as the others have been. The sword of Damocles is hanging over his head right now, and I want you to help me save him, and ourselves too."[13]

Before Grant returned from Memphis, Wilson got to know the other members of the general's staff, whom he was to join as chief topographical engineer and all-purpose troubleshooter. Rawlins had warned him about those aides whose influence on Grant he considered "wholly bad," including Colonels Hillyer, Lagow, and John Riggin, Jr. Among the more estimable specimens were Major William R. Rowley and Captain Theodore S. Bowers. A few days later Wilson got to meet the general himself. Although a bit disappointed by his "simple and unmilitary bearing," the newcomer was won over by Grant's friendly welcome. Wilson found him "at first somewhat reserved . . . [but] he warmed up and became both fluent and interesting." He added:

> While he showed little of that smartness of carriage and dress and none of that hauteur or affectation of rank and superior knowledge which were so noticeable in McClellan as well as in many other regular army men, he seemed self-contained, simple-minded, and direct in all his thoughts and ways. Putting on no airs whatever and using nothing but the mildest and cleanest language, he treated me from the start with cordiality and without the slightest assumption of personal or official superiority.[14]

It did not take long for Wilson to decide that he had made the right move in hitching his star to Grant's. This was a man who, despite his faults and weaknesses, deserved to be given the chance to show what common sense and clear thinking, buttressed by high rank and great authority, could do in the way of winning the war and saving the Union. Wilson quickly vowed to do all in his power to smooth Grant's ways and deflect the blows liable to rain down on him at any time and from any direction.

★ ★ ★

Within days of Wilson's coming, Grant inaugurated a chain of events fated to embroil him in a controversy that would take another toll of his personal and professional standing. This time, not even John Rawlins could shield his boss from the consequences of his actions—and his prejudices.

Grant had long turned a jaundiced eye on the hordes of traders and speculators who swarmed over his department like so many locusts, nibbling away as they did at the army's physical health, moral stamina, and good name. Sutlers, peddlers, and other merchants overcharged soldiers for basic goods, cheated them of hard-earned pay through ingenious swindles, and covertly purchased contraband items for resale in the North at inflated prices. By this autumn of 1862, Grant, who had briefly been a member of the anti-immigrant Know-Nothing Party and who shared the prevailing nativist attitudes toward certain ethnic groups, had begun to notice that many of the unscrupulous entrepreneurs who passed through his department were of Jewish extraction. The stereotypical "Jew peddler" of mid-nineteenth-century America was shrewd, avaricious, amoral, and unpatriotic. Grant would have added another characteristic to the list: ubiquitous. He appeared to believe that Jews doing business in a war zone could pass, chameleon-like, from North to South and back again virtually unnoticed and generally unhindered. This facility made them more of a menace than equally corrupt Christian businessmen.

In July 1862, Grant directed some of his post commanders in Kentucky and Tennessee to inspect carefully the baggage of all speculators come down from the North and to arrest those found to be carrying contraband. He added, significantly: "Jews should receive special attention." Four months later, they were still receiving special attention. One day after Lieutenant Wilson reported at La Grange, Grant ordered General Hurlbut to "refuse all permits to come south of Jackson [Tennessee]" for the time being. He added, "The Israelites especially should be kept out." The next day, he ordered McPherson's successor as superintendent of departmental railroads to instruct all conductors that "no Jews [were] to be permitted to travel on the Rail Road southward from any point[.]" They could, he said, "go north and be encouraged in it but they [were] such an intolerable nuisance . . . the Department [had to] be purged [of] them." At his order, various subordinates issued edicts expelling "Cotton Speculators, Jews and other Vagrants" from areas of occupation within Grant's jurisdiction.[15]

Grant's intensified efforts to rid himself of Jewish merchants appear to have been triggered by his father's unexpected visit to departmental headquarters in the autumn of 1862. The determinedly acquisitive Jesse was in Mississippi to purchase cotton on behalf of some Jewish businessmen from Cincinnati. Grant was outraged by the influence-peddling by which his father hoped to purchase a large quantity of the embargoed commodity. The resale of the cotton in the North would reap Jesse's partners a sizable profit, one-quarter of which he stood to receive. The general may have blamed the Jewish businessmen for ensnaring his father in a corrupt enterprise. Whatever the reason, on December 17 he composed and issued General Orders No. 11 for immediate implementation throughout his realm. The order read as follows:

I. The Jews, as a class, violating every regulation of trade established by the Treasury Department, and also Department orders, are hereby expelled from the Department. II. Within twenty-four hours from the receipt of this order by Post Commanders, they will see that all of this class

of people are furnished with passes and required to leave, and any one returning after such notification, will be arrested and held in confinement
until an opportunity occurs of sending them out as prisoners unless furnished with permits from these Head Quarters. III. No permits will be
given these people to visit Head Quarters for the purpose of making personal application for trade permits.[16]

Within days of its issuance, General Orders No. 11 became a cause
célèbre throughout the Union, especially when it caused Jews—whole families, regardless of occupation or sectional loyalty—to be driven from towns
and cities within the department's limits. First in Tennessee and Mississippi, then across the North, Jewish leaders protested the order. Their numbers, swelled by liberal-minded Gentiles, grew so large and their message so
strident that government officials took note. On January 4, 1863, Halleck
telegraphed Grant inquiring about the edict—specifically, whether it expelled Jews from Grant's department. If it did, it would be "immediately revoked." Grant took steps to comply.[17]

The following day, one of Halleck's subordinates, Colonel John C. Kelton,
informed Grant of Halleck's reasoning: "It excluded a whole class, instead of
certain obnoxious individuals. Had the word 'peddler' been inserted after
Jew I do not suppose any exception would have been taken to the order."
Kelton pointed out that "several officers and a number of enlisted men in
[Grant's] Dept." were Jews, and he noted that these men would be grossly
offended by such a decree. On January 21, Halleck wrote again, explaining
that Lincoln had been behind the revocation: "The President has no objection to your expelling traders & Jew peddlers, which I suppose was the object of your order, but as it in terms prescribed an entire religious class,
some of whom are fighting in our ranks, the President deemed it necessary
to revoke it."[18]

Grant's quick compliance with Halleck's order resulted in the tabling of
resolutions of censure in both the Senate and House of Representatives—
resolutions that some of Grant's defenders, including Congressman Washburne, vocally condemned. Thus it prevented lasting damage to Grant's
reputation. It helped, too, that for once his newspaper critics did not pounce
on a misstep of his and give it wide circulation.

Whether Grant was truly sorry for issuing the decree, however, is a matter
of conjecture. Five years later, when running for the presidency, he had to
readdress the matter when his Democratic opponents dredged it up and
made it a campaign issue. As he explained at that time:

I do not pretend to sustain the order. At the time of its publication I was incensed by a reprimand from Washington for permitting acts which Jews within my lines were engaged in. There were many other persons within my lines equally bad with the worst of them, but the difference was that the Jews could pass with impunity from one army to the other, and gold, in violation of orders, was being smuggled through the lines at least so it was reported. The order was issued and sent without any reflection and without thinking of the Jews as a sect or race to themselves, but simply as persons who had successfully . . . violated an order, which greatly inured to the help of the rebels.[19]

Even if Grant regretted having condemned Jews as a group, his explanation fails to absolve him of the offense of characterizing the Jew as primary beneficiary of the illicit trade that Grant intended to curtail. Nor does it prove that Grant repented his action, either at the time or years afterwards when he could reconsider it from a political perspective. It seems unlikely that he ever rid himself of the notion that certain ethnic groups tended to less than respectable behavior and were more likely than others to engage in illegal acts for personal gain.

During this same period, Grant dealt more fairly and honorably with another minority, the African American. Whereas no government decree forbade the exclusion of white men from the army's areas of occupation, laws specifically prohibited the expulsion of blacks—moreover, as Grant put it, "humanity forbade allowing them to starve." By the time he began his advance through Mississippi, Grant found his army hamstrung by having to care for thousand of runaway slaves "of all ages and both sexes," most of whom had congregated at his supply base at Grand Junction. There was, as he observed, no special provision for feeding and caring for displaced persons of color except those employed by the army as teamsters, cooks, and laborers. Relatively few blacks were needed for these occupations; the rest were totally dependent on the army's support and exerted a slow but steady drain on its resources. Grant noticed, however, that the deeper he penetrated the state the more plantations came within the range of his authority. All but a few had been abandoned by their masters and deserted by their workforces. Crops—principally cotton and corn—lay untended in the fields, giving Grant the idea to employ all "men, women and children above ten years of age" in their harvesting.[20]

For the plan to work, it was imperative that he find a competent—ideally, an efficient—directing hand. Until he did, the situation was liable to become chaotic, with unseen consequences for the conduct of military operations. Watching the daily influx of chattels bent on seeking refuge with the military, Chaplain John Eaton of the 27th Ohio Volunteers observed:

> There was no plan in this exodus, no Moses to lead it. Unlettered reason or the more inarticulate decision of instinct brought them to us. Often the slaves met prejudices against their own color more bitter than any they had left behind. But their own interests were identical, they felt, with the objects of our armies; a blind terror stung them, an equally blind hope allured them, and to us they came.[21]

Upon making inquiries, Grant learned that no better man could be tapped for the job of shepherding these people than Eaton himself. When first apprised of the general's intentions, however, the good chaplain wanted no part of it—and he intended to tell Grant so at the first chance he got. Years later, he recalled what happened when this opportunity arose. Called to departmental headquarters at LaGrange, Eaton braced himself for a confrontation with a commander whose questionable morals were as well known as his military achievements. Expecting the worst, Eaton was relieved to find that everything about his superior "beckoned moderation and simplicity." Grant was also disarmingly direct; when Eaton introduced himself, Grant's first words were: "Oh, you are the man who has all these darkies on his shoulders."[22]

Without preamble, Eaton loosed a barrage of arguments against his being named superintendent of freedmen for the department, including the incontrovertible fact that he had no experience in such duty. Yet: "All that I said had no more effect upon that quiet, attentive face than a similar appeal might have had upon a stone wall. When my arguments were exhausted, the General simply remarked, 'Mr. Eaton, I have ordered you to report to me in person, and I will take care of you.' And so he did."[23]

Until the operation was up and running, Eaton would consult with Grant virtually every day. Despite a hectic schedule, the general always made time for him, listening attentively to his problems, working with him to devise solutions. Grant supported him by directing subordinates and staff personnel to do everything in their power to cut his mammoth job down to size. Grant's solicitude ensured that Eaton would succeed to such an extent that in postwar years he would oversee two state chapters of the Freedmen's Bureau, the government's primary agency for supervising the welfare of former slaves.

The prompt and continued assistance he gave the chaplain indicated that Grant's views on slavery and emancipation had evolved in tune with the war itself. While always opposed to chattel slavery as an abstract principle, and desirous of curbing its spread into the territories, Grant had considered it illegal and impractical to eradicate the institution where it already existed. Over time, he came to regard slavery as liable to extinction through military expediency, a legitimate means of eroding the enemy's ability to make and sustain war.

Although he had rarely, if ever, expressed such a thought to those around him—even to those who would appreciate it, such as Elihu Washburne—Grant had also come to believe that African Americans would make effective soldiers should the government see fit to enlist them. In fact, just such a policy was in the offing. Although McClellan had failed to overwhelm Lee at Antietam, he had turned back the enemy invasion. The outcome looked enough like a victory that Lincoln used it as a forum to announce a preliminary declaration that would grant freedom to slaves in rebellious sections of the country and bar the army from returning fugitive chattels to their masters (the practice had virtually ceased, but now it was officially outlawed). The edict would not go into effect until the first day of 1863, but even now its implications were clear to anyone with a modicum of perceptivity.

Grant not only understood the motivation behind the law but foresaw the logical next step—the recruiting of blacks into the ranks of the Union armies. The policy, a radical extension of executive power, would provoke an outcry among conservative Northerners, and outrage Southerners. Yet Grant suspected that Lincoln had both the clout and the backbone to pull it off. Grant would avoid becoming involved in a debate over the constitutionality of emancipation and the arming of freedmen and fugitive slaves, but he would strive mightily to support both policies in the context of doing everything necessary to "whip the rebellion" and punish the rebel.[24]

On November 15, 1862, Grant sent Sherman at Memphis an order to meet him at Columbus, Kentucky, on November 20, and added an instruction: "If you have a good map of the country south of you, take it up with you." When the two men met on the appointed date, Sherman was informed that the Army of the Tennessee was prepared to advance against Vicksburg. Grant intended to execute a plan that Halleck had proposed to him, whereby instead of trying to attack the stronghold on its swamp- and bayou-infested north side, the army would follow the line of the Mississippi Central through Oxford and Grenada to Jackson, the state capital, then westward to take the city over more accessible terrain. Grant directed Sherman to leave an adequate force to hold Memphis, and, with the balance of his command, to march cross-country to the Tallahatchie River. Simultaneously, Grant would move from Holly Springs at the head of two divisions, his column moving east of, and parallel to, Sherman's. By the time both forces reached the Tallahatchie, they would be within mutual supporting distance.[25]

During their confab at Columbus, Grant and Sherman must have discussed the threat to Halleck's strategy posed by McClernand, who would soon reach Memphis to take command of his new regiments and plan with David Porter an amphibious operation against Vicksburg. Now, however, thanks to Halleck's assistance, Grant expected to get a jump on his erstwhile subordinate. When he left Memphis on November 24 to join Grant on the Tallahatchie, Sherman marched at the head of three divisions; they included many of those raw recruits McClernand had enlisted for his own purpose.[26]

Grant's column reached the Tallahatchie first. On December 1, it found Pemberton's troops ensconced behind well-built works on the south bank. Union cavalry crossed downstream, threatening the Rebel rear, and Pemberton promptly abandoned his position. The enemy was pursued to a point eighteen miles below the college town of Oxford, where Grant's people halted to rebuild a part of the Mississippi Central that Pemberton had torn up, now needed as an artery of Union supply.

On December 8, while waiting for the railroad work to end, Grant received a dispatch from Halleck calling on him to expedite operations and releasing him of his commitment to approach Vicksburg as his superior desired. Grant immediately ordered Sherman, whose force was a few miles to the west, to return as quickly as possible to Memphis with one or two of his divisions. At Memphis he should enlist the assistance of David Porter (who felt no obligation to support McClernand only) in moving down the Mississippi, then up the Yazoo River to Chickasaw Bluffs, just north of the citadel. Sherman should disembark there and attack the fort from that side while Grant pinned Pemberton to Grenada, 120 miles northeast of Vicksburg.[27]

Saluting smartly, Sherman hastened back to Memphis, where he organized an expeditionary force thirty thousand strong. By December 18, his transports were paddling downriver, convoyed by Porter's fleet. Meanwhile, Grant was marching briskly toward Grenada, which he erroneously believed was already in friendly hands. By now he had begun to worry about his elongated line of communications, which stretched almost two hundred miles north to Columbus via the newly built-up supply depot at Holly Springs. Grant's fears were well-founded. On December 19, he learned that Nathan Bedford Forrest, now a brigadier general, with two thousand troopers had raided the army's supply lines in West Tennessee, destroying critical stretches of the Mississippi Central and Mobile & Ohio Railroads. The blow troubled Grant so much that he halted his movement and took steps to secure his communications.[28]

The following day, the enemy landed the second half of a one-two combination, ending Grant's overland advance. Earl Van Dorn, who after his failure at Corinth had been demoted to command of Pemberton's cavalry, led thirty-five hundred troopers on a surprise raid on Holly Springs. On December 20, he swept down on the railroad town where, until recently, Julia Dent Grant, her father-in-law (on his cotton-buying excursion), and the youngest Grant child, Jesse (whose siblings were in school and could not get away), had been staying during an extended visit to the army. Van Dorn forced the surrender of the garrison; then he systematically destroyed two million dollars worth of rations, forage, and supplies. His men also tore up the railroad above and below the depot and downed miles of telegraph line. Late in the day, the raiders rode on, bathed in the glow of the flames that were consuming everything needed to sustain Grant's expedition. Van Dorn marched them swiftly enough to avoid being overtaken by the pursuit forces that took up his trail. By December 28, he had returned in triumph to the camps near Grenada he had left sixteen days earlier.[29]

The destruction of his advanced supply base and the damage done to his remote communications persuaded Grant that he must abort his drive down the Mississippi Central. On December 21, he turned north and started Old Jack back toward Holly Springs. After pausing there to inspect the destruction Van Dorn had wrought, he moved on to Memphis, where he arrived on January 10. As he withdrew, he sent a communiqué to Sherman explaining his change of plan and warning that he could not keep Pemberton from interfering with the attack on Chickasaw Bluffs. The damage Van Dorn had done to Grant's telegraph network prevented the message from reaching Sherman until after New Year's. By then, Grant's favorite subordinate had landed his own troops as well as twelve thousand others from the command of Brigadier General Frederick Steele, based in Helena, Arkansas, and lent him for the operation.

The combined force encountered not only heavy detachments of the Vicksburg garrison and some of the troops out of Grenada but also natural obstacles including impassable swamps, flooded terrain, and bitter weather. The attack Sherman felt compelled to launch on the twenty-ninth was repulsed with the loss of two thousand men, ten times as many as Pemberton and his subordinates absorbed. At first anxious to strike again from more advantageous positions, an angry and frustrated Sherman changed his mind and on January 2 recalled his troops to the mouth of the Yazoo River. There he received Grant's long-delayed message, which persuaded him to suspend operations. Grant's initial attempt to take Vicksburg and open the Mississippi had been reduced to ruins.[30]

★ ★ ★

As he withdrew on January 2, Sherman learned that McClernand had reached the Yazoo with orders to take control of the Vicksburg expedition. When the two generals met, McClernand provided details of Grant's retreat to Holly Springs and points north. "This, then," Sherman recalled, "fully explained how Vicksburg was being reenforced [sic]. I saw that any attempt on the place from the Yazoo was hopeless; and, with General McClernand's full approval we all came out of the Yazoo [country], and on the 3d of January rendezvoused at Milliken's Bend, about ten miles above." The following day, McClernand, angry about having his army stolen from him, assumed command of the forces that had failed at Chickasaw Bluffs.[31]

On January 9, just before he left Holly Springs for Memphis, Grant received a telegram from Halleck asking how many troops he could send to Sherman. Grant had been out of contact with his subordinate for almost three weeks and did not know whether Sherman had received the telegram telling of his withdrawal; but he assured Halleck that he would do "everything possible for the capture of Vicksburg." As soon as he reached Memphis, Grant swallowed his pride and notified McClernand, whom he addressed as "Comd.g Expedition of Vicksburg," that having been out of contact with him for so long, his "wants and requirements all [had] to be guessed at." He added: "I am prepared to reinforce you immediately with one Division from my old command[,] one brigade from Gen. [Samuel R.] Curtis' and one brigade coming from Gen. Wright's Dept." The last item was a reference to Major General Horatio G. Wright, the current commander of the Department of the Ohio, headquartered at Cincinnati. Grant was willing to do this much for a colleague he disliked and distrusted because "this expedition must not fail."[32]

At the time he wrote, he did not know that McClernand had decided to forgo an immediate advance against Vicksburg. He had instead taken Sherman's advice to attack and neutralize Fort Hindman, also known as Post of Arkansas, fifty miles above the mouth of the Arkansas River and 120 miles below Vicksburg. This bastioned position, held by five thousand Confederates under Brigadier General Thomas J. Churchill, commanded a staging area for gunboats that could be sent into the Mississippi to complicate an advance on Vicksburg. On January 11, after Admiral Porter's ironclads and gunboats had softened up the position, McClernand assaulted it with ground forces that had landed on both sides of the river. The poorly planned and uncoordinated attack was beaten back, but the accurate shelling of Porter's fleet silenced all but one of the fort's seventeen guns and persuaded the garrison to surrender.[33]

When Grant, on January 11, learned of the attack, he was far from impressed. He cabled Halleck that McClernand had "gone on a wild goose chase"—criticism he softened only after receiving a message from Sherman assuming responsibility for suggesting the operation and explaining why he considered it necessary ("As long as the Post of Ark. Existed on our flanks with boats to ship cannon & men to the mouth of Arkansas [River] we would be annoyed beyond measure whilst operating below").[34]

In the same communiqué, Sherman expressed concern that disaster would result from McClernand's taking charge of the Vicksburg expedition. To win fame and glory, he feared, the man "may attempt impossibilities" with the troops at his disposal. For this reason, Sherman wished that Grant "would come down & see" what was going on along the Arkansas. Admiral Porter, who also doubted McClernand's ability to head a successful expedition, issued a similar plea to Grant.[35]

Grant, who required little additional persuading, made up his mind to intervene after receiving Halleck's January 12 telegram authorizing him "to relieve Genl McClernand from command of the Expedition against Vicksburg, giving it to [his] next in rank, or taking it [him]self." That same day, Grant had John Rawlins notify the Illinois general that he was relieved of command of the Vicksburg operation and would "turn over the same to [his] next in rank." But Grant never sent the message. Instead, four days later he boarded a steamer that would take him to Napoleon, Arkansas, eighteen miles southeast of Fort Hindman. There he intended to confront McClernand and lay out the local lines of authority once and for all.[36]

Even before he reached Napoleon, a showdown with McClernand had come and gone without Grant's knowledge. By choosing not to send the order relieving the politician-general Grant had offered the Illinoisan an olive branch of sorts, but it had been spurned. Instead of attempting to reconcile his differences with his senior, McClernand, who still beamed with pride over the reduction of Post of Arkansas, wrote to Abraham Lincoln to complain: "My success here is gall and wormwood to the clique of West Pointers who have been persecuting me for months. How can you expect success when the men controlling the military destinies of the country are more chagrined at the success of your volunteer officers than the very enemy beaten by the latter in battle?" He called on Lincoln to declare unambiguously his earlier intention (as McClernand understood it) to make him independent of Grant.[37]

To McClernand's surprise and dismay, he found the president unwilling to take sides in an unseemly confrontation between two high-powered commanders, one a successful professional, the other an apparently successful but injudicious and indiscreet citizen-soldier. In his reply to McClernand's demand for autonomy, Lincoln congratulated his fellow Illinoisan on his recent "brilliant and valuable" victory but added a plea: "I have too many family controversies (so to speak) already on my hands, to voluntarily, or so long as I can avoid it, take up another." He begged McClernand not to start a war with either Grant or Halleck (McClernand had called for Halleck's relief as punishment for his behind-the-scenes role in the scheme to take McClernand's expedition from him and give it to another). Had Lincoln's correspondent been able to read between the lines he would have perceived that the president would not support him in a quarrel with his seniors, either in the field or in Washington.[38]

On January 17, Grant reached Napoleon, where he met not only with McClernand but also with Sherman and Admiral Porter. The visit confirmed what Grant already believed: "Both the army and navy were so distrustful of McClernand's fitness to command that, while they would do all they could to insure success, this distrust was an element of weakness. It would have been criminal to send troops under these circumstances into such danger."

Because he had too much respect for long-standing army practice to assign McClernand's expedition to an officer junior to him, Grant determined to take command himself. On January 20, he ordered McClernand, Sherman, and the troops to Young's Point and Milliken's Bend while he retraced his trip upriver to "make all the necessary preparation for leaving the territory behind [him] secure."[39]

Once at Memphis, he briefed the local commander, Hurlbut (now also leader of the XVI Army Corps), about his recent decision and discussed its possible repercussions. After a final inspection of the headquarters he was leaving behind, on January 29, he kissed Julia and the children goodbye—they would remain in Memphis for several weeks after his departure—and again headed south, to take command of the expedition John McClernand had almost stolen from him through covert insubordination and political manipulation.

Looking back on this point of the war, and of his career, he would observe: "The real work of the campaign and siege of Vicksburg now began." Fortunately, the man who would oversee this work was not the cautious, tentative commander Grant had become after Shiloh. The bold, assertive, risk-taking side of his personality had resurfaced—just in time to elevate his career to the next level.[40]

★ *Chapter 9* ★

A DEGREE OF RELIEF
SCARCELY EVER EQUALED

Having established his control over the forces that would operate against Vicksburg, Grant applied himself to the problem of placing those forces on dry ground east of the city. He had organized his sixty-thousand-man army into three corps: the XIII, under the disgruntled but temporarily silenced McClernand; the XV, led by the volatile but dependable Sherman, and the XVII, which Grant had assigned to the brilliant, fast-rising Major General James B. McPherson. It was a formidable command—Grant only hoped he could find it maneuvering room. To the north of Vicksburg, the land was cut up by bayous formed by the Mississippi. Many of these water-ways would have been navigable by steamers were it not for their twisting, turning course, their narrow channels, and the gnarly, low-hanging trees that clogged their banks. Grant believed that "marching across this country in the face of an enemy was impossible."[1]

Unable to operate north of the fort, he considered retracing his path along the Mississippi Central as far as Jackson, then turning west toward the city. But to make another go of this strategy would require returning the army to Memphis, which would have to be built up as a major supply base and would have to be held so strongly that no reprise of Holly Springs would be possible. Sherman preferred this strategy and strongly urged his superior to consider it.

Grant, who had become more and more politically conscious as the war progressed, refused to consider a return to Memphis because of its psychological ramifications. He realized that the Northern public was becoming war weary and discouraged. As McClernand had pointed out to Lincoln (as if Lincoln needed reminding), state elections already had placed many antiwar

Democrats in office; moreover, volunteer enlistments had fallen off drastically. The most significant factor in the low morale of the North was the lack of visible progress in the field. In mid-December, George B. McClellan's successor, Major General Ambrose E. Burnside, had nearly destroyed the Army of the Potomac by attacking impregnable Confederate positions outside Fredericksburg, Virginia. Burnside's tactical ineptitude and near-criminal stubbornness had cost him almost thirteen thousand casualties as against little more than five thousand for Robert E. Lee. Meanwhile, in Middle Tennessee Rosecrans's Army of the Cumberland had forced the retreat of Braxton Bragg's Army of Tennessee after a two-day slugging match outside Murfreesboro and along Stones River, but in essence the battle had been a draw. No clear-cut Union victories had followed Iuka, Stones River, and Pea Ridge, and there had been no major triumph since Shiloh.[2]

"It was my judgment at the time," Grant later wrote,

that to make a backward movement so long as that from Vicksburg to Memphis, would be interpreted, by many of those yet full of hope for the preservation of the Union, as a defeat, and that the draft would be resisted, desertions ensue and the power to capture and punish deserters lost. This was in my mind from the moment I took command in person at Young's Point [on the Louisiana side of the river seven miles west of Vicksburg].[3]

Because the winter promised heavy rain and high water on the Mississippi, Grant suspected that no large-scale land movement would be possible until the end of March or the beginning of April. If he was committed to remaining on the river, he would have to take steps to keep his troops busy and well-conditioned throughout that season. If he allowed them to remain idle, "friends in the North would have grown more and more discouraged, and enemies in the same section more and more insolent in their gibes and denunciations of the cause and those engaged in it." Therefore, after consulting with his subordinates, Grant developed projects to cut land or water routes through the bayou-infested country north of the fort and onto terra firma on its east side. He never entertained hopes that any would achieve dramatic success. Yet by working on them, the army would stay physically and mentally fit. Moreover, they would give Vicksburg's defenders something to worry about.[4]

Grant's military-political thinking resulted in four separate attempts to open a water route to Vicksburg from west and north through new or existing canals. The first began as an effort to deepen an artificial channel that had been cut across a peninsula known as DeSoto Point; thus vessels might be able to move south without rounding a bend within range of Vicksburg's guns. The project had begun the previous summer under the supervision of Brigadier General Thomas Williams, then stationed in occupied New Orleans. The base of DeSoto Point was only a mile and a half wide, which seemed a manageable distance. But the project failed because the river's customary summer drop in sea level had caused the banks of the thirteen-foot-deep canal to cave in when digging stopped on July 11.

Taking his cue from Williams, when he resumed the project with the intention of digging the canal even deeper—fifty feet, if necessary—Grant employed a work force of some one thousand soldiers augmented by slaves impressed from local plantations (eventually most of the laborers would be replaced by powerful steam dredges). From the beginning, the diggers encountered daunting problems. High water, ubiquitous mud, tropical-style humidity, and a smallpox outbreak made their lives miserable and precarious. Still they labored on, hopeful that their exertions would help shorten the war.[5]

Long before the canal was finished, Grant began to question its usefulness. For one thing, it was uncertain whether the Mississippi could be properly harnessed. Sylvanus Cadwallader, a correspondent of the *Chicago Times* (and later of the *New York Herald*) traveling with the army, observed that soon after digging began the canal "was standing full of still water, without any current whatever and quite as much inclined to empty itself into the river above Vicksburg as below it." Moreover, when the canal was finished, Pemberton could neutralize it by erecting defenses opposite its outlet. In fact, the Confederate commander built heavy works at Warrenton, nine miles below Vicksburg, protected by long-range guns that would blast boats using the canal. "This battery," Grant recalled, "soon drove out our dredges, two in number, which were doing the work of thousands of men." By March, following a rise in the river that flooded Young's Point and the surrounding countryside, he ordered the canal abandoned.[6]

Grant's next attempt to bypass Vicksburg involved clearing an existing but constricted route from Lake Providence, thirty miles north of the stronghold, via the Tensas, Black, and Red Rivers to a point sixty miles below the city. Grant assigned the task of pushing through the interconnecting waterways to General McPherson, whose engineering experience would prove critical to success. The XVII Corps commander put his men to work clearing the rivers and bayous of a myriad of obstructions and removing the trees that overhung the water. The task was made easier by a huge circular saw mounted on a platform that could be submerged to whatever depth was needed to remove underwater obstructions.

By early March, McPherson's men had cut their way through treacherous Bayou Baxter, but much clearing and deepening remained to be done. At that point, Grant "saw there was scarcely a chance of this ever becoming a practicable route for moving troops through an enemy's country." The project was fatally compromised by the proximity of its mouth to the defenses at Port Hudson and to points on the Tensas and Red Rivers accessible to the defenders of Vicksburg.[7]

Even before the Lake Providence effort was halted, Grant's engineers suggested that Vicksburg might be reachable from above via the Yazoo River and two of its tributaries, the Coldwater and Tallahatchie Rivers. Troops could be transported 160 miles down the Yazoo to the fortress if an abandoned cotton canal near Helena, Arkansas, known as the Yazoo Pass, was opened by breaking a six-foot-high, one hundred-foot-wide dike. An amphibious expedition using this route might not only reach Vicksburg from above but also destroy railroad bridges that connected Rebel bases in the Yazoo Delta, sink steamboats in the Yazoo River, and stop the flow of cattle and grain into Vicksburg from the surrounding country.

When Grant decided to attempt this venture, he sent his newest and most ambitious aide, Lieutenant Wilson, to Helena. The young engineer called on the local commander, Brigadier General Willis A. Gorman, who provided a five-hundred-man fatigue party to reopen the canal. Wilson planted explosives in the dike and on February 3 detonated them, creating an eighty-foot gap through which the muddy waters of the Mississippi poured like a runaway locomotive. Once the water level in river and canal equalized, the laborers began clearing snags and logs and removing the trees that the enemy was tossing into the canal in hopes of damming it up.[8]

It took two weeks to clear the pass to the point that it was navigable by a cooperating fleet of gunboats under Lieutenant Commander Watson Smith. Just as Wilson began to believe that the project would succeed, Smith found his passage down the Tallahatchie blocked by Fort Pemberton, a hastily erected but well-defended earthwork near Greenwood, commanded by Lloyd Tilghman, who had been paroled and exchanged after his capture at Fort Henry. This time, Tilghman had the upper hand: His heavy guns thwarted four attempts by Smith in as many days to run past the fort or to shell it into surrender. A cooperating force of forty-five hundred infantry under Brigadier General Leonard F. Ross, which Grant, anticipating success, had sent to Wilson, attempted a ground assault, but could make no headway against Tilghman's formidable weaponry. The impasse drove the high-strung Wilson into a furor. In diary entries, as well as in dispatches to Grant, he castigated everyone involved in the project, especially the hapless Smith. When a desperate attempt to salvage success by cutting the Yazoo levee near its entrance to the pass and flooding Fort Pemberton failed to drive out the defenders, a disgusted Wilson despaired of ultimate success.[9]

The stalemate on the Tallahatchie led indirectly to Grant's fourth and final attempt at forging an alternative water route to Vicksburg. By mid-March, he had begun to fear that Ross's troops as well as a column of reinforcements under Grant's West Point classmate Brigadier General Isaac F. Quinby might be cut off and captured by Confederates dispatched from Vicksburg. So that he could send Ross additional supports, Grant had his engineers survey a promising but tortuous route from the Yazoo River opposite Haynes's Bluff northward through Steele's Bayou to a point on the Big Sunflower River about twenty-five miles west of Fort Pemberton. On March 16, he placed Sherman, with one of his divisions, aboard transports and sent him, preceded by Porter's ironclads and gunboats, up the bayou.[10]

The relief expedition, which Grant briefly accompanied, was slowed by floating debris and then halted by hundreds of sharpshooters on the banks of the bayou. Porter, whose ships were moving well ahead of the transports, "could do nothing against sharp-shooters," Grant observed. "The rebels, learning his route, had sent in about 4,000 men—many more than there were sailors in the fleet." Accordingly, the admiral hove to and rounded about—barely in time to avoid being cut off by the fast-arriving Confederates. He escaped through the assistance of Sherman, who rushed his troops to the front in time to counter Pemberton's reinforcements.[11]

Porter's withdrawal, which Sherman emulated, ended the operation against Fort Pemberton. In response to Grant's recall, by April 5, Wilson, Smith, Ross, and Quinby were returning to their respective starting points. The outcome forced Grant—with only a few weeks remaining before the resumption of active operations—to devise some other way of reaching his objective.

In actuality, the solution to Grant's problem had surfaced as early as January when his staff began to discuss alternative proposals to Sherman's disastrous Chickasaw Bluffs expedition. It was suggested that the army should march down the Louisiana side of the river while the navy, towing empty transports, ran the Vicksburg batteries. Once the ships were below Vicksburg, they would ferry the troops across to the proper side to stage an assault. Rawlins and Wilson both entertained this idea (in later years, Wilson would claim it originated with him and that he had persuaded Rawlins to make it his own). Wilson also maintained that General Sherman argued vehemently against it, warning that the transports "wouldn't live a minute" under Vicksburg's shelling. Wilson alleged, however, that Rawlins so clearly explained the reasoning behind the plan that in the end Grant adopted it.[12]

Wilson seems to have claimed too much for himself and his friend Rawlins. He might have arrived at the idea independent of his superior, but it is difficult to dismiss Grant's assertion in his memoirs that he had been contemplating something similar for weeks, perhaps months. He chose not to divulge the plan—which he realized would be inoperable until the river receded in the spring—to his staff. The first person he remembered broaching it to was Admiral Porter, who "fell into the plan at once" despite the evident risks.[13]

The plan to run the Vicksburg batteries had yet another earnest supporter— a civilian visitor from Washington, who, being an outsider, could be considered a disinterested judge of the proposal. This was Charles Dana, who had arrived at Grant's headquarters at Milliken's Bend on April 6 in his official capacity as investigator of the workings of the pay service in the western armies. His unofficial and highly confidential mission was to spy on Grant for Edwin Stanton and, through him, for Abraham Lincoln.

During his years as a newspaperman, Dana had gained a reputation for uncovering not only the facts of a story but also the details that gave it flavor and import. This talent made him invaluable to his current superiors. Even from Washington it was obvious that Grant was the coming man in this war, but he served in such a distant theater that the civilians in power knew little about him. To run the war effectively, the president and his war secretary needed more information, and they needed to hear it from someone who could deliver it properly, with the rumor, the speculation, the extraneous matter, and the drama filtered out. Specifically, they needed to know whether the personal and professional flaws so roundly attributed to Grant had any substance and, if they did, whether they outweighed his obvious usefulness. Dana was to remain at army headquarters until he could determine which of the countless conflicting stories about Grant held water and which leaked like a sieve.[14]

From the outset, Dana's cover story fooled no one at army headquarters, but Rawlins believed he could make the man's assignment work to Grant's advantage. If the War Department wanted regular reports on Grant's habits and plans, Dana could do much to make Grant not only known to the powers that be but also approved of and trusted by them. As soon as he was convinced that the former journalist was patriotic and fair-minded, Rawlins admitted him fully to the inner sanctum of the departmental staff. He filled Dana in on the many obstacles that Grant faced in realizing his potential as the most effective field commander the Union possessed. He spoke frankly of Grant's tendency to drink, but pointed out that he struggled with the weakness only on occasion, usually when beset by stress, boredom, and the loneliness that came from being separated from his family. The pernicious habit could be, and had been, controlled, and it had yet to affect Grant's performance in the field. The overall problem, as Rawlins saw it—and which, over time, Dana accepted—was not that Grant drank occasionally but that those intent on harming him for their own selfish purposes (and here Rawlins would have been forgiven for inserting the name of John A. McClernand) insisted on making the problem worse, and more deleterious to the war effort, than it was.[15]

Even apart from Rawlins's coaching, it did not take Dana long to form a favorable overall opinion of the man he had been sent to shadow. It took him years, however, to render a fully rounded portrait of Grant as a soldier and a man. He was, Dana believed, an extraordinary person in thought and deed, although a very ordinary one in outward appearance, speech, and behavior. By the 1890s, when he wrote his memoirs, Dana had come to appreciate Grant; he was, he said, "the most modest, the most disinterested and the most honest man" he had ever known.

> [He had] a temper that nothing could disturb and a judgment that was judicial in its comprehensiveness and wisdom. Not a great man except morally; not an original or brilliant man, but sincere, thoughtful, deep and gifted with courage that never faltered; when the time came to risk all he went in like a simple-hearted, unaffected, unpretending hero, whom no ill omens could deject and no triumph unduly exalt. A social, friendly man, too, fond of a pleasant joke and also ready with one; but liking above all a long chat of an evening, and ready to sit up all night talking in the cool breeze in front of his tent. Not a man of sentimentality, nor demonstrative in friendship, but always holding to his friends and just even to the enemies he hated.[16]

This was a man who deserved to be cut some slack, not only for the sake of his good name but for that of his bleeding, suffering nation.

★ ★ ★

Julia Grant, who, along with their children, was still visiting at army headquarters, remembered that in mid-April her husband, without going into the
details, told her of a plan he described as "running the blockade." The general explained:

> I have ordered three transports to be prepared, and tonight after dark they
> are to drop silently down the river as far as possible and then put on all
> steam and go flying past Vicksburg and its batteries to where I want to use
> them. Porter, who is a gallant fellow, insists on taking two or more gun-
> boats as escort and to return the rebel fire. He says it would not look well
> to run past and not return their broadside.[17]

By April 16, Grant had been collecting—from points as far afield as
Chicago—a fleet of barges and yawls that could be used to ferry the troops
across the river once the navy arrived below the fort. To place the vessels
where needed, he took steps to open a water route from Milliken's Bend to
New Carthage, thirty miles below Vicksburg on the Louisiana side. At his
order, troops were set to clear the intervening bayous of obstructions. Navigation was also aided by diverting water from the Mississippi by means of a
canal dug opposite Young's Point.[18]

Efforts were also being made by April 16 to prevent Pemberton from getting wise to Grant's intentions. General Steele was preparing a diversionary
expedition toward Greenville, 150 miles above Vicksburg; at the same time,
a seventeen-hundred-man column of cavalry under Colonel Benjamin H.
Grierson was about to raid down the corridor of eastern Mississippi. Grierson intended to down telegraph lines, sack supply depots, break the railroad
from Meridian to Vicksburg (via Jackson), and draw enough pursuers from
Pemberton's department to expedite Grant's crossing.[19]

These diversions would not only distract Pemberton but thoroughly be-
fuddle him, causing him to make wrong decisions and unwise troop transfers. They would also confuse his superior, General Joseph E. Johnston,
Robert E. Lee's predecessor in command of the Army of Northern Virginia
and now the ranking Confederate west of the Alleghenies. Johnston did not
expect any dramatic moves from Grant; he believed the Union commander
had been so demoralized by his inability to reach Vicksburg by roundabout
routes that he was about to return to Memphis, either to plan anew or to detach troops to more promising venues such as Middle Tennessee.

At 10:00 P.M. on April 16, Porter began his run, heading downriver with
eight gunboats and the three transports. Initially shrouded in darkness, the
vessels were soon illuminated by shoreline bonfires lit by Pemberton's

troops. Their targets now visible, Vicksburg's guns opened with an unearthly roar. The bombardment continued for two hours, Porter's boats returning fire (however ineffectually) from close up under the bluffs. Grant, who witnessed the shelling from the deck of a river steamer that had been run as close to the fort as was safe, pronounced the sight "magnificent, but terrible." Pemberton's gunners did themselves proud, but to little profit. Every vessel in the flotilla took several hits, but only one—a transport—was rendered inoperable.[20]

The opening act of Grant's drama having been judged a success, his troops were cued for their performance. Originally he intended to cross them at New Carthage, about thirty miles below Vicksburg. McClernand's corps, the advance element of the army, had massed there by April 20 with the intent of landing on the opposite bank at Grand Gulf. When he arrived at New Carthage, however, Grant found the place inundated by flood waters and decided that Grand Gulf was too strongly defended. He changed the staging site to Hard Times Landing and the point of debarkation to Bruinsburg, ten miles south of Grand Gulf. He fixed April 28 as the day the operation would begin.

At the appointed hour, the troops—McClernand's corps and one of McPherson's divisions—were in place at and near Hard Times. The rest of McPherson's men were still marching crosscountry to the jumping-off point, and Sherman's command was far upriver at Haynes's Bluff, eleven miles above Vicksburg, engaged in a demonstration so effective that Pemberton feared more for the safety of his right flank than for his left.[21]

At 8:00 A.M., Porter's gunboats, having pushed off from Hard Times, began to engage the cannons at Grand Gulf. Within five hours, the Confederate batteries had fallen silent; but, fearing they might reopen suddenly, Grant refused to cross the troops until after nightfall. By morning of April 30, McClernand's corps and McPherson's division were on the Mississippi side of the river. "When this was effected," Grant remarked, "I felt a degree of relief scarcely ever equalled since. Vicksburg was not yet taken it is true. . . . But I was on dry ground on the same side of the river with the enemy. All the campaigns, labors, hardships and exposures from the month of December previous to this time that had been made and endured, were for the accomplishment of this one object."[22]

When the march inland began, he directed it toward not only Vicksburg but also Jackson, fifty miles farther east. By capturing Mississippi's capital he would neutralize the threat posed by a force of unknown size that had assembled there. The movement got off to a sluggish start. Foul-ups in issuing marching rations made McClernand's soldiers hours late in leaving

Bruinsburg. Had Pemberton attempted to occupy the heights surrounding the town, the movement might have been jeopardized; but he declined to contest the precarious foothold his enemy had gained. By sunset on April 30, McClernand had secured the local bluffs and was making headway toward his next objective, Port Gibson. West of that village, five thousand Confederates lay in wait, and three thousand more under a hard-fighting brigadier, John Stevens Bowen, were hastening there from Grand Gulf.[23]

At 7:00 A.M. on May 1, McClernand's advance encountered Port Gibson's defenders, whom they dislodged with relative ease. When reinforced by Bowen, however, the Confederates rallied and held on for several hours. Only in late afternoon, when McPherson's troops arrived to threaten their right flank, did the Rebels relinquish the town. The next day, the Federals occupied Port Gibson, then pushed east by way of some partially dismounted bridges over the Bayou Pierre. The bridges had been repaired by work crews supervised by the able and energetic Wilson, now a lieutenant colonel of volunteers thanks to Grant's patronage.[24]

A lull in the fighting now occurred, during which Pemberton destroyed his batteries at Grand Gulf and concentrated his scattered forces along the upper bank of the Big Black River. Grant used the respite to secure his foothold at Bruinsburg, to bring up his supply trains, to study the dramatic results of the diversions by Sherman, Steele, and Grierson, and to try to contact Nathaniel Banks opposite Port Hudson. Halleck had directed Grant to cooperate closely with his colleague, formerly the Speaker of the U.S. House of Representatives. Grant—probably thinking it poetic justice to reinforce one politician general with another—had intended to send McClernand's entire corps to Banks's assistance. Now, however, Grant learned that Banks had temporarily turned his back on Port Hudson to try to run to earth a detached force cooperating with the garrison and did not expect to renew his siege for several days. The news persuaded Grant to leave Port Hudson entirely to Banks and devote the full range of his own resources to taking Vicksburg.

He would do this by abandoning the base he had established at now-occupied Grand Gulf and, like Winfield Scott during his advance on Mexico City, living off the land. His men would travel with only five days' prepared rations and would have to rely on their foraging abilities to extend this supply to cover the campaigning that lay ahead.[25]

On May 6, Sherman's corps, having returned from Haynes's Bluff, crossed the river to secure the rear of Grant's army. At the same time, McPherson conducted a reconnaissance north of the Big Black River and learned that Pemberton had concentrated his troops and was preparing to defend against an attack from the south. McPherson's progress was such that Grant believed the army might then have besieged Vicksburg from the south. After careful deliberation, he decided that the terrain in that area was so wild and broken that the siege lines could have been made sufficiently tight; instead, he would approach the citadel by way of the railroad east of it. Thus he kept McPherson on the south side of the stream and then sent him eastward toward Raymond, fifteen miles from Jackson.

On the morning of May 12, McPherson, on the right of the army (Sherman held the center on Fourteen Mile Creek and McClernand was on the left near Edwards's Station), advanced on Raymond. Two miles south of the town, the XVII Corps met stiff resistance from Brigadier General John Gregg's brigade. Although outnumbered perhaps three-to-one, Gregg held off the Yankees until late afternoon when John Logan—who had orated to Grant's regiment at Springfield before it was mustered into federal service—attacked, as Grant said, "with vigor, carrying the enemy's position easily, sending Gregg flying from the field not to appear against [the Union's] front again until [they] met at Jackson."[26]

Having pushed to within twenty miles of the capital, Grant decided to assault its defenders, drive them out of the city, and destroy that strategic rail center. Only when that job was complete would he return his full attention to Pemberton and Vicksburg: "All the enemy's supplies of men and stores would come by that point [Jackson]. As I hoped in the end to besiege Vicksburg I must first destroy all possibility of aid. . . . I then had no fears for my communications, and if I moved quickly enough [I] could turn upon Pemberton before he could attack me in the rear."[27]

One day before Grant reached Jackson, General Johnston arrived there in response to orders from Richmond. He did what he could to organize the small force available for local defense—four brigades, no more than six thousand men under some admittedly mediocre generals. When he learned the approximate size of the enemy moving against him and discovered that it already had interposed between him and Pemberton near Edwards's Station, Johnston realized that resistance was hopeless. Before dawn on May 14, he decided to evacuate the city. He passed command to John Gregg, who would cover the evacuation of the stores on which Vicksburg's continued existence might depend.

Shortly after 9:00 A.M., Sherman came up to the western outskirts of Jackson. Although hindered by heavy rain and bottomless roads, he attacked at once and uprooted part of Gregg's brigade. However, McPherson, approaching from the west, delayed his supporting assault because he feared the rain would ruin his men's ammunition. When he finally advanced on

Sherman's left flank, he was stymied by the well-entrenched brigade of Brigadier General William H. T. Walker. After a few hours under growing pressure, Walker's men emulated Gregg's by fleeing out the north end of town, Johnston at their head. Eight hundred other Confederates had been left behind, dead, wounded, or in enemy hands.[28]

By 4:00 P.M., the town itself was in Sherman's possession. His men were soon hard at work mangling tracks and ties, rolling stock, and a vast quantity of supplies earmarked for shipment to Vicksburg. The occupiers burned every factory in Jackson as well as many of its public buildings and more than a few private homes. The work of destruction—which almost got out of hand when some Federals got drunk on a cache of whiskey and began to burn and loot indiscriminately—was in full swing when Grant entered and rode to the state capitol, from which the Stars and Stripes already flew. "I slept that night," he reported proudly, "in the room that Johnston was said to have occupied the night before." There, presumably, he began to plan his final approach to Vicksburg.[29]

★ ★ ★

As Grant had foreseen, while he was attacking Jackson Pemberton was moving to cut the Union line of supply, which no longer existed. The indecisive Pemberton aborted the move when he had trouble crossing rain-swollen Bakers Creek. On May 14, Johnston had ordered him to withdraw his troops from Vicksburg, which the latter considered a death trap, and join Johnston in striking the rear of Grant's army near Clinton. However, Jefferson Davis had ordered Pemberton to hold Vicksburg at all costs. Early on May 16, by which time he had returned his troops to Edwards's Station, Pemberton resolved the conflict in Johnston's favor; but by then it was too late. Soon after sunrise, Grant, at the head of McClernand's and McPherson's troops, advanced against Pemberton's latest position, a heavily wooded ridge, the northern end of which, known as Champion Hill, rose to a height of seventy-five feet.[30]

Because local reports led Grant to believe he was facing as many as fifty thousand Confederates, more than twice the number at Pemberton's disposal, he called up Sherman's corps, which had just begun to depart the thoroughly ruined town of Jackson. Fighting erupted at about 10:30 A.M., when Brigadier General Alvin P. Hovey's division of McClernand's corps assaulted Major General Carter H. Stevenson's division on the Confederate left. Stevenson's line was already caving in when McPherson came up and committed Logan's division. The added pressure forced Pemberton, who had suffered several thousand casualties and the loss of sixteen cannons, to haul his entire line half a mile to the rear.

Although forced from his commanding position, Pemberton rallied and counterattacked with Bowen's division, which had fought so stoutly at Port Gibson. Concentrating against Hovey, Bowen drove the Union division from the ground Pemberton had lost; he also recovered every captured artillery piece. Hovey's command suffered heavily, and the ordnance trains in rear of Grant's lines came within an ace of being seized before reinforcements contained Bowen's thrust.[31]

When Pemberton strengthened Bowen's division as if for a further attack, Hovey asked for more support. His plea was answered when Grant ordered to his assistance a brigade that had circumvented the Confederate left and was nearly in position to prevent the possibility of a successful retreat. When his counterattack stalled, Pemberton, at about 4:00 P.M., began to withdraw, having suffered forty-three hundred casualties, almost twice as many as Grant. Thanks to the removal of the brigade that had nearly cut his line of retreat, Pemberton was able to reach the river in his rear. Looking back, Grant deeply regretted the shifting of that force, for which he blamed McClernand.[32]

Pemberton's tired and bloodied troops fell back to prepared defenses along the right bank of the Big Black. A fresh brigade occupied the works while the main body crossed the stream. On the north side, the retreating troops struck the road to Vicksburg, twelve miles away. There Pemberton planned to regroup his shattered forces, and there—in violation of the instructions he had received from Johnston—he would dare Grant to come and get him.

Grant accepted the challenge with alacrity. As soon as they could clear Champion Hill and cross Bakers Creek, the troops of McClernand and McPherson pursued along the direct road to Vicksburg. Grant had Sherman, then moving from Jackson to Bolton's Station, shift toward the Confederate left in hopes of interposing between Pemberton and Vicksburg. Sherman was unable to move quickly enough to cut off the enemy; but early on May 17, McClernand's advance, the division of Brigadier General Michael J. Lawler, struck Pemberton's rear guard a stunning blow along the banks of the Big Black. A bayonet charge across four hundred yards of open ground— a risky maneuver under any conditions—broke the left center of the well-entrenched line, capturing hundreds of Rebels and sending thousands of others scrambling across the river in panic and consternation, dozens of them drowning in the attempt. Watching from a position close to the starting point of Lawler's charge, Grant marveled at its speed and power, which he attributed to its commander, an Irish-born veteran of the Mexican War famed for his Falstaffian girth and formidable fighting qualities. Later, Grant would declare: "When it comes to just plain hard fighting I would rather trust old Mike Lawler than any of them."[33]

Just as Lawler's assault got underway, Grant was paged by a courier bearing a letter from Halleck, sent from Washington on May 11. It called on the army to return to the Mississippi and move to attack Port Hudson. Only after cooperating with General Banks against the lower citadel should Grant return and, with Banks's assistance, attack or besiege Vicksburg. As Grant recalled, "I told the officer that the order came too late, and that Halleck would not give it now if he knew our position." The courier was brash enough to insist that the order be carried out. Instead of coming down hard on the youngster, Grant "immediately mounted [his] horse and rode in the direction of the charge, and saw no more of the officer who delivered the dispatch."[34]

With Pemberton in full, though disorganized, retreat to his supposed place of sanctuary, Grant saw that Vicksburg was virtually in his hands. Yet it was not for another two days that he gained the foothold that would doom Pemberton's garrison. On the morning of May 18, having rebuilt the bridge over the Big Black, his army approached the fortified city deliberately and confidently, McClernand's corps on the left, McPherson's in the center, and Sherman's on the right. Grant, who rode with Sherman, shared his subordinate's hope that a base of supply could be gained on the Yazoo above the city, a perquisite to a successful siege. "Our impatience," Grant wrote, "led us to move in advance of the [XV Corps] column and well up with the advanced skirmishers." In that exposed position, both generals became the focus of Rebel sharpshooters; but they forged on, anxious to secure a lodgment on Walnut Hills, a wooded ridge that commanded Vicksburg. Their risk-taking was rewarded: "In a few minutes Sherman had the pleasure of looking down from the spot coveted so much by him the December before on the ground where his command had been so helpless for offensive action."[35]

As his columns passed him to take up a position from which they could not be dislodged by any such force as Pemberton's, Sherman turned to Grant and made a heartfelt admission. The corps leader confessed that until then he had entertained "no positive assurance of success," as Grant quoted him. "This, however, he said was the end of one of the greatest campaigns in history and I ought to make a report of it at once. Vicksburg was not yet captured, and there was no telling what might happen before it was taken; but whether captured or not, this was a complete and successful campaign."[36]

Grant shared this view but it seems doubtful that he replied to Sherman's pronouncement with more than a modest shrug or a clasp of hands. Or perhaps Grant offered a few words of thanks for the unfailing support his favorite subordinate had given him at every step since the day he had asked Sherman to meet him in Columbus and to bring a good map of Mississippi.

★ ★ ★

Having been so consistently beaten and forced into retreat, Pemberton's troops, Grant believed, were too demoralized to offer effective resistance, even though they were now battened down behind Vicksburg's defenses. Thus he launched an attack all along the line almost as soon as his army went into position north and east of the city. To his surprise, the assault, launched early on May 19, was repulsed handily and with heavy loss. No sector of the works was penetrated, and few defenders were driven from their well-entrenched positions. The attack was especially costly on Sherman's front, where a division led by now-Major General Frank Blair, the early-war defender of federal assets in St. Louis, was caught in a vicious crossfire while attempting to seize the so-called Stockade Redan. Blair's men had advanced so close to their objective that not until after dark could they disengage and withdraw. Grant put the best face on events when he observed that the attack "resulted in securing more advanced positions for all [the] troops where they were fully covered from the fire of the enemy."[37]

Choosing to regard the outcome as an aberration, he planned another attack as soon as late-arriving forces filed into the lines. He spent May 20 and 21 consolidating the few gains that had been made on May 19 and in cutting roads to the Yazoo that would expedite the passage of troops and supplies to the front. He also spent time addressing the needs of his soldiers. While riding along the lines on May 21, he drew a vocal complaint from troops, who had stretched their five-day rations beyond the limit. Having gone without their customary bread ration for the past three weeks, the men he passed gathered in groups and began to chant: "Hardtack! Hardtack!" The chorus was taken up along the length of Grant's route.

To rebuke one's commander in this fashion might appear to be an act of insubordination. Another general would have taken offense, but Grant did not. For one thing, he was used to the refusal of his soldiers to be cowed or even impressed by the image he projected. He was too short, too common-looking, too carelessly dressed to evoke reverence or awe. As Grant's civilian telegrapher recalled: "He was not what would be called an imposing figure. . . . When the weather was mild he generally wore while riding a regulation blue blouse within his coat. He seldom carried a sword and manifestly had no liking for the trappings and show of rank."[38]

Perhaps because he never lost the common touch, Grant took the needs and complaints of his soldiers to heart. On the present occasion, he reined in and, as the men clustered about him, made a rare impromptu announcement. Those newly constructed roads, he told the men, would soon—within hours—be bringing to the front all the rations they could want, including hard and soft bread. The news was everything his audience wished to hear; the men responded with cheers and shouts. As he rode on and the crowds dispersed, the men remained in a cheerful mood. When the promised rations were issued to them after nightfall, they were jubilant. Grant observed, quite unnecessarily: "The bread and coffee were highly appreciated."[39]

No one appreciated the results of Grant's second assault, which began at 5:00 A.M. on May 22 with an artillery bombardment. To this barrage, which went on for an hour, Admiral Porter added shells from his gunboats in the river west and north of the city. When the guns quieted, the infantry swept forward in a general attack; it was spearheaded by McClernand's corps, which targeted the formidable position known as the Railroad Redoubt. A portion of Lawler's division seized a section of the redoubt but, buffeted by a thunderstorm of musketry and artillery-fire, could advance no farther. Observing from the rear, the Chicago correspondent Sylvanus Cadwallader recorded that in a matter of minutes the main body of the XIII Corps "had been so mercilessly torn to pieces by Confederate shot and shell that it had lost nearly all resemblance to a line of battle, or the formation of a storming column." He added: "A straggling line, continually growing thinner and weaker, finally reached the summit, when all who were not instantly shot down were literally pulled over the rebel breastworks as prisoners."[40]

McPherson's corps, which attacked farther to the right against the Great Redoubt, and Sherman's command, which attempted to storm the Stockade Redan, achieved no more success than McClernand had before grinding to a halt in front of impassable works. Both commands, however, were forced to resume their advance when, late in the afternoon, McClernand sent Grant a message saying that he was in the process of carrying the works in his front but would fail without the close support of his colleagues. Skeptical of McClernand's claim but feeling compelled to exploit any chance for a breakthrough, Grant got McPherson and Sherman moving again, only to see their commands cut to pieces by a converging fire from many points of the defenses. Grant was further dismayed when he learned that McClernand had ordered a column of reinforcements under Isaac Quinby to attack, without close support, the Second Texas Lunette. Predictably, Quinby's command was nearly annihilated without compensatory gain. The day ended with McClernand holding no greater advantage than he had when he sent his plea

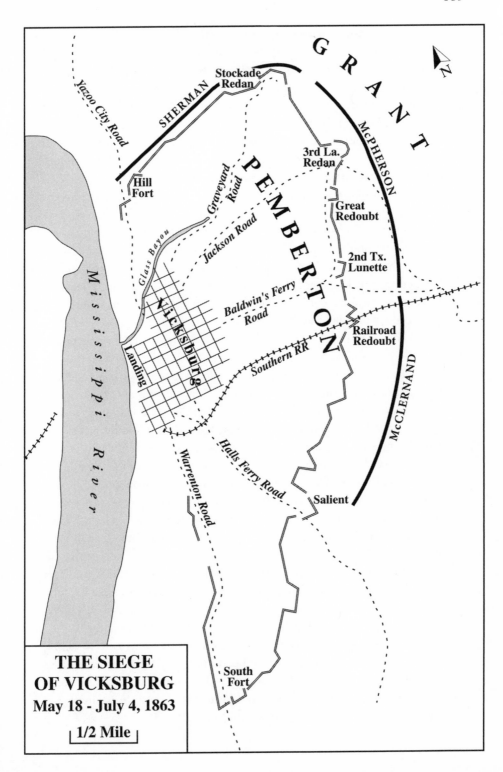

**THE SIEGE
OF VICKSBURG**
May 18 - July 4, 1863

| 1/2 Mile |

to Grant for support. In a series of futile attacks, the Federals had suffered more than three thousand casualties—an unknown number of which had been sacrificed to McClernand's tactical ineptitude and personal ambition.[41]

Grant's patience with McClernand had been worn threadbare. The politician in uniform had been a thorn in his superior's flesh long before he had conspired to gain an independent command in Grant's department. Since demoted to the position of corps commander, he had been even more surly and disputatious than ever. In some instances, McClernand's anger with Grant appears to have been justified, for the commanding general had grown so ill-disposed toward him that he had allowed his feelings to affect his inherent sense of fair play. For example, on May 20, he had verbally blasted McClernand for countermanding a directive from army headquarters that one of his divisions remain on the Big Black to guard a strategic bridge. As Grant knew, or ought to have known, McClernand's order withdrawing the division had been issued the previous day, before Grant made known his desire. Then, too, in his report of the assault of May 22, Grant threw all blame for its failure, and for the excessive bloodletting that resulted, on the politician-general. He also appended an unnecessarily harsh characterization. McClernand was "entirely unfit for the position of corps commander, both on the march and on the battlefield," Grant asserted. "Looking after his corps gives me more labor and infinitely more uneasiness than all the remainder of my department."[42]

McClernand became fed up with being criticized by his superior and blamed for what he perceived to be the mistakes of Grant and his other subordinates. When, on or about May 23, Grant sent Lieutenant Colonel Wilson to McClernand's field headquarters with a peremptory order to strengthen a guard force on the Big Black, McClernand exploded. Wilson quoted him as shouting, "I'll be God damned if I do it—I am tired of being dictated to—I won't stand it any longer, and you can go back and tell General Grant!" Then the corps commanded loosed a "volley of oaths" apparently aimed at all West Pointers. As an Academy graduate, young Wilson took such umbrage that, as he later claimed, he threatened to pull McClernand out of the saddle and beat him up. At this display of naked outrage, the general suddenly regained his composure and offered an apology, explaining that he had not been cursing Wilson but "simply expressing [his] intense vehemence on the subject matter."[43]

For a time the incident, which Wilson recounted word-by-word to Grant, furnished some comic relief at army headquarters. Afterward, whenever Rawlins or some other staff officer was provoked to profanity, Grant would smile; "He's not cursing," he would tell other listeners. "He is simply expressing his intense vehemence on the subject matter!"[44]

The headquarters staff did not stay amused for long. As Grant told Wilson in the aftermath of McClernand's outburst, he intended to rid himself of the troublesome subordinate at the first opportunity. That opportunity arose as a result of an order the corps commander issued on May 30 congratulating his men on the success they had achieved over the past month. The address was typical of its author—verbose, hyperbolic, overly laudatory to the corps and, by extension to its commander, critical of the performance of the rest of the army, and especially of Grant. Indiscreet and insubordinate, the order was just the sort of misstep that Grant had been waiting for McClernand to make.

Apparently, the document did not come to Grant's attention until June 17 when Sherman sent him an issue of a newspaper that had printed it verbatim. Incensed not only by what McClernand had written but that he had contrived to make his exaggerations and criticisms public, Sherman opined that its intended audience was not the XIII Corps but McClernand's political constituency. James McPherson was similarly outraged; he told Grant that the address had been designed "to impress the public mind with the magnificent strategy, superior tactics, and brilliant deeds" of John McClernand.[45]

Grant had had enough. Because McClernand had violated an order of long standing that prohibited the publication of official documents without first clearing it with army headquarters, he had a pretext to fire McClernand, who, when confronted with the newspaper account, admitted his infraction. Just after midnight on June 18, he sent Wilson back to XIII Corps headquarters, this time carrying an order relieving McClernand of his command. Wilson took delight in waking the politician-general from a sound sleep and placing the order in his hand. After perusing it, McClernand responded, "Well, sir, I am relieved!" Then he added: "By God, sir, we are both relieved!"[46]

Wilson took McClernand's comment as a threat to use his influence with Lincoln to bring about Grant's downfall and his own reinstatement. But it was not to be. McClernand bitterly protested his relief and his replacement by General Ord, but to no avail. The best he was able to achieve was to regain command of the XIII Corps the following February, when it was serving apart from Grant during the Red River Campaign in Louisiana. But he held the command for less than a month before shattered health forced him to quit the field for good. He spent the rest of the war trying to recuperate and trying to fathom how such a promising military and political career could have gone so terribly awry.[47]

★ ★ ★

The failure of the May 22 offensive persuaded Grant to invest Vicksburg, a strategy he knew would prove effective but time-consuming. During the next six weeks, his troops slowly tightened their death-grip on the city's defenders and its civilian occupants, thousands of whom, refusing to evacuate, literally dug in to withstand the siege despite the extraordinary hardships and widespread suffering it caused. Many of the inhabitants were forced to tunnel into the river bluffs and huddle in caves to escape the almost constant shower of shot and shell from Grant's strategically emplaced batteries.

Every day the siege forces advanced their lines closer to those of the enemy. The Federals threw up breastworks, dug trenches, and erected covered ways to protect themselves against sniper and artillery fire as well as the baking heat and heavy rains common to a Mississippi summer. Ex-miners in the ranks dug shafts under two sectors of Pemberton's lines; on June 25 and again six days later, they detonated the explosives stored in the tunnels. Grant reaped no strategic advantage from either action, but they kept the enemy's nerves on edge lest other mines be under construction.[48]

As soon as Grant established his foothold on the Yazoo, reinforcements began to arrive in great numbers, courtesy of Halleck. Meanwhile, Pemberton's garrison was depleted by desertions, which steadily increased as the city's food supply dwindled away. By the end of June, the garrison was subsisting on mule meat and pea bread. Numerous Confederates later declared they had been reduced to cooking and devouring rats, but this oft-stated claim cannot be verified.

Although never doubting its ultimate success, Grant was bothered by the pace of the siege, which he appeared powerless to expedite. His starving, dirty, ragged, and sleep-deprived enemy seemed determined to hold out to the bitterest end imaginable. This was especially taxing to the Northern public, whose morale was again sagging under the weight of the recent failure by the Army of the Potomac, now under Joseph ("Fighting Joe") Hooker, to best Lee's Army of Northern Virginia in battle. Despite outnumbering his opponent almost two-to-one and having concocted a promising plan to evict him from his impregnable position at Fredericksburg, during four days of bitter struggle (May 1–4) in the tangled forest known as the Virginia Wilderness Hooker had permitted Lee to outsmart, outmaneuver, and outfight him. The result was another round of heavy casualties followed by another disheartening retreat. This one would end the tenure of Fighting Joe.[49]

Worse in its strategic implications than the sense of gloom it spread across the North, his latest success emboldened Robert E. Lee to launch his second invasion of Northern soil. By late June, his soldiers, poorly armed and equipped but brimming over with confidence, were making their way virtually unmolested through lower Pennsylvania, bound, perhaps, for Washington, D.C., or another major city. Hooker, crippled psychologically and having lost the confidence of Lincoln and Stanton, was pursuing slowly and at a distance. To military observers and political prognosticators alike, the war was at its most critical stage. The next few days or weeks would decide whether the republic would survive intact or be torn forever asunder.

Grant's awareness that the morale of the North was dependent on a successful conclusion to his campaign weighed heavily on his mind, but the static nature and stultifying effects of the siege, the progress of which seemed imperceptible, left him bored, weary, and at times dispirited, especially in the absence of his wife. Julia and three of the children had left the war zone on April 24, although Fred, who had just entered his teens, would remain with his father through the campaign.[50]

As had happened on past occasions when beset by similar pressures and influences, Grant gave in to his longing for alcohol. Already he may have succumbed to its temptations; in mid-March, McClernand had relayed to Lincoln a second-hand allegation that Grant had been "gloriously drunk" two days earlier and had spent a considerable time sleeping off the effects. The charge emanated from a source neither reliable nor disinterested, but in his postwar writings the more credible Sylvanus Cadwallader, who had full access to army headquarters, confirmed that Grant did drink on another occasion. Grant, Cadwallader claimed, downed as many as three "generous" portions from a canteen filled with whiskey furnished by one of his staff officers, Lieutenant Colonel William L. Duff. The aide, Cadwallader claimed, "had catered to Grant's inordinate desire for stimulants long before this." Cadwallader did not assert that Grant became intoxicated but noted that he drank "with great apparent satisfaction."[51]

Drinking at his headquarters when his presence was not required at the front was one thing. But on June 6, Grant imbibed again, this time while on duty and in quantity sufficient to become very drunk. The occasion was an inspection trip up the Yazoo River to the village of Satartia, where he had posted an infantry division to stop potential reinforcements for Pemberton. A coterie of staff officers—not including Rawlins or Wilson—accompanied him on the journey, as did Charles Dana. When Grant and his retinue, en route from Haynes's Bluff on horseback, met the steamboat *Diligent* coming downriver, Grant persuaded her captain to turn about and convey them all to Satartia. On board the steamer was Sylvanus Cadwallader, who thereafter joined Grant's party.

Grant "had been drinking heavily, and . . . was still keeping it up," the newspaperman quickly discovered. "He made several trips to the bar room of the boat in a short time, and became stupid in speech and staggering in gait. This was the first time he had shown symptoms of intoxication in my presence, and I was greatly alarmed by his condition, which was fast becoming worse."[52]

Cadwallader claimed that he took it upon himself, in light of inaction by Grant's staff, to entice the general into a stateroom. The reporter locked the door and then tossed several bottles of whiskey he found in the room out the cabin's portholes and into the Yazoo. Grant took umbrage at Cadwallader's actions and ordered him out of the cabin, but Cadwallader stayed long enough to get Grant into bed; the journalist "soon fanned him to sleep." When Grant awoke from his stupor, Cadwallader managed to dissuade him from going ashore, as the general wished, and put him back to bed. That night, the boat returned to Haynes's Bluff; but in the morning Grant debarked, slipped away from Cadwallader, procured whiskey ashore, and soon "was quite as much intoxicated as the day before."[53]

Cadwallader somehow got Grant back on board and the *Diligent* continued on to army headquarters at Chickasaw Bayou. But when the steamer docked there that night, she was boarded by a party of carousing officers and army sutlers, in whose merriment Grant joined, much to Cadwallader's horror. Again intoxicated, Grant staggered ashore, where he mounted—rather unsteadily, one imagines—for the ride to headquarters. The horse he chose had a reputation for wildness, and as soon as the general was in the saddle the beast "darted away at full speed before anyone was ready to follow."[54]

Reminiscent of his wild ride the previous spring with William Smith in pursuit, Grant allowed the horse to carry him over hill and dale as well as through the camps of troops who shouted and cursed as he rode over them. Behind him came his worried staff officers and escort troopers along with an equally concerned Charles Dana and a positively appalled Sylvanus Cadwallader. Only when Grant's horse slowed to a walk and Cadwallader overtook him and grabbed his bridle rein was the dangerous escapade over. The reporter persuaded Grant to lie down on a grassy patch; the general was soon asleep. He was awakened when an ambulance ordered by Cadwallader arrived. By the time the conveyance reached headquarters a little after midnight, Grant had recovered his faculties to the extent that he made his way without assistance to his tent, where he fell back to sleep.

When Grant and the rest of the party arrived, John Rawlins, a stricken look on his face, interrogated Cadwallader intensively, gleaning the details of his boss's escapade ("I have a right to know them," the straightlaced staff officer told Cadwallader, "and I will know them"). He appreciated the thoroughness and candor the reporter displayed in recounting the events of the past two days—thereafter Cadwallader was given unparalleled access to the workings of the headquarters staff. Because he never brought up the subject of the trip when in Grant's presence, the journalist maintained a place at, or at least near, Grant's right hand for the rest of the war, a position that enabled him to send his editor accounts of plans and operations that only a headquarters insider could provide.[55]

For his part, Rawlins not only spoke to Grant about the escapade but warned him in pungent language of the dangers it posed to his reputation and position, especially given the unresolved situation at Vicksburg, which threatened Grant's tenure in command. Then, too, upon the cessation of offensive operations, distinguished visitors had begun to arrive at headquarters to observe the siege, Governor Yates and other Illinois state officials being among the first. Had any of these men observed Grant's out-of-control behavior, it would have been the talk of the entire Northwest within days.

Supposedly Rawlins had an additional reason for upbraiding Grant. Shortly before starting for Satartia, the adjutant had discovered an empty wine bottle inside Grant's tent as well as an unopened case of wine that was to be tapped when word came of Pemberton's surrender. The finding had provoked the long-suffering Rawlins to compose a letter that began: "The great solicitude I feel for the safety of this army leads me to mention what I had hoped never again to do, the subject of your drinking." It ended with a fervent plea that Grant not "touch a single drop of any kind of liquor no matter by whom asked or under what circumstances." If Grant refused to pledge himself to stop drinking, Rawlins would immediately resign from Grant's staff. James Wilson, who later published a biography of Rawlins, claimed to have learned that although harshly worded and sharply delivered, his "admonitions were not resented but heeded for a season."[56]

Historians have argued about the accuracy of Cadwallader's account of the episode ever since the publication of his memoirs in 1955. The general consensus is that Cadwallader was not on hand for many of the events he claims to have observed or taken part in. Details of the trip may have come to him from second- or third-hand sources; in old age, when he put his recollections on paper, he might have confused the events he had witnessed with those reported to him later. Even so, the gist of his story—that Grant got very drunk while on an inspection tour, shocking observers, worrying his companions, and incurring the wrath of John Rawlins—has never been credibly challenged.

Some of those who have attacked Cadwallader's narrative as fiction do so because when he wrote his postwar memoirs, Charles Dana, who was along on the trip and presumably witnessed Grant's antics, presented an account much at odds with Cadwallader's, and not nearly so sensationalistic. (For one thing, Dana described Grant during much of the trip as "ill" rather than intoxicated, although the euphemism is transparent.) Yet Dana is also generally acknowledged to be the author of an editorial published in a January 1887 issue of the *New York Sun,* a newspaper he was editing. The editorial, "General Grant's Occasional Intoxication," mentions the Satartia trip as one instance in which the general got "stupidly drunk" and behaved so recklessly as to imperil his career.[57]

That neither Cadwallader nor Dana divulged details of the episode for many years after it happened suggests the effectiveness of the conspiracy of silence by which those close to Grant protected his public image. Dana might have torpedoed Grant's career all by himself had he mentioned the event, even in passing, in his dispatches to Stanton and Lincoln. For the sake of the army, and of the cause, he chose not to. As Wilson commented years later: "One cannot help reflecting that the consequences of this episode might have been far different had Dana been . . . a narrow minded and unreasonable bigot."[58]

★ *Chapter 10* ★

THE IDOL OF THE HOUR

GRANT'S REPUTATION, SO RECENTLY SALVAGED THROUGH THE EFFORTS OF HIS inner circle, soared dramatically when Pemberton surrendered Vicksburg. With his garrison and the city's civilian population on the brink of starvation, and without hope of lifting the siege or fighting his way out of the city, early on July 3 Pemberton authorized the flying of white flags. Hostilities ceased immediately. Then General Bowen, who had been a neighbor of Grant's in prewar St. Louis, entered the Union lines under a flag of truce, carrying an armistice proposal from his superior. That afternoon, Grant and Pemberton met between the lines to discuss the terms of capitulation.

At first, Grant, hearkening back to Fort Donelson, demanded an unconditional surrender. Pemberton, who wanted his men to march out of the city with full honors of war and be paroled instead of sent to a POW compound, reacted by breaking off the parlay. After returning to his headquarters, Grant reconsidered the matter. After giving it some thought, he agreed to permit the Confederates to sign their paroles and "march out of [the Union] lines." The officers could take their side-arms and clothing, the field, staff, and cavalry officers one horse each. The rank and file could take "all their clothing, but no other property." After some additional haggling, Pemberton accepted Grant's terms. Surrender ceremonies took place the next morning, Independence Day, and the Union forces took immediate possession of the defenses they had been unable to breach. Grant had notched the greatest victory of his career in arms. Looking back years later, he asserted confidently that "the fate of the Confederacy was sealed when Vicksburg fell."[1]

Vicksburg's surrender—coming as it did on the heels of Robert E. Lee's defeat at Gettysburg at the hands of Major General George Gordon Meade, ending Lee's sojourn in the North—gave the greatest possible boost to

Union morale. When, as Grant foresaw, Port Hudson quickly followed suit, a chorus of cheers greeted Abraham Lincoln's pronouncement: At long last, "the Father of Waters goes unvexed to the sea."[2]

Once again Ulysses S. Grant was a hero to the loyal people of the North, the acknowledged master of every Confederate in the western theater of the war. His achievement, however, was downgraded by those who considered his decision to parole Pemberton's garrison a mistake that invited the Confederates to retake the field once exchanged. Grant consistently defended his action by citing his limited transportation capacity, which would have been overtaxed had he been forced to convey the Rebels to distant prison camps. He also reasoned that a majority of Pemberton's people had lost the heart to wage war and, once exchanged, would go home and stay there. This supposition was more wishful thinking than anything else; but, given Grant's situation, it may well have been the wisest course.[3]

Grant then tended to some unfinished business. On the day after Vicksburg's surrender, three corps under Sherman began to cross the Big Black, converging toward Bolton's Station. They drove Joe Johnston's command all the way to Jackson, where the Confederate leader hunkered down. On July 11, Sherman laid siege to the town and began shelling it. His artillery set fire to so many houses, leaving only their stone portions standing, that Jackson became known as "Chimneyville." Johnston's troops resisted bravely for a week, but by July 17 they had evacuated; they fled toward Brandon so quickly that they outdistanced their pursuers. Believing that enough success had been achieved, Grant recalled Sherman to Vicksburg, which the latter reached on July 27, effectively ending the campaign in Mississippi.[4]

Grant had barely begun to savor his latest round of success when he was dealt a defeat by his superiors. For some time he had favored, as soon as the Vicksburg operations were wrapped up, a drive down the Mississippi to capture Mobile, one of the Confederacy's most valuable ports, then to invade Georgia. Believing that his success in Mississippi had given him the leverage to impress this strategy on Washington, he placed such a proposal before General Halleck, only to have it promptly rejected. Lincoln, Halleck explained, was more interested in gaining a foothold inside Texas, an objective that had political and diplomatic as well as military value. A Union presence on the Rio Grande would foil, or at least complicate, the expansionist ambitions of France, which was setting up a puppet government in Mexico in violation of the Monroe Doctrine. Lincoln's desire to raise the flag in Texas would heavily influence Union war planning in 1864.[5]

When turning down Grant's plan for Mobile, Halleck also denied his request to visit New Orleans and confer with General Banks, who also favored a drive to the Gulf Coast. Thus Grant was "obliged to settle down" and see himself "put again on the defensive as [he] had been a year before in west Tennessee." At Halleck's behest, he depleted his forces by sending four thousand men to Banks, dispatching the IX Corps—which had joined him at Vicksburg in June—to Kentucky, detaching five thousand troops to Major General John M. Schofield in Missouri, and detailing a brigade under Brigadier General Thomas E. G. Ransom—a young volunteer officer whom Grant thought highly of—to permanent garrison duty in strategic Natchez. By early August, he had also divested himself of the XIII Corps. Ord's troops went to Banks, with whom Grant had been directed to cooperate on movements west of the Mississippi River.[6]

On the basis of that mission, Grant won approval to visit New Orleans, where Banks had his headquarters. He went in the last days of August. Because the venture in which he and Banks were to cooperate came to naught, his visit was notable only for two incidents. While reviewing Banks's army near Carrollton, Louisiana, Grant rode a borrowed horse, known for his sometimes overly spirited behavior. At some point the mount, spooked by a passing locomotive, ran away with his rider, then fell, knocking Grant unconscious and laying him up for weeks with a bruise so severe that his body was swollen from knee to arm-pit "almost to the point of bursting." He described the pain as "almost beyond endurance."[7]

The second noteworthy incident derived from the first. The inability of Grant, a master horseman and horse gentler, to quell his fractious steed suggested to many witnesses that the general had been drinking. Whether he had remains uncertain, although one observer who should have had first-hand knowledge of Grant's behavior that day—Nathaniel Banks—believed that he was indeed drunk. As he told his wife, the accident was the result of Grant's overindulging at a pre-review banquet honoring the conqueror of Vicksburg. One of Banks's subordinates, Major General William B. Franklin, who also attended the review, agreed. Franklin called the accident a fortunate occurrence for Grant because it ended a "frolic" that "would have ruined his body and reputation in a week."[8]

If Grant did drink to excess, the root cause may well have been that old bugaboo, separation from loved ones. Julia and the children, including Fred, had recently ended another stay with him by returning via Memphis to their new home in St. Louis (Grant had used his army pay to purchase both White Haven and Wish-ton-Wish). Presumably John Rawlins was not at the banquet—had he been, the accident might never have occurred.

Whatever the cause, Grant was laid up in Louisiana for almost two weeks. On September 16, a steamboat returned him to Vicksburg, where he completed his slow and painful recovery in a twenty-six-room mansion he had transformed into his headquarters. As soon as she could, Julia returned from St. Louis to nurse him. Her presence ensured that his recuperation would include no prohibited stimulants.[9]

He could not afford to be inactive for long, for a new and challenging assignment was in the works even as he lay abed. It involved a rescue of the Army of the Cumberland, which had met disaster in battle in northern Georgia four days after Grant was transported from New Orleans to Vicksburg. The assignment threatened to reunite Grant with a former subordinate he disliked and distrusted nearly as much as he had John McClernand.

While the siege of Vicksburg was winding down, William Rosecrans had been winning kudos—but not a commensurate amount of newspaper publicity—for a masterly campaign of maneuver, bluff, feint, and fighting in Middle Tennessee. In the last week of June, the victor at Stones River had engineered an even greater victory by driving Bragg's Confederates out of the Tullahoma, Tennessee, region, then forcing them to abandon the communications hub of Chattanooga. Although overshadowed by the press coverage given to Grant's triumph in Mississippi and Meade's victory in Pennsylvania, the Tullahoma Campaign would stand as a brilliant achievement, the crowning glory of a career otherwise steeped in controversy and defeat.[10]

Then, with astonishing speed, Rosecrans lost everything he had gained, the result of a careless and overconfident pursuit of Bragg's supposedly demoralized troops into Georgia. Along Chickamauga Creek, near Rossville, on September 19 Bragg suddenly attacked Rosecrans's fatally dispersed command. The first day's fighting was inconclusive, but on September 20, thanks to an opportune assault by reinforcements sent from Virginia under James Longstreet, Bragg routed Rosecrans and sent his army flying pell-mell to Chattanooga. Only a resolute stand by troops under George Thomas—who thereby gained the title "Rock of Chickamauga"—allowed the Army of the Cumberland to escape annihilation.

As if determined to prove correct those critics—and they were legion—who considered him incompetent, Bragg failed to reap the fruits of victory through pursuit. Still, by month's end he had moved his army into siege positions atop commanding eminences west and southwest of the city (Raccoon Mountain), on the southwest (Lookout Mountain), and on the east and southeast (Missionary Ridge). Bragg's movement cut most of the supply lines into the garrison, threatening Rosecrans's troops with the same fate that Pemberton's had faced—starvation.[11]

On September 29—by which time Grant had recovered from his injuries to the extent that he could mount a horse—Halleck wired him details of

Rosecrans's disaster and word that Meade was dispatching reinforcements to Chattanooga. For his part, Grant was to send as many troops as he could spare, headed by a competent subordinate such as Sherman or McPherson. Grant himself should prepare to move to Nashville via Louisville to supervise the troop transfer. On October 10, the day before he saw off Sherman at the head of thousands of troops, Grant was directed to move his headquarters as previously indicated. Still quite sore and hobbling about on crutches, later that same day he left Vicksburg accompanied by Julia, who was looking forward to visiting her Louisville-area relations.[12]

A subsequent dispatch, which Grant received during a stopover at Cairo, informed him that an officer of the War Department carrying detailed instructions would meet him in Louisville. But Grant got only as far as Indianapolis before the emissary—Secretary Stanton himself—flagged down his train. When he entered Grant's car, Stanton, who had never met Grant, announced that he would recognize him anywhere by his soldierly appearance. He proved it by pumping the hand of Dr. Edward D. Kittoe, Grant's tall, imposing-looking medical director, and addressing him by the general's name. Once the mix-up was cleared up, Stanton dismissed the special train that had brought him from Washington and accompanied Grant all the way to Louisville.

As they rode, the two men discussed strategy and tactics, general war news, and the successes and disappointments of the recent campaigns. At some point Stanton handed his companion two orders; these were "identical in all but one particular," Grant recalled.

> Both created the Military Division of the Mississippi, giving me the command, composed of the Departments of the Ohio, the Cumberland, and the Tennessee, and all the territory from the Alleghenies to the Mississippi River, north of Banks's command in the south-west. One order left the department commanders as they were, while the other relieved Rosecrans and assigned Thomas to his place.

Grant did not have to wrack his brain to determine which was preferable: "I accepted the latter."[13]

Upon reaching Louisville, Stanton learned by telegraph from Charles Dana, then at Chattanooga, that Rosecrans was thinking about evacuating the city. Both Grant and Stanton considered such a move potentially disastrous. Grant got on the telegraph and informed Rosecrans of his assumption of overall command and of Rosecrans's replacement by Thomas. To Thomas he sent a peremptory order to hold the city at all hazards—Grant would join him there as soon as possible.

★ ★ ★

On October 20, having spent one day in Louisville, Grant kissed Julia good-bye and, along with his staff, proceeded south to Nashville, where he paid a courtesy call on Tennessee's provisional governor, Andrew Johnson. While in the city he telegraphed orders to some of his new subordinates, including Thomas at Chattanooga (who was told to hasten the construction of alternate supply routes to the city) and Major General Ambrose E. Burnside at Knoxville, Tennessee (ordered to strengthen his fortifications against attack). Burnside, who had led the Army of the Potomac to disaster at Fredericksburg nearly a year earlier, had been assigned to command the Department of the Ohio, which now comprised the IX and XXIII Corps. Originally directed to invade Kentucky, Burnside had been holed up in Knoxville since early September; thus he was fulfilling Abraham Lincoln's desire that a military presence be felt in heavily Unionist East Tennessee.

The day after his audience with Governor Johnson, Grant and his party moved on to Stevenson, Alabama, where they met Rosecrans on his way north. Understandably dejected by his failure and relief from command, Old Rosy nevertheless "described very clearly the situation in Chattanooga and made some excellent suggestions as to what should be done," Grant wrote. "My only wonder was that he had not carried them out."[14]

From Stevenson, Grant was conveyed to Bridgeport, Alabama, where the railroad crossed the Tennessee River into a region controlled by Bragg's army. Unable to proceed farther, the general alighted from the train, picked up an escort and several horses, and started for Chattanooga via Jasper and a crossing of Walden's Ridge. The terrain he and his companions crossed was awash in water, and in places knee-deep in mud. Grant had to be carried on a litter over places too unsafe to be crossed on horseback. After dark on October 23, the travelers reached General Thomas's headquarters at Chattanooga, where Grant planned to board until he could establish a headquarters of his own.

The greeting Grant received from the man he had just elevated to army command was anything but cordial. Colonel Wilson—only days away from his own promotion, to brigadier general of volunteers—had ridden ahead of the party to meet Thomas and study the local defenses in company with an old friend, Brigadier General William Farrar ("Baldy") Smith, Thomas's chief engineer officer. Wilson had been in Chattanooga for two days when Grant and his group slipped inside the city. Upon joining them at Thomas's head-quarters, Wilson found the atmosphere as stiff and as cold as the new arrivals after riding for hours in a frigid rain: "Grant was sitting on one side of the fire[place] over a puddle of water that had run out of his clothes; Thomas, glum and silent, was sitting on the other, while Rawlins and the rest were scattered about in disorder." Wilson attributed Thomas's poor hospitality to pique at being subordinated to Grant after outranking him in the Regular Army and having effectively superseded him after Shiloh, when he had a field command and Grant did not. Only at Wilson's brash insistence did Thomas bustle about to make Grant and his staff dry and comfortable. The young engineer wondered whether the generals could team cordially to manage the critical work that lay ahead.[15]

Wilson need not have worried. Although the generals had their differences of opinion, they worked together from the first, largely the result of Thomas's self-effacing nature. A man of dignity and lofty bearing, Thomas was also, as Rosecrans would have testified, a loyal and trustworthy subordinate who carried out given orders faithfully and precisely, although with a degree of deliberation that was reflected in another of Thomas's nicknames, "Old Slow Trot."

Now that he was on the scene, Grant's first task was to restore the Army of the Cumberland's supply line to Bridgeport. This he accomplished with little difficulty thanks to the expertise of Baldy Smith. Working closely with Rosecrans, himself a skilled engineer, Smith had devised a plan to lay pontoons across two prongs of a horseshoe-shaped bend in the Tennessee River (west of Chattanooga) enclosing a peninsula called Moccasin Point. Wagons passing from Brown's Ferry, on the far side of the more westerly prong, across the peninsula and into the city would bypass Confederate artillery positions atop Lookout Mountain that commanded supply ship navigation.

Grant was impressed by Smith's ability to explain his plan clearly and concisely and by the energy with which he was producing the requisite resources, including pontoon boats and bridge planking. Grant decided to permit the engineer, whom he had known briefly at West Point (Smith had been two years behind him) to command many of the troops required to execute his plan. Smith had gained enough field experience to recommend him for the assignment. From late 1861 until the battle of Fredericksburg he had commanded, successively, a brigade, a division, and a corps in the Army of the Potomac before being forced onto inactive duty and seeing his nominations as major general rejected by the Senate.[16]

Grant knew that Smith had run afoul of his former commander, Burnside, but he attributed the man's travail to personality clashes and army politics rather than any culpability on Smith's part. In fact, the sharp-tongued, prickly tempered Smith had lost his command because he had shamelessly intrigued against Burnside, whom he considered grossly incompetent, thereby losing the respect and confidence of Stanton and Lincoln. Smith's greatest liability was a towering ego—he saw himself as a giant surrounded by pigmies, a man of action in an army of thumbsuckers. Seeking reinstatement in the East and hopeful that Grant would secure it for him, he was careful not to condescend toward the new theater commander. His single-minded effort to use Grant for his own purposes would bear some fruit, but in the end his penchant for criticizing his superiors would ruin their relationship and bring on his final downfall.[17]

Smith's plan was ready for implantation by October 26. Put into effect that day and the next, it worked almost flawlessly. First, the troops sent from Virginia under another deposed leader of the Army of the Potomac, Joe Hooker, crossed the Tennessee from Bridgeport. Once on the south bank, Hooker's column marched upriver to Brown's Ferry. At the same time, Major General John M. Palmer, commanding the XIV Corps, Army of the Cumberland, moved downriver on the north bank, then crossed to secure the road Hooker had taken to Brown's Ferry.

Before daylight on October 27, the second phase of the operation got under way as four thousand troops under Smith's direction moved out of Chattanooga. About half of them paddled downriver toward Brown's Ferry in sixty newly constructed pontoon boats, their passing undetected by Confederate pickets at the northern base of Lookout Mountain. Landing on the south side of the river at about 5:00 A.M., the neophyte sailors captured or drove out the Rebels stationed nearby. Like clockwork, the troops were joined by the two thousand or more men under Smith, who came marching down the north side, bridge materials in tow.

By 7:00 A.M., Smith's entire force had crossed the river; by 10:00 A.M. the ferry had been fortified against attack and the bridge linking it to Moccasin Point was in place. At this point, the "extreme right, now in Lookout valley [between Lookout and Raccoon Mountains], was fortified and connected with the rest of the army," Grant wrote. "The two bridges over the Tennessee River—a flying one at Chattanooga and the new one at Brown's Ferry—with the road north of the river, covered from both the fire and the view of the enemy, made the connection complete."[18]

To support the bridging operation, Hooker's soldiers emerged into Lookout Valley near the town of Wauhatchie, split into detachments, and entrapped those Rebels who had been picketing below the bend of the river. By morning of October 30, the first shipload of supplies to use the new route was carted into Chattanooga; it consisted of forty thousand tons of edibles ranging from forage for cavalry horses to that staple of the soldier's diet, hardtack. The importance the men attached to their bread ration was evident in the name they gave the new route—"The Cracker Line."[19]

★ ★ ★

Having reacted too slowly to prevent the restoration of Chattanooga's communications, after dark on October 28 an angry Braxton Bragg ordered an attack against one of Hooker's divisions, which had taken up an isolated position outside Wauhatchie. Eighteen hundred members of Longstreet's corps made the effort, which was beaten back by belated reinforcements, but only after several hours of some of the most confused fighting of the war. Casualties were heavy on both sides, in part because, in the dark, trigger-happy troops had fired on their own comrades. Also involved in the fighting were several dozen U.S. Army mules who, spooked by the heavy firing, broke away from their skinners, stampeded through the lines, and overran a Confederate position. Although Grant's old friend had withdrawn before the stampede began, in a postwar article for *Century Magazine* Grant took delight in blaming the retreat on the "mule charge," which, as he claimed, Longstreet's troops mistook for a cavalry attack.[20]

Whatever the facts of the combat at Wauhatchie, it marked the last time Bragg would take the initiative against Grant. Throughout the remainder of the campaign, he would react—belatedly, ineptly, and unluckily—to the deceptively simple strategy and effective tactics of his opponent. Yet even before Grant moved against him, Bragg had sealed his own fate by engaging in an unseemly dispute with Longstreet and then acquiescing in a faulty decision by President Davis, who had begun an extended visit to the Army of Tennessee early in October in hopes of resolving its command problems. Shaken by the hostility and distrust dividing the ranking generals, Davis decreed that they should part ways: Bragg would remain at Chattanooga while Longstreet took some twenty thousand troops—those he had brought from Virginia augmented by most of Bragg's cavalry under Major General Joseph Wheeler—to attack or besiege Burnside at Knoxville. The troop transfer began by both rail and overland march on November 5.[21]

When Grant got wind of the detaching, he saw an opportunity to breach Bragg's porous but still constrictive siege. He was not in a position to do so, however, until the middle of the month, when the troops from Vicksburg under Sherman—Grant's successor as commander of the Army of the Tennessee—finally drew near. They had been slowed by foul weather, wretched roads, and the need to mend the disrupted railroad that paralleled their route so that it could be used to supply their needs. The delay this requirement caused proved so severe that Grant finally ordered Sherman to forgo track reconstruction and hasten to Chattanooga. Sherman arrived ahead of his troops, and by October 23 he, as well as Thomas and Hooker, had been briefed on Grant's strategy and were ready to execute it.[22]

The battle plan was simplicity itself. It was predicated on striking Bragg's right flank at the top of Missionary Ridge, driving down the crest, and rolling up the Confederate line like a flimsy piece of gray carpeting. Originally Grant assigned the main effort to Thomas, but the conservative old soldier demurred, arguing that his command was not large enough to make the assault and hold its position at Chattanooga. Grant reluctantly passed the job to Sherman, whose troops would have to travel a much greater distance to get into position to attack. Diversionary movements would pin down other sectors of Bragg's line, but the plan hinged on the strength and savvy of Sherman's new arrivals.[23]

The day before Sherman moved to the attack, his comrades in the Army of the Cumberland achieved dramatic success against the advance elements of Bragg's army. At about 2:00 P.M. on October 23, the divisions of Thomas J. Wood and Philip H. Sheridan drove a heavy Rebel force from a foothill of Missionary Ridge known as Orchard Knob. Looking on from a vantage point above Chattanooga, Grant was gratified by Thomas's achievement. He was particularly impressed by the power and verve displayed by the troops under Sheridan, a feisty, bandy-legged Irishman who had performed admirably at Perryville under Buell and at Stones River under Rosecrans. The capture of Orchard Knob showed Grant, who feared the Army of the Cumberland had been fatally demoralized at Chickamauga, that Thomas's troops retained their fighting spirit.[24]

He was also pleased to discover that, although Bragg had lost his advanced position, he showed no signs of retreating to more defensible ground. "The advantage was greatly to our side now," Grant reasoned, "and if I could only have been assured that Burnside could hold out ten days longer I should have rested more easily." That was how long it would take, he calculated, to defeat Bragg and move to the relief of Knoxville. Already Lincoln and Stanton were importuning him to overtake Longstreet before he challenged Burnside's garrison. But Grant was intent on first things first—he would defeat the manpower-depleted army opposite him before rescuing the well-meaning but hapless defender of East Tennessee.[25]

★ ★ ★

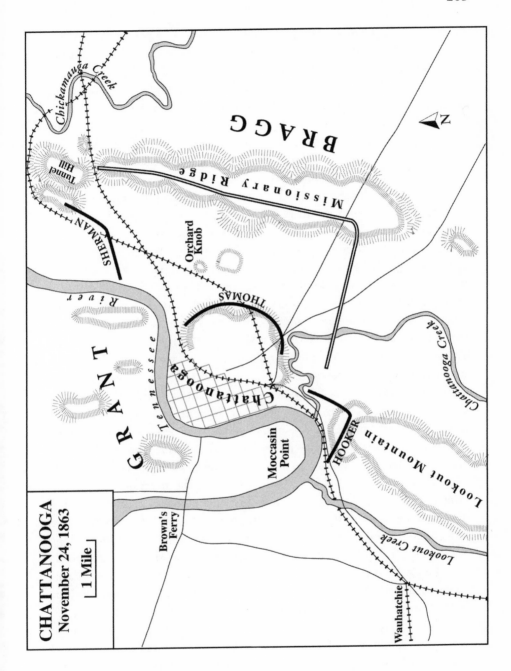

CHATTANOOGA
November 24, 1863

1 Mile

GRANT

BRAGG

Chickamauga Creek

Tunnel Hill

SHERMAN

Missionary Ridge

Orchard Knob

THOMAS

River

Tennessee

Chattanooga

Moccasin Point

Brown's Ferry

HOOKER

Lookout Mountain

Chattanooga Creek

Lookout Creek

Wauhatchie

N

Before dawn on October 24, Sherman was to move into position to play his critical role in Grant's plan. He was to cross the river on the new bridge at Brown's Ferry, and then South Chickamauga Creek via a bridge to be laid by his engineers. But problems with the stability of both bridges delayed his advance and not until 1:00 P.M. was he in position to challenge the Rebels on the northern end of Missionary Ridge. At first he met light resistance—by 4:00 P.M. he had seized a foothold on the ridgeline. But when he attempted to move toward strategic Tunnel Hill, he found himself stymied by a wide depression between the eminence and Missionary Ridge. Moreover, Tunnel Hill was held by the division of Bragg's most combative subordinate, Major General Patrick Cleburne. In response to orders to reinforce Longstreet, Bragg had nearly detached Cleburne from his army. Now the division was Bragg's salvation—as long as it maintained its strategic foothold.[26]

While Sherman tried to get his men moving again, Hooker's troops from the Army of the Potomac, reinforced by some of Thomas's divisions and later by one of Sherman's, were to cross Lookout Valley, drive the enemy from the mountain of the same name, and advance to Rossville, a village nestled between two crests at the lower end of Missionary Ridge. Hooker's drive, designed to take pressure off Sherman's offensive and prevent reinforcements from opposing him, began at 8:00 A.M. on October 24 with a division crossing Lookout Creek north of Wauhatchie and ramming into a Confederate force near Craven's Farm. The fighting that gyrated for hours across this farm and adjacent properties was shrouded in a thick fog that caused the engagement to be known in some circles as the "Battle Above the Clouds."

At noon, Hooker managed to drive the enemy from Craven's to a position close to the base of Lookout Mountain. There the defenders were reinforced by two brigades brought down from the summit. Fighting raged in this area from about 2:00 P.M. until after midnight, when the Confederates broke contact and withdrew to Missionary Ridge. As the historian Glenn Tucker explained it, Hooker's success "gave Grant a straight line of battle with Lookout on the right, extending to the outer works at Chattanooga, through Orchard Knob, and on to where Sherman had come into position facing the north end of Missionary Ridge."[27]

The next day, October 25, it was Thomas's turn to go forward—once Sherman turned the Confederate right—against the center of Bragg's line on Missionary Ridge. At dawn on that "beautiful clear cold day," as Grant's visiting in-law William W. Smith described it, Sherman resumed his drive against Cleburne and his supports, and Hooker began moving through Lookout Valley toward Rossville, threatening Bragg's left. Smith, following the progress of the fight from a lofty crest north of the city, noted that around 11:00 A.M. Sherman—who this day had at his disposal two corps of the Army of the Tennessee, Major General O. O. Howard's corps of the Army of the Potomac, and two divisions of Thomas's command—became heavily engaged, "every inch of his attempted progress along the ridge being severly [sic] contested." Sherman gained ground, but no lodgement beyond his position at the break of day. To the south, meanwhile, Hooker was being held up by delays in rebuilding a bridge over Chattanooga Creek; he was not in position to engage troops along the Rebel left until late in the afternoon. His difficulties enabled Bragg—as Grant had feared—to bolster his embattled right.

Grant was unhappy about Sherman's and Hooker's lack of progress, but, characteristically, he blamed only Hooker. He ordered reinforcements to Sherman's sector, but Sherman gained little additional ground. Fearing that the battle would soon be halted by darkness, Grant determined to send in the Army of the Cumberland. Shortly after 3:00 P.M., he ordered to be fired the signal guns that told four of Thomas's divisions, including Wood's and Sheridan's, to move forward. "Such an immense roar I never conceived of," wrote William Smith. "All our guns together with those of the enemy all along Missionary Ridge seemed to open up at once. . . . the roll of musketry from our lines (about two miles in length) and the reply from the enemies [sic] rifle pits near the foot of the ridge, was terrific."[28]

Grant's intent was for the attackers to fight their way to the base of the mountain, penetrate Bragg's first line of defense, then halt and reorganize prior to ascending the rocky face of the ridge. But when Thomas's men achieved their breakthrough, they came under such a murderous fire from Bragg's artillery on the summit that they felt they had nowhere to go but up. On their own initiative—initially against the remonstrations of their officers—they began scaling the steep mountain wall. Peering through his binoculars, Grant was stunned, then concerned, and then angry, lest the troops be slaughtered either during their climb or after (or if) they reached the crest. "Who ordered those men up that ridge?" he supposedly asked Thomas and his subordinates. "Some one will suffer for it, if it turns out badly." No one had an answer, for no such order had been given. Finally, Major General Gordon Granger, the commander of the corps to which Wood's and Sheridan's troops belonged, spoke up. His voice quavering with emotion, he told Grant: "When these men get going, all hell can't stop them!"[29]

As they clambered up the ridge, Granger's men were protected by the sheerness of the incline from artillery fire—Bragg's gunners could not depress their pieces enough to strike them. "Regiment after regiment gained the top," observed William Smith, "and planted their colors—most of them gaining it by the many roads that passed from the valley to the top of the ridge." Once on level ground, the Federals began to clear the crest with deadly precision, driving the flabbergasted enemy from one rallying point after another. By nightfall, much to Grant's astonishment, two thousand Confederates and almost forty of their cannons had been captured; and Bragg's army, with the exception of one division, was in disorderly flight down the mountain in the direction of Ringgold Gap and Dalton. Thanks to Cleburne's against-all-odds defense, however, Grant's troops failed to mount a pursuit worthy of the name.[30]

Although he regretted his inability to overtake his opponent, Grant contented himself with the indisputable fact that Bragg's army had been shattered. A later count revealed that during the past three days the Army of Tennessee had absorbed nearly sixty-seven hundred casualties, 14 percent of its strength, as against fewer than six thousand Federal losses, 10 percent of the manpower available to Grant when the battle began. Grant suspected that when what remained of Bragg's command reached Dalton, it would lay down to die.[31]

That night, he sent Halleck word of the great victory while stressing that a relief force would soon be on its way to Knoxville. It took longer than he anticipated, however, to put the relief column in motion. At first, he assigned the task to Granger's corps of Thomas's army, but Granger failed to move out on time, and Thomas failed to prod him; this made Grant fear that Burnside, whose men were down to five or six days' rations, would be forced to surrender to Longstreet. Accordingly, Grant directed Sherman to lead the expedition. Sherman started promptly on October 29 and by December 4 was near enough to Knoxville to force Longstreet to end the siege and retreat into the mountains north of the city. There he would spend the coming winter; the following spring, he would rejoin Lee in Virginia.

For his most recent triumphs, Grant received the congratulations of his civilian superiors, who sounded more relieved by Burnside's rescue than by Bragg's defeat. On December 8, Lincoln expressed his pleasure to Grant and his soldiers: "I wish to tender you, and all under your command, my more than thanks, my profoundest gratitude for the skill, courage, and perseverance which you and they, over so great difficulties, have effected that important object. God bless you all."[32]

★ ★ ★

Grant spent a fortnight tying up business in Chattanooga. Five days before Christmas, he returned local command to General Thomas and repaired to

Nashville, "the most central point from which to communicate with [the] entire military division, and also with the authorities at Washington." In his memoirs, he declares that nothing worthy of mention occurred over the following winter. His fondest memory of this period was of being presented with a diamond-studded sword and a golden scabbard engraved with the names of the battles he had fought, a gift of the good citizens of Jo Daviess County.[33]

In early January 1864, just back from an inspection tour of Knoxville and its environs, Grant arranged with Sherman—himself recently returned from Knoxville—to put into effect, on a limited scale, the raiding strategy Sherman had proposed to Grant at the start of the Vicksburg Campaign. The plan, predicated on striking, with heavy but highly mobile forces, selected targets of strategic value instead of tying down manpower by occupying enemy territory, would influence Sherman's operations throughout the coming year. Its initial application was the Meridian Campaign of February and March, the object of which was to drive out enemy units that remained on the east bank of the Mississippi River, impeding Union navigation. The operation achieved mixed results. Although supporting movements by cavalry gotten up by General Hurlbut ended in humiliating defeat at the hands of Bedford Forrest, Sherman's forces succeeded in clearing away outposts on the Mississippi and the Big Black and devastating the rail center of Meridian, Mississippi.[34]

Grant spent part of January in Chattanooga, where he arranged a movement of some of Thomas's troops in support of Sherman's expedition. The end of the month found him in St. Louis, where he had gone to see his eldest son. Fred had contracted a virulent illness while visiting his father's headquarters during the Vicksburg Campaign, and Grant feared that when he reached Missouri he would find his firstborn dead. If so, he would experience the same self-reproach that beset Sherman, whose ten-year-old son Willie had succumbed in October to typhoid fever, contracted during an extended stay with his father in the field. Fortunately, Grant's journey had a happier ending, Fred having passed his crisis and regained his health by the time his father arrived.[35]

Grant spent a few days in St. Louis visiting old friends and attending the theater, one of his favorite diversions. When it was learned that he was in the audience, the other playgoers demanded that he stand so that he could be greeted with raucous applause. Two nights later, he was the guest of honor at a banquet attended by two hundred citizens of St. Louis. He enjoyed the dinner, but he refused to acknowledge the good wishes of the audience with anything more than a brief expression of thanks. A guest recalled that he accepted the tribute of the diners with "great modesty and evident embarrassment."[36]

Modesty aside, it must have given him great satisfaction to know that his achievements were deemed worthy of public recognition—especially as those seated at his table included his old business partner Harry Boggs and his unrepentant Rebel of a father-in-law, Colonel Dent. Ulysses Grant had come a long way since Boggs had pronounced him a failure and Dent had scorned him as unworthy of his daughter's hand. One wonders whether the crotchety Colonel recalled his late wife's dream, in which their son-in-law basked in the adulation of an adoring crowd. That once-unlikely vision had come true this evening.[37]

Accolades of a different sort awaited Grant's return to his Nashville headquarters. In January, Elihu Washburne had introduced in the House a bill to revive the long-dormant grade of lieutenant general in the United States Army. The bill, which was held up in Congress for a time but in the end passed by a healthy majority, was clearly intended to benefit one officer only. Grant's capture of Vicksburg had brought him the rank of major general in the Regular Army, but the pending promotion would give him unprecedented authority and prestige, ensuring that when the war was carried to its conclusion it would bear his imprint.[38]

Grant's nomination for three-star rank went to the U.S. Senate on March 1; it was confirmed the following day. On March 3, he was ordered to Washington to receive the commission from Lincoln himself at a White House ceremony. The next day, Grant started east accompanied by his staff. His retinue included not only Baldy Smith, for whom he proposed to find a command in Virginia, but also Fred Grant, fully recovered from his bout with sickness and looking forward to his first visit to the nation's capital. Conspicuous by his absence was Brigadier General Wilson, who had been called to the capital six weeks earlier to take charge of a relatively new War Department agency, the Cavalry Bureau.[39]

The party traveled by way of Louisville, Cincinnati, Pittsburgh, Harrisburg, and Baltimore. At various stops along the way, delegations of public officials and crowds of ordinary citizens turned out to hail the great commander. Apparently, however, when Grant reached Washington, no one met him. The oft-told story is that he arrived a day early and without fanfare, accompanied only by Fred—the rest of the party had been dropped off at various and sundry places to run errands for their boss. This may or may not be true; some sources suggest that when the train pulled into Washington, the general was accompanied by at least a few of his traveling companions.[40]

As the story goes, in keeping with Grant's unprepossessing appearance and unmilitary image—he hid his insignia of rank beneath an old coat—he carried his own bags to Willard's Hotel; there, he went unrecognized by the staff at he front desk, who assigned him a poorly furnished room on an upper floor. Only when he and Fred went down to supper did people at the next table realize they were sitting beside the most important soldier in the Union. The story ends with a roomful of well-wishers descending upon Grant and his son, neither of whom was able to finish his meal.

Later that night, Grant was whisked off to the White House, where the Lincolns were hosting an evening reception. As Bruce Catton described the scene, the guests were awed by Grant's arrival:

> The crowd parted like the Red Sea waves, leaving an open lane for him, everybody telling his neighbor that this really was General Grant, and at the far end of the lane there was Abraham Lincoln, all lanky six feet four of him. . . . Lincoln stepped forward, his hand outstretched, a smile on his face, and Grant walked toward him . . . and when the walk ended and the two men shook hands President Lincoln's three-year search for a general had ended.[41]

From the moment they met, Lincoln became Grant's guide to, and buffer against, the world of Washington politics, a world that Grant had no desire to enter. Lincoln was pleased, and relieved, to know that Grant had no desire for political advancement. He had gone to some lengths to determine this; in fact, he might not have approved Grant's promotion had the general not made his position clear. Indeed, Grant had informed his boyhood friend Daniel Ammen of his sentiments only a month earlier: "I have always thought the most slavish life any man could lead was that of a politician. Besides, I do not believe any man can be successful as a soldier whilst he has an anchor ahead for other advancement. I know of no circumstances likely to arise which could induce me to accept of any political office whatever."[42]

Lincoln's role as tour guide began when he ushered Grant through the evening's star-struck throng: He saw to it that he met everyone of note in attendance, including the First Lady, Mary Todd Lincoln, and Secretary of State William H. Seward. So that everyone in the crowd could gaze upon the honored guest, Grant, at the president's request, mounted a sofa and stood there rather like a sideshow attraction for the better part of an hour, bowing right and left and doing his best to look natural in a most unnatural setting. "For once at least the President of the United States was not the chief figure in the picture," wrote the Washington correspondent Noah Brooks. "The little, scared-looking man who stood on a crimson-covered sofa was the idol of the hour."[43]

The morning after his somewhat overwhelming introduction to official Washington, Grant returned to the Executive Mansion in company with political officials, including Congressman Washburne, for a brief ceremony formalizing his promotion. To a smaller audience than the night before, but one no less enthusiastic, Lincoln offered a few remarks, including a reminder to the warrior he was about to knight: "With this high honor devolves upon you also a corresponding responsibility. As the country herein trusts you, so, under God, it will sustain you." Grant responded with an acceptance speech equally brief and to the point, in which he acknowledged the high expectations of the country and pledged to strive mightily to meet them.[44]

Over the next twenty-four hours, Grant conferred not only with the president but also with Secretary Stanton and Grant's old superior, General Halleck, who was vacating the post of commanding general in Grant's favor while preparing to take over the lesser post of chief of staff of the army. In company with his reassembled staff, including Brigadier General Rawlins (now installed as Grant's personal chief of staff), Grant, sporting his three-star shoulder straps, confidently strode the halls of the War Department, the office that in 1861 had pigeon-holed his request for a colonel's commission.

Grant would return to the capital several times during the next six weeks for further consultations, military and political, but his first priority was to visit the Army of the Potomac in its winter camp near Brandy Station, Virginia. Early on March 10, he boarded a down train, and later that day was welcomed at General Meade's headquarters. For weeks rumor had it that if promoted to commanding general, Grant would replace Meade with a subordinate of his own choosing. Although Meade was the author of the great victory at Gettysburg, he had no later successes to his credit. He had been unable to prevent Lee from reinforcing Bragg, nor had he capitalized on Lee's weakening. Washington had been forced to prod him into taking the war to Lee's army, which was now ensconced on the south bank of the Rapidan River, its headquarters at Orange Court House. In November, Meade had finally made an attempt to envelop Lee's right flank by attacking across Mine Run, but the effort ended in embarrassing failure.[45]

The prevailing wisdom was that Lincoln had lost faith in the commander of "his" army but was unwilling to remove him unless Grant acquiesced in it. For his part, Meade, as he wrote to his wife in Philadelphia, believed that Grant had come east "indoctrinated with the notion of the superiority of western armies and that the failure of the Army of the Potomac to accomplish anything [was] due to their commanders." If so, it would not surprise Meade if high-level changes were in the offing.[46]

In fact, Grant had considered replacing Meade with someone of proven ability, well known to him, such as Baldy Smith, whom General Wilson, among others, considered Meade's tactical superior. By the time Grant came down to Brandy Station, however, he had begun to consider the effect such a change would have on an army to whom he was a stranger, a proud and sensitive command understandably resentful of outside intervention and disposed to regard Grant warily until he proved himself worthy of his third star.

Grant's thinking underwent further alteration after he conferred with Meade, who began by assuring his visitor that he would promptly and without complaint step down in favor of anyone Grant wished to place over him and would serve faithfully in any capacity Grant considered him qualified to fill. Disarmed by the obvious sincerity of Meade's gesture, Grant immediately decided to keep him in command. He spent the rest of his visit giving Meade a broad outline of his plans for the mammoth (120,000-man) Army of the Potomac and receiving a brief tour of its area of operations. Grant also called on some of Meade's subordinates, members of the army's II, V, and VI Corps (Burnside's IX Corps would be added to the command before the spring campaign began, but because its commander was senior to Meade, initially he would report directly to Grant). In time, Grant would come to know well, and form decided opinions about, the commanders of the other corps—respectively, Major Generals Winfield Scott Hancock, Gouverneur K. Warren, and John Sedgwick.

On his first visit to Brandy Station, Grant renewed his acquaintance with a few officers who had served with him in the West or in the prewar Regulars. One of the most cherished of these was his West Point classmate, Brigadier General Rufus Ingalls, quartermaster general of Meade's army. Another with whom he had served long ago was Meade's chief of artillery, Brigadier General Henry Jackson Hunt, the older brother of Lewis Cass Hunt, Grant's comrade at Fort Humboldt.

Hunt reminded Grant that they had last met shortly after the fall of Mexico City when both were junior lieutenants. On that day, the artillerist recalled, Grant had asked Hunt to corroborate his recent heroics at the San Cosme gate—they had escaped the attention of his immediate superior and would therefore be left out of his official report of the action. Hunt had disappointed his colleague by pleading that he, too, had overlooked Lieutenant Grant's feat, although he did not doubt it had taken place as Grant described. Grant had been disconsolate: "The war is nearly done," he lamented. "So there goes the last chance I shall ever have of military distinction." It now appeared, as Hunt wryly suggested, that Grant had been unduly pessimistic.[47]

★ ★ ★

Returning to Washington after his visit with Meade, Grant tackled some command and personnel issues, including his own place in the spring campaign.

Before coming east to receive his promotion, he had intended to return to the headquarters of his Military Division of the Mississippi. This course was strongly urged on him by Sherman, who believed that if Grant remained in the East he would be forever troubled by politicians looking over his shoulder and either questioning or dictating his every move. Yet almost from the time he set foot in the capital, Grant saw that it "was the point for the commanding general to be." He added: "No one else could, probably, resist the pressure that would be brought to bear upon him to desist from his own plans and pursue others." He would return to the West, but only for brief consultations with the men who would take over for him: "I determined, therefore, before I started back to have Sherman advanced to my late position, McPherson to Sherman's in command of the department [of West Tennessee], and Logan to the command of McPherson's corps. These changes were all made on my recommendation and without hesitation."[48]

His decision to stay in the eastern theater would create a dual command situation. Although Meade would retain operational as well as nominal command of the Army of the Potomac, Grant would travel with it, making the strategic decisions that Meade and his subordinates would execute at the tactical level. Given his future proximity to Meade's headquarters, Grant resolved to make personnel changes. To begin with, he wanted a new commander for the army's cavalry, which since before Gettysburg had been led by Major General Alfred Pleasonton, a flashy personality but a middling tactician who had never won the confidence of his superior or the respect of his troopers. Consequently, Meade's cavalry had consistently underachieved. Although they had made a quantum leap in experience and ability since the war's beginning, the horsemen of the Army of the Potomac still appeared to be overmatched by the cavaliers of the Army of Northern Virginia under the dashing James Ewell Brown Stuart.

During early talks with Lincoln and Halleck, Grant accepted the latter's suggestion that the able, aggressive, and charismatic Phil Sheridan—who enjoyed mounted as well as infantry experience—be called from Tennessee to Virginia. To the same arm, Grant added another energetic and versatile officer whom he knew well. Through his intercession, Wilson was transferred from the Cavalry Bureau to head one of the three divisions in Sheridan's new command.[49]

If Meade was to retain his position, what should be done with Baldy Smith, who had been promised a field command in Virginia? During his early days in the capital, Grant learned from various sources that Smith's unseemly intriguing against Burnside had not faded from the corporate memory of the Army of the Potomac, many of whose officers considered him a "perfect Ishmaelite." Grant nevertheless remained committed to placing Smith in a position of some prominence and gaining for him the second star that the Senate had denied him. He succeeded on both counts: Smith was reappointed a major general to rank from early March, and Stanton and Halleck permitted him to become second-in-command of the smaller Union army that would operate in Virginia during the coming campaign.[50]

This was the Army of the James. Eventually thirty-six thousand strong, it was led by a politician-general even more notorious than John McClernand: Benjamin Franklin Butler, a former Massachusetts congressman who had become one of the war's earliest, and least likely, heroes. A shrewd lawyer and adept administrator, but a military amateur, in 1861 he had made a name as the occupier of secessionist-leaning Baltimore; then as the captor of Hatteras Inlet, North Carolina; and, from April to December 1862, as the military governor of occupied New Orleans. Butler's repressive policies had cost him his job in Louisiana, but had won the approval of hard-war advocates across the North.

By late 1863, Butler's standing as one of the country's most influential War Democrats had impelled Lincoln, who coveted the man's support in the coming presidential campaign, to return him to field command. Butler's role in the spring campaign was to advance on Richmond from the Virginia Peninsula, either to capture the city outright or to join with Meade—once the latter drove Lee's army from the Rapidan to the James—in besieging the Rebel capital.[51]

Because Butler was the only nonprofessional soldier to lead more than a single corps (his army would embrace the X Corps, to be brought up from Charleston and the XVIII, composed of troops formerly in garrison on the Peninsula), Stanton and Halleck desired that his ranking subordinates should be West Pointers. Major General Quincy Adams Gillmore (Class of 1849) would lead the troops from South Carolina, and the XVIII Corps would go to Smith.

On April 1–2, when Grant paid his initial visit to Butler's headquarters at Fort Monroe, Smith was there; the three officers worked out a preliminary blueprint of operations for the peninsula army. Smith was silent for much of the conference, but Grant was surprised to find Butler not only voluble but strategically acute. In the end, he substantially adopted Butler's carefully crafted plan to move his army—simultaneous with Meade's advance against Lee—up the James River, debarking at Bermuda Hundred, a peninsula formed by the James and the Appomattox Rivers about twelve miles below Richmond—and, once his base of operations was secure, advancing overland against the town Jeff Davis called home.[52]

On April 3, Grant left Butler to return to his newly established headquarters at Culpeper, six miles southwest of Brandy Station. There he assembled his expanded staff, briefed its members on some of his plans that had been taking form in his head, and discussed with them the most effective way of interfacing with Meade's staff. Grant now had at his beck and call a coterie of young professionals who were passionately committed to translating his commands into action. Gone were the old cronies like Hillyer and Lagow, who would rather drink and gamble than carry a dispatch across a shell-blasted battlefield or ride all night through rain and mud to inspect a distant outpost.

The staff of the Commander of the Armies of the United States included a few leftovers such as Chief of Staff Rawlins and Adjutant General Bowers, but it abounded in newcomers such as Lieutenant Colonels Cyrus B. Comstock, Orville E. Babcock, and Horace Porter (three "honor Graduates of West Point, of excellent character and first-class ability each in his own line," in the words of James Wilson). Other new faces included the bronzed mien of Captain Ely S. Parker, a full-blooded Seneca sachem and trained engineer who served as Grant's military secretary; Lieutenant Colonel Adam Badeau, the prissy, pedantic ex-newspaperman who handled Grant's personal correspondence; the lanky Captain Henry W. Janes, headquarters quartermaster; and the stocky Lieutenant Colonel Michael R. Morgan, chief commissary of subsistence. Men of varying backgrounds and experience, they would in time form a cohesive, well-integrated team of coadjutors on whom Grant would unhesitatingly rely.[53]

Between mid-March and the close of April, the lieutenant general regularly traveled to and from Washington, honing his strategic vision in consultation with the lords of the War Department. The dominant theme to emerge from these skull sessions was the necessity of closely coordinating the operations of the sundry forces under Grant's command, which comprised more than half a million officers and men. It struck Grant that unity of action had never been attempted at any time during this war. Could it be achieved, the Confederacy, with its limited resources, would be hard-pressed to assemble enough mobile resources to counter it. He proposed to capitalize on that deficiency by projecting simultaneous advances on several fronts by armies cooperating with one another across great distances.

As per Grant vision, while Meade and Butler operated, respectively, against Lee's army and Richmond, other armies would advance toward carefully chosen objectives in Georgia, West Virginia, and the Shenandoah Valley. At the head of three of those armies (McPherson's Army of the Tennessee, Thomas's Army of the Cumberland, and the Army of the Ohio, now led by John Schofield), Sherman would advance from Chattanooga toward the industrial and rail center of Atlanta, en route engaging the reinforced and reorganized Army of Tennessee, now under Joe Johnston. In the Shenandoah, a Union force entrusted to Major General Franz Sigel would drive up (i.e., southward through) the Valley toward Staunton, opening the "Breadbasket of the Confederacy" to occupation, confiscation, and destruction, while safeguarding the all-important Baltimore & Ohio Railroad. Farther west, Major General George Crook was to advance from Charles Town, West Virginia, and disrupt a rail line equally valuable to the enemy, the Virginia & Tennessee, before moving against the supply depots in and around Lynchburg, Virginia. Grant would have liked to add Nathaniel Banks's command to this strategic equation for a drive against Mobile; but the commander of the Department of the Gulf was already heavily involved in the ill-starred Red River Campaign, which was fated to fall well short of Lincoln's dream of an occupied Texas. Grant hoped, at some future point, to add expeditions against Mobile as well as other as-yet-unthreatened points in the Confederate interior; but because his superiors were not as anxious to venture into such distant reaches, these operations would be delayed for almost a year.[54]

To activate to the fullest the cooperative spirit of his many subordinates, Grant visited some of the more far-flung points in his domain. In late March, he returned to Nashville for a strategy conference with Sherman. The old friends developed a methodology for long-distance cooperation, one Grant knew Sherman would strive to execute. He felt deeply indebted to Sherman, as he did to James McPherson, for the unflagging support they had provided him thus far. Upon learning that Lincoln had submitted his name to fill the position of lieutenant general, Grant had written the two subordinates: "I want to express my thanks to you and McPherson, as the men to whom, above all others, I feel indebted for whatever I have had of success." Both men had replied with becoming modesty and in a spirit of true friendship. Grant was confident that in their newly elevated positions they would push the war in the West to a successful conclusion.

He owed his biggest debt to Sherman. Although he regretted his inability to heed his friend's well-intentioned advice to avoid political entanglements ("for God's sake and for your country's sake, come out of Washington"), he fully endorsed the man's operational suggestions. He gave Sherman free rein: "You I propose to move against Johnston's army, to break it up, and to get into the interior of the enemy's country as far as you can, inflicting all the damage you can against their war resources." With these words, Grant approved the large-scale raiding strategy Sherman had been fine-tuning for months and hungered to apply to the operations in Georgia.[55]

In these and other ways, Grant emphasized that Sherman enjoyed his full support in making his campaign the death blow of the western Confederacy. Upon returning to Washington, Grant received a similar pledge from his commander in chief. Up to the commencement of active operations, every time general and president met, Lincoln restated his determination to sustain Grant in all possible ways and against all opposition. He made this intention clear in a letter he sent to Grant's headquarters only days before the Army of the Potomac broke camp and headed south to oppose Robert E. Lee:

> I wish to express in this way my entire satisfaction with what you have done, up to this time, so far as I understand it. The particulars of your plans I neither know or seek to know. You are vigilant and self-reliant; and, pleased with this, I wish not to obtrude any constraints or restraints upon you. . . . If there is anything wanting which is within my power to give, do not fail to let me know it. And now with a brave army, and a just cause, may God sustain you.[56]

Grant heartily returned the president's expressions of high regard and unshakable confidence: "Should my success be less than I desire, and expect, the least I can say is, the fault is not with you." Unlike his predecessors in command here in Virginia, Grant did not regard loyalty as flowing in only one direction. Any success enjoyed by Union arms during the coming campaign would be his; it was only right that any blame for failure would accrue to him as well. He would not try to shift the responsibility to the man who had made him the highest-ranking officer in the United States Army since George Washington.

★ *Chapter 11* ★

No Turning Back

AFTER CONSULTING WITH MEADE, GRANT DECIDED THAT IT WOULD BE folly to attack Lee in his strong defensive works below the Rapidan; nor would it be possible to turn Lee's right along Mine Run as Meade had failed to do in the fall. The Army of the Potomac must cross well upstream or downstream from Lee's position, then head toward Richmond. That would force him out of his position, either to follow the invaders or to fight them.

When May brought warmer weather and drier roads, Grant grappled with the question of whether the army should cross the Rapidan by its right or its left flank. Both routes had advantages and drawbacks. If Meade moved by his right, crossing west of the Rebels, the angle of his advance would block Lee from moving north to attack his enemy's capital should he choose not to protect his own. This route, however, would place Lee between Meade and Butler and thus prevent the Armies of the Potomac and the James from joining forces against Richmond; it would also leave Meade's communications vulnerable, forcing the Army of the Potomac to carry all its rations, forage, and supplies. If Meade crossed the river by his left flank, the many waterways he would encounter on the way to the James would help support the building and maintaining of supply lines. But this route would remove the barrier between the Confederates and Washington, a prohibition that had been a major element of Union planning since the war's start.[1]

Grant, believing that Lee could not afford to leave his own capital exposed, decided to have Meade move by the left. The ability to safeguard its seat of government gave legitimacy to a fledgling nation such as the Confederacy, which had yet to establish itself as a viable entity in the eyes of much of the world. If Richmond fell, the Confederacy was likely to fall with it. Militarily, the loss of Richmond would cost Lee's army its base of operations and supply, dooming it to wander west or south in search of a nonexistent sanctuary. Jeff Davis's favorite general would not permit this.

The final, extended campaign of the war in the East got underway when the Army of the Potomac broke camp and marched toward the Rapidan just after midnight on May 4, 1864. By starting at such an early hour, Grant hoped to make substantial progress before Lee detected his advance and perhaps advanced to meet it. Immediately below the Rapidan was the Wilderness, that seemingly unending tract of scrub oak, second-growth pine, and devilishly entangled thicket that exactly one year earlier had cost Joe Hooker a battle, his reputation, and very nearly his army. Should Lee react to Grant's strategy by abandoning his defenses and giving battle in the forest, the Army of the Potomac's two-to-one edge in strength would be neutralized. The foliage below the river was so thick and constricting that infantry would be unable to mass; cavalry would be brought to a standstill; and artillery would lack adequate fields of fire. Grant's strategy was a gamble, but one he believed worth taking.

The magnitude of the gamble may have cost Grant some sleep; at the least, it preyed on his mind. As he wrote to Julia on May 2: "I know the greatest anxiety is now felt in the North for the success of this move, and that the anxiety will increase when it is once known that the Army is in motion. . . . [I] do not know that this is any criterion to judge results because I have never felt otherwise." Lest she misconstrue his habitual anxiety as paralyzing fear, he added a half-serious, half-jocular observation: "I believe it has never been my misfortune to be placed where I lost my presence of mind, unless indeed it has been when thrown in strange company, particularly of ladies. Under such circumstances I know I must appear like a fool."[2]

In the early morning darkness of May 4, Meade's army marched, trotted, and trundled south in two columns. The western column was led by Warren's V Corps; it was preceded by Wilson's division of Sheridan's cavalry corps and followed by the VI Corps of John Sedgwick. It would cross at Germanna Ford, eight miles below Lee's position. Six miles farther east, Hancock's II Corps, shielded by the horsemen of Brigadier General David McMurtrie Gregg, would cross at Ely's Ford. Behind Hancock came the almost three hundred artillery pieces of the army under the overall supervision of General Hunt. In the rear of both columns came four thousand densely packed supply wagons, protected by the cavalry of Brigadier General Alfred Torbert. Well to the rear was Burnside's IX Corps, which had been guarding Meade's principal supply line, the Orange & Alexandria Railroad. Burnside's troops would remain in their camps near Warrenton until the rest of the army completed crossing and opened the roads for their use.[3]

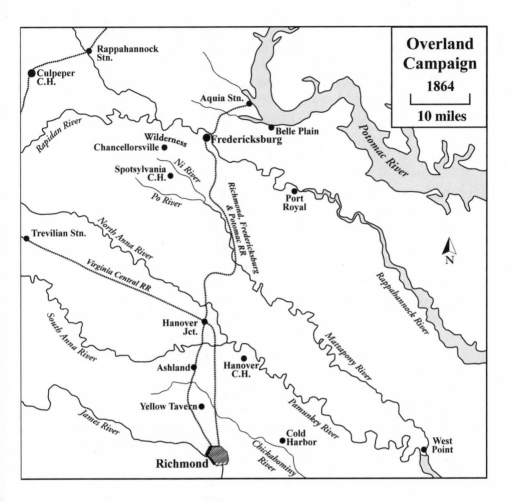

Overland
Campaign
1864

10 miles

Rappahannock
Stn.

Culpeper
C.H.

Aquia Stn.

Belle Plain

Rapidan River

Wilderness
Chancellorsville

Fredericksburg

Ni River

Spotsylvania
C.H.

Po River

Richmond, Fredericksburg & Potomac RR

Port
Royal

Potomac River

Trevilian Stn.

North Anna River

Virginia Central RR

Rappahannock River

N

South Anna River

Hanover
Jct.

Ashland

Hanover
C.H.

Mattapony River

Yellow Tavern

Pamunkey River

James River

Cold
Harbor

West
Point

Richmond

Chickahominy River

At about 4:00 A.M., Wilson's troopers reached Germanna Ford, which they cleared of enemy pickets, permitting Meade's engineers to lay a canvas-topped pontoon bridge atop the water. Within three hours, Warren's corps was crossing the floating bridge to the south side. At approximately the same time, Hancock's soldiers began to cross at Ely's Ford on a portable wooden bridge. At 5:00 A.M., General Meade joined his army on the march. Three hours later, Grant and his staff broke camp at Culpeper and headed for Germanna Ford. Chomping on his ubiquitous cigar, Grant trotted south aboard Cincinnati, a magnificent war horse, powerfully built and seventeen hands high. The deathbed gift of a St. Louis admirer of Grant's following the battles outside Chattanooga, the stallion was the son of Lexington, a celebrated thoroughbred who had run the fastest four miles ever recorded up to that time.[4]

At about noon, Cincinnati bore his rider across the river and into the trees on the south bank. Almost as soon as they reached dry ground, Grant was handed a message from one of the army's signal stations. According to an intercepted dispatch, the Second Corps of Lee's army under Lieutenant General Richard Ewell (who had expedited Grant's transfer from Jefferson Barracks to Louisiana in 1844) was approaching along the Orange Turnpike, one of very few east-west roads that cut through the Wilderness. Evidently, Lee was not about to allow his enemy to move unmolested around his flank. If he wished to slug it out in the woods, Grant would have to oblige, for Meade, who could not afford to move too far ahead of his trains, would not clear the Wilderness until tomorrow. Concerned that he must concentrate his forces, Grant sent a message to Burnside ordering him to move with all speed to and across Germanna Ford.[5]

By midafternoon, the army appeared to have made good progress. Warren's and Sedgwick's soldiers were grouped just west of Wilderness Tavern; almost five miles to the east, Hancock's men had reached the strategic crossroads known as Chancellorsville, not far from the edge of the woods. In these locations, the army spent the balance of the day waiting for the ponderous wagons to close up. Grant had no desire to abort an offensive for the second time in two and a half years because of a strike against his source of supply. That was the sort of thing one might expect of James Ewell Brown Stuart, an even bolder raiding leader than Earl Van Dorn.

Meade's march resumed just before dawn on May 5. Although most of Warren's corps passed south of Wilderness Tavern, one of its divisions, Brigadier General Charles Griffin's, remained on the Orange Pike facing toward the reported location of Ewell's Confederates. Sedgwick's corps followed Warren's main body, while Hancock moved southwest from Chancellorsville toward a junction with both of his colleagues. Burnside's troops were still on the north side of the river, closing up on Germanna Ford.[6]

About 7:30 A.M., a courier from Meade alerted Grant that Griffin's men had made contact with a body of the enemy that appeared to be forming lines of battle across the turnpike. Meade had ordered Warren to send Griffin forward to the attack while the rest of the V Corps formed farther south. It sounded like a simple maneuver, but the trees and brush were so thick that it took more than five hours for Meade to communicate with Warren and for Griffin to organize an attack column.

When it was finally launched at 1:00 P.M., the assault produced the first clash of arms between Grant, the preeminent hero of the Union, and Lee, the Confederacy's finest field general. Griffin, as Grant later put it, attacked "with favorable though not decisive results." The effort drove in Ewell's leading division, but it rallied, counterattacked, and shoved Griffin back in turn. The tangled woods quickly filled with the crackle of musketry and the roar of artillery, most of the salvos shattering tree trunks and severing branches instead of striking enemy soldiers.[7]

Griffin's repulse led to an ironic scene featuring Grant, who was known for his equanimity under stress, and the often excitable Meade. Incensed that Brigadier General Horatio G. Wright's division of the VI Corps had failed to come to his support until almost too late, Griffin rode to army headquarters, where he sought out Meade, and—oblivious to Grant's presence within earshot—began to curse his colleague's incapacity and that of the army in general. Griffin's tirade was so laden with venom and so sweepingly critical that both Grant and John Rawlins, who also heard it, considered the outburst prejudicial to good conduct and perhaps even mutinous. When Griffin stalked off, Grant angrily suggested that Meade relieve him from command and then arrest him. But Meade—perhaps because of his own temper problems—habitually made allowances for his subordinates' tantrums. He managed to calm Grant down, insisting that it was "only his way of talking." No action was taken against Griffin who, despite wearing his emotions on his sleeve was, as Grant would learn, an able leader and a good man.[8]

With the exception of this incident, Grant kept his composure throughout the day. The object of Griffin's ire, General Wright, had been a comrade of Grant's in the West before coming to Virginia to take a division under Meade. He had been slow to support Griffin because he had been ambushed en route to the battlefield by the tree-shielded Rebel infantry, including the celebrated Stonewall Brigade. At one point, the Rebels had rushed Wright's field headquarters, capturing several members of his staff and, as Grant feared, Wright himself. Shortly after the assault had been repulsed, Grant came upon the division leader and hailed him with a cheery "Hello, Wright, I thought you had gone to Richmond"—meaning, to prison in the enemy capital. When Wright explained otherwise, Grant replied matter-of-factly: "All right. I guess you'll fix up things properly." To Wright, the exchange demonstrated that Grant "didn't seem to be a bit shaken," a pleasant contrast to the often agitated, impulsive Meade. "He was just the man," Wright added, that "we needed" when the battle hung in the balance and the army was under extreme stress.[9]

Lieutenant Colonel Horace Porter was similarly impressed by Grant's coolness under pressure. While the fighting raged on the first day, Grant stayed mainly at his field headquarters, where he was easily accessible to his subordinates:

> He would at times walk slowly up and down [the aide reported], but most of the day he sat upon the stump of a tree, or on the ground, with his back leaning against a tree. . . . a lighted cigar was in his mouth almost constantly, and his penknife was kept in active use whittling sticks. He would pick up one small twig after another, and sometimes holding the small end away from him would rapidly shave it down to a point; at other times he would turn the point toward him and work on it as if sharpening a lead-pencil; then he would girdle it, cut it in two, throw it away, and begin on another.[10]

The commanding general appeared impervious to rumor, good or bad. Porter recalled one general officer, whom he refused to identify, who came running to Grant's tent "laboring under considerable excitement." The officer was convinced that a terrible crisis was at hand; he claimed to know, from long experience, Lee's methods: "He will throw his whole army between us and the Rapidan, and cut us off completely from our communications," he reported breathlessly. Porter saw Grant rise, face the general, and slowly remove his cigar so that he spoke clearly and with emphasis: "I am heartily tired of hearing about what Lee is going to do. Some of you always seem to think he is suddenly going to turn a double somersault, and land in our rear and on both of our flanks at the same time. Go back to your command, and try to think what we are going to do ourselves, instead of what Lee is going to do!"[11]

★ ★ ★

As Grant spoke, the battle expanded with the arrival of two of the divisions in Lieutenant General A. P. Hill's Third Corps, Army of Northern Virginia. The Confederates advanced up the Orange Plank Road, south of and parallel to the Orange Pike, scattered Wilson's isolated cavalry, then plowed into the head of the VI Corps. Brigadier General George W. Getty's division of Sedgwick's command arrived barely in time to secure a vital crossroads clearing, the intersection of the Orange Plank Road and the Brock Road, but Getty's men had to fight like demons to hold their ground. Not until late in the afternoon did Hancock's troops—who had moved south of the scene of fighting until recalled north by Grant—reach the field and form on Getty's left. At bout 4:00 P.M., two II Corps divisions went forward to add their weight to the fight at the crossroads.

The confused and desperate fighting that gyrated across turnpike and plank road and over the two-mile stretch in between ranked among the fiercest the Army of the Potomac had ever experienced. One Federal later described it as "simply bushwhacking on a grand scale in brush where all formation beyond that of regiments or companies was soon lost, and where such a thing as a constant line of battle on either side was impossible." Casualties ran unusually high on both sides even though it was difficult for a man to get a clear shot at his foe. Among the slain was Brigadier General Alexander Hays, one of Grant's closest comrades in the prewar army who, in this war, had distinguished himself in many battles, but especially on the third day at Gettysburg. Grant eulogized the II Corps brigade leader in these words: "He was a most gallant officer, ready to lead his command wherever ordered. With him it was 'Come, boys,' not 'Go.'"[12]

The fighting raged at white heat until well after dark. By then both armies had launched numerous attacks and counterattacks. Each had run out of steam or been repulsed with heavy loss, as a summary of the final actions of the day indicates. Meade's attempt to outflank Ewell's corps and reach its rear had failed; Hill's effort to capture the Brock Road intersection had been beaten back—barely; Warren's 7:00 P.M. attack on Hill's left flank had been halted just short of success; and Hancock's 8:00 P.M. assault on Hill's other flank had been curtailed by darkness. For all their movements and countermovements, when the fighting petered out in the night the armies held approximately the same positions they had occupied at the start of the fighting. A second day of attack and counterattack, death and devastation would be needed to settle the issue.[13]

The fighting of May 6 began at about 4:00 A.M. when one of Ewell's divisions, Major General Jubal Anderson Early's, attacked Sedgwick's troops along the turnpike, only to be thrown back bloodily. Promptly at 5:00 A.M., on Grant's orders, Hancock's corps and one of Warren's divisions went forward on either side of the plank road. Initially, Hancock's thrust was dramatically successful, Hill's troops being driven westward for more than a mile. Hancock's gains, added to those of the V Corps, which struck Hill's left, and the advance of Burnside's late-arriving IX Corps into the area between turnpike and plank road, for a time threatened to cut Lee's army in two.

Just as it appeared the Army of Northern Virginia was doomed, Longstreet's First Corps, which had made a grueling, all-night march from the far Confederate left at Gordonsville, arrived by way of the plank road. Grant's West Point cohort and poker partner assisted Hill in neutralizing the threat to his left, then met and slowed Hancock's and Burnside's advances. At about 10:00 A.M., a lull settled over this portion of the field as both Longstreet and his opponents re-formed for further offensive action.[14]

An hour later, Longstreet's well-aligned ranks sprang to the attack. He sent four brigades south of the plank road and along a railroad cut toward the lower flank of the II Corps while pressing straight ahead with the body of his command. The two-pronged offensive achieved surprise and at first gained considerable ground—for a time Lee had hopes of rolling up the Union left. But then Longstreet's men became entangled with Hills's, costing the attack much of its momentum, and Longstreet himself fell severely wounded. He would require five months of recuperation before able to re-take the field.[15]

Another lull in the fighting ensued, during which Grant had Meade called for counterattacks by Hancock and Burnside. Before either commander could go forward, however, Lee personally led Longstreet's corps in another assault on Hancock's position. Again the effort was initially successful, but it eventually ran out of steam. This time, the attackers were stymied by strongly built breastworks of logs that their opponents had erected along the Brock Road. Sparks from rifles and cannon discharges had set fire to dry leaves and twigs on both sides of these barriers; soon the works were engulfed in flames, a blaze that facilitated their defense. The same fires ravaged the ground between the armies, where hundreds of wounded men lay, many immobilized by their injuries. Informal truces were called throughout the day so that rescue teams could drag their injured comrades to safety; nonetheless, dozens perished horribly because they were unable to escape the advance of the flames.[16]

Although halted at the log works, elsewhere Lee's attack succeeded in routing a II Corps division. Again, success appeared to be in the grasp of the Army of Northern Virginia, but the Confederates could not hold it. Hancock rushed up reserves that parried Lee's thrust, and Burnside's units finally made their presence felt by striking the upper flank of the attacking force. Although Burnside was eventually forced to withdraw, so was Lee. The dual retreats ended the major action of this day, although small-unit fighting raged until well after dark.[17]

By then, both armies were bone-tired and woozy from blood loss. The Army of the Potomac, which had initiated the fighting and had maintained the offensive throughout both days, had suffered considerably more than its opponent. Its losses were later estimated at 17,700. Lee's losses, never officially tabulated, were estimated to be about 7,500, although Union veterans insisted they were much higher.

The bloodletting had a profound effect on Grant, who had not witnessed battle at such close quarters since Shiloh.

> It was noticed [Horace Porter remarked] that he was visibly affected by his proximity to the wounded, and especially by the sight of blood. He would turn his face away from such scenes, and show by the expression of his countenance, and sometimes by a pause in his conversation, that he felt most keenly the painful spectacle presented by the field of battle. Some reference was made to the subject in camp that evening, and the general said: "I cannot bear the sight of suffering."[18]

James H. Wilson would claim in print that at some point in the battle Grant, overwhelmed by the carnage and especially by the deaths caused by fire, "went into his tent, and, throwing himself face downward on his cot, gave way to the greatest emotion but without uttering any word of doubt or discouragement," thus disproving the myth that he was "the stolid and indifferent man, without sensibility or emotion." Wilson admitted that the story had come to him secondhand. Grant could well have behaved as he described, but the underlying cause is open to question. Grant's distress may have had physical as well as emotional origins. Throughout May 5 and 6, he had suffered acutely from migraines. That malady sometimes drove him to his bed, where for hours he would writhe in agony.[19]

When Wilson encountered his commander early on May 7, his cavalry division was in desperate shape, having barely escaped destruction when cut off by Hill's infantry and, later in the fight, when nearly surrounded by Stuart's horsemen. Wilson knew his was not the only command to have suffered severely; the entire army was reeling after two terrible days of combat in this godforsaken forest. Grant's protégé—in common with many another officer and man in blue—wondered whether they would all be returning to the north side of the Rapidan to catch their breath, salve their wounds, and plan a new effort against Lee. Most of Grant's predecessors, including Meade after Mine Run, had done just that. Would the new man continue the pattern?

Wilson need not have worried. When he approached Grant's headquarters that morning, he observed the commanding general, hand upraised, advancing to meet him. Before Wilson reined in, Grant, as if anticipating the question, exclaimed: "It's all right, Wilson, the army is moving toward Richmond!" And so it was. Meade's troops had been fought to a standstill, but so had Lee's—in Grant's book, being stalemated did not mean being stymied. Besides, a retreat would have flown in the face of Grant's boyhood aversion to turning back, a course that invited failure.[20]

Already, in fact, Meade had gained a notable advantage. "Our victory," Grant wrote, "consisted in having successfully crossed a formidable stream, almost in the face of an enemy, and in getting the army together as a unit." As a unit it must now move on, breaking contact with Lee and trying to find another path around his right in the direction of Richmond. Within hours of Wilson's visit to Grant's headquarters, Meade's soldiers would be trudging south and east toward their next port of call, Spotsylvania Court House.[21]

★ ★ ★

On the afternoon of May 7, while the army rested after its exertions of the past two days, Grant heard from Washington that at least two other major offensives had gotten off to a promising start. In northern Georgia, Sherman had attacked Johnston, driving the Confederates along Tunnel Hill Ridge; while below the James, Butler had moved his army by water to City Point, a landing on the Appomattox River about nine miles northeast of Petersburg and sixteen miles below Richmond, which he occupied as a staging area for his movement against the Confederate capital.[22]

Soon it was time for the Army of the Potomac to hit the road. Early that evening, it left its woodland bivouacs for the open ground around Spotsylvania, Warren and Hancock by the most direct route, the Brock Road, Sedgwick and Burnside by paths farther east. The columns would unite at a crossroads west of the courthouse, one of whose radii led to Richmond.

Despite Grant's and Meade's careful planning, the movement got off to an unpropitious start. Because Meade believed the lower reaches of the Brock Road were unobstructed, he ordered most of Sheridan's horsemen—then located at Todd's Tavern, near the southeastern edge of the Wilderness, scene of a major action that day with Stuart's cavaliers—to advance down that thoroughfare. While Torbert's and Gregg's divisions (the former now headed by Brigadier General Wesley Merritt) spearheaded Warren's and

Hancock's advance, Wilson's troopers would move crosscountry to Spotsylvania, holding the village until the main army joined it. But although the V Corps started out at 8:30 P.M. on May 7, Meade did not give Merritt and Gregg their marching orders until after midnight on May 8. Moreover, the dispositions he called for conflicted sharply with Sheridan's plans for his command.

The Meade-Sheridan conflict would cause tempers to flare, but it was the resistance of Stuart's horsemen, fighting dismounted, that crossed up Grant's strategy. Shortly after dawn, they brought the army's advance to a standstill. Warren's footsoldiers came down the narrow tree-lined road to find their way blocked by horses and riders, mounted artillery, and some of Sheridan's wagons. At Warren's strident, expletive-laden protest, Meade had Sheridan's people clear the way so that the infantry could forge ahead. Slowly but surely, Warren's column pushed Stuart's dismounted troopers out of its path, opening the way to Spotsylvania.[23]

Shortly after noon, when Sheridan caught up with Meade, the ill-suited pair lashed out at each other within earshot of officers and men. Meade accused Sheridan of botching his troopers' advance, and Sheridan scored his superior for giving orders to his subordinates without his knowledge or permission. The clash ended with Sheridan's heated claim that if Meade would cease meddling in its affairs, the cavalry would head for Richmond and draw Stuart into a finish fight.[24]

When Grant learned of the shouting match, he was troubled. In only a few days of campaigning, he had witnessed or had had brought to his attention several confrontations involving senior subordinates. The arguments confirmed his preconceived notion that the Army of the Potomac was riven by cliquishness and internal dissent. He was especially disturbed by Warren's shrill and profane outburst of that morning, which suggested emotional instability. Grant was also concerned with Warren's slow response to some of the orders given him during the previous two days; indeed, his tardiness had compromised the effectiveness of the assaults his corps had launched. Grant was similarly troubled by the glacial pace at which Burnside had moved the IX Corps to within striking range of the enemy. Such behavior contrasted markedly with the speed, power, and well-coordinated efficiency of Hancock's and Sedgwick's operations on May 5 and 6.

Grant sided with Sheridan in his confrontation with Meade. Late on May 8, he gave the cavalry leader permission to cut loose from the army and make good on his boast to beat Stuart. Grant reasoned that even if "Little Phil" merely lured his opponent into pursuing him, Stuart's detaching would compromise Lee's ability to detect and counter Meade's next move while also limiting the possibility of an attack on Meade's trains. The following morning, Sheridan's entire corps started for Richmond by detouring around the army's left flank, its elated leader riding proudly at its head.[25]

Meade's interference with Sheridan's plans for May 8 had left unguarded a bridge over the Po River that enabled the vanguard of the Army of Northern Virginia—two divisions under Major General Richard H. Anderson, Longstreet's designated successor—to reach Spotsylvania Court House after Wilson's arrival but before Warren came up to support him. The result was that Wilson's troopers were again roughly handled and forced to retreat. When word reached him that Yankee infantry were heading his way along the Brock Road, Anderson built a line two miles northwest of the court house. For the second time that day, Warren's column was brought to a halt by a gray roadblock.[26]

Anderson's stubborn defense of his position foreshadowed the success Lee's army was to enjoy over the next nine days in denying Union access to the strategic crossroads. By the morning of May 9, after both armies had dug in along a several-mile line, Meade's army found itself facing Anderson on the left; Ewell in the center, north of the crossroads, inside a U-shaped salient; and Early on the right. (The latter had taken over for A. P. Hill, temporarily incapacitated by illness). The next morning, Grant had Meade attack the Confederate left center with the troops of Warren, Hancock, and Horatio Wright, who had succeeded to the command of the VI Corps following the death by sniper fire of John Sedgwick the previous afternoon. At first, the Federals gained much ground and Grant was elated. Employing novel tactics predicated on speed of maneuver rather than brute strength, early that evening Colonel Emory Upton's brigade of Wright's corps broke through Ewell's "Mule Shoe" salient, overran several lines of defense, and took hundreds of prisoners. But Upton's success proved temporary; failing to gain the support needed to sustain momentum, his men were forced to withdraw to their starting point.[27]

On May 11, the day he sent Washington a dispatch proclaiming his intent to "fight it out on this line if it takes all summer," Grant determined to attack the same sector that Upton had penetrated but with a heavier force. Before daylight the next morning, Hancock's entire corps, supported by most of the army, assaulted the Mule Shoe in a misty rain. Within minutes, Ewell's salient was caving in under the weight of a raging blue torrent. But instead of filing off to right and left, expanding its penetration as Upton's lighter force had done, Hancock's column plowed straight ahead and became jammed up in the narrow confines of the salient. While confusion reigned in the Union ranks, Early's troops on the right fell back to take cover behind a prepared line of defense. They poured a vicious fire into Hancock's front and left flank, effectively halting the advance. Then Lee committed reserve forces that steadily forced the II Corps back to the entrenchments it had seized inside the Mule Shoe.[28]

Under a now-steady rain, Hancock held onto the trench line but found no opportunity to recover the ground he had given up. Late-day assaults by Warren and Wright, ordered by Grant, failed to achieve a breakthrough, although some elements of the VI Corps grappled hand-to-hand at bayonet point with the defenders of the "Bloody Angle," where the line of trenches made a sharp bend to the south. An oak tree between the opposing forces was cut in two by a torrent of rifle balls and a section of a disputed breastwork was so riddled that a Confederate officer described it as "whipped into basket-stuff." At least one historian has described the fighting in this sector as "probably the most desperate engagement in the history of modern warfare."[29]

Despite its unprecedented savagery, the encounter settled nothing—the Bloody Angle's defenders were forced to withdraw but the Federals could not advance beyond the mutilated works they had seized. Farther to the east, one of Burnside's divisions penetrated another sector of the salient, but the break was quickly repaired. As it had in the Wilderness, this day the IX Corps had disappointed Grant by its lack of staying-power as well as by its failure to prevent Early's corps from counterattacking against Hancock.

Because the Mule Shoe remained in Union hands, Lee personally led his army in a series of attacks aimed at repossessing it, but to no avail. The assaults did, however, buy time for defenders to cobble together a new line farther to the rear, which blocked additional penetration. When Lee led his weary and embattled troops behind this cover, the day's fighting finally closed. A survivor in blue, speaking for many comrades, wrote: "This has been the most terrible day I have ever lived."[30]

Since his opening assaults on May 9, Grant had lost seventeen thousand troops at Spotsylvania. He was appalled by the losses, but they did not shake his intention to keep moving toward Richmond. Instead, he cabled Washington for reinforcements that would include many of those artillerists who for months had led sheltered lives inside the capital's fortifications—they would take the field as foot soldiers. The Confederates sensed this degree of determination, fearing that Grant would continue to fight to the last man. "We have met a man this time," one Rebel declared, "who either does not know when he is whipped, or who cares not if he loses his whole Army."[31]

★ ★ ★

The rain that had hampered the fighting on May 12 continued for several days, turning roads into soup and making further efforts to breach Lee's lines unlikely. By now, Grant had decided to forgo additional offensives and to return to his strategy of outflanking the enemy. Despite the difficulties he had encountered, he remained confident of eventual success. On June 13, he wrote to Julia:

> The ninth day of battle is just closing with victory so far on our side. But the enemy are fighting with great desperation[,] entrenching themselves in every position they take up. We have lost many thousand men killed and wounded and the enemy have no doubt lost more. We have taken about eight thousand prisoners and lost likely three thousand. . . . I am very well and full of hope. I see from the papers the country is also hopeful.[32]

He made one last attempt to press the enemy, principally to determine his position and strength, but Hancock's renewed assault on the Mule Shoe ended quickly and disastrously on May 18 in the face of a devastating barrage by massed artillery. On May 19 and 20, Grant shifted around Meade's forces so that the VI and IX Corps would face the Confederate left, allowing Hancock to move around the right and head southeastward along the line of the Richmond, Fredericksburg & Potomac Railroad. Grant hoped that by placing the II Corps in advance of the rest of the army, Lee would leave his works and attack it, "in which case the main army could follow Lee up and attack him before he had time to intrench." When on May 20 Lee did nothing to foil this strategy, the movement by Meade's left flank began.

When he departed Spotsylvania, Grant was in good spirits, not merely because he was leaving behind one of the war's bloodiest venues but because he had received promising news from the commanders of his more distant forces. Butler had advanced from City Point to cut the railroad between Richmond and Petersburg and to capture the defenses at Drewry's Bluff on the southern doorstep of the capital. Sherman, meanwhile, had driven Johnston's Confederates from their winter camps around Dalton and was pursuing at full tilt. General Crook had destroyed Confederate supply caches in West Virginia while torching a major bridge on the Virginia & Tennessee Railroad. And Phil Sheridan had bested Stuart's pursuers at Yellow Tavern, twelve miles above Richmond, challenging the defenders of the capital. As Grant happily supposed, "the prospect must now have been dismal in Richmond." It would be more so when word reached the city late on May 12 that Stuart had succumbed to the effects of a mortal wound received at Yellow Tavern.[33]

Grant's mood would not endure. Although the news out of Sherman's and Crook's headquarters continued to be positive, Grant would learn that Butler had failed to take his objective. Faulty dispositions, poor generalship, and a reluctance to attack the inner works of Drewry's Bluff had forced the politician-general into retreat. He had been assaulted by a much smaller enemy force on May 16—most of it hustled up from the Carolinas via the still largely intact railroad to Richmond—under the peripatetic Beauregard. Butler's withdrawal ended with his dispirited army at Bermuda Hundred, a peninsula formed by the James and Appomattox, which he had heavily fortified. This was bad enough, but in subsequent days Beauregard would entrap the Federals inside their own works, ensuring that Butler would be unable to cooperate with Meade, at least not in the way Grant envisioned.[34]

On the heels of this disheartening news, Grant would learn that Sigel's thrust up the Shenandoah had been turned back forty miles short of its objective, Staunton. At New Market on May 15, Sigel's nine-thousand-man command was throttled by a Rebel force so small that it required augmenting by 258 cadets of the Virginia Military Institute. Then, too, by mid-May, the Red River Campaign was nearing its disastrous conclusion as Nathaniel Banks's beaten and demoralized army, having failed to plant the Stars and Stripes in Texas, retreated from Alexandria to Donaldsonville, Louisiana. It soon became clear that three of the legs that had supported Grant's multitheater strategy had been irreparably broken. What was worse, with Sigel routed and Butler "bottled up" at Bermuda Hundred, Lee could expect to receive substantial reinforcements in a matter of weeks, perhaps even days.[35]

After evacuating its trenches around Spotsylvania, Hancock's corps spent the night of May 20 trudging southeastward over unfamiliar territory toward Guiney's Station on the Richmond, Fredericksburg & Potomac. Isolated from the rest of the army, which departed the recent battlefield more slowly, the II Corps, although screened by cavalry, should have been an inviting target. Lee, however, refused to take the bait Grant was dangling before him. Still feeling the losses he had suffered on May 10 and 12, at least until augmented by troops from Richmond or the Shenandoah, Lee was incapable of an early offensive. His single intention was to remain between his enemy and his nation's capital. Thus, as soon as he learned of Hancock's pullout, he withdrew his army by degrees toward Hanover Junction, where the R, F & P connected with the Virginia Central, eighteen miles south of Guiney's and twenty-four miles north of Richmond.

From Hanover Junction, which was situated less than a mile below the North Anna River, Lee could dispute, if he chose, Meade's crossing of the stream. He decided to do so but without committing maximum resources. The north bank of the river was higher than the side Lee would be compelled to occupy; Meade could plant enough artillery on his side to ensure a crossing in force. And Meade had plenty of guns, though not nearly as many as before. The rough and broken ground Meade's army had crossed since passing the Rapidan had persuaded Grant that it "had more artillery than could ever be brought into action at any one time." Over the objections of General Hunt, he recently had ordered more than one hundred cannons to be transferred to the defenses of Washington.[36]

By noon of May 23, when Meade's advance reached the North Anna, Lee's soldiers had hunkered down behind earthworks across the water. At 4:30 P.M., Warren's corps crossed the newly laid floating bridge at Jericho Mills; once on the south side, it, too, entrenched. Wright's troops came up on Warren's left but, like Hancock's farther downstream, did not cross till the next day. Slow-moving Burnside finally pushed one of his divisions across the stream at Ox Ford, between Jericho Mills and Hancock's crossing point, Chesterfield Bridge, but the Confederates in that sector rose up and shoved it to the north bank.

Burnside's repulse was disconcerting, but of even greater dismay to Grant was the position of the entire army, which, he conceded, was faulty. The sharp bends in the river prevented any of Meade's corps from easily supporting the others. Furthermore, Lee was so deeply entrenched that a direct attack on his line would, as Grant informed the War Department, "cause a slaughter of [his] men that even success would not justify." On his part, Lee was more hopeful. On the evening of May 23, he attacked Warren's isolated corps with Major General Cadmus Wilcox's division. The spirited attack failed to drive the Yankees out of their works, but Brigadier General Lysander Cutler's division of Warren's corps suffered heavily while repulsing it. Wilcox withdrew, but only after absorbing upwards of 650 casualties.[37]

Grant's suspicion that Lee would be heavily reinforced had been confirmed. On May 20 and 21, the Army of Northern Virginia had added approximately eight thousand officers and men. The augmentees included five infantry brigades from Beauregard's lines south of Richmond and two from the Shenandoah under the officer who had defeated Franz Sigel, Major General John C. Breckinridge. Although unaware of Meade's suddenly diminished advantage in strength, Grant decided he could accomplish nothing of value in his present position. After dark on May 26, he began to withdraw Meade's troops in the same direction—southeastward—that the army had taken from the Wilderness and Spotsylvania, still hopeful of an opportunity to skirt Lee's lower flank. The route now led to the Pamunkey River in the vicinity of Hanover Town. Grant directed Sheridan—who had rejoined the army after threatening but not breaching the defenses of Richmond—to spearhead the movement by crossing the river and seizing a vital crossroads near Cold Harbor, ten miles northeast of Richmond.[38]

As the army plodded south, Grant's mood plummeted. He was suffering from another sick headache, and a chloroform treatment failed to alleviate his suffering. Then, too, he was disturbed by the hard knocks the army had taken almost every time it stopped marching and gave battle. He was further distressed by the realization that Meade was quickly running out of maneuvering room. This latest movement would place the army more to the east of Richmond than north of it, and major waterways—the Chickahominy and James Rivers—were looming up in its path.

Grant rid himself of pent-up frustration when he came upon a teamster whose wagon had sunk into a marsh and refused to be extricated. As Horace Porter told the story, Grant reined in when he witnessed the man "beating his horses brutally in the face with the butt-end of his whip, and swearing with a volubility calculated to give a sulphurous odor to all the surrounding atmosphere." Grant had an aversion to profanity, but he could not tolerate cruelty to animals, especially horses. He vented his anger in an explosive outburst that shocked Porter, who had never seen him so overcome with emotion. At his order, the teamster was tied to a tree where he remained for hours as the army trudged past, jeering and cursing him.[39]

Over the next few days, Grant had further occasion to display his temper. As the army neared Cold Harbor, staff work suffered a major breakdown. To counter Lee's reinforcing, Grant found it possible to call up ten thousand troops from Butler's base at Bermuda Hundred. This force, consisting of elements of both of Butler's corps under overall command of Baldy Smith, had been sent by transport to Fort Monroe and then up the York and Pamunkey Rivers to link with Meade's army in advance of its next confrontation with Lee.

At first ignorant of where he was to link with Meade, on May 30 Smith learned that the Army of the Potomac would cross the Pamunkey at Hanover Town. Yet instead of being directed there, Smith was ordered to New Castle, several miles away. After a long, hot, dusty trek, Smith's column reached its supposed destination on May 31, only to be informed next day by a courier from Grant's headquarters that it should be at New Castle *Ferry*, a long march to the north and west.

Another stamina-draining march brought the expeditionary force to the ferry late that morning, where it found no one waiting for them. An angry and frustrated Smith—whose well-known temper had been ignited several times during the recent campaigning under Butler, whom he had come to loathe—sent a courier to locate Meade's headquarters. Before the man returned, Lieutenant Colonel Babcock of Grant's staff came galloping up to offer apologies for a series of errors by someone on Grant's staff, perhaps a telegrapher. Babcock explained that Smith's destination all along had been Cold Harbor, which he was to reach as soon as possible. The foul-up provoked a volley of oaths from Smith, but there was no help for it; he turned his command about and followed Babcock to Cold Harbor, which he finally reached on the afternoon of June 1.[40]

For all his travail in getting there, Smith came to regret that he had completed his journey. Grant and Meade came to share his feelings, for the attacks that the former ordered, and the latter conducted, over the next two days later ranked among the costliest ever made in the Virginia theater of the war. Lee's interior lines of movement and supply, which had enabled him to beat his opponent to Spotsylvania and the North Anna, brought him to Cold Harbor in advance of Grant, Smith, and Meade. Meade's slow crossing of the Pamunkey and Smith's marching and countermarching gave Lee the time to entrench along a line west of Cold Harbor, to shield that line with field works, and to brace it with banks of cannons.

Lee's position was impregnable, but Grant refused to concede the point. Frustrated beyond measure to find his flank attempt once again thwarted, he gave vent to his emotion by twice ordering frontal assaults across open ground susceptible of frontal and enfilading fire. On June 1 and 3, the attacking columns were blown apart by musketry and cannon-fire well short of their objective. On June 1, Smith alone lost one thousand men killed, wounded, or captured. On June 3, the combined Union forces suffered five times as many casualties, most during the first hour of fighting. Survivors got no farther than fifty yards from the Rebel line before being forced to lie down to escape a murderous torrent of missiles. Unable to advance or retreat by daylight, they lay on the sun-scorched earth until darkness permitted them to crawl to the rear over the bodies of their dead comrades.[41]

The disastrous results of June 1 and 3 profoundly affected Grant and made him repent his rashness. He would group the second attack at Cold Harbor with the May 22, 1863, assault on Vicksburg as the most regrettable tactical errors of his career. The unacceptable losses suffered by the Federals at Cold Harbor would sharpen the image of "Grant the Butcher" long popular in Confederate circles and now alluded to in some Northern newspapers. The fact that the armies under Grant's supervision had suffered almost fifty thousand casualties—more than 40 percent of their original strength—since crossing the Rapidan bolstered his claim to the undesirable title. Few of his critics considered that the losses were largely the result of Grant's being forced to initiate combat and to maintain the offensive while his opponent attacked only when it suited his purposes. Then too, the "Butcher" label flew in the face of Grant's determined attempt to outflank his opponent rather than attack him directly.[42]

In addition to confirming him as a heartless aggressor in the minds of many North and South, the disastrous assaults of June 1 and 3 appeared to give Lee's army renewed hope of ultimate victory. As Grant wrote, before Cold Harbor, "the Army of Northern Virginia seemed to have acquired a wholesome regard for the courage, endurance, and soldierly qualities generally of the Army of the Potomac. They no longer wanted to fight them 'one Confederate to five Yanks'. . . . This charge [of June 3] seemed to revive their hopes." It was his job to ensure that this change in the enemy's outlook was of short duration.[43]

★ ★ ★

On June 15, Grant wrote to Julia and discussed the previous three days: "We have been engaged in one of the most perilous movements ever executed by a large army, that of withdrawing from the front of an enemy and moving past his flank[,] crossing two rivers over which the enemy has bridges and rail-roads whilst we have bridges to improvise. So far it has been eminently successful and I hope will prove so to the end."[44]

The perilous movement had occurred when Grant drove Lee so close to Richmond that the only way to get between the enemy and his capital was through the swamps and marshes that festered on both sides of the Chickahominy, an obstacle that gave Grant pause. As early as June 5, he had written General Halleck that "a full survey of all the ground" suggested the impracticality of maintaining a long, vulnerable line of communications on the north side of the Chickahominy and the James. Furthermore, the tactical pattern Lee had displayed since the Wilderness showed that he preferred "to act purely on the defensive behind breastworks, or feebly on the offensive immediately in front of them."[45]

With Lee refusing to fight in the open and able to use interior lines to fend off any flanking movements, Grant saw no profit in continuing to operate north of the James. Instead, he would cross that river and fight against Richmond and Lee from below, as Butler had attempted to do. In that quarter he could cut the communications that linked Richmond and Lee's army to the Deep South, leaving only the Shenandoah Valley as a source of supply.

Grant hoped that a force operating in the Valley under David Hunter would break this link as well.

Grant's objective south of the James was Petersburg, a major supply conduit twenty-two miles below Richmond. Railroads ran from that city—which was believed to be lightly defended—not only north to the capital but south to Weldon, North Carolina, east to Norfolk, Virginia, and west to the country around Appomattox Court House. Breaking any of those lines, especially the Petersburg & Weldon, would isolate Lee from his sources of supply, forcing him to come out from behind his cherished works and fight on open ground where Meade's numbers would prove telling.

The move to Petersburg entailed heavy risks even if, as Grant hoped, his opponent failed to detect his pull-out from Cold Harbor. If Lee did learn where Meade and Smith were heading and elected not to pursue, he could either turn against Butler and crush him or make for Lynchburg to defeat Hunter, en route subsisting his army in the lush Valley of Virginia. "But the move had to be made," Grant declared, "and I relied upon Lee not seeing my danger as I saw it."[46]

He began to execute his change of base on June 6 when he detached two-thirds of Sheridan's cavalry—only Wilson's division would remain with the main army—and sent it on an expedition toward Gordonsville and Charlottesville, well to the north and west of Richmond. He instructed Little Phil to break the Virginia Central and the James River canal while making contact with Hunter and escorting his force to Grant's new location below the James. Sheridan rode off on June 7. As Grant had hoped, he drew most of Lee's cavalry, now under Major General Wade Hampton, after him. The result would be the largest all-cavalry clash of the war, near the Virginia Central depot of Trevilian Station, on June 11 and 12. Sheridan would emerge from the fight much the worse for wear, but by then he would have assisted Grant's descent on Petersburg.[47]

By June 12, Grant's engineers had fixed the proper place at which to bridge the James—the high ground between Wilcox's Landing and Windmill Point, twenty-three miles southeast of Cold Harbor. There the fast-moving river was twenty-two hundred feet wide and as much as fifteen fathoms deep. Because the Southside (i.e., the area south of the James) was in Butler's department, Grant's subordinate was charged with providing a floating bridge long enough to support the crossing and an engineer officer to supervise its construction. Butler responded effectively; working closely with his counterpart in the Army of the Potomac, between late afternoon and midnight on June 14, Butler's engineering chief supervised the placement of one hundred pontoon boots, which were then anchored side-by-side and topped with planking. By the early hours of June 15, one of the greatest engineering feats of the war was complete. Despite its vaunted intelligence-gathering prowess, Lee's army did not learn of the bridge's presence until well after the first troops began to cross it.[48]

On the evening of June 12, Meade's army had begun to slip away from Cold Harbor, moving to the rear in detachments carefully screened from enemy view. Hancock's corps, which had occupied the southern end of Meade's battle line, was first to make the overland trek to the James. It was preceded, however, by Smith's command, which Grant had designated to reach Petersburg by water, there to launch the initial attack on the city. On June 12, Smith had begun to vacate his position in the center of the army's line. He led his troops back toward White House, where waiting transports carried them down the Pamunkey and the York, then up the James to Bermuda Hundred. At Butler's enclave they debarked, reassembled, and headed for Petersburg on foot.[49]

After Smith moved out, Hancock's men, followed by Wright's corps, began the long march to the James. They were screened on the west side by Warren's corps, preceded by Wilson's horsemen; both commands had crossed the Chickahominy to take position northeast of Richmond as if Grant intended to attack the capital. Lee, who remained ignorant of Grant's intentions, left a small force in the trenches at Cold Harbor and sent the greater part of his army—Anderson's and Hill's corps—to defend the White Oak Swamp-Malvern Hill area. Warren's and Wilson's screening operation would end on June 15 with their men marching and trotting across the floating bridge. The crossing would be complete by 7:00 P.M. on June 18, whereupon the bridge would be broken up and floated to City Point.[50]

The head of Hancock's column reached Wilcox's Wharf late on the afternoon of June 13, while the engineers were still collecting their bridging materials. Because they represented the second wave of attack on Petersburg, the soldiers did not wait for the pontoons to be laid. Throughout June 14, transports conducted them across the water to Windmill Point. By the morning of June 15, the last member of the II Corps had set foot on dry ground, sixteen miles from Petersburg. Additional manpower was close at hand in the form of Wright's and Burnside's corps. Lee was still far to the west of the crossing points, ignorant of what was in store for Petersburg.[51]

The operation appeared to be an unalloyed success. On the evening of June 16, Lieutenant Colonel Theodore Lyman of Meade's staff arrived at Grant's headquarters—where he found the lieutenant general about to turn in for the night—to deliver a progress report on the crossing. After Lyman had finished speaking, Grant "smiled, like one who has done a clever thing, and said, 'I think it is pretty well to get across a great river, and come up here and attack Lee in his rear before he is ready for us!'"[52]

But by then Grant's plan was in grave jeopardy, and the fault was largely his own. Baldy Smith had arrived opposite Petersburg's northern defenses on schedule on the morning of June 15. Smith had nine thousand men with which to oppose the twenty-two hundred defenders of the "Cockade City" commanded by Beauregard. But Smith had only the vaguest notion of what was expected of him. Grant hoped that he would penetrate to the heart of the city, capture successive lines of works, and, when Hancock arrived, team with the II Corps to take full possession of the city. But Smith believed he was to do no more than force Beauregard's troops inside their inner works. He also had a dim conception of how he was to cooperate with Meade's advance. Moreover, he was ill, having suffered an attack of an old malady, malaria, and he was still suffering the psychological effects of the carnage his command had undergone at Cold Harbor, for which he held Grant and Meade equally responsible.

The result of these factors was that Smith delayed his attack until he made a through reconnaissance of the lightly held works in his front. Then, when finally ready to go forward, he found that his artillery teams were watering from a stream well in the rear. By the time guns and men were in place and Rebel positions two miles in advance of the city had been carried—largely through the valor and determination of the many African American units in Smith's command—it was close to 7:00 P.M.

Smith's attack, launched in gathering darkness but made with power and speed, appeared successful enough. By 8:30 P.M., his men had captured several detached batteries north and northeast of the city, opening a gap in Beauregard's defenses fully three and a half miles wide. But Smith, fearing to continue the attack in the dark, went no further. Nor did Hancock when the head of the II Corps reached Petersburg after Smith's attack ended. The same faulty staff work that had hamstrung the advance on Cold Harbor had prevented Hancock from being informed of his mission to support Smith in an attack on the city—in fact, he did not realize an attack was imminent. The destination originally assigned him this day had proven to be inside Beauregard's lines. Finally, his march from the James had started late as a result of the nonarrival of rations from Butler's commissariat, rations that Hancock had been ordered to issue to his troops before starting for Petersburg.[53]

When he reached the scene of action, Hancock did little more than have his men relieve Smith's in the captured works. In the interim, Smith went to the rear on sick leave. No further attacks were made that night, although many of Hancock's soldiers expressed themselves as "furiously" upset that a strike was withheld, fearing "they were to be sacrificed on the morrow."[54]

The men knew, better than their commanders, what was in store for them. After his main line was breached, Beauregard fell back to a hastily selected position two miles farther south, which he built up through the night, manning it not only with the city's garrison but with troops stripped from the lines opposite Bermuda Hundred. At the same time, he put in a desperate call for help from Lee. The army commander, however, remained unconvinced that all, or even most, of Meade's troops had vacated the Cold Harbor defenses. Lee would not send units to Beauregard's assistance until June 17; they would not occupy the Petersburg works until early the next day.[55]

That timetable gave Grant and Meade three days to straighten out their tangled strategy and renew their assault on what had become the most valuable piece of real estate in the entire Confederacy. But, as if the Army of the Potomac had succumbed to an inherent, fatal weakness, it failed to take advantage of its gleaming opportunity. By June 16, it had closed up on the disputed ground but was not yet ready to strike. That morning, Grant scheduled an all-out assault for 6:00 P.M.; when it was made, however, the effort succeeded in capturing some batteries south of Smith's breakthrough, but little more. Similarly, limited success was gained on June 17, mainly along the IX Corps' front, but a counterattack by troops hustled down from the Richmond defenses recaptured most of the lost ground.

During the night, Beauregard withdrew even closer to Petersburg. When Meade attacked early on June 18, he breached his opponent's original line; but his commanders moved slowly and tentatively toward the new position, fearing to attack it until the ground leading to it could be surveyed. When assaults were finally launched later in the day, they failed through a lack of cohesion and coordination. In these actions, the heavy artillerists who had been transformed into infantry and knew nothing of attacking fortifications exposed themselves unwisely and suffered extraordinary losses.[56]

By late that afternoon, the Confederates out of Cold Harbor began to file inside Beauregard's works, and Grant saw that his chance to take Petersburg by storm had vanished. In four days of confused and misdirected operations, Meade's army had suffered eleven thousand casualties. No more was to be gained by direct assault; Grant would have to submit to that unsatisfying alternative, a siege. On June 19, he dashed off a letter to Julia: "There has been some very hard fighting here the last four days, but now I hope it is over." He wanted her and the children to visit him "if a suitable place [could] be found," perhaps at Fort Monroe, where he could see her occasionally.[57]

Here was the only advantage to stationary operations: Grant could have his loved ones with him to help take his mind off the failures, the dashed hopes, and the horrific carnage that had followed him almost since the day he took the field against Robert Edward Lee.

Chapter 12

ADDITIONAL AND
MAGNIFICENT SUCCESSES

GRANT HOPED TO THE LAST THAT HE WOULD NOT HAVE TO RESORT TO "regular approaches" against Petersburg. As he had learned when investing Vicksburg, a lengthy, drawn-out siege would sap the energy and morale of the army, and of the public at large. Grant hated to disappoint the people of the North and even more so the government officials who had placed him in command. Only days before, Lincoln, upon hearing of Grant's plans to cross the James, had cabled the general: "I begin to see it; you will succeed. God bless you all." But Grant could not tell the president when or how that success would come. He must have felt something akin to a sense of failure when, on June 20, Lincoln came down to City Point to visit the Headquarters of the Armies of the United States and tour the siege lines. Gazing at the multilayered defenses that had already acquired a look of permanence, Grant's guest must have felt discouraged and perhaps also disheartened, especially with the election little more than four months off.[1]

By the time of the presidential visit, the forces of Meade and Butler had gone into fixed positions outside Petersburg. The Army of the Potomac and Smith's troops of the Army of the James held the works and trenches that stretched east and southeast of the city, and the rest of Butler's army manned the perimeter between the James and the Appomattox. The two armies had at last joined hands against Lee, although weeks later than Grant had anticipated. Already both were suffering from the hardships inherent to siege operations, enemy fire being only one. Before June was out, a newspaper correspondent with Butler's army would make a dramatic complaint to his readers: "Suffocating heat! Blinding dust! Torturing flies!"[2]

Desperate to drive Lee from his works before the armies truly began to suffer, on June 20 Grant sent Wilson's cavalry to raid the railroads south and west of Petersburg in hopes of forcing Lee to evacuate as a result of disrupted supply lines. Wilson, augmented by the small cavalry division from Butler's army under Brigadier General August V. Kautz, succeeded in tearing up sixty miles of tracks and ties; but before he could complete his mission, he was set upon by cavalry under Hampton and infantry under Hill. The defenders inflicted so many casualties that Wilson and Kautz barely made it back to Petersburg with enough men to keep their commands alive. Their exertions and achievements availed Grant nothing. In less than a week, repair crews had the battered railroads back in operation.[3]

While the cavalry raided, portions of the II Corps (temporarily under Major General David Bell Birney, Hancock having been disabled by the reopening of a nasty wound received at Gettysburg), supported by the VI Corps, shifted southward in an attempt to do greater damage to one of the rail lines the raiders had struck, the Petersburg & Weldon. If they secured a lodgment, they were to sweep westward toward another major supply artery, the Boydton Plank Road. But Birney was new to corps command and the effort was carelessly conducted. When he permitted a gap to open between his column and Wright's, Rebel infantry under Major General William Mahone advanced through it, attacked to right and left, and came away with almost two thousand prisoners. The attackers fought back but withdrew after making little headway.[4]

The Federals did, however, secure one notable acquisition, the Jerusalem Plank Road, which ran southeast from the city. The possession of that vital thoroughfare forced Lee to extend his lines to cover the position. This was cold comfort to some observers. Lieutenant Colonel Comstock of Grant's staff noted in his diary that the "troops did not fight nearly as well as when [they] started"—meaning when the Rapidan was crossed, six weeks ago. Comstock entertained the gloomy notion that the army's "best officers & best men [were] gone—losses enormous—between 60 & 70,000 since campaign began."[5]

The seemingly meager results of Wilson's and Birney's efforts convinced Grant that he must truly besiege Petersburg, the supervision of which he divided between two capable professionals, General Hunt and Brigadier General Henry W. Benham, Meade's chief engineer officer. The Union armies settled in for the duration, strengthening their breastworks, digging newer and deeper trenches, and erecting "bombproofs" and covered ways to deflect rifle balls and (it was hoped) artillery rounds. It was dirty, grueling work conducted under conditions so stressful that, where possible, troops spent twenty-four hours on the front lines and a day of relative peace in the rear.

The hardships and frustrations of siege duty caused nerves to fray and tempers to flare. One of the first episodes pitted Baldy Smith against Ben Butler. Following their partially successful assault on June 15, Smith's troops crossed the Appomattox to rejoin their army at Bermuda Hundred, but at Grant's order they had been returned to the Petersburg lines on June 21. In the interim, Smith had feuded several times with his superior, and when he was on his way back to Petersburg the two engaged in an especially heated argument provoked by Smith's erroneous belief that Butler had criticized his supervision of the marching column. "I can stand as much as most men, but I cannot live under this man much longer," Smith complained in a letter to his wife in Vermont. To Grant, he pleaded to be transferred out of Butler's command and went so far as to ask how Grant could "keep in command of two army corps a man who is as helpless as a child on the field of battle and as visionary as an opium eater in council."[6]

Grant had never thought much of Butler as a field leader, but he continued to regard the tart-tongued Smith as an able tactician. Grant thus began to conspire with Halleck toward the issuance of orders remanding Butler to a desk job at Fort Monroe and giving Smith effective command of the Army of the James. Butler got wind of the effort, however, and, according to Smith, developed a plan to thwart it. On June 29, Grant, accompanied by Butler, made an inspection tour of Smith's lines at Petersburg. Smith claimed that at every stop along the way—corps, division, brigade headquarters—Butler saw to it that Grant was offered one or more drinks of whiskey. By the end of the day, said Smith, the commanding general was "in a most disgusting state after having vomited all over his horse's neck & shoulders."[7]

Revulsed by Grant's condition, Smith commented to one of his staff officers: "General Grant has gone away drunk; General Butler has seen it, and will never fail to use the weapon which has been put into his hands." Smith then wrote a detailed report of the event and handed it to John Rawlins, who had not accompanied Grant on his tour. After reading Smith's account, Rawlins assured him: "Being thus advised of the slippery ground he is on, I shall not fail to use my endeavors to stay him from failing."[8]

Later events appeared to confirm Smith's conviction that Butler intended to blackmail his superior. On July 10, Grant suspended the order for Butler's transfer to Fort Monroe, a preliminary version of which Halleck had sent him three days earlier. Smith saw this as a bad sign, but he had no idea that he would be taking Butler's place on the sidelines. While on a brief furlough in Vermont, Smith learned that Grant had issued an order relieving him of his command. Smith rushed back to the army and demanded an explanation, but Grant refused to discuss the matter other than to tell Smith that he talked too much. For his part, Smith assumed that Butler was responsible, having forced Grant to fire him by threatening to bring new charges and lurid details of Grant's alcoholism to the attention of the many reporters traveling with the Army of the James.

Many historians—especially committed defenders of Grant's good name—refuse to believe that he got drunk on this occasion. In the main they do so because of Smith's fanciful claim of blackmail. In truth, Grant did not act out of compulsion; he decided to jettison Smith because he learned that the man had been feuding not only with his immediate superior but also with other officers, including Meade, whose job Smith had coveted since before coming east with Grant. Over the weeks since Cold Harbor, Smith's criticisms of his superiors and colleagues had been increasingly shrill and biting. Just before going on leave, he had complained directly to Grant about the butchery of June 1 and 3, and in doing so he gave Grant the impression that he as well as Meade was being condemned. Grant, who wanted nothing so much as harmony among his ranking subordinates, thought highly of Meade and had consistently supported him against the baseless charges of reporters and politicians. He was incensed that Smith should add to the wave of unfair criticism against the man. At last convinced that Smith must go, Grant saw to it without further hesitation.

But just because Grant, in firing Smith, was not motivated by the fear of bad publicity does not prove that he was not intoxicated in public on June 29. Various witnesses in addition to Smith, including the visiting assistant secretary of war, St. John Tucker, testified to seeing Grant drunk. Once again, under the effects of stress, frustration, or inactive duty, the commanding general had given way to a weakness the consequences of which, as Smith warned, might have played hob with his career. With the armies bogged down at Petersburg, and no end to the fighting in sight, renewed publicity of Grant's drinking might have threatened his continuance in command. But the only publicist was Smith, who, after being relieved, loudly denounced his unfair treatment at the hands of a drunken coward. Fortunately for Grant, Smith was widely regarded as a disgruntled seeker of revenge, and no one paid him much attention.[9]

★ ★ ★

Early in July, Grant learned that the stalemate at Petersburg was not his only concern. On June 12, Lee had dispatched Jubal Early, with the corps that once belonged to Dick Ewell, to block David Hunter's advance on Lynchburg. Six days later, Early helped local forces repulse Hunter's assault on

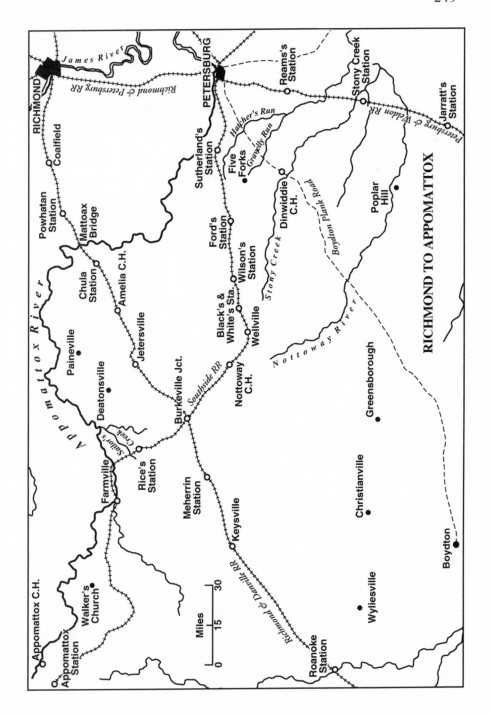

RICHMOND TO APPOMATTOX

that vital supply center. Beaten and cowed, Hunter made a circuitous but speedy retreat; Early pursued briefly before allowing his demoralized opponent to escape. He lingered for a time in that quarter of the state; then, at Lee's suggestion, he entered the Shenandoah Valley, where he organized his ten thousand soldiers into a strike force with which he planned to invade the North. Lee viewed the expedition as a means of forcing Grant to detach troops from Meade's army to run Early down.

By Independence Day, Early was threatening the garrison of Harpers Ferry at the bottom (i.e., the northern end) of the Valley. Electing not to attack that formidable outpost, he turned away, crossed the Potomac into southern Maryland, and kept moving. Only now did Washington became sufficiently alarmed to order Grant to do something about the audacious Virginian whose fiery temper and salty language led Lee to refer to him as "my bad old man."[10]

Lee's opponent came under a wave of criticism for permitting Early to menace the capital. Grant, who had initially counted on Hunter's troops to keep Early south of the Potomac, admitted to having been caught flat-footed, that his plans had been "upset" by "that Maryland raid." Halleck and Stanton scored him for failing to reinforce the capital with troops from Petersburg. When Lieutenant Colonel Comstock reached Washington ahead of a belated relief effort, Halleck asked the aide "in a rather sneering way" when they were going "to do something" about Early.[11]

Even Grant's long-time supporter Charles Dana, then in Washington, wrote to John Rawlins condemning his boss for denuding the capital's defenses and accusing Grant of "poltroonery and stupidity," which were likely to cause "the defeat of Mr. Lincoln and the election of Gen. McClellan to the Presidency." Dana was referring to the widely anticipated nomination of George B. McClellan to oppose Lincoln's reelection bid. Little Mac would indeed get the nod at the Democratic National Convention late in August. Although he attempted to disavow his party's platform, which called the war a failure and held out the hope of a negotiated peace, the former army commander would find himself chained to that ominous position.[12]

On July 6, as Early made his way through the Maryland countryside toward Baltimore, Grant dispatched five thousand members of the VI Corps and three thousand cavalrymen who had been unhorsed and not yet remounted. The troopers went directly to Washington. Wright's troops joined a scratch force under Lew Wallace which, on July 9, blocked Early's path along the Monocacy River southeast of Frederick. After a several-hour fight, the outmanned Federals broke and fled, but the check given Early delayed his arrival at Washington long enough for Wright's corps to reach and man the capital's works. Later, a division of General Banks's XIX Corps, freed for service in the East following the failure of the Red River Campaign, reached Petersburg minus its leader. Grant also sent this force to Washington, but it arrived too late to deter Early.[13]

On July 10, a worried Lincoln wired Grant, suggesting but not demanding that he accompany the reinforcements. Grant considered doing so, but in the end declined, explaining that if he left Petersburg it would be interpreted by the Northern public as a sign of weakness in the war effort. Lincoln readily accepted Grant's view of things; he was not afraid of what Early might do to the capital, merely concerned that the man would slip away and return to the Valley. His fears would be validated.[14]

Early reached the outskirts of Washington about noon on July 11, shortly before the main body of General Wright's column filed inside the capital's defenses. During the rest of the day, he planned an assault, to be launched early on July 12. During the night, however, Early learned of Wright's presence and called off the attack; throughout the next day, he contented himself with skirmishing with the defenders. At one point, Lincoln, who was observing the fighting from Fort Stevens, came under sharpshooter fire. That night, Early withdrew. He crossed the Potomac on July 14 and two days later was back in his Valley sanctuary.[15]

Grant understood that a major enemy presence in that strategic corridor could no longer be tolerated. Prolonged discussions with Halleck and Stanton produced a consensus to retain the VI and XIX Corps in the Washington area while four geographical commands whose operations were not properly coordinated—the Middle Department and the Departments of Washington, West Virginia, and the Susquehanna—would be reduced to districts and combined into one department, the forces of which would be empowered to evict Early from the Valley. Negotiations toward this end stalled when the War Department balked at Grant's first choice to head the new command, William B. Franklin. Grant had long considered Franklin a skilled and dependable field commander, but he was persona non grata to Lincoln, Stanton, and Halleck, who remembered only that the man had served less than capably under Burnside at Fredericksburg and afterwards had joined Baldy Smith in intriguing against their superior.[16]

His first choice rejected, Grant proposed that George Meade head the consolidated Middle Department, Hancock to command the Army of the Potomac in his stead. Meade was quite willing to accept the position. Although he had faithfully and without complaint filled his subordinate position, he was weary of serving in Grant's shadow. His poor relations with newspaper correspondents, whom he considered meddlers in army business and violators of military security, had placed Meade in the frustrating position of being blamed for his army's every setback and defeat; meanwhile, credit for its successes uniformly went to Grant. The lieutenant general felt grateful to Meade for having made the best of an anomalous command situation laden with pressures and susceptible of friction and tension. His only complaint was that the prideful Meade sometimes seemed more concerned with slights to his own reputation than with internal or external attacks on the skill and tenacity of his army.

The present situation ended with Grant unintentionally adding another wound to Meade's pride. Meade believed Grant had promised him the departmental command; thus, he was surprised and hurt when at Lincoln's insistence it went to another. Meade's biographer, Freeman Cleaves, noted: "As Grant later explained matters, the President did not wish to separate him [Meade] from the Army of the Potomac, since that action might be viewed as disapproval. This explanation did not go down easily, and Meade felt that other factors were involved." Cleaves is correct: When he had a chance to rethink his selection, Grant decided that Phil Sheridan would be a better fit than Meade. He believed the younger man would act more quickly and decisively to engage Early and would be more aggressive in combat. Despite initial objections that Sheridan was too young and inexperienced for the position, Washington eventually endorsed Grant's third choice for the job, sending Sheridan to the Valley and giving him command not only of the VI and a portion of the XIX Corps but also of the VIII Corps (the so-called Army of West Virginia, under Crook) as well as Wilson's and Torbert's cavalry.[17]

Grant felt he could not share his reasoning with Meade without hurting the latter's feelings. By not being forthcoming with his subordinate, he did just that. His selection of a man whom Meade neither liked nor trusted only aggravated Meade's resentment, although both he and Grant seemed determined to prevent the contretemps from injuring their delicate, awkward, but critically important relationship. To some extent, Grant made amends through his insistence that Meade be elevated to major general in the Regular Army, a promotion that came through in November.

★ ★ ★

Even with the siege six weeks along, Grant grasped at the hope that it could be ended by one decisive stratagem. Since June 25, a Pennsylvania infantry regiment in Burnside's corps, composed of coal miners commanded by a mining engineer, had been hard at work digging a shaft under an enemy salient only four hundred yards from the IX Corps' position southeast of

Petersburg. At first, neither Grant nor Meade gave the project much chance of success—the two mines Grant's army had exploded at Vicksburg had done relatively little damage—but by late July the tunnel was all but complete: The miners had filled it and two lateral galleries with 320 kegs—four tons—of blasting powder connected to a multispliced fuse that ran almost the length of the shaft.

At this point, Burnside, who had favored the project all along as a means of burnishing a reputation tarnished by poor generalship, persuaded Grant to plan an attack on Lee's lines if the powder should blast a hole through them. At first with lingering reluctance, then with moderate enthusiasm, Grant authorized Burnside to organize and train an assault column. At Grant's behest, Meade and Butler made available supporting troops, and General Hunt trained dozens of cannons on the ground above the mine.[18]

On his own, Grant moved to draw Lee's troops out of their defenses on each side of the salient. His action was also designed to forestall an attack on Grant's lines that Confederate deserters swore was imminent. On July 27, the II Corps (Hancock back in command), most of Sheridan's cavalry, and some of Kautz's crossed the James via a bridgehead that Butler had established at Deep Bottom, ten miles southeast of Richmond. As Grant foresaw, Lee responded by augmenting his defenses on the north side with two divisions of infantry and two of cavalry drawn from Petersburg and the Bermuda Hundred front. Even with Grant for a time on the scene, the commitment of heavy forces on both sides ensured a stalemate. Unable to make much headway toward the outermost of three lines of defenses that ringed the enemy capital, Hancock, Sheridan, and Kautz returned to Petersburg hours before the mine was to be detonated.[19]

Grant had made no objection to Burnside's original selection of the force to attack in the wake of the mine blast, Brigadier General Edward Ferrero's 3rd Division, IX Corps, composed entirely of African American enlisted men and white officers. As a long-time believer in the military potential of the black man, and an early convert to arming both freedmen and liberated slaves, Grant was amenable to giving African American troops an opportunity to prove themselves in an action that would capture the attention of the nation. But as July 30, the date set for the detonation of the mine, approached, Grant changed his mind at the urging of Meade.

Many historians accuse the army leader of intervening from fear of the political repercussions—especially in an election year—should the attack fail and the black soldiers be slaughtered. Some historians suspect that Meade, who was not a negrophile, feared the assault would succeed and that Ferrero's men would receive a disproportionate share of the credit. Few historians heed the claim of Meade's chief of staff, Major General Andrew A. Humphreys, that his superior acted because Ferrero's troops were too inexperienced to carry off a major assault. Whatever the true reason or reasons, the black soldiers, who had been drilling in quick-strike tactics for some time, were replaced at the eleventh hour by a division of untrained white troops under Brigadier General James H. Ledlie, who would prove not only incompetent but also cowardly.[20]

Predictably, perhaps, the mine proved a resounding success and the assault a costly failure. When it exploded on July 30 at 4:45 A.M., the powder cache blew a hole in the enemy salient almost two hundred feet long, fifty feet wide, and twenty-five feet deep. Suddenly, a path into downtown Petersburg stared Burnside in the face. "There was nothing . . . to prevent our walking in and taking possession," Grant later wrote to Dan Ammen. But when the attack column went forward, it did so tentatively, aimlessly, and without Ledlie, who spent the day ensconced in a bombproof well to the rear, occasionally joined by General Ferrero.[21]

The attackers failed to capitalize on the demolition of the Rebel works in their front. Some officers led their men into the smoking crater instead of around it. Others called retreat as soon as the Confederates recovered from the shock of the blast and rushed up from other sectors to close the breach. Neither the availability of reinforcements nor Hunt's well-directed covering fire could salvage the assault. Despite Grant's early realization that the attack must fail, Burnside committed more and more troops to it. After several efforts by white units were handily repulsed, Burnside committed Ferrero's division—too late to save the day. Predictably, the African Americans—especially those who followed their white comrades into the "horrid pit"—were cut down in droves.

Grant was sickened by the botched offensive and the losses that resulted, for whom he blamed Burnside, Ledlie, and Ferrero. He agreed to Meade's request for a formal court of inquiry, which eventually confirmed his belief as to culpability. In the wake of the investigation, Burnside and Ledlie resigned their commissions, Burnside being replaced by Major General John G. Parke. Ferrero was transferred to a relatively unimportant command on Butler's front. Yet these actions, although satisfying Grant's passion for accountability, did nothing to redeem the tragedy: "It was the saddest affair I have witnessed in the war," Grant wrote. "Such opportunity for carrying fortifications I have never seen and do not expect again to have."[22]

★ ★ ★

By late August, Grant had good reason to be depressed, but he refused to give in to the emotion. Not only had the Petersburg mine failed, so had a second offensive above the James. Launched on August 13, the operation, which involved elements of both Meade's and Butler's armies, was designed to take advantage of a rumored diminishing of the Confederate defenses opposite Deep Bottom. Instead of depleted, those works had been reinforced; from behind them Lee's troops repulsed successive advances aimed at breaching and/or circumventing Richmond's outer works. The closest the Federals got to the city was seven miles, where Gregg's cavalry division was brought to a halt on August 16. On the evening of August 20, Grant conceded defeat and recalled most of the forces involved, principally the II Corps, to the south side.[23]

Having failed to gain a permanent hold on one end of Lee's lines, Grant had better luck at the other end. On August 18, he had sent Warren's corps three miles to the south and west of Petersburg to gain possession of a stretch of the Weldon Railroad, thus forcing Lee to extend his already thin right flank to counter the incursion. The V Corps seized the railroad at Globe Tavern, about four miles south of the city, and, thanks to supports hustled down from Deep Bottom, held it next day and again two days later against desperate attacks by A. P. Hill.[24]

Warren's success signified that Grant's efforts to extend his reach, and to stretch Lee's lines to the breaking point, were bearing fruit. But to the public at large, and official Washington in particular, the advantage thus gained was microscopic. Grant believed it would prove decisive in the long run; in a letter to Congressman Washburne on August 16, he declared: "The end is visible if we but be true to ourselves." Yet only a week later, a gloomy President Lincoln, running for reelection on the ticket of the Union Party (comprising Republicans and War Democrats) composed a memorandum to his cabinet calling his defeat in November "exceedingly probable" and pledging to assist the likely victor in saving the Union prior to McClellan's inauguration, "as he will have secured his election on such ground that he can not possibly save it afterwards."[25]

Another reason for Lincoln's pessimism, and Grant's unease, was the war news out of Georgia, which, although inconclusive, suggested that Sherman's drive against the Army of Tennessee had fatally stalled. Sherman's armies had been closing in on Atlanta since early July when they crossed the Chattahoochee River, the last natural barrier to their objective. Jefferson Davis, unable to secure a pledge from Joe Johnston that he would fight to the last to hold Atlanta, had replaced him with a more aggressive fighter, but a less astute tactician, Lieutenant General John Bell Hood. Hood promptly attacked out of his defenses, but his smaller numbers and faulty dispositions ensured his army of defeat and heavy casualties. Hood inflicted many losses as well; during his second sortie, on July 22, the genial and much-loved James McPherson was killed at the head of Grant's old Army of the Tennessee. Grant took the news hard; eyewitnesses testified that this general who supposedly sent men to their deaths without batting an eye retired to his tent and wept uncontrollably. Reportedly he also gave way to tears when, three months later, he learned of the death from disease of another former subordinate for whom he felt a warm personal regard, T.E.G. Ransom.[26]

By late August, reports from Sherman's area of operations had become sketchy and irregular, then nonexistent. Unknown to Grant and the authorities in Washington, Sherman had begun to mass his forces for a climactic effort to turn Hood's western flank. He moved so stealthily to a point below the city that Hood lost track of him, relocating him only when it was too late. On the last day of August and the first of September, Hood's subordinates encountered a large body of Yankees near Jonesboro on the railroad south of the city. They attacked, but failed to break Sherman's grip on that critical supply line; thus the city was doomed to capture.[27]

According to Cyrus Comstock, everything was "totally quiet" at City Point on the evening of September 2. Meade was on leave and Grant was returning from Washington, where he had been testifying at Burnside's court of inquiry and spending time with Julia and the children, who were staying at Fort Monroe. That night, the headquarters telegraph clicked out the news that Sherman had entered Atlanta on the heels of Hood's departing troops. "God grant it [the news] may be true," Comstock wrote in his diary.[28]

It was true. Reports of the occupation began to pour into headquarters the next day, as well as across the nation. The news had a galvanic effect on public opinion throughout the North. Suddenly, the war to save the Union was showing progress—if not in the East, at least in a major theater of operations. The twin goals of victory and peace no longer seemed so distant, so unreachable.

Grant wired Sherman his heartiest congratulations and his thanks for a victory that relieved some of the public pressure to force an evacuation of Petersburg. At about the same time, Grant tried to expedite progress in another theater, one not so distant as Georgia. Phil Sheridan had spent the first month of his Valley operations avoiding a confrontation with Early, who in mid-August had been reinforced with two divisions—one of infantry, one of horsemen—dispatched by Lee. The additions made Washington believe that Sheridan was outnumbered, and the War Department urged a policy of caution on the new department commander.

Grant, who dutifully directed Sheridan to remain on the defensive until further notice, believed the Lincoln administration "was a little afraid to have a decisive battle fought at that time, for fear it might go against [them] and have a bad effect on the November elections." Although he understood this reasoning, Grant argued that a decisive victory in the Shenandoah would be "the most effective campaign argument" in favor of the Union Party.[29]

Sheridan's unaggressive maneuvering, his unwillingness to take the offensive when his adversary offered it to him, made Early believe Little Phil was cut from the same cloth as David Hunter—weak-kneed, unenterprising, even cowardly. Sheridan appeared so willing to let him roam at will through the lower Valley that Early readily assented to return his infantry reinforcements to Petersburg. When Grant got word of the detaching in mid-September he traveled to Charles Town, where he met with Sheridan. He ordered the feisty Irishman to engage and defeat Early, then denude the Valley of foodstuffs, livestock, and anything else that might sustain Lee's army at Petersburg.

Grant returned to City Point on September 19. That day Sheridan attacked, overwhelmed, and routed Early's depleted force at Winchester. Closely pursuing the fugitives, Sheridan overtook them on September 22 at Fisher's Hill and continued the drubbing he had administered three days earlier. Whereas at Winchester Sheridan had suffered more heavily than his opponent, at Fisher's Hill he inflicted more than twice as many casualties as he absorbed. Heartened by the dramatic victories and pleased by Sheridan's subsequent, systematic "peeling" of the Valley of Virginia, the North again rejoiced that the defenders of the Union were making critical progress.[30]

In mid-October, Sheridan defeated his once-overconfident antagonist a third time, thereby ending Early's effective contributions to the Confederacy and removing the threat he had posed to the territory above the Potomac. This victory was the most dramatic of the three, highlighted as it was by a hell-for-leather ride Sheridan made from Winchester to his army's camps on Cedar Creek, which Early had overrun during a surprise attack hours earlier. Although historians would disagree, soldiers and civilians alike gave Sheridan credit for personally turning near-defeat into overwhelming victory, reorganizing his scattered forces, restoring their morale, and delivering a counterattack that recovered the lost ground and sent his enemy whirling southward in abject defeat.[31]

The victory at Cedar Creek was at least partly attributable to the foresight of Grant, who had gone to great lengths to ensure that Lee did not reinforce

Early a second time. To hold his enemy in place at Petersburg and threaten Richmond anew, three weeks before Cedar Creek, Grant launched a major offensive on the Army of the James' front against Lee's far left flank. On the morning of September 28, Grant ordered large elements of both of Butler's corps—now under Edward Ord (whom Grant had brought in to take Baldy Smith's place) and David Birney (who had replaced the inept and unlucky Quincy Gillmore)—to cross the James on pontoons and attack the intricate defenses near Chaffin's Farm and on New Market Heights.

Although the offensive fell short of full success, it did result in the capture of Fort Harrison (renamed Fort Burnham in honor of the slain general whose troops had taken it), a key work on the outer defense lines of Richmond. Lee was so alarmed by the fort's loss that he crossed the river accompanied by several brigades and personally directed three successive attempts to retake it—all of which failed. The seizure of Harrison gave the Federals an important foothold on the Northside. In October, Butler would twice fail to extend his gains along the New Market, Darbytown, and Charles City Roads, stymied by works recently constructed in advance of Richmond's intermediate defense line. Even so, he would not relinquish his lodgment at Fort Burnham, from which his troops would constantly threaten the capital over the next six months.[32]

While Butler struck above the James, Grant ordered Meade to make a diversion on the other end of the siege lines. A reconnaissance in force conducted by four divisions, two each from the V and IX Corps, overran the Rebel defenses at Peebles's Farm, three miles south and a little west of Petersburg. The Federals dug in there as well as along the Squirrel Level Road, which ran south from the captured position. When the newly taken ground was connected by breastworks and rifle pits to the defenses at Globe Tavern, Grant had extended his left flank almost two miles beyond the railroad.

The following month, he attempted to reach even farther west, to the Boydton Plank Road, which gave access to the South Side Railroad, Petersburg's last line of supply. Hancock's and Warren's corps made the move but—reminiscent of the first attack on the city almost three months earlier—the columns permitted a gap to form between them; Confederate forces interposed and thrust the attackers back. The Federals would finally seize the plank road on February 5, 1865, credit for which would go to the II Corps; but none would go to Hancock, who had been invalided out of the army in November, replaced by Meade's erstwhile chief of staff, the capable and steadygoing General Humphreys.[33]

Again Lee was forced to distend his thinning lines to cover the encroachment. He was now trying to hold thirty-five miles of defenses with fewer than fifty thousand troops. As his correspondence with the Confederate government indicates, the recent gains by Butler and Meade had made him pessimistic, an emotion never before attributed to Robert E. Lee. "Without some increase in strength," he warned Jefferson Davis, "I cannot see how we can escape the natural military consequences of the enemy's numerical superiority. If things thus continue, the most serious consequences must result."[34]

While Lee descended into gloom, supporters of the Union rejoiced. The triumphs wrought by Sherman and Sheridan and the steady if unspectacular progress made at Petersburg helped revive the war spirit of the North. On November 8, Lincoln won reelection, defeating his erstwhile field commander by a plurality of almost half a million votes. Two days later, when the final tally was in, Grant cabled Stanton with a request: "Congratulate the President for me for . . . a victory worth more to the country than a battle won." The result not only vindicated Lincoln's stewardship of the war effort but ensured that the conflict would be determined on the field of battle, not the negotiating table, and that Ulysses S. Grant would be the principal determinant.[35]

★ ★ ★

Ever since Sherman took Atlanta, his next move had been an issue of as much importance to Grant and the officials of the government as to Sherman himself. His armies could not remain in the captured city forever, and Grant wanted "to keep the enemy constantly pressed to the end of the war." The circuitous route that Hood had taken after evacuating the city suggested that Sherman would wear himself out trying to bring him to battle. Surely the victorious Federals could find more productive employment.[36]

Sherman believed he knew what should be done. Within days of occupying Atlanta, he proposed that he move east to Macon or Milledgeville, the state capital, then to the coast, perhaps capturing Savannah in the process. Initially, Lincoln and Halleck voiced strong opposition to the plan, as did some of Grant's closest advisors, including John Rawlins. It made no sense, they argued, for Sherman to turn his back on Hood, who would then be free to march into Tennessee and perhaps all the way to the Ohio River (which is exactly what the Rebel commander proposed to do).

Grant was not as strongly opposed to Sherman's project as his superiors or his chief of staff. For one thing, he was confident that, as Sherman predicted, Hood could be contained by heavy detachments from the Military Division of the Mississippi sent to Tennessee under George Thomas. Yet Grant had never given up his hope of taking Mobile, and Sherman might be the instrument to that end. The previous month, Admiral Farragut, with four monitor-class gunboats and fourteen wooden men-of-war, had captured Mobile Bay, effectively ending its role as a conduit of Rebel commerce. Farragut had not neutralized the fortifications at the mouth of the bay, however, and the city remained open for business. Closing it down was a task for a formidable army such as Sherman's.

On September 12, Grant sent Horace Porter to Georgia to provide Sherman with details of a strategic vision predicated on capturing not only Mobile but also Wilmington, North Carolina, the last Atlantic Coast port of value to the Confederacy. Grant wished Sherman to provide him, through Porter, his views on the subject. Barely two weeks after Porter left City Point, however, Grant's thinking took a wide turn upon learning that Hood had gotten into the rear of Sherman's armies and was heading north. Grant immediately endorsed the plan to send Thomas to Chattanooga, and later to Nashville, where an army would be assembled from forces sent to him by Sherman and augmented by units elsewhere in the theater. The additions included a full corps of cavalry under now-Brevet Major General James Wilson, whom Grant had detached from the Shenandoah Valley to command Sherman's mounted arm.

On October 13, Grant informed Secretary Stanton that he had approved Sherman's march through Georgia to the coast. One month later, having completed his job of destroying Atlanta's capacity for war production, Sherman started east at the forefront of sixty thousand infantrymen and artillerymen and a division of horse soldiers. As he had informed Grant, he intended not only to capture objectives of strategic importance but by living off the land he covered to "make Georgia howl."[37]

★ ★ ★

With one expedition to the Atlantic seaboard underway, Grant turned to the outfitting of another. Before he did, however, he greeted a couple of semipermanent guests—Julia and young Jesse, who came to share the snug cabin that had been built for their general as a combination office-living quarters by a fatigue detail supervised by Rufus Ingalls. Grant's loved ones arrived in early January from Burlington, New Jersey, in one of whose celebrated private schools Julia had placed the children at the commencement of the fall term. The older children were still at their studies, watched over by the wife of Julia's brother, Fred (the latter was now a member of Grant's staff, with rank of brigadier general); although the oldest, fourteen-year-old Frederick Dent Grant, had just ended a Christmas holiday visit to Fort Monroe, which included frequent trips to his father's headquarters.

Julia and Jesse would spend the next three months at City Point, "domiciled in this little cabin," as she noted, "enjoying not only the society of the Commanding General but all of the distinguished men and generals that visited headquarters that winter." Visitors who failed to knock sometimes encountered Grant and Julia kissing like teenaged sweethearts or the general on the cabin floor tussling with Jesse. And when they left Virginia in April, the family had a new home to move into: a stately row house in Philadelphia, completely furnished, presented to the general by several patriotic gentlemen of the city as a token of their esteem.[38]

Since late 1862, the Navy Department had been struggling to launch an operation against Wilmington, North Carolina, the closing of which it considered tantamount to "severing the jugular vein" of the Confederacy. Since then, blockade-runners out of Europe, Canada, the Bahamas, and Bermuda had smuggled almost thirty million dollars worth of war goods—weapons, ammunition, medicines, supplies of all kinds—into the Confederacy via that port, which lay beyond the effective reach of the North Atlantic Blockading Squadron. Every attempt to stanch the flow had failed, largely because of Fort Fisher, the massive, heavily armed earthwork that commanded the water approach to Wilmington from a sandy peninsula, Confederate Point, almost twenty miles below the city.[39]

Only when Grant interested himself in the project was a full-size expedition fitted out to capture the earthwork, close the port, and occupy Wilmington. A reported strengthening of Colonel William Lamb's garrison, however, caused the operation, originally planned for October, to be postponed for two months. When the project was revived in early December, extensive planning went into it and substantial resources were committed—sixty-five hundred members of the Army of the James stripped from the siege lines above the James, supported by a flotilla of sixty warships under Grant's old naval colleague, David Dixon Porter. The able and energetic Porter was a good choice for the mission, but Grant made the mistake of permitting Ben Butler to command the army contingent. Butler was ordered to attack or besiege the fort as soon as he landed on Confederate Point. Under no circumstances was he to return to Virginia without doing one or the other.

Butler failed to heed his instructions. He seemed more interested in testing a "powder boat," an old mail packet laden with explosives that he intended to beach near the fort. The politician-general's inability to cooperate with the navy, unforeseen delays and difficulties, and the spectacular failure of the powder boat unsettled Butler and doomed his assault. Landing north of Fisher's land face on Christmas Day, he found the surf running dangerously high and Lamb's garrison undeterred by a massive but misdirected barrage by

Porter's gunboats. The army commander suddenly lost heart, cancelled the operation, and withdrew. He pulled out to sea so quickly that hundreds of his men were left stranded on the beach beneath the fort's guns.

When Butler returned to Fort Monroe empty-handed, a furious Grant made plans to relieve him of his command. He did so on January 8, replacing him with Edward Ord—a move sustained by Lincoln, who no longer needed Butler's political support. Grant immediately notified Admiral Porter that a second attempt would be made against Fisher. A better organized and slightly larger expeditionary force was formed, which Grant entrusted to one of Butler's more aggressive subordinates, Brevet Major General Alfred Terry. The force sailed from Hampton Roads on January 4, 1865, and eleven days later, supported closely by Porter's seamen and guns, attacked the fort in successive waves. After five hours of some of the most desperate close-quarters fighting of the war, the Federals forced the garrison to surrender and slammed shut the last door connecting the Confederacy to the outside world.[40]

Grant rejoiced over Terry's victory, as did Secretary of War Stanton, who visited Fisher only hours after it fell. "When he heard the good news he promoted all the officers of any considerable rank for their conspicuous gallantry," Grant reported. Terry, now a full-rank major general of volunteers, was ordered to operate against the city itself, surmounting the various other fortifications that protected it.

In cooperation with John Schofield's XXIII Corps, then en route from Tennessee at Grant's behest, Terry was also to support Sherman's column once it reached the coast at Savannah. This occurred on December 10, four weeks after Sherman had departed Atlanta. Barely slowed by their ragtag opposition—mainly the Georgia militia and the poorly disciplined cavalry of Joseph Wheeler—Sherman and his "bummers" cut a swath of destruction sixty miles wide and stripped the state of every resource of conceivable use to the Confederacy, especially railroads, bridges, and farms. On December 21, twelve days after the Federals began to invest Savannah, the local commander, William Hardee, evacuated. The next day, an elated Sherman sent a telegram to Lincoln offering him the city, with all its captures, as a Christmas gift.[41]

★ ★ ★

Although Sherman's foray through Georgia had been spectacularly successful, by choosing to make it he had permitted Hood's Army of Tennessee to invade the state it was named for. Hood did not do so, however, until mid-November, which gave George Thomas, now at Nashville, the time he needed to assimilate the forces coming to him from many quarters. His was a heterogeneous command, but a formidable one. Grant calculated that by the time Hood entered Tennessee, Thomas had in and around Nashville at least seventy thousand men. A large detachment contested Hood's march at Columbia and Spring Hill, then repulsed the several attacks Hood launched at Franklin on November 30. The Confederate dead included five general officers, one being the redoubtable Pat Cleburne.[42]

After Franklin, Thomas concentrated his troops at Nashville, which Hood advanced against early the following month with twenty-three thousand troops, including cavalry under Bedford Forrest. Rather than challenge Hood, Thomas spent the next two weeks reinforcing and organizing his infantry and remounting Wilson's horse-poor cavalry. Hood, who attempted to lay siege to well-fortified Nashville, appeared willing to wait for Thomas to attack. But Grant, recalling the nerve-wracking deliberation with which Old Slow Trot had moved at and after Chattanooga, worried that Hood would slip away and invade Kentucky: "I consequently urged Thomas in frequent dispatches sent from City Point to make the attack at once. The country was alarmed, the administration was alarmed, and I was alarmed lest . . . Hood would go north."[43]

When winter weather further delayed Thomas's advance, Grant made plans to relieve him and personally oversee the effort against Hood. He got as far as Washington, where on December 15 he learned that Thomas was finally on the march, moving with a power and confidence that validated his lengthy preparations. Over the next two days, Thomas inflicted on his enemy one of the severest beatings an American army ever absorbed. In the fight, whose outcome was never in doubt, Hood lost almost six thousand men, most of them captured, almost twice as many as Thomas. By late on November 16, the Confederates who remained were scrambling for the safety of the Tennessee River, Wilson's horsemen in warm pursuit.

Only Hood's head-start and the rear-guard heroics of Bedford Forrest prevented the annihilation of the Army of Tennessee. Although later reconstituted yet again, this time under Joe Johnston, it would be made up of the scrapings of the Confederate military barrel. It would never regain its former potency, which had been so often diminished by inept leadership, inefficient organization, and the numerical superiority of its enemy.[44]

★ ★ ★

By mid-January 1865, it was obvious to the least insightful observer that the war was winding down. With Savannah occupied, Wilmington about to be, and with the threats posed by Early and Hood effectively erased (Sheridan would drub Old Jube once more, for good measure, at Waynesboro in early March), Grant could plan for the closing operations of the war. He still favored a strike against the forts and troops in Mobile, and this time appeared to have the manpower and high-level support to launch it. He assigned the command to Major General E.R.S. Canby, Nathaniel Banks's successor at New Orleans, who, once he took the coastal city, was to operate against the interior of Alabama. At about the same time, Grant directed Thomas to send a cavalry force against Forrest in Mississippi. Both operations were designed to prevent Confederate forces in the West from opposing Sherman as he moved from Savannah toward Petersburg. This journey Sherman had originally considered making via water; for want of transportation, he decided to conduct it by overland march through the Carolinas, a course Grant favored.

Grant's expectations for Alabama and Mississippi were never fulfilled. Canby and his forty-five thousand troops did not start for Mobile until mid-March. By then Sherman was well into North Carolina, having defeated a force led by Hardee at Averasboro, and on the verge of confronting a larger body under Johnston at Bentonville. After the latter battle, a two-day affair (March 19 and 21) that began well for the Confederates but ended, predictably enough, in their retreat, Sherman would move toward a union with Schofield and Terry, who had teamed to capture and occupy Wilmington four weeks earlier.[45]

If Canby got off to a late start, Thomas did not start at all. On January 31, a disappointed Grant canceled his expedition and instead ordered a pair of cavalry raids. Like Canby's movement, both started too late to contribute materially to Union strategy. Major General George Stoneman raided from Tennessee through parts of North Carolina and into western Virginia in belated and distant cooperation with Sherman; at the same time, James Wilson's horse soldiers, 12,500 strong—the largest mounted force assembled at any point in the war—were sent into Alabama and western Georgia in equally remote support of Canby.

Stoneman achieved mixed success, but Wilson's troopers rewrote the record books for mounted raids. Over a four-week period, they captured Selma and Montgomery, Alabama, along with almost seven thousand enemy troops; destroyed dozens of miles of railroad track and telegraph cable; demolished countless supply depots, factories, and mills; and, for the first time in the conflict, consistently defeated Forrest's cavalry in open combat. Because he had downed so many telegraph lines, however, Wilson could neither communicate with his superiors nor keep abreast of the war news. By the time his ride ended at Macon, Georgia, on April 20, the shooting had stopped in that theater. Thus Wilson's hugely successful expedition counted for naught in the long run—just as Ulysses Grant had anticipated and feared.[46]

With the Confederacy crumbling before its leaders' eyes, it was logical that they should put out peace feelers. These proved frequent and attractive enough to prompt Lincoln to meet with three commissioners sent by Jefferson Davis to discuss ending the conflict short of a climactic orgy of violence and death. Grant did his part to facilitate the meeting, which took place aboard a steamer anchored in Hampton Roads not far from Fort Monroe. When Davis's emissaries arrived at his City Point headquarters in advance of the conference, Grant conversed pleasantly enough with the "very agreeable gentlemen," especially Confederate Vice-President Alexander H. Stephens, although he was careful to avoid discussing the import of their mission.[47]

On the other hand, Grant would declare, "I never had admitted, and never was ready to admit, that they were the representatives of a government. There had been too great a waste of blood and treasure to concede anything of the kind." Thus he was not hugely disappointed when the conference foundered and broke apart on the issues of Confederate independence and the perpetuation of slavery. Nor was he eager to join other army officers in negotiating a separate peace. A few weeks after Lincoln met with Stephens and his associates, General Ord attempted to arrange an armistice with Grant's old friend James Longstreet, now in command of Confederate forces north of the James. As soon as he learned of the covert parlay Grant tried to stop it. And when Robert E. Lee wrote to him regarding a "military convention" that the two generals had proposed, Grant forwarded the correspondence to his superiors in Washington, who saw to it that the unauthorized negotiations went no further.[48]

The day after the Hampton Roads conference broke up, Lincoln visited Grant at City Point. He explained to his host—if an explanation was needed—why he had broken off talks with the commissioners. Grant appreciated being taken into the president's confidence and thought highly of his motivations in the matter. Lincoln's evident lack of malice impressed Grant, as it had in the past: "He always showed a generous and kindly spirit toward the Southern people, and I never heard him abuse an enemy. . . . Never in my presence did he evince a revengeful disposition—and I saw a great deal of him at City Point, for he seemed glad to get away from the cares and anxieties of the capital."[49]

The president enjoyed Grant's hospitality so much that he returned to his headquarters six weeks later, this time in company with the First Lady and their son, "Tad," during an inspection tour of the armies on the eve of their final campaign. Aboard the presidential yacht *River Queen*, Lincoln discussed strategy not only with his commanding general but also with distinguished visitors, including Sheridan, just returned from the Valley at the head of two divisions of cavalry; Sherman, up from North Carolina; and Admiral Porter, who had moved his headquarters to Hampton Roads.

When not talking strategy and tactics, Lincoln took his exercise aboard Grant's colossal war horse, Cincinnati, whom he rode when reviewing Grant's troops, the lieutenant general riding beside him on a much smaller mount named Jeff Davis, captured during the Vicksburg Campaign from a plantation owned by the brother of the Confederate president. Lincoln welcomed the diversion and exercise that riding afforded: "The enormous expense of the war seemed to weigh upon him like an incubus," Admiral Porter observed. "He could not keep away from General Grant's tent, and was constantly inquiring when he was going to move."[50]

★ ★ ★

That same question had long preyed on Grant's mind. After the war, he recalled,

> One of the most anxious periods of my experience during the rebellion, was the last few weeks before Petersburg. I felt that the situation of the Confederate army was such that they would try to make an escape at the earliest practicable moment, and I was afraid, every morning, that I would awake from my sleep to find that Lee had gone, and that nothing was left but a picket line.

As Horace Porter would put it, "General Grant . . . had been sleeping with one eye open and one foot out of bed for many weeks, in the fear that Lee would thus give him the slip." In fact, everyone at headquarters waited anxiously for the weather to warm and the roads to solidify. The pace of seasonal progression seemed agonizingly slow.[51]

Grant was right to fear a breakout; Lee attempted it before his enemy could move against him. Before daylight on March 25, he sent several casualty-depleted divisions to capture Fort Stedman, along the eastern face of the siege lines. Lee hoped that a lodgment there would prompt Grant to contract his line sufficiently to leave weak spots elsewhere that could be exploited. Lee's ultimate goal was to breach the investment lines, exit Petersburg en masse, and head for North Carolina. There he could join with Johnston in defeating Sherman, then attack Meade and Ord. Shortly after Stedman's fall, however, the surprise assault lost momentum. Units of General Parke's corps rushed up to seal the break, and a crossfire of musketry and shell ripped into the thin gray ranks. Those attackers who could withdraw did so speedily; four thousand others became casualties. Lee's final offensive of the conflict was history. If he was going to join with Joe Johnston, he would have to do so by evacuation, not by assault.[52]

Eight days later, Lee did evacuate, the direct result of a massive turning-movement Grant finally put in motion on March 29. That morning, the foot soldiers of Humphreys and Warren left their siege works bound for Lee's far right flank beyond the Boydton Plank Road. At the same time, Sheridan departed a staging area near Globe Tavern with nine thousand cavalrymen—those he had brought back from the Valley and additions from Meade's and Ord's forces. While the II and V Corps pushed toward Lee's main line of defense along the White Oak and Quaker Roads, Sheridan, following Grant's strategy, looped around the infantry and made for Dinwiddie Court House, five miles from the Rebel flank and almost within striking distance of the all-important South Side Railroad.

Lee responded to Sheridan's advance by sending a ten-thousand-man expeditionary force under the tragic Gettysburg hero George Pickett, including three divisions of cavalry under the army commander's nephew, Major General Fitzhugh Lee, to Five Forks, a crossroads eighteen miles southwest of Petersburg and five miles above Dinwiddie. Pickett dug in astride the intersection, but the works his men erected there would not withstand a well-conducted assault in even moderate strength. During the next two days he left his works to spar with Sheridan's troopers; but when Grant sent Warren's corps to Little Phil's assistance before daylight on April 1, Pickett retreated to his works, where he battened down to await help from Petersburg that would never come.

Sheridan was ready to attack Five Forks early on All Fools Day, but, due partly to lapses on his part and partly to circumstances beyond his control, Warren did not take position opposite Pickett's left until late afternoon, a delay that caused Sheridan's temper to boil. When infantry and cavalry finally went forward, Warren's attack went slightly awry. Even so, in less than ninety minutes, Pickett's line was in shambles and his men were retreating in confusion and panic across Hatcher's Run. The three thousand men who failed to cross to safety were taken prisoner. Sheridan was ecstatic; but even as shouts of triumph went up from the ranks, he made use of the authority recently given him to relieve Warren of his command. That authority had come from Grant, who had become fed up with Warren's chronic slowness and tendency to question given orders, habits that had nearly caused his removal on at least one other occasion.[53]

★ ★ ★

Five Forks overrun, his right flank broken, Lee had no alternative to evacuating Petersburg. Of necessity, Richmond also had to be abandoned. Throughout the second, Jefferson Davis and scores of lesser officials made plans to flee the capital. White and African American troops whom Ord had left behind when he moved his main army to Petersburg prepared for an unopposed entry into the city that had been a linchpin of Union strategy in the East since the war's earliest days.

While Richmond prepared to empty, on the night of April 1–2, Petersburg underwent an hours-long barrage followed next day by assaults on its outer works. Sensing coming victory, Ord's men wrested Fort Gregg, one of the strongest bastions in the city's defense line, from its defenders at bayonet-point. Farther west, Wright's VI Corps broke through the works that covered the Boydton Plank Road into the city, rolling up the Rebel lines and reaching the long-coveted South Side Railroad. Other attackers surmounted what remained of Lee's line along Hatcher's Run.[54]

After dark on April 2, Lee began to evacuate Petersburg along the only escape route left to him, which led north across the Appomattox River. Once on the upper bank, his troops turned west and were soon moving through the countryside of Amelia County. As it trudged along, the column neared a junction populated by a wave of fugitive soldiers and civilian refugees out of Richmond. The columns would meet in the vicinity of Amelia Court House, thirty-some miles west of Petersburg. At Amelia, Lee, still hopeful of escaping into North Carolina, planned to place his troops aboard trains on the Richmond & Danville Railroad that would shuttle them to Joe Johnston's area of operations.

★ ★ ★

Early on April 3, Grant, who had transferred his headquarters from City Point to the outskirts of Petersburg, rode into the evacuated city. There he conferred with officers in charge of the occupation forces and, presently, with Abraham Lincoln, who had not returned to Washington following the recent strategy session aboard the *River Queen*. Grant had been keeping him posted on the progress of his turning-movement, and its effects. Anticipating Petersburg's emptying, the previous afternoon Grant had sent the president a telegram inviting him to visit army headquarters in the city. The president agreed, adding a warm postscript: "Allow me to tender you, and all with you, the nation's grateful thanks for the additional and magnificent successes."[55]

Late on April 3, the two men met at a house on Market Street. Lincoln seized Grant's hand and "stood shaking it for some time, and pouring out his thanks and congratulations with all the fervor of a heart which seemed overflowing with its fullness of joy," Horace Porter noted. "I doubt whether Mr. Lincoln ever experienced a happier moment in his life." He quoted the chief executive as telling Grant, with a sly smile: "Do you know, general, I had a sort of sneaking idea all along that you intended to do something like this." Grant smiled, made an appropriate reply, and engaged the president in pleasant talk for an hour or more. It would be the last time he did so.[56]

At length, it was time to go. The two men who had done more than anyone else to end this war went their separate ways. When word of Richmond's capture and occupation reached Lincoln a few hours after he and Grant parted, the president headed north to take a symbolic walk through the streets of that city. Grant mounted Cincinnati and rode toward Sutherland's Station on the South Side Railroad. Already he had sent the troops of Meade and Ord westward to press Lee's column while ordering Phil Sheridan and his horsemen to circle southward and make for Jetersville, on the R & D ten miles southwest of Amelia Court House. Sheridan arrived at that depot in time to block Lee's path to North Carolina. The fugitive Rebels would have to keep moving west in the direction of Lynchburg. As they did so, Grant hoped, they would be cut off and brought to bay.

On the morning of April 4, Grant, who was accompanying Meade's column, left Sutherland's Station after only a few hours of sleep and pushed westward. "The pursuit," Horace Porter recalled, "had now become swift, unflagging, relentless." Now Grant joined Ord's troops, whose line of march paralleled Sheridan's on the south. Before dark he reached Wilson's Station, twenty-seven miles out of Petersburg. Meade and Ord had yet to make contact with the Rebels, but they were closing in; and Sheridan was straining every muscle and nerve to get ahead of the enemy.[57]

Late on April 5, Grant received a message from Sheridan at Jetersville, where Meade's advance was closing up on the cavalry's column. At Little Phil's urging, Grant moved to the front, reaching the depot at 10:00 P.M. and conferring with his generals. With Grant's reluctant approval, the next morning Meade started up the railroad in hopes of catching Lee at Amelia Court

House. Sheridan, who was convinced that Lee would not wait for Meade, pushed west parallel to the enemy's line of march, Ord's infantry following. Presently, Little Phil was proved correct: Meade reached Amelia to find the enemy well ahead of him and forging west. Meade was forced to follow, sniping at the Rebel rear, but he was unable to bring the fugitives to heel.[58]

By late on April 7, Grant, again traveling with Ord's column, began to feel confident of overtaking his opponent and forcing him to surrender. Late the previous day, a large detachment of Lee's column had suffered a disastrous defeat when overtaken by Sheridan and forward elements of Meade's infantry at Little Sailor's Creek. In the lopsided fight, the Confederates lost about seventy-five hundred men, most of them captured, including six general officers. It seemed a matter of time before Lee's main body was also run to earth and badly whipped. So thinking, while at Farmville, twenty-odd miles west of Amelia Court House, Grant at 5:00 P.M. on April 7 sent through the lines a letter that began: "The results of the last week must convince you of the hopelessness of further resistance." The balance of the letter called on Lee to lay down his arms and avoid "any further effusion of blood." Grant knew that the hopelessness he spoke of extended to Joe Johnston's army as well. Once Lee surrendered, the capitulation of every other Confederate command would be a matter of time.[59]

Hours later, Lee replied by flag-of-truce courier that he did not believe his situation without hope; nevertheless he inquired about the terms Grant would offer in the event of a surrender. In response, Grant listed one condition: that Lee's troops disarm, accept parole, and return to their homes until or unless exchanged. Again Lee sent a negative reply, although he did suggest negotiations toward a truce. He offered to meet Grant between the lines to discuss the proposal, but Grant, who sensed another attempt to broker a separate peace, declined.[60]

The situation changed dramatically at about 2:00 P.M. on April 8, when Sheridan's hard-riding horsemen forged ahead of Lee's column, turned north, and occupied Appomattox Station, near where Lee hoped to meet a train sent from Lynchburg that was filled with rations for his famished troops. A message to that effect had fallen into the hands of Sheridan's scouts, and Little Phil, by a clever stratagem, had arranged to have the trains sent, instead, inside his own lines. The loss of the rations, coupled with Sheridan's presence across his path and the rapid approach of Ord's troops in the cavalry's rear, told Lee that the race was over and he had lost.[61]

On the morning of April 9, the Confederate leader made a desperate attempt to break through Sheridan's lines west of Appomattox Court House. The blow was strongly delivered, but Sheridan parried it long enough for the

Army of the James to reach the scene and spell his troopers on the firing line. The presence of large numbers of infantry and artillery both in front and in the rear meant that the Army of Northern Virginia had reached the end of its tether.[62]

Early that morning, Grant, who was suffering from one of his migraines, had ridden with Meade's troops as they closed in on the enemy rear and engaged what remained of the once-proud command of James Longstreet. Suddenly eager to view the fighting on Sheridan's and Ord's front, Grant spurred Cincinnati across the fields to the south, trailed by his staff. On the way, he was met by another courier from Lee. Unlike his predecessors, this man carried a note expressing his commander's willingness to meet at Appomattox Court House to talk surrender. Until that moment, Grant's sick headache had been beating like a trip-hammer against the inside of his skull. He recalled, "The instant I saw the contents of the note, I was cured." At his order, a cease-fire took effect all along the line, the guns falling silent one by one. Collecting his staff and accompanied by Sheridan and Ord, Grant rode slowly toward the courthouse village that sat between the lines suddenly gone quiet as if with anticipation and wonder.[63]

This was a ride heavy with significance for a man who had completed the climb from the bottom rung of life to the summit of achievement and honor. Although not one to look to the past for direction, Grant would have been forgiven had the journey evoked memories both poignant and pleasant—memories of adversity endured and misgivings overcome at West Point, in Mexico, and in the peacetime army, of failure and poverty erased by war, of trial and error at Belmont and Fort Henry, of success and travail at Donelson and Shiloh, of triumph and redemption at Vicksburg and Chattanooga, of frustration and perseverance on the tortuous, bloody route from the Wilderness to Petersburg.

All these things were behind him now—he was riding toward final victory, propelled by a combination of uncommon qualities concealed beneath a most common exterior, qualities capable of transcending human weakness. One quality, more than any other, which he had acquired at an early age, had brought him this far—a determination to forge ahead, once he had set a course, and never turn back, no matter how many swollen, angry rivers barred his path.

NOTES

ABBREVIATIONS:

B&L   *Battles and Leaders of the Civil War*
CWTI   *Civil War Times Illustrated*
JDG   Julia Dent Grant
HG   Hamlin Garland
LC   Library of Congress
MSS   Correspondence, Papers
OR   *The War of the Rebellion: A Compilation of the Official Records of the Union and Confederate Armies*
ORN   *Official Records of the Union and Confederate Navies During the War of the Rebellion*
USC   Doheny Library, University of Southern California
USG   Ulysses S. Grant

CHAPTER 1

1. *New York Times,* July 24, 1885; Jeffry D. Wert, *General James Longstreet, the Confederacy's Most Controversial Soldier: A Biography* (New York, 1993), 50; HG interview of James Longstreet, March 20, 1897, HG MSS, USC.

2. HG interview of James Longstreet, March 20, 1897, HG MSS, USC.

3. *New York Times,* July 24, 1885.

4. USG, *Personal Memoirs of U. S. Grant,* ed. E. B. Long (New York, 2001), 6; HG, *Ulysses S. Grant: His Life and Character* (New York, 1898), 1–2.

5. USG, *Personal Memoirs,* 3–5; Henry Coppée, *Grant and His Campaigns: A Military Biography* (New York, 1866), 18–19; Albert D. Richardson, *A Personal History of Ulysses S. Grant* (Hartford, Conn., 1868), 17–32; Charles A. Dana and James Harrison Wilson, *The Life of Ulysses S. Grant, General of the Armies of the United States* (Springfield, Mass., 1868), 17–19; Louis A. Coolidge, *Ulysses S. Grant,* 2 vols. (Boston, 1917), 1:7–8; William Conant Church, *Ulysses S. Grant and the Period of National Preservation and Reconstruction* (New York, 1926), 4–6; William E. Woodward, *Meet General Grant* (New York, 1939), 11–12; Lloyd Lewis, *Captain Sam Grant* (Boston, 1950), 5–8; William S. McFeely, *Grant* (New York, 1981), 3–6; Geoffrey Perret, *Ulysses S. Grant, Soldier & President* (New York, 1997), 4–7; Jean Edward Smith, *Grant* (New York, 2001), 21–22.

6. Richardson, *Personal History of Ulysses S. Grant,* 49–53; Church, *Ulysses S. Grant,* 6; Lewis, *Captain Sam Grant,* 9–10.

7. Richardson, *Personal History of Ulysses S. Grant,* 49–53; HG, *Ulysses S. Grant,* 2; Lewis, *Captain Sam Grant,* 9–11.

8. USG, *Personal Memoirs,* 6; Lewis, *Captain Sam Grant,* 12–14.

9. Church, *Ulysses S. Grant,* 7; Lewis, *Captain Sam Grant,* 14–15.

10. Lewis, *Captain Sam Grant,* 14–16; R. J. Smith, "Man Proposes and God Disposes: The Religious Faith of Ulysses S. Grant," *Cavalry Journal* 26 (June 2001): 13–14; Church, *Ulysses S. Grant,* 6–7; Michael J. Cramer, *Ulysses S. Grant: Conversations and Unpublished Letters* (New York, 1897), 60; John H. Wigger, *Taking Heaven by Storm: Methodism and the Rise of Popular Christianity in America* (New York, 1998), 12–13.

11. Richardson, *Personal History of Ulysses S. Grant,* 71; USG, *Personal Memoirs,* 4, 6, 8, 10; Perret, *Ulysses S. Grant,* 15; Smith, "Man Proposes and God Disposes," 14.

12. Smith, "Man Proposes and God Disposes," 14; Perret, *Ulysses S. Grant,* 19; HG interview of Jesse Root Grant (son of USG), n.d., HG MSS, USC.

13. HG, *Ulysses S. Grant,* 6–7; Michael Korda, *Ulysses S. Grant, the Unlikely Hero* (New York, 2004), 13; Josiah Bunting, III, *Ulysses S. Grant* (New York, 2004), 9–10; William B. Hesseltine, *Ulysses S. Grant, Politician* (New York, 1935), 2–3; Woodward, *Meet General Grant,* 13–14.

14. Richardson, *Personal History of Ulysses S. Grant,* 69; Oliver Optic [William Taylor Adams], *Our Standard-Bearer; or, The Life of General Ulysses S. Grant: His Youth, His Manhood, His Campaigns, and His Eminent Services in the Reconstruction of the Nation His Sword Has Redeemed* (Boston, 1868), 50–51; HG, *Ulysses S. Grant,* 5–6; Church, *Ulysses S. Grant,* 7–8; Coolidge, *Ulysses S. Grant,* 1:4; Lewis, *Captain Sam Grant,* 17; Korda, *Ulysses S. Grant,* 14–15.

15. Lewis, *Captain Sam Grant,* 21–22; Perret, *Ulysses S. Grant,* 11; John S. C. Abbott, *The Life of General Ulysses S. Grant, Containing a Brief but Faithful Narrative of Those Military and Diplomatic Achievements . . .* (Boston, 1868), 12.

16. HG, *Ulysses S. Grant,* 10–11; Church, *Ulysses S. Grant,* 13.

17. Richardson, *Personal History of Ulysses S. Grant,* 56; HG, *Ulysses S. Grant,* 13–14; Abbott, *Life of General Ulysses S. Grant,* 13–14.

18. Richardson, *Personal History of Ulysses S. Grant,* 56; Coolidge, *Ulysses S. Grant,* 1:10.

19. USG, *Personal Memoirs,* 8; Richardson, *Personal History of Ulysses S. Grant,* 67; Perret, *Ulysses S. Grant,* 14.

20. Richardson, *Personal History of Ulysses S. Grant,* 63–65; [Adams], *Our Standard-Bearer,* 43–44.

21. Ishbel Ross, *The General's Wife: The Life of Mrs. Ulysses S. Grant* (New York, 1959), 93.

22. Coolidge, *Ulysses S. Grant,* 1:9; Woodward, *Meet General Grant,* 14; McFeely, *Grant,* 9.

23. HG, *Ulysses S. Grant,* 6–7.

24. Woodward, *Meet General Grant,* 14; Korda, *Ulysses S. Grant,* 14; McFeely, *Grant,* 10.

25. Richardson, *Personal History of Ulysses S. Grant,* 57; HG, "The Early Life of Ulysses Grant," *McClure's Magazine* 8 (1897): 134; USG, *Personal Memoirs,* 9–10; Hesseltine, *Ulysses S. Grant, Politician,* 4.

26. Coolidge, *Ulysses S. Grant,* 1:13.

27. Adam Badeau, *Military History of Ulysses S. Grant, from April, 1861, to April, 1865,* 3 vols. (New York, 1868–1881), 2:21; David L. Wilson and John Y. Simon, eds., *Ulysses S. Grant: Essays and Documents* (Carbondale, Ill., 1981), 94.

28. Smith, "Man Proposes and God Disposes," 9.

29. Ibid., 14–15; Richardson, *Personal History of Ulysses S. Grant,* 59–60, 169–170; Wilson and Simon, eds., *Ulysses S. Grant: Essays and Documents,* 92; Cramer, *Ulysses S. Grant: Conversations and Unpublished Letters,* 177–178, 202–203; Dana and Wilson, *Life of Ulysses S. Grant,* 403; HG interview of William Wrenshall Smith, n.d., HG MSS, USC; Woodward, *Meet General Grant,* 23.

30. Cramer, *Ulysses S. Grant: Conversations and Unpublished Letters,* 82; Jesse Root Grant, *In the Days of My Father, General Grant* (New York, 1925), 16–18.

31. Richardson, *Personal History of Ulysses S. Grant,* 58; HG, *Ulysses S. Grant,* 12n–13n; Smith, "Man Proposes and God Disposes," 6; Cramer, *Ulysses S. Grant: Conversations and Unpublished Letters,* 65–66; USG, *General Grant's Letters to a Friend, 1861–1880* (New York, 1897), 28; HG interview of W. T. Burke, September 26, 1896, HG MSS, USC; Brooks D. Simpson, *Let Us Have Peace: Ulysses S. Grant and the Politics of War and Reconstruction, 1861–1868* (Chapel Hill, N.C., 1991), 12; Lyle W. Dorsett, "The Problem of Ulysses S. Grant's Drinking during the Civil War," *Hayes Historical Journal* 4 (Fall 1983): 39.

32. Brian P. Quinn, *The Depression Sourcebook* (Los Angeles, 2000), 6–8; Jules R. Bemporad, "Individual Psychotherapy," in Ira D. Glick, ed., *Treating Depression* (San Francisco, 1995): 109–115; Bruce Catton, *U. S. Grant and the American Military Tradition* (Boston, 1954), 11; Daniel Ammen, *The Old Navy and the New . . . with an Appendix of Personal Letters from General Grant* (Philadelphia, 1891), 16.

33. USG, *Personal Memoirs,* 34; Richardson, *Personal History of Ulysses S. Grant,* 58–59.

34. USG, *Personal Memoirs,* 7; Richardson, *Personal History of Ulysses S. Grant,* 71; HG, *Ulysses S. Grant,* 17–18, 27–29.

35. USG, *Personal Memoirs,* 7.

36. USG, *Personal Memoirs,* 7; Richardson, *Personal History of Ulysses S. Grant,* 69.

37. USG, *Personal Memoirs,* 8; Richardson, *Personal History of Ulysses S. Grant,* 63, 73; HG, *Ulysses S. Grant,* 21.

38. USG, *Personal Memoirs,* 11; Richardson, *Personal History of Ulysses S. Grant,* 74; HG, *Ulysses S. Grant,* 21–22.

39. Richardson, *Personal History of Ulysses S. Grant,* 68, 75; HG, *Ulysses S. Grant,* 25–27; Lewis, *Captain Sam Grant,* 19–20.

40. Richardson, *Personal History of Ulysses S. Grant,* 75, 91; HG, *Ulysses S. Grant,* 32, 42.

41. USG, *Personal Memoirs,* 12–14; Richardson, *Personal History of Ulysses S. Grant,* 76; HG, *Ulysses S. Grant,* 30–31.

42. USG, *Personal Memoirs,* 14–15; *New York Herald,* April 7, 1885; Transcript of anon. interview of Frederick T. Dent. n.d., HG MSS, USC.

43. USG, *Personal Memoirs,* 17; Richardson, *Personal History of Ulysses S. Grant,* 76; Dana and Wilson, *Life of Ulysses S. Grant,* 27–28; Church, *Ulysses S. Grant,* 20.

44. USG, *Personal Memoirs,* 17; HG interview of James Longstreet, March 20, 1897, HG MSS, USC.

45. USG, *Personal Memoirs,* 15; USG, *Papers of Ulysses S. Grant,* ed. John Y. Simon et al., 28 vols. to date (Carbondale, Ill., 1967–), 1:4, 8.

46. USG, *Personal Memoirs,* 14.

47. Richardson, *Personal History of Ulysses S. Grant,* 91; James Grant Wilson, *General Grant* (New York, 1897), 38–39; Church, *Ulysses S. Grant,* 15–16.

48. USG, *Personal Memoirs,* 14–15; HG, *Ulysses S. Grant,* 46.

49. HG, *Ulysses S. Grant,* 43.

50. Richardson, *Personal History of Ulysses S. Grant,* 90; Coolidge, *Ulysses S. Grant,* 1:23; Church, *Ulysses S. Grant,* 17–18.

51. USG, *Personal Memoirs,* 29; Michael B. Ballard, *U. S. Grant: The Making of a General, 1861–1863* (Lanham, Md., 2005), 7; *New York Herald,* April 7, 1885; HG interview of James Longstreet, March 20, 1897, HG MSS, USC; Church, *Ulysses S. Grant,* 179.

52. USG, *Personal Memoirs,* 15–16.

53. HG, *Ulysses S. Grant,* 43, 45–46; Church, *Ulysses S. Grant,* 17; HG, "Grant at West Point: The Story of His Cadet Days," *McClure's Magazine* 8 (1897): 199; HG interview of James Longstreet, March 20, 1897, HG MSS, USC; Wilson, *General Grant,* 25–36; Coppée, *Grant and His Campaigns,* 22; [Adams], *Our Standard-Bearer,* 54–55; Coolidge, *Ulysses S. Grant,* 1:21–22.

54. USG, *Personal Memoirs,* 16.

55. Charles Winslow Elliott, *Winfield Scott, the Soldier and the Man* (New York, 1937), 757–759.

Chapter 2

1. USG, *Personal Memoirs of U. S. Grant,* ed. E. B. Long (New York, 2001), 16; Theophilus F. Rodenbough and William A. Haskin, eds., *The Army of the United States: Historical Sketches of Staff and Line . . .* (New York, 1896), 153–158; Theophilus F. Rodenbough, comp., *From Everglade to Cañyon with the Second United States Dragoons . . .* (New York, 1875), 18n, 77–82.

2. Albert D. Richardson, *A Personal History of Ulysses S. Grant* (Hartford, Conn., 1868), 92–93.

3. Louis A. Coolidge, *Ulysses S. Grant,* 2 vols. (Boston, 1917), 1:22–23; James Grant Wilson, *General Grant* (New York, 1897), 27–28; Geoffrey Perret, *Ulysses S. Grant, Soldier & President* (New York, 1997), 33.

4. USG, *Personal Memoirs,* 17; HG interview of W. T. Burke, September 26, 1896, HG MSS, USC.

5. Richardson, *Personal History of Ulysses S. Grant,* 91.

6. USG, *Personal Memoirs,* 17.

7. HG, *Ulysses S. Grant: His Life and Character* (New York, 1898), 47–48.

8. USG, *Personal Memoirs,* 17.

9. Ibid., 17–18.

10. Ibid., 18, 26; Robert W. Frazer, *Forts of the West: Military Forts . . . West of the Mississippi River to 1898* (Norman, Okla., 1965), xxi, xxiii.

11. Perret, *Ulysses S. Grant,* 41–42; Charles G. Ellington, *The Trial of U. S. Grant: The Pacific Coast Years, 1852–1854* (Glendale, Calif., 1987), 132–133.

12. USG, *Personal Memoirs,* 18–19; HG interview of Julia Dent Grant, n.d., HG MSS, USC.

13. JDG, *The Personal Memoirs of Julia Dent Grant (Mrs. Ulysses S. Grant),* ed. John Y. Simon (Carbondale, Ill., 1975), 47–48; Thomas Sharp, "Colonel Dent of Whitehaven: The Father-in-Law of General Grant," *McClure's Magazine* 9 (1897): 66; HG interview of Eliza M. Shaw, n.d., HG MSS, USC.

14. USG, *Personal Memoirs,* 19; Perret, *Ulysses S. Grant,* 40.

15. USG, *Personal Memoirs,* 19.

16. Ibid., 19–20; K. Jack Bauer, *The Mexican War, 1846–1848* (New York, 1974), 1–12.

17. USG, *Personal Memoirs,* 19–20; JDG, *Personal Memoirs,* 48–49.

18. USG, *Personal Memoirs,* 20.

19. Ibid., 20–21.

20. JDG, *Personal Memoirs,* 49–50.

21. Ibid., 50.

22. James M. McPherson, *Ordeal by Fire: The Civil War and Reconstruction* (New York, 1982), 51–52, 60–61, 86.

23. Frazer, *Forts of the West,* 60–62; HG interview of James Longstreet, March 20, 1897, HG MSS, USC.

24. USG to JDG, June 4, 1844, USG MSS, LC.

25. USG to JDG, January 12, 1855, ibid.

26. Bauer, *Mexican War, 1846–1848,* 8–12, 16–19.

27. JDG, *Personal Memoirs,* 51.

28. Ibid.; USG, *Personal Memoirs,* 21.

29. JDG, *Personal Memoirs,* 51; USG, *Personal Memoirs,* 21–22.

30. HG interview of Mrs. Louisa Boggs, n.d., HG MSS, USC; Richardson, *Personal History of Ulysses S. Grant,* 153–154.

31. USG to JDG, May 6, 1845, USG MSS, LC.

32. USG, *Personal Memoirs,* 25.

33. Ibid., 26; Lloyd Lewis, *Captain Sam Grant* (Boston, 1950), 123.

34. USG, *Personal Memoirs,* 26–29.

35. Ibid., 29–30, 47; Jean Edward Smith, *Grant* (New York, 2001), 39.

36. USG, *Personal Memoirs,* 67.

37. Ibid., 31, 35; Charles A. Dana and James Harrison Wilson, *The Life of Ulysses S. Grant, General of the Armies of the United States* (Springfield, Mass., 1868), 32.

38. USG, *Personal Memoirs,* 34–35.

39. Bauer, *Mexican War, 1846–1848,* 35, 46; Francis B. Heitman, comp., *Historical Register and Dictionary of the United States Army . . . ,* 2 vols. (Washington, D.C., 1903), 1:800.

40. USG, *Personal Memoirs,* 30.

41. Ibid., 32, 38–40; Bauer, *Mexican War, 1846–1848,* 46–52; Alfred Hoyt Bill, *Rehearsal for Conflict* (New York, 1947), 50–106.

42. Lewis, *Captain Sam Grant,* 144–151; Smith, *Grant,* 47–49; Bauer, *Mexican War, 1846–1848,* 52–65; USG, *Personal Memoirs,* 42–46.

43. Bauer, *Mexican War, 1846–1848,* 81–82; USG, *Personal Memoirs,* 48; USG, *Papers of Ulysses S. Grant,* ed. John Y. Simon et al., 28 vols. to date (Carbondale, Ill., 1967–), 1:121.

44. USG, *Papers of Ulysses S. Grant,* 1:121n.

45. USG to JDG, June 5, 1846, USG MSS, LC; Bauer, *Mexican War, 1846–1848,* 85–96.

46. USG, *Personal Memoirs,* 52–53; William S. McFeely, *Grant* (New York, 1981), 33.

47. USG, *Personal Memoirs,* 54–55; Lewis, *Captain Sam Grant,* 179–180.

48. Bauer, *Mexican War, 1846–1848,* 96–101.

49. Ibid., 201–202; USG, *Personal Memoirs,* 56–57; Bill, *Rehearsal for Conflict,* 278–283; Smith, *Grant,* 58–59.

50. Bauer, *Mexican War, 1846–1848,* 232–253; USG, *Personal Memoirs,* 58–61.

51. Bauer, *Mexican War, 1846–1848,* 263–274, 283; USG, *Personal Memoirs,* 64–65; Lewis, *Captain Sam Grant,* 207–208.

52. USG, *Personal Memoirs,* 66–67. Although supposedly superseded by later works, the most comprehensive biography of Scott is Charles Winslow Elliott, *Winfield Scott, the Soldier and the Man* (New York, 1937).

53. Bauer, *Mexican War, 1846–1848,* 291–297; USG, *Personal Memoirs,* 63, 79n.

54. Bauer, *Mexican War, 1846–1848,* 292–301, 308–311.

55. USG, *Personal Memoirs,* 73–75; HG interview of James Elderkin, n.d., HG MSS, USC; Lewis, *Captain Sam Grant,* 239–241; Perret, *Ulysses S. Grant,* 68–69.

56. Bauer, *Mexican War, 1846–1848,* 319–321; Lewis, *Captain Sam Grant,* 249–253; Perret, *Ulysses S. Grant,* 71.

CHAPTER 3

1. USG to JDG, September 1847, USG MSS, LC.

2. USG, *Personal Memoirs of U. S. Grant,* ed. E. B. Long (New York, 2001), 81.

3. Ibid., 90.

4. Ibid., 90–91.

5. USG to JDG, September 1847, March 22, 1848, USG MSS, LC.

6. HG interview of James Elderkin, n.d., HG MSS, USC.

7. Carl M. Becker, "Was Grant Drinking in Mexico?" *Bulletin of the Cincinnati Historical Society* 24 (1966): 70–71; Albert D. Richardson, *A Personal History of Ulysses S. Grant* (Hartford, Conn., 1868), 138.

8. USG, *Personal Memoirs,* 88–93; USG to JDG, May 7, 1848, USG MSS, LC.

9. USG to JDG, September 1847, ISG MSS, LC.

10. USG, *The Papers of Ulysses S. Grant,* ed. John Y. Simon et al., 28 vols. to date (Carbondale, Ill., 1967–), 1:164n.

11. Ibid.; JDG, *The Personal Memoirs of Julia Dent Grant (Mrs. Ulysses S. Grant),* ed. John Y. Simon (Carbondale, Ill., 1975), 52, 54.

12. William M. Thayer, *From Tannery to the White House: The Life of Ulysses S. Grant, His Boyhood, Youth, Manhood and Private Life and Services* (New York, 1885), 130.

13. JDG, *Personal Memoirs,* 55; HG interview of JDG, n.d.; HG interview of Louisa Boggs, n.d.; both, HG MSS, USC.

14. JDG, *Personal Memoirs,* 55.

15. Ibid.

16. Ibid., 56–57; HG interview of Louisa Boggs, n.d.; HG interview of Eliza M. Shaw, n.d.; HG interview of Dr. W. Lee Wright, n.d.; all, HG MSS, USC.

17. JDG, *Personal Memoirs,* 57.

18. HG interview of W. T. Burke, September 26, 1896, HG MSS, USC.

19. JDG, *Personal Memoirs,* 57–58.

20. Ibid., 58–59; *Detroit Free Press,* Nov. 17, 21, 1848; Richardson, *Personal History of Ulysses S. Grant,* 129.

21. JDG, *Personal Memoirs,* 59–61.

22. HG, "Grant's Quiet Years at Northern Posts," *McClure's Magazine* 8 (1897): 403.

23. JDG, *Personal Memoirs,* 59.

24. Ibid., 65–66.

25. USG, *Personal Memoirs,* 97; Richardson, *Personal History of Ulysses S. Grant,* 134–135.

26. JDG, *Personal Memoirs,* 67.

27. Ibid., 69–70.

28. Lyle W. Dorsett, "The Problem of Ulysses S. Grant's Drinking During the Civil War," *Hayes Historical Journal* 4 (Fall 1983): 40.

29. Mark Edward Lender and James Kirby Martin, *Drinking in America: A History* (New York, 1987), 64–74; Jack H. Mendelson and Nancy K. Mello, *Alcohol: Use and Abuse in America* (Boston, 1985), 27–40; HG, "Grant's Quiet Years at Northern Posts," 403.

30. John R. Bumgarner, *The Health of the Presidents: The 41 United States Presidents through 1993 from a Physician's Point of View* (Jefferson, N.C., 1994), 103; HG, "Grant's Quiet Years," 403.

31. JDG, *Personal Memoirs,* 71.

32. USG, *Personal Memoirs,* 97–98; Dorsett, "Grant's Drinking during the Civil War," 40; HG interview of James Elderkin, n.d., HG MSS, USC.

33. USG, *Personal Memoirs,* 98.

34. From the poem "Beyond the Chagres," by James Stanley Gilbert (1894–1913).

35. USG, *Personal Memoirs,* 99.

36. HG interview of James Elderkin, n.d., HG MSS, USC.

37. USG, *Personal Memoirs,* 99; David L. Wilson and John Y. Simon, eds., *Ulysses S. Grant: Essays and Documents* (Carbondale, Ill., 1981), 37–38; JDG, *Personal Memoirs,* 71.

38. HG, "Grant's Quiet Years," 408; Wilson and Simon, eds., *Ulysses S. Grant: Essays and Documents,* 40–45.

39. USG, *Personal Memoirs,* 99; Wilson and Simon, eds., *Ulysses S. Grant: Essays and Documents,* 43.

40. USG, *Personal Memoirs,* 100–102.

41. Ibid., 102.

42. Ibid.; Bruce Catton, *U. S. Grant and the American Military Tradition* (Boston, 1954), 48–49; HG interview of James Elderkin, n.d., HG MSS, USC; Richardson, *Personal History of Ulysses S. Grant,* 146; Charles G. Ellington, *The Trial of U. S. Grant: The Pacific Coast Years, 1852–1854* (Glendale, Calif., 1987), 114–115, 119–122.

43. HG interview of James Elderkin, n.d., HG MSS, USC; Louis A. Coolidge, *Ulysses S. Grant,* 2 vols. (Boston, 1917), 1:33; James Grant Wilson, *General Grant* (New York, 1897), 379.

44. Ellington, *Trial of U. S. Grant,* 146–147; USG to JDG, February 2, 1854, USG MSS, LC.

45. Ellington, *Trial of U. S. Grant,* 155–156; USG to JDG, February 6, March 6, 25, 1854, USG MSS, LC.

46. Charles King, *The True Ulysses S. Grant* (Philadelphia, 1914), 127; Bumgarner, *Health of the Presidents,* 102; Ellington, *Trial of U. S. Grant,* 167–181; Coolidge, *Ulysses S. Grant,* 1:33; HG interview of Henry Heth, n.d., HG MSS, USC.

47. HG, "Notes from a Talk by General Chetlain," n.d., 3–4, HG MSS, USC.

48. William Conant Church, *Ulysses S. Grant and the Period of National Preservation and Reconstruction* (New York, 1926), 52–53; Josiah Bunting, III, *Ulysses S. Grant* (New York, 2004), 31–32; Catton, *U. S. Grant and the American Military Tradition,* 50–51.

49. Ellington, *Trial of U. S. Grant,* 181–184, attacks several points made by Professor Dorsett in his journal article on Grant's drinking habits. Ellington's approach is to set up straw men and knock them down. He misstates Dorsett's thesis that Grant had no military reputation to lose at the outset of the Civil War. He distorts Dorsett's view of why Grant became a Son of Temperance. He disregards—strictly because it cannot be proven—Dorsett's suggestion that Grant might have inherited his alcoholic tendencies from his grandfather. And

he builds his arguments on the dubious assertion—which Dorsett disproves—that alcohol never interfered with Grant's performance as a soldier.

50. Ibid., 191–192; Richardson, *Personal History of Ulysses S. Grant,* 148.

51. HG interview of JDG, n.d., HG MSS, USC; Richardson, *Personal History of Ulysses S. Grant,* 149–150; Ellington, *Trial of U. S. Grant,* 192–98.

52. HG interview of Simon B. Buckner, n.d., HG MSS, USC.

53. HG, *Ulysses S. Grant: His Life and Character* (New York, 1898), 125–129; HG interview of Dr. W. Lee Wright, n.d., HG MSS, USC.

54. USG, *Personal Memoirs,* 106; JDG, *Personal Memoirs,* 75.

CHAPTER 4

1. JDG, *The Personal Memoirs of Julia Dent Grant (Mrs. Ulysses S. Grant),* ed. John Y. Simon (Carbondale, Ill., 1975), 76; Albert D. Richardson, *A Personal History of Ulysses S. Grant* (Hartford, Conn., 1868), 150; HG, *Ulysses S. Grant: His Life and Character* (New York, 1898), 129–130; HG interview of Dr. F. Lee Wright, n.d.; Mary Grant Cramer questionnaire, n.d.; both HG MSS, USC.

2. USG, *Personal Memoirs of U. S. Grant,* ed. E. B. Long (New York, 2001), 106; JDG, *Personal Memoirs,* 75–76.

3. Richardson, *Personal History of Ulysses S. Grant,* 151; JDG, *Personal Memoirs,* 77; Charles King, *The True Ulysses S. Grant* (Philadelphia, 1914), 133; William Conant Church, *Ulysses S. Grant and the Period of National Preservation and Reconstruction* (New York, 1926), 57; Charles A. Dana and James Harrison Wilson, *The Life of Ulysses S. Grant, General of the Armies of the United States* (Springfield, Mass., 1868), 37.

4. HG interview of Louisa Boggs, n.d., HG MSS, USC; Dana and Wilson, *Life of Ulysses S. Grant,* 37–38.

5. HG, *Ulysses S. Grant,* 137.

6. Church, *Ulysses S. Grant,* 59.

7. Ibid., 57n; *New York Times,* September 10, 1885.

8. Richardson, *Personal History of Ulysses S. Grant,* 151–152; JDG, *Personal Memoirs,* 76, 78–80; HG interview of William Wrenshall Smith, n.d., HG MSS, USC; Alan W. O'Bright and Kristen R. Marolf, *The Farm on the Gravois: Ulysses S. Grant National Historic Site, St. Louis, Missouri* (St. Louis, 1999), 2:57–58; HG, "Grant's Life in Missouri," *McClure's Magazine* 8 (1897): 515.

9. Geoffrey Perret, *Ulysses S. Grant, Soldier & President* (New York, 1997), 110; Ishbel Ross, *The General's Wife: The Life of Mrs. Ulysses S. Grant* (New York, 1959), 90–92; Lyle W. Dorsett, "The Problem of Ulysses S. Grant's Drinking during the Civil War," *Hayes Historical Journal* 4 (Fall 1983): 45.

10. USG, *Personal Memoirs,* 106; JDG, *Personal Memoirs,* 80; James Grant Wilson, *General Grant* (New York, 1897), 78; John R. Bumgarner, *The Health of the Presidents: The 41 United States Presidents through 1993 from a Physician's Point of View* (Jefferson, N.C., 1994), 105; USG, *Letters of Ulysses S. Grant to His Father and His Youngest Sister, 1857 to 1878,* ed. Jesse Grant Cramer (New York, 1912), 9–11.

11. JDG, *Personal Memoirs,* 80; USG, *Personal Memoirs,* 106; USG, *Letters of Ulysses S. Grant to His Father and Sister,* 11–12; Church, *Ulysses S. Grant,* 58; William E. Woodward, *Meet General Grant* (New York, 1939), 123.

12. USG, *Personal Memoirs,* 106; USG, *Letters of Ulysses S. Grant to His Father and Sister,* 13–14; JDG, *Personal Memoirs,* 80–81; Richardson, *Personal History of Ulysses S. Grant,* 157–158.

13. Richardson, *Personal History of Ulysses S. Grant,* 159–160, 162; William M. Thayer, *From Tannery to the White House: The Life of Ulysses S. Grant, His Boyhood, Youth, Manhood and Private Life and Services* (New York, 1885), 138.

14. HG interview of Louisa Boggs, n.d.; HG interview of "Mrs. Dr. Baker," n.d.; both, HG MSS, USC.

15. HG interview of Louisa Boggs, n.d., ibid.

16. Richardson, *Personal History of Ulysses S. Grant,* 161; King, *True Ulysses S. Grant,* 134–135; Louis A. Coolidge, *Ulysses S. Grant,* 2 vols. (Boston, 1917), 1:3; Michael J. Cramer, *Ulysses S. Grant: Conversations and Unpublished Letters* (New York, 1897), 31.

17. USG, *Personal Memoirs,* 106; Richardson, *Personal History of Ulysses S. Grant,* 161–163.

18. USG, *Personal Memoirs,* 106; USG, *Letters of Ulysses S. Grant to His Father and Sister,* 17–18; Richardson, *Personal History of Ulysses S. Grant,* 164–167.

19. USG, *Personal Memoirs,* 108; USG, *Letters of Ulysses S. Grant to His Father and Sister,* 20–21.

20. USG, *Letters of Ulysses S. Grant to His Father and Sister,* 12, 19, 23; USG, *Papers of Ulysses S. Grant,* ed. John Y. Simon et al., 28 vols. to date (Carbondale, Ill., 1967–), 1:347; Perret, *Ulysses S. Grant,* 108; Richardson, *Personal History of Ulysses S. Grant,* 167–168.

21. USG, *Letters of Ulysses S. Grant to His Father and Sister,* 22–23; Richardson, *Personal History of Ulysses S. Grant,* 169.

22. JDG, *Personal Memoirs,* 82; Wilson, *General Grant,* 78–79.

23. USG, *Personal Memoirs,* 108–109; HG, *Ulysses S. Grant,* 146; HG interview of W. T. Burke, September 26, 1896, HG MSS, USC.

24. USG, *Personal Memoirs,* 106–107.

25. JDG, *Personal Memoirs,* 83–84; Richardson, *Personal History of Ulysses S. Grant,* 172.

26. Richardson, *Personal History of Ulysses S. Grant,* 172; Thayer, *From Tannery to White House,* 143–144; Perret, *Ulysses S. Grant,* 115–116.

27. USG, *Personal Memoirs,* 112; HG, *Ulysses S. Grant,* 151.

28. King, *True Ulysses S. Grant,* 135–136.

29. Richardson, *Personal History of Ulysses S. Grant,* 172.

30. JDG, *Personal Memoirs,* 84–86.

31. Thayer, *From Tannery to White House,* 142; Bumgarner, *Health of the Presidents,* 106.

32. USG, *Personal Memoirs,* 112–113.

33. Richardson, *Personal History of Ulysses S. Grant,* 174; Thayer, *From Tannery to White House,* 145.

34. Thayer, *From Tannery to White House,* 146; USG, *Personal Memoirs,* 109; HG interview of W. T. Burke, September 26, 1896, HG MSS, USC.

35. Richardson, *Personal History of Ulysses S. Grant,* 175.

36. Ibid., 175–176.

37. HG, *Ulysses S. Grant,* 152–153; USG, *Papers of Ulysses S. Grant,* 2:3–4.

38. HG interview of Louisa Boggs, n.d., HG MSS, USC.

39. Cramer, *Ulysses S. Grant: Conversations and Unpublished Letters,* 24–25; USG, *Papers of Ulysses S. Grant,* 2:6–7.

40. USG, *Papers of Ulysses S. Grant,* 2:8n.

41. Richardson, *Personal History of Ulysses S. Grant,* 177–178; HG, *Ulysses S. Grant,* 154–156; HG interview of W. T. Burke, September 26, 1896, HG MSS, USC; James Harrison Wilson, *Life of John A. Rawlins Lawyer, Assistant Adjutant-General, Chief of Staff, Major General of Volunteers, and Secretary of War* (New York, 1916), 46–49.

42. HG interview of W. T. Burke, September 26, 1896, HG MSS, USC.

43. Richardson, *Personal History of Ulysses S. Grant,* 179.

44. USG, *Papers of Ulysses S. Grant,* 2:35–36; USG, *Personal Memoirs,* 122.

45. USG, *Personal Memoirs,* 116; HG, *Ulysses S. Grant,* 156–158.

46. USG, *Personal Memoirs,* 116–117.

47. Ibid., 117–118; Lloyd Lewis, *Captain Sam Grant* (Boston, 1950), 402–406; HG, "Notes from a Talk by General Chetlain," n.d., 1; HG interview of J. Russell Jones, n.d.; both, HG MSS, USC.

48. HG interview of John E. Smith, n.d., HG MSS, USC.

49. Ibid.; USG, *Personal Memoirs,* 117–119; HG, *Ulysses S. Grant,* 161–163.

50. Lewis, *Captain Sam Grant,* 415–416; USG, *Papers of Ulysses S. Grant,* 12, 12n–13n.

51. USG, *Personal Memoirs,* 118–119; HG, "Notes from a Talk by General Chetlain," n.d., 2; HG interview of John E. Smith, n.d.; both, HG MSS, USC.

52. USG, *Personal Memoirs,* 119–120; Wilson, *General Grant,* 86.

53. USG, *Personal Memoirs,* 120–121.

54. Elden E. Billings, ed. "Letters end Diaries: The St. Louis Riots," *CWTI* 2 (June 1963): 39–40.

55. USG, *Personal Memoirs,* 121; HG interview of Frank Parker, n.d., HG MSS, USC; Lewis, *Captain Sam Grant,* 423.

56. HG, *Ulysses S. Grant,* 165–166; Lewis, *Captain Sam Grant,* 423–424.

57. HG, "Notes from a Talk by General Chetlain," n.d., 3, HG MSS, USC; USG, *Letters of Ulysses S. Grant to His Father and Sister,* 32–35.

58. USG, *Personal Memoirs,* 122–123; HG, *Ulysses S. Grant,* 168; John Russell Young, *Around the World with General Grant: A Narrative of the Visit of General U. S. Grant, Ex-President of the United States, to Various Countries in Europe, Asia, and Africa, in 1877, 1878, 1879,* 2 vols. (New York, 1879), 2:214–215.

59. E. B. Long and Barbara Long, *The Civil War Day by Day: An Almanac, 1861–1865* (Garden City, N.Y., 1971), 84–85.

60. HG interview of Ed Harland, January 14, 1897, HG MSS, USC; HG, *Ulysses S. Grant,* 169–170.

61. HG interview of Ed Harland, January 14, 1897, HG MSS, USC; HG, *Ulysses S. Grant,* 170–171.

62. Wilson, *General Grant,* 85.

CHAPTER 5

1. HG, *Ulysses S. Grant: His Life and Character* (New York, 1898), 169; Lloyd Lewis, *Captain Sam Grant* (Boston, 1950), 427.

2. Lewis, *Captain Sam Grant,* 427.

3. HG, *Ulysses S. Grant,* 173; Nancy Scott Anderson and Dwight Anderson, *The Generals: Ulysses S. Grant and Robert E. Lee* (New York, 1988), 192–193.

4. USG, *Papers of Ulysses S. Grant,* ed. John Y. Simon et al., 28 vols. to date (Carbondale, Ill., 1967–), 2:46, 46n–47n.

5. Ibid.

6. Bruce Catton, *Grant Moves South* (Boston, 1960), 5.

7. HG interview of Ed Harland, January 14, 1897, HG MSS, USC.

8. HG, *Ulysses S. Grant,* 174.

9. Ibid., 175.

10. Ibid.

11. HG interview of W. T. Burke, September 26, 1896; HG interview of Ed Harland, January 14, 1897; both, HG MSS, USC; Lewis, *Captain Sam Grant,* 428.

12. USG, *Personal Memoirs of U. S. Grant,* ed. E. B. Long (New York, 2001), 124–125.

13. HG, *Ulysses S. Grant,* 172; Louis A. Coolidge, *Ulysses S. Grant,* 2 vols. (Boston, 1917), 1:51–52; Lewis, *Captain Sam Grant,* 429–430.

14. J.F.C. Fuller, *The Generalship of Ulysses S. Grant* (London, 1929), 189–190.

15. USG, *Personal Memoirs,* 125–126; Catton, *Grant Moves South,* 9–10; *Illinois State Journal* (Springfield), July 1861, copy in HG MSS, USC.

16. Bruce Catton, *U. S. Grant and the American Military Tradition* (Boston, 1954), 59; HG interview of Ed Harland, February 4, 1897, HG MSS, USC.

17. USG, *Letters of Ulysses S. Grant to His Father and His Youngest Sister, 1857 to 1878,* ed. Jesse Grant Cramer (New York, 1912), 41–42; HG interview of Ed Harland, February 4, 1897, HG MSS, USC.

18. Catton, *Grant Moves South,* 10–11; USG, *Papers of Ulysses S. Grant,* 2:61 and n–62n; Theophilus F. Rodenbough, "War-Horses," in Francis Trevelyan Miller, ed., *The Photographic History of the Civil War,* 10 vols. (New York, 1911), 4:292, 294.

19. USG, *Personal Memoirs,* 126.

20. Ibid., 126–127; USG, *Letters of Ulysses S. Grant to His Father and Sister,* 41; USG to JDG, July 13, 19, 1861, USG MSS, LC; Arthur L. Conger, *The Rise of U. S. Grant* (New York, 1931), 5–6.

21. USG, *Personal Memoirs,* 127.

22. Ibid.

23. Ibid., 128; USG, *Letters of Ulysses S. Grant to His Father and Sister,* 43n; USG to JDG, August 3, 4, 1861, USG MSS, LC; Conger, *Rise of U. S. Grant,* 7; USG, *Papers of Ulysses S. Grant,* 2:80–81, 84–85; Catton, *Grant Moves South,* 13; William E. Parrish, "Frémont in Missouri," *CWTI* 17 (April 1978): 4.

24. USG, *Personal Memoirs,* 128–130; USG, *Letters of Ulysses S. Grant to His Father and Sister,* 45–46; USG to JDG, August 3, 4, 1861, USG MSS, LC; USG, *Papers of Ulysses S. Grant,* 2:80–81, 82n; Michael J. Cramer, *Ulysses S. Grant: Conversations and Unpublished Letters* (New York, 1897), 200.

25. USG, *Personal Memoirs,* 130; Henry Coppée, *Grant and His Campaigns: A Military Biography* (New York, 1866), 465–466; HG interview of James H. Wilson, March 1897, HG MSS, USC.

26. USG, *Personal Memoirs,* 130; James Harrison Wilson, *Life of John A. Rawlins, Lawyer, Assistant Adjutant-General, Chief of Staff, Major General of Volunteers, and Secretary of War* (New York, 1916), 52–53.

27. USG, *Personal Memoirs,* 130–131; USG to JDG, August 10, 1861, USG MSS, LC.

28. USG, *Personal Memoirs,* 130–131; USG to JDG, August 10, 1861, USG MSS, LC; USG, *Letters of Ulysses S. Grant to His Father and Sister,* 47.

29. The finest modern book-length works on First Bull Run (First Manassas) are William C. Davis, *Battle at Bull Run: A History of the First Major Campaign of the Civil War* (Garden City, N.Y., 1977), John Hennessy, *The First Battle of Manassas: An End to Innocence, July 18–21, 1861* (Lynchburg, Va., 1989), and David Detzer, *Donnybrook: The Battle of Bull Run, 1861* (New York, 2004).

30. USG, *Letters of Ulysses S. Grant to His Father and Sister,* 48.

31. USG, *Personal Memoirs,* 131, 134–135; Conger, *Rise of U. S. Grant,* 26–29; Kenneth P. Williams, *Lincoln Finds a General: A Military Study of the Civil War,* 5 vols. (New York, 1949–1959), 3:50–51; Catton, *Grant Moves South,* 27–28.

32. OR, I, 3:452; USG, *Personal Memoirs,* 133.

33. USG, *Personal Memoirs,* 133–134; USG, *Papers of Ulysses S. Grant,* 2:124n; USG, *Letters of Ulysses S. Grant to His Father and Sister,* 54.

34. USG, *Personal Memoirs,* 134; USG, *Papers of Ulysses S. Grant,* 2:184–185. The only modern biography of Grant's opponent is James J. Monaghan, *Swamp Fox of the Confederacy: The Life and Military Services of M. Jeff Thompson* (Tuscaloosa, Ala., 1956).

35. USG, *Personal Memoirs,* 135; OR, I, 3:470; Catton, *Grant Moves South,* 25.

36. USG, General *Grant's Letters to a Friend, 1861–1880* (New York, 1897), 1–2; *OR,* I, 3:699; R. M. Kelly, "Holding Kentucky for the Union," *B&L* 1:378–379.

37. USG, *Personal Memoirs,* 135–136.

38. Ibid., 136; USG, *Papers of Ulysses S. Grant,* 2:194–195; JDG, *The Personal Memoirs of Julia Dent Grant (Mrs. Ulysses S. Grant),* ed. John Y. Simon (Carbondale, Ill., 1975), 101–102.

39. Brooks D. Simpson, *Let Us Have Peace: Ulysses S. Grant and the Politics of War and Reconstruction, 1861–1868* (Chapel Hill, N.C., 1991), 17–18; Parrish, "Frémont in Missouri," 8–9, 44–45.

40. USG, *Letters of Ulysses S. Grant to His Father and Sister,* 59.

41. Ibid., 78; USG, *Personal Memoirs,* 137.

42. USG, *Personal Memoirs,* 138.

43. Ibid., 139; *OR,* I, 3:273.

44. *OR,* I, 3:267–270; *ORN,* I, 22:399–403; USG, *Personal Memoirs,* 139–140; USG, *Letters of Ulysses S. Grant to His Father and Sister,* 64–66.

45. *OR,* I, 3:270–271; USG, *Personal Memoirs,* 140–141; Henry I. Kurtz, "The Battle of Belmont," *CWTI* 2 (June 1963): 21, 24; Williams, *Lincoln Finds a General,* 3:93–94; Conger, *Rise of U. S. Grant,* 86–95, 365–376. The most comprehensive account of Grant's first Civil War battle is Nathaniel Cheairs Hughes, *The Battle of Belmont: Grant Strikes South* (Chapel Hill, N.C., 1991).

46. *OR,* I, 3:271–272; USG, *Personal Memoirs,* 141, 143.

47. USG, *Personal Memoirs,* 141–143.

48. *OR,* I, 3:274.

49. Clarence E. Macartney, *Grant and His Generals* (New York, 1953), 79.

50. Ibid., 79–80; Albert D. Richardson, *A Personal History of Ulysses S. Grant* (Hartford, Conn., 1868), 195–196; Wilson, *Life of John A. Rawlins,* 67; Catton, *Grant Moves South,* 95–97.

51. JDG, *Personal Memoirs,* 93; Anderson and Anderson, *The Generals,* 212.

52. JDG, *Personal Memoirs,* 94; Catton, *Grant Moves South,* 105.

53. JDG, *Personal Memoirs,* 95–97.

54. USG, *Personal Memoirs,* 146; Kelly, "Holding Kentucky for the Union," 385–386.

55. USG, *Personal Memoirs,* 146; USG, *Letters of Ulysses S. Grant to His Father and Sister,* 77, 77n–78n.

56. Kelly, "Holding Kentucky for the Union," 387–392.

57. USG, *Personal Memoirs,* 147.

58. Ibid.; *OR,* I, 7:577.

59. USG, *Personal Memoirs,* 147–148.

60. Ibid., 148–149; *OR,* I, 7:122–130; *ORN,* I, 22:535–537.

61. USG, *Personal Memoirs,* 149–150; Conger, *Rise of U. S. Grant,* 158–159; Catton, *Grant Moves South,* 145; *OR,* I, 7:124; *ORN,* I, 22:537–339, 547.

CHAPTER 6

1. USG, *Personal Memoirs of U. S. Grant,* ed. E. B. Long (New York, 2001), 150–151, 153.

2. Ibid., 151–152; USG, *Papers of Ulysses S. Grant,* ed. John Y. Simon et al., 28 vols. to date (Carbondale, Ill., 1967), 5:215–216; John F. Marszalek, "'A Full Share of All the Credit': Sherman and Grant to the Fall of Vicksburg," in Steven E. Woodworth, ed., *Grant's Lieutenants: From Cairo to Vicksburg* (Lawrence, Kan., 2001): 5–9.

3. USG, *Personal Memoirs,* 152.

4. *OR,* I, 7:159, 161–162.

5. USG, *Personal Memoirs,* 153; *OR,* I, 7: 172–174; *ORN,* I, 22:590–591, 598; Benjamin F. Cooling, *Forts Henry and Donelson: The Key to the Confederate Heartland* (Knoxville, Tenn., 1987), 140–146.

6. USG, *Personal Memoirs,* 154; *OR,* I, 7: 159, 165–166; *ORN,* I, 22:584–586; Stephen E. Ambrose, "Fort Donelson a 'Disastrous' Blow to South," *CWTI* 5 (June 1966): 8.

7. USG, *Personal Memoirs,* 155–156; Cooling, *Forts Henry and Donelson,* 166–183.

8. USG, *Personal Memoirs,* 156–157; *OR,* I, 7:159, 175–180.

9. Ambrose, "Fort Donelson a 'Disastrous' Blow," 12; Cooling, *Forts Henry and Donelson,* 183–184; HG, "Donelson (2)," HG MSS, USC; Jean Edward Smith, *Grant* (New York, 2001), 157–158; William S. McFeely, *Grant* (New York, 1981), 99–100.

10. USG, *Personal Memoirs,* 157; Cooling, *Forts Henry and Donelson,* 166–169, 171–177, 179–182.

11. USG, *Personal Memoirs,* 157; Cooling, *Forts Henry and Donelson,* 185.

12. USG, *Personal Memoirs,* 157; *OR,* I, 7:159–160; Ambrose, "Fort Donelson a 'Disastrous' Blow," 13.

13. USG, *Personal Memoirs,* 157; Cooling, *Forts Henry and Donelson,* 200–207.

14. Cooling, *Forts Henry and Donelson,* 203, 207–208; Ambrose, "Fort Donelson a 'Disastrous' Blow," 13, 42; HG interview of Simon B. Buckner, n.d., HG MSS, USC.

15. *OR,* I, 7:160–161.

16. Cooling, *Forts Henry and Donelson,* 215; USG, *Papers of Ulysses S. Grant,* 4:221n–222n.

17. *OR,* I, 7:159, 625.

18. Nancy Scott Anderson and Dwight Anderson, *The Generals: Ulysses S. Grant and Robert E. Lee* (New York, 1988), 228; T. Harry Williams, *McClellan, Sherman, and Grant* (New Brunswick, N.J., 1962), 87–88; James Grant Wilson, *General Grant* (New York, 1897), 118–119.

19. USG to JDG, February 16, 1862, USG MSS, LC; USG, *General Grant's Letters to a Friend, 1861–1880* (New York, 1897), 4–5.

20. *OR,* I, 7:628; 637; Arthur L. Conger, *The Rise of U. S. Grant* (New York, 1931), 191–192.

21. USG, *Personal Memoirs,* 162.

22. Ibid., 163–164.

23. Ibid., 164.

24. Ibid., 165.

25. Ibid., 167; Bruce Catton, *Grant Moves South* (Boston, 1960), 193.

26. USG, *Personal Memoirs,* 167.

27. Catton, *Grant Moves South,* 186–187.

28. *OR,* I, 7:674, 679–680; John F. Marszalek, *Commander of All Lincoln's Armies: A Life of General Henry W. Halleck* (Cambridge, Mass., 2004), 118–119.

29. *OR*, I, 7:680.

30. Ibid., 682; USG, *Personal Memoirs,* 168.

31. *OR*, I, 10, pt. 2:15, 21; Conger, *Rise of U. S. Grant,* 211–212.

32. HG interview of John M. Thayer, n.d., HG MSS, USC; HG, *Ulysses S. Grant: His Life and Character* (New York, 1898), 198; USG, *Papers of Ulysses S. Grant,* 4:189n–190n, 343n.

33. USG, *Papers of Ulysses S. Grant,* 4:443–444; Grenville M. Dodge, *Personal Recollections of President Abraham Lincoln, General Ulysses S. Grant and General William T. Sherman* (Council Bluffs, Iowa, 1914), 37–38.

34. *OR*, I, 7:674–675; 10, pt. 2:4–5.

35. *OR*, I, 10, pt. 2:13.

36. Ibid., 17, 21, 30.

37. *OR*, I, 7:683.

38. *OR*, I, 10, pt. 2:28–29.

39. Ibid., 32.

40. USG, *Personal Memoirs,* 170; Wiley Sword, *Shiloh: Bloody April* (New York, 1974), 20–22.

41. USG, *Personal Memoirs,* 170–171; Benjamin F. Cooling, "The Reliable First Team: Grant and Charles Ferguson Smith," in Steven E. Woodworth, ed., *Grant's Lieutenants: From Cairo to Vicksburg* (Lawrence, Kan., 2001): 57–60.

42. USG, *Personal Memoirs,* 171; USG, "The Battle of Shiloh," *B&L* 1:481; William T. Sherman, *Memoirs of General William T. Sherman, by Himself,* 2 vols. (Bloomington, Ind., 1957), 1:247; Conger, *Rise of U. S. Grant,* 264–265; Larry J. Daniel, *Shiloh: The Battle That Changed the Civil War* (New York, 1997), 132; Kenneth P. Williams, *Lincoln Finds a General: A Military Study of the Civil War,* 5 vols. (New York, 1949–1959), 3:331–333.

43. USG, *Personal Memoirs,* 172–173; USG, "Battle of Shiloh," 466–468; *OR*, I, 10, pt. 1:108–109; pt. 2:95–96; Daniel, *Shiloh,* 139–141, 173–176; Geoffrey Perret, *Ulysses S. Grant, Soldier & President* (New York, 1997), 186–189.

44. USG, *Personal Memoirs,* 174; *OR*, I, 10, pt. 1:114–119, 203–205, 248–250, 278–279.

45. USG, *Personal Memoirs,* 177 and n; Daniel, *Shiloh,* 202–214; Sword, *Shiloh,* 234–256.

46. USG, *Personal Memoirs,* 177–178.

47. Daniel, *Shiloh,* 214–266; Sword, *Shiloh,* 257–382; Jean Edward Smith, *Grant* (New York, 2001), 194–200.

CHAPTER 7

1. USG, *Personal Memoirs of U. S. Grant,* ed. E. B. Long (New York, 2001), 179.

2. Ibid., 180–182.

3. Ibid., 180–181.

4. *OR*, I, 10, pt. 1:108–109, 119–121, 205–206, 251–252; pt. 2:96–97; Larry J. Daniel, *Shiloh: The Battle That Changed the Civil War* (New York, 1997), 267–292; Wiley Sword, *Shiloh: Bloody April* (New York, 1974), 383–412.

5. USG, *Personal Memoirs,* 182; Daniel, *Shiloh,* 292, 294–296; Sword, *Shiloh,* 413–417.

6. USG, *Personal Memoirs,* 184; *OR,* I, 10, pt. 2:97; Daniel, *Shiloh,* 296–297; Sword, *Shiloh,* 423–426.

7. USG to JDG, April 8, 1862, USG MSS, LC.

8. *New York Tribune,* April 16, 1862; William E. Woodward, *Meet General Grant* (New York, 1939), 255.

9. USG, *Personal Memoirs,* 194; Michael B. Ballard, *U. S. Grant: The Making of a General, 1861–1863* (Lanham, Md., 2005), 57–58; *New York Tribune,* April 17, May 3, 1862.

10. Woodward, *Meet General Grant,* 256.

11. William T. Sherman, *Home Letters of General Sherman,* ed. M. A. De-Wolfe Howe (New York, 1909), 224–225; William T. Sherman, *Memoirs of General William T. Sherman, by Himself,* 2 vols. (Bloomington, Ind., 1957), 1:246.

12. Alexander K. McClure, *Abraham Lincoln and Men of War-Times: Some Personal Recollections of War and Politics During the Lincoln Administration* (Philadelphia, 1892), 194–196. For one historian's contention that this conversation never took place, see Brooks D. Simpson, *Ulysses S. Grant: Triumph over Adversity, 1822–1865* (Boston, 2000), 136.

13. Michael Korda, *Ulysses S. Grant, the Unlikely Hero* (New York, 2004), 78; 10–12; USG, General *Grant's Letters to a Friend, 1861–1880* (New York, 1897), 10–12.

14. USG, *Papers of Ulysses S. Grant,* ed. John Y. Simon et al., 28 vols. to date (Carbondale, Ill., 1967–), 5:78–83; USG to JDG, May 11, 1862, USG MSS, LC.

15. *OR,* I, 10, pt. 2:99.

16. USG, *Personal Memoirs,* 193; USG, *Papers of Ulysses S. Grant,* 5:114–115.

17. USG, *Personal Memoirs,* 115n; *OR,* I, 10, pt. 2:182–183.

18. USG, *Personal Memoirs,* 197; Adam Badeau, *Military History of Ulysses S. Grant, from April, 1861, to April, 1865,* 3 vols. (New York, 1868–1881), 1:102; Evan Rowland Jones, *Lincoln, Stanton and Grant: Historical Sketches* (London, 1875), 204.

19. HG interview of William Wrenshall Smith, n.d., HG MSS, USC.

20. USG to JDG, May 11, 16, 20, 24, 1862, USG MSS, LC.

21. Michael Fellman, *Citizen Sherman: A Life of William Tecumseh Sherman* (New York, 1995), 116–117; Joseph T. Glatthaar, *Partners in Command: The Relationships between Leaders in the Civil War* (New York, 1994), 142.

22. *OR,* I, 10, pt. 2:288; USG, *Personal Memoirs,* 200.

23. USG, *Personal Memoirs,* 200–202; HG interview of Thomas W. Brown, n.d., HG MSS, USC.

24. HG notes on recollections of J. Preston Young, HG MSS, USC.

25. Harry J. Maihafer, *The General and the Journalists: Ulysses S. Grant, Horace Greeley, and Charles Dana* (Washington, D.C., 1998), 126–127.

26. The most readable and comprehensive account of the Peninsula Campaign is Stephen W. Sears, *To the Gates of Richmond: The Peninsula Campaign* (New York, 1992).

27. Maihafer, *General and the Journalists,* 127; Ballard, *U. S. Grant,* 92.

28. *OR,* I, 17, pt. 2:90; Kenneth P. Williams, *Lincoln Finds a General: A Military Study of the Civil War,* 5 vols. (New York, 1949–1959), 5:276–277.

29. USG, *Personal Memoirs,* 204; Ballard, *U. S. Grant,* 66; Bruce Catton, *Grant Moves South* (Boston, 1960), 286–288; *OR,* I, 12, pt. 3:435; 17, pt. 2:237, 240.

30. USG, *Personal Memoirs,* 205.

31. Thomas Lawrence Connelly, *Army of the Heartland: The Army of Tennessee, 1861–1862* (Baton Rouge, La., 1967), 177–204.

32. USG, *Personal Memoirs,* 205–207.

33. Ibid., 206–207.

34. Ibid., 207–208.

35. Clarence E. Macartney, *Grant and His Generals* (New York, 1953), 305–306.

36. USG, *Personal Memoirs,* 211.

37. The best modern-day accounts of the Antietam (Sharpsburg) Campaign are Stephen W. Sears, *Landscape Turned Red: The Battle of Antietam* (New Haven, Conn., 1893), and James V. Murfin, *The Gleam of Bayonets: The Battle of Antietam and the Maryland Campaign of 1862* (New York, 1965). For the Perryville Campaign, see Kenneth W. Noe, *Perryville: This Grand Havoc of Battle* (Lexington, Ky., 2001).

38. USG, *Personal Memoirs,* 210–214; USG, *Letters of Ulysses S. Grant to His Father and His Youngest Sister, 1857 to 1878,* ed. Jesse Grant Cramer (New York, 1912), 93–94; USG, *General Grant's Letters to a Friend,* 22. A detailed account of the battles of Iuka and Corinth may be found in Peter Cozzens, *The Darkest Days of the War: The Battles of Iuka & Corinth* (Chapel Hill, N.C., 1997).

39. USG, *Personal Memoirs,* 215–278.

40. Ibid., 217–218.

41. Ibid., 218–219; *OR,* I, 17, pt. 1:160–166.

42. Lesley J. Gordon, "'I Could Not Make Him Do As I Wished': The Failed Relationship of William S. Rosecrans and Grant," in Steven W. Woodworth, ed., *Grant's Lieutenants: From Cairo to Vicksburg* (Lawrence, Kan., 2001), 118–119; Catton, *Grant Moves South,* 317–318; Ballard, *U. S. Grant,* 75–79; Lyle W. Dorsett, "The Problem of Ulysses S. Grant's Drinking during the Civil War," *Hayes Historical Journal* 4 (Fall 1983): 46–47.

CHAPTER 8

1. *OR,* I, 17, pt. 2:259–262.

2. *ORN,* I, 18:608–611.

3. *OR,* I, 17, pt. 2:294, 296–297.

4. Ibid., 314–220; USG, *Personal Memoirs of U. S. Grant,* ed. E. B. Long (New York, 2001), 219–220, 222.

5. USG, *Papers of Ulysses S. Grant,* ed. John Y. Simon et al., 28 vols. to date (Carbondale, Ill., 1967–), 6:286n; William S. McFeely, *Grant* (New York, 1981), 123.

6. *OR,* I, 3:277; 7:170–182; 10, pt. 1:113.

7. Richard L. Kiper, *Major General John Alexander McClernand, Politician in Uniform* (Kent, Ohio, 1999), 129–131; Bruce Catton, *Grant Moves South* (Boston, 1960), 324–326.

8. *OR*, I, 17, pt. 2:282; Catton, *Grant Moves South*, 326, 522n.

9. *OR*, I, 17, pt. 2:282.

10. USG, *Personal Memoirs*, 222.

11. *OR*, I, 17, pt. 1:469; USG, *Papers of Ulysses S. Grant*, 6:288 and n.

12. James Harrison Wilson, *Under the Old Flag: Recollections of Military Operations in the War for the Union, the Spanish War, the Boxer Rebellion, etc.*, 2 vols. (New York, 1912), 1:119–132; Edward G. Longacre, *Grant's Cavalryman: The Life and Wars of General James H. Wilson* (Mechanicsburg, Pa., 1996), 56–62.

13. Wilson, *Under the Old Flag*, 1:133; James Harrison Wilson, *Life of John A. Rawlins, Lawyer, Assistant Adjutant-General, Chief of Staff, Major General of Volunteers, and Secretary of War* (New York, 1916), 99–101; HG interview of James H. Wilson, March 1897, HG MSS, USC.

14. Wilson, *Under the Old Flag*, 1:134–139; HG interview of James H. Wilson, March 1897, HG MSS, USC.

15. *OR*, I, 17, pt. 2:337; USG, *Papers of Ulysses S. Grant*, 5:238 and n–241n; 6:283 and n; John Y. Simon, "That Obnoxious Order," *CWTI* 23 (October 1984): 14–15.

16. *OR*, I, 17, pt. 2: 421–422, 424; Simon, "That Obnoxious Order," 13, 15; Kenneth P. Williams, *Lincoln Finds a General: A Military Study of the Civil War*, 5 vols. (New York, 1949–1959), 4:165–166, 178–179; Michael Korda, *Ulysses S. Grant, the Unlikely Hero* (New York, 2004), 80.

17. *OR*, I, 17, pt. 2:530.

18. Simon, "That Obnoxious Order," 17.

19. JDG, *The Personal Memoirs of Julia Dent Grant (Mrs. Ulysses S. Grant)*, ed. John Y. Simon (Carbondale, Ill., 1975), 107; Korda, *Ulysses S. Grant*, 81; Simon, "That Obnoxious Order," 15–17.

20. USG, *Personal Memoirs*, 22; USG, *Papers of Ulysses S. Grant*, 6:315 and n–317n.

21. John Eaton and Ethel O. Mason, *Grant, Lincoln, and the Freedmen: Reminiscences of the Civil War with Special Reference to the Work of the Contrabands and Freemen of the Mississippi Valley* (New York, 1907), 2–3; Catton, *Grant Moves South*, 356–357.

22. *OR*, I, 17, pt. 2:396; Catton, *Grant Moves South*, 358–359.

23. Catton, *Grant Moves South*, 359.

24. Ibid., 359–382; USG, *Papers of Ulysses S. Grant*, 6:329, 330n–31n, 456; Williams, *Lincoln Finds a General*, 4:164–165; Joseph T. Glatthaar, *Partners in Command: The Relationships Between Leaders in the Civil War* (New York, 1994), 196–198.

25. William T. Sherman, *Memoirs of General William T. Sherman, by Himself*, 2 vols. (Bloomington, Ind., 1957), 1:279; *OR*, I, 17, pt. 2:347–348.

26. Sherman, *Memoirs*, 1:279–280; Lee Kennett, *Sherman: A Soldier's Life* (New York, 2001), 188.

27. USG, *Personal Memoirs*, 222–224; Sherman, *Memoirs*, 1:281–283; USG, *Papers of Ulysses S. Grant*, 6:404, 406–407; Kennett, *Sherman*, 188.

28. USG, *Personal Memoirs*, 225.

29. Ibid.; Edward G. Longacre, *Mounted Raids of the Civil War* (South Brunswick, N.J., 1975), 46–65; JDG, *Personal Memoirs*, 105, 107; HG interview of John Hay, n.d., HG MSS, USC.

30. USG, *Personal Memoirs*, 228; Sherman, *Memoirs*, 1:285–294.

31. Sherman, *Memoirs*, 1:294–296.

32. *OR*, I, 17, pt. 2:549, 551.

33. Ibid., pt. 1:699–710, 754–759; pt. 2:552, 562; Sherman, *Memoirs*, 1:296–302.

34. *OR*, I, 17, pt. 2:553, 570–571; USG, *Personal Memoirs*, 228–229.

35. *OR*, I, 17, pt. 2:571; USG, *Personal Memoirs*, 229.

36. *OR*, I, 17, pt. 2:555; USG, *Personal Memoirs*, 229; USG, *Papers of Ulysses S. Grant*, 6:210n.

37. Kiper, *Major General John Alexander McClernand*, 180–181.

38. Ibid., 182.

39. USG, *Personal Memoirs*, 229.

40. Ibid., 230.

CHAPTER 9

1. USG, *Personal Memoirs of U. S. Grant*, ed. E. B. Long (New York, 2001), 231.

2. The most comprehensive studies of the Fredericksburg Campaign are George C. Rable, *Fredericksburg! Fredericksburg!* (Chapel Hill, N.C., 2002), and Francis Augustin O'Reilly, *The Fredericksburg Campaign: Winter War on the Rappahannock* (Baton Rouge, La., 2003). For Stones River, see Peter Cozzens, *No Better Place to Die: The Battle of Stones River* (Urbana, Ill., 1990), and James Lee McDonough, *Stones River—Bloody Winter in Tennessee* (Knoxville, Tenn., 1980).

3. USG, *Personal Memoirs*, 231; William T. Sherman, *Memoirs of General William T. Sherman, by Himself*, 2 vols. (Bloomington, Ind., 1957), 1:315–317; John F. Marszalek, "'A Full Share of All the Credit': Sherman and Grant to the Fall of Vicksburg," in Steven E. Woodworth, ed., *Grant's Lieutenants: From Cairo to Vicksburg* (Lawrence, Kan., 2001), 17–18.

4. USG, *Personal Memoirs*, 231–232.

5. Ibid., 232–233; *OR*, I, 24, pt. 1:8–9, 44–45.

6. Sylvanus Cadwallader, *Three Years with Grant, as Recalled by War Correspondent Sylvanus Cadwallader*, ed. Benjamin P. Thomas (New York, 1955), 46, 48; USG, *Personal Memoirs*, 233.

7. USG, *Personal Memoirs*, 233–234; *OR*, I, 24, pt. 1:45.

8. USG, *Personal Memoirs*, 234; *OR*, I, 24, pt. 1:45–46; James Harrison Wilson, *Under the Old Flag: Recollections of Military Operations in the War for the Union, the Spanish War, the Boxer Rebellion, etc.*, 2 vols. (New York, 1912),

1:150–152; Edward G. Longacre, *Grant's Cavalryman: The Life and Wars of General James H. Wilson* (Mechanicsburg, Pa., 1996), 68–70; Cadwallader, *Three Years with Grant*, 50–51.

9. USG, *Personal Memoirs*, 235; *OR*, I, 24, pt. 1:46; Wilson, *Under the Old Flag*, 1:152–153; Longacre, *Grant's Cavalryman*, 71–75.

10. USG, *Personal Memoirs*, 235–236; Cadwallader, *Three Years with Grant*, 51.

11. USG, *Personal Memoirs*, 236–237; Sherman, *Memoirs*, 1:306–311; Cadwallader, *Three Years with Grant*, 52.

12. HG interview of James H. Wilson, March 1897, HG MSS, USC; Wilson, *Under the Old Flag*, 1:156–160.

13. USG, *Personal Memoirs*, 240.

14. Bruce Catton, *Grant Moves South* (Boston, 1960), 388–389; Joseph T. Glatthaar, *Partners in Command: The Relationships between Leaders in the Civil War* (New York, 1994), 194. The best source on Dana's Civil War activities apart from his *Recollections of the Civil War* (New York, 1899)—which is not always reliable and must be used with care—is Harry J. Maihafer, *The General and the Journalists: Ulysses S. Grant, Horace Greeley, and Charles Dana* (Washington, D.C., 1998).

15. HG interview of M. H. Strong, n.d., HG MSS, USC; Catton, *Grant Moves South*, 389; Nancy Scott Anderson and Dwight Anderson, *The Generals: Ulysses S. Grant and Robert E. Lee* (New York, 1988), 282; Michael B. Ballard, *U. S. Grant: The Making of a General, 1861–1863* (Lanham, Md., 2005), 92. At least two persons whom Hamlin Garland interviewed while researching his biography of Grant, including the general's youngest son, claimed that by 1865 the general had come to form an unfavorable opinion of Dana: HG interview of Jesse Root Grant, n.d.; HG interview of William Wrenshall Smith, n.d.; both, HG MSS, USC.

16. Dana, *Recollections of the Civil War*, 61–62; Catton, *Grant Moves South*, 389–390.

17. JDG, *The Personal Memoirs of Julia Dent Grant (Mrs. Ulysses S. Grant)*, ed. John Y. Simon (Carbondale, Ill., 1975), 112.

18. USG, *Personal Memoirs*, 241.

19. *OR*, I, 24, pt. 1:501–502, 519–522.

20. USG, *Personal Memoirs*, 241; *ORN*, I, 24:550–554.

21. *OR*, I, 24, pt. 1: 47–48, 576–577; Sherman, *Memoirs*, 1:317–321.

22. USG, *Personal Memoirs*, 241–242, 245–252.

23. Ibid., 252–253; Stephen E. Ambrose, "Struggle for Vicksburg: The Battle & Siege That Decided the Civil War," *CWTI* 6 (July 1967): 13–14; Phillip Thomas Tucker, *The Forgotten "Stonewall of the West": Major General John Stevens Bowen* (Macon, Ga., 1997), 234–235.

24. USG, *Personal Memoirs*, 253–254; *OR*, I, 24, pt. 1:48–49, 144–146, 634–635.

25. USG, *Personal Memoirs*, 254–259.

26. Ibid., 260–261; *OR*, I, 24, pt. 1:49–51, 635–638, 752–753.

27. USG, *Personal Memoirs*, 262.

28. Joseph E. Johnston, *Narrative of Military Operations During the Civil War* (New York, 1874), 174–177; Craig L. Symonds, *Joseph E. Johnston: A Civil War Biography* (New York, 1992), 205, 207–208; *OR,* I, 24, pt. 1:50–51, 753–754.

29. USG, *Personal Memoirs*, 265.

30. *OR,* I, 24, pt. 1:260–263, 321–322; Ambrose, "Struggle for Vicksburg," 21–24.

31. USG, *Personal Memoirs*, 269–271; *OR,* I, 24, pt. 1:52–53, 148–150, 263–266, 639–640; Tucker, *Forgotten "Stonewall of the West,"* 274–283.

32. USG, *Personal Memoirs*, 271–272.

33. Ibid., 274–275; *OR,* I, 24, pt. 1:754–755; Wilson, *Under the Old Flag,* 1:177–178.

34. USG, *Personal Memoirs*, 274.

35. Ibid., 275–276; Sherman, *Memoirs,* 1:325.

36. USG, *Personal Memoirs*, 276.

37. Ibid., 276; *OR,* I, 24, pt. 1:54, 153–154, 756; Sherman, *Memoirs,* 1:324–325; James R. Arnold, *Grant Wins the War: Decision at Vicksburg* (New York, 1997), 241–245.

38. USG, *Personal Memoirs*, 276–277; *OR,* I, 24, pt. 1:54–55; David L. Wilson and John Y. Simon, eds., *Ulysses S. Grant: Essays and Documents* (Carbondale, Ill., 1981), 94–95.

39. USG, *Personal Memoirs*, 277.

40. Cadwallader, *Three Years with Grant,* 90.

41. USG, *Personal Memoirs*, 277; *OR,* I, 24, pt. 1:55–56, 154–156, 765–758; pt. 3:338–341; Arnold, *Grant Wins the War,* 248–256; Sherman, *Memoirs,* 1:326–328; Jean Edward Smith, *Grant* (New York, 2001), 252–253; William S. McFeely, *Grant* (New York, 1981), 131–132; Catton, *Grant Moves South,* 452–453; Richard L. Kiper, *Major General John Alexander McClernand, Politician in Uniform* (Kent, Ohio, 1999), 260–263, 268–269, 277, 280–281, 304.

42. *OR,* I, 24, pt. 1:37–39; Kiper, *Major General John Alexander McClernand,* 256–257, 265.

43. Wilson, *Under the Old Flag,* 1:182–183.

44. Ibid., 183.

45. Ibid.; *OR,* I, 24, pt. 1:159–166; Kiper, *Major General John Alexander Mc-Clernand,* 268–269, 271, 273, 282, 305.

46. Wilson, *Under the Old Flag,* 1:184–186.

47. Kiper, *Major General John Alexander McClernand,* 267–268, 270–271, 273, 275, 301; Ezra J. Warner, *Generals in Blue: Lives of the Union Commanders* (Baton Rouge, La., 1964), 293.

48. USG, *Personal Memoirs*, 280–282; *OR,* I, 24, pt. 3:438–441, 456–457.

49. The finest accounts of the Chancellorsville Campaign are John Bigelow, Jr., *The Campaign of Chancellorsville: A Strategic and Tactical Study* (New Haven, Conn., 1910), and Stephen W. Sears, *Chancellorsville* (Boston, 1996).

50. JDG, *Personal Memoirs,* 113.

51. Kenneth P. Williams, *Lincoln Finds a General: A Military Study of the Civil War,* 5 vols. (New York, 1949–1959), 4:330–331, 446; Cadwallader, *Three Years with Grant,* 70–72.

52. Cadwallader, *Three Years with Grant,* 102–103.

53. Ibid., 103–108.

54. Ibid., 106–107.

55. Ibid., 107–109; James Harrison Wilson diary, June 7, 1863, Wilson MSS, Historical Society of Delaware.

56. Catton, *Grant Moves South,* 463–464; Clarence E. Macartney, *Grant and His Generals* (New York, 1953), 83–85; John R. Bumgarner, *The Health of the Presidents: The 41 United States Presidents through 1993 from a Physician's Point of View* (Jefferson, N.C., 1994), 109; McFeely, *Grant,* 132–135; James Harrison Wilson, *Life of John A. Rawlins, Lawyer, Assistant Adjutant-General, Chief of Staff, Major General of Volunteers, and Secretary of War* (New York, 1916), 128–130; USG, *Personal Memoirs,* 282.

57. Dana, *Recollections of the Civil War,* 82–83; *New York Sun,* January 20, 1887.

58. Maihafer, *The General and the Journalists,* 162–163. For a passionate denial that this incident never happened, at least not as Cadwallader describes it, see Williams, *Lincoln Finds a General,* 4:402, 441–451. The most thorough and objective study of the incident—which concludes that it happened substantially as Cadwallader describes it and that a conspiracy of silence shielded Grant from the consequences of his behavior—is Dan Bauer, "The Big Bender," *CWTI* 27 (December 1988): 35–43.

CHAPTER 10

1. USG, *Personal Memoirs of U. S. Grant,* ed. E. B. Long (New York, 2001), 291–297; Phillip Thomas Tucker, *The Forgotten "Stonewall of the West": Major General John Stevens Bowen* (Macon, Ga., 1997), 303–309; USG to John C. Pemberton, July 3, 1863, Century-Civil War Collection, New York Public Library.

2. Abraham Lincoln, *Complete Works of Abraham Lincoln,* ed. John G. Nicolay and John Hay, 12 vols. (New York, 1905), 9:100–101.

3. USG, *Personal Memoirs,* 293, 297–298.

4. OR, I, 24, pt. 2: 520–542; William T. Sherman, *Memoirs of General William T. Sherman, by Himself,* 2 vols. (Bloomington, Ind., 1957), 1:331–332.

5. Ibid., 303; USG, "Chattanooga," *B&L* 3:679–680; Herman Hattaway and Archer Jones, *How the North Won: A Military History of the Civil War* (Urbana, Ill., 1983), 493–496; Joseph T. Glatthaar, *Partners in Command: The Relationships between Leaders in the Civil War* (New York, 1994), 200–201.

6. USG, *Personal Memoirs,* 303–304.

7. Ibid., 304–306; Kenneth P. Williams, *Lincoln Finds a General: A Military Study of the Civil War,* 5 vols. (New York, 1949–1959), 5:137–138; Bruce Catton, *Grant Takes Command* (Boston, 1968), 22–25.

8. David L. Wilson and John Y. Simon, eds., *Ulysses S. Grant: Essays and Documents* (Carbondale, Ill., 1981), 11; Catton, *Grant Takes Command*, 26.

9. JDG, *The Personal Memoirs of Julia Dent Grant (Mrs. Ulysses S. Grant)*, ed. John Y. Simon (Carbondale, Ill., 1975), 113, 119–121; Catton, *Grant Takes Command*, 27.

10. Lesley J. Gordon, "'I Could Not Make Him Do as I Wished': The Failed Relationship of William S. Rosecrans and Grant," in Steven W. Woodworth, ed., *Grant's Lieutenants: From Cairo to Vicksburg* (Lawrence, Kan., 2001), 123–124; *OR*, I, 23, pt. 2:7–10, 402–411.

11. The most reliable sources on the Chickamauga Campaign include Peter Cozzens, *This Terrible Sound: The Battle of Chickamauga* (Urbana, Ill., 1992), and Glenn Tucker, *Chickamauga, Bloody Battle in the West* (Indianapolis, 1961).

12. USG, *Personal Memoirs*, 307–308; JDG, *Personal Memoirs*, 123–124; USG, "Chattanooga," 681.

13. James Harrison Wilson, *Under the Old Flag: Recollections of Military Operations in the War for the Union, the Spanish War, the Boxer Rebellion, etc.*, 2 vols. (New York, 1912), 1:259–260; USG, *Personal Memoirs*, 308–309; Wilson and Simon, eds., *Ulysses S. Grant: Essays and Documents*, 95.

14. USG, *Personal Memoirs*, 309–313; JDG, *Personal Memoirs*, 124.

15. USG, *Personal Memoirs*, 313–314; Horace Porter, *Campaigning with Grant* (New York, 1897), 1–9; Wilson, *Under the Old Flag*, 1:268–276; HG interview of James H. Wilson, March 1897, HG MSS, USC.

16. USG, *Personal Memoirs*, 315–317; Ezra J. Warner, *Generals in Blue: Lives of the Union Commanders* (Baton Rouge, La., 1964), 462–463.

17. USG, *Personal Memoirs*, 349; Edward G. Longacre, "'A Perfect Ishmaelite': General 'Baldy' Smith," *CWTI* 15 (December 1976): 10–14.

18. USG, *Personal Memoirs*, 317–318; *OR*, I, 31, pt. 1:50–59, 77–78; pt. 2:27–29. Smith's own accounts of the opening of the communications line are *The Relief of the Army of the Cumberland, and the Opening of the Short Line of Communication Between Chattanooga, Tenn., and Bridgeport, Ala., in October 1863* (Wilmington, Del., 1891), and *The Re-Opening of the Tennessee River near Chattanooga, October 1863, as Related by Major General George H. Thomas and the Official Record* (Wilmington, Del., n.d.).

19. USG, *Personal Memoirs*, 318–319; *OR*, I, 31, pt. 1:477–478, 842, 844.

20. USG, *Personal Memoirs*, 319–320; USG, "Chattanooga," 690 and n.

21. Thomas Lawrence Connelly, *Autumn of Glory: The Army of Tennessee, 1862–65* (Baton Rouge, La., 1971), 259–264; Jeffry D. Wert, *General James Longstreet, the Confederacy's Most Controversial Soldier: A Biography* (New York, 1993), 338–340.

22. USG, *Personal Memoirs*, 321–322; Sherman, *Memoirs*, 1:347–361.

23. USG, *Personal Memoirs*, 326–328; J.F.C. Fuller, *The Generalship of Ulysses S. Grant* (London, 1929), 169–170.

24. USG, *Personal Memoirs*, 331–332; *OR*, I, 31, pt. 2:24, 33, 90, 188–189, 251–256.

25. USG, *Personal Memoirs*, 331–332.

26. Ibid., 333–334, 338; *OR*, I, 31, pt. 2:24, 34, 574–575; Sherman, *Memoirs*, 1:364–365; HG interview of James H. Wilson, March 1897, HG MSS, USC; Lee Kennett, *Sherman: A Soldier's Life* (New York, 2001), 214–215.

27. USG, *Personal Memoirs*, 335–336 and n, 341–342; *OR*, I, 31, pt. 2:34, 314–317; Glenn Tucker, "The Battles for Chattanooga," *CWTI* 10 (August 1971): 32.

28. USG, *Personal Memoirs*, 337–340; *OR*, I, 31, pt. 2:25, 34–35, 90–91, 189–192, 252, 257–259; William Wrenshall Smith, "Holocaust Holiday: Vacationing at Chattanooga, 1863," *CWTI* 18 (October 1979): 35–36.

29. USG, *Personal Memoirs*, 340–341; Tucker, "Battles for Chattanooga," 40–41.

30. Smith, "Holocaust Holiday," 36; Connelly, *Autumn of Glory*, 275–277.

31. Mark Mayo Boatner III, *The Civil War Dictionary* (New York, 1959), 147.

32. Sherman, *Memoirs*, 1:365–368; USG, *Personal Memoirs*, 346–348, 350n.

33. USG, *Personal Memoirs*, 350–351, 351n; JDG, *Personal Memoirs*, 128.

34. USG, *Personal Memoirs*, 354–356; J.F.C. Fuller, *The Generalship of Ulysses S. Grant* (London, 1929), 180–181; Sherman, *Memoirs*, 1:386–395; William T. Sherman, *The Sherman Letters: Correspondence Between General Sherman and Senator* [John] *Sherman from 1837 to 1891*, ed. Rachel Sherman Thorndike (New York, 1969), 221; Catton, *Grant Takes Command*, 112; Glatthaar, *Partners in Command*, 154; Hattaway and Jones, *How the North Won*, 506–511.

35. USG, *Personal Memoirs*, 356; Catton, *Grant Takes Command*, 113–114; Sherman, *Memoirs*, 1:348–349.

36. Catton, *Grant Takes Command*, 114.

37. Adam Badeau, *Military History of Ulysses S. Grant, from April, 1861, to April, 1865*, 3 vols. (New York, 1868–1881), 1:560; Albert D. Richardson, *A Personal History of Ulysses S. Grant* (Hartford, Conn., 1868), 375–376.

38. USG, *Personal Memoirs*, 357 and n–358; Catton, *Grant Takes Command*, 118–120.

39. USG, *Personal Memoirs*, 358; Cyrus Ballou Comstock, *The Diary of Cyrus B. Comstock*, ed. Merlin E. Sumner (Dayton, Ohio, 1987), 259–260; Wilson, *Under the Old Flag*, 1:325–327.

40. Comstock, *Diary*, 260; JDG, *Personal Memoirs*, 127–128.

41. Catton, *Grant Takes Command*, 124–125.

42. Richardson, *Personal History of Ulysses S. Grant*, 384–385; William M. Thayer, *From Tannery to the White House: The Life of Ulysses S. Grant, His Boyhood, Youth, Manhood and Private Life and Services* (New York, 1885), 262–263; USG, *Letters of Ulysses S. Grant to His Father and His Youngest Sister, 1857 to 1878*, ed. Jesse Grant Cramer (New York, 1912), 100–101; Daniel Ammen, *The Old Navy and the New . . . with an Appendix of Personal Letters from General Grant* (Philadelphia, 1891), 530.

43. Porter, *Campaigning with Grant*, 18–21; Noah Brooks, *Washington, D.C., in Lincoln's Time*, ed. Herbert Mitgang (Chicago, 1971), 135.

44. Catton, *Grant Takes Command,* 127; Grenville M. Dodge, *Personal Recollections of President Abraham Lincoln, General Ulysses S. Grant and General William T. Sherman* (Council Bluffs, Iowa, 1914), 67; Porter, *Campaigning with Grant,* 21–22.

45. Comstock, *Diary,* 260; USG, *Personal Memoirs,* 358; Porter, *Campaigning with Grant,* 22.

46. George Meade, *The Life and Letters of George Gordon Meade, Major-General, United States Army,* 2 vols. (New York, 1913), 2:176.

47. USG, *Personal Memoirs,* 359; Porter, *Campaigning with Grant,* 29; Theodore Lyman, *Meade's Headquarters, 1863–1865: Letters of Colonel Theodore Lyman from the Wilderness to Appomattox,* ed. George R. Agassiz (Boston, 1922), 313.

48. USG, *Personal Memoirs,* 358–359.

49. Ibid., 368; Wilson, *Under the Old Flag,* 1:358–363.

50. USG, *Personal Memoirs,* 349, 367; Freeman Cleaves, *Meade of Gettysburg* (Norman, Okla., 1960), 225, 228.

51. Edward G. Longacre, *Army of Amateurs: General Benjamin F. Butler and the Army of the James, 1863–1865* (Mechanicsburg, Pa., 1997), 33–39.

52. USG, *Personal Memoirs,* 367, 369n; *OR,* I, 33:794–795; William F. Smith, "Butler's Attack on Drewry's Bluff," *B&L* 4:206–207.

53. Henry Coppée, *Grant and His Campaigns: A Military Biography* (New York, 1866), 459–465; James Harrison Wilson, *Life of John A. Rawlins, Lawyer, Assistant Adjutant-General, Chief of Staff, Major General of Volunteers, and Secretary of War* (New York, 1916), 193–194.

54. USG, *Personal Memoirs,* 363–366, 366n–369n; *OR,* I, 33:827–828.

55. USG, *Personal Memoirs,* 360–361, 366; James Grant Wilson, *General Grant* (New York, 1897), 209–211; Sherman, *Memoirs,* 1:398–400; *OR,* I, 32, pt. 3:245–246; Glatthaar, *Partners in Command,* 156.

56. Lincoln, *Complete Works,* 9:90–91.

CHAPTER 11

1. USG, *Personal Memoirs of U. S. Grant,* ed. E. B. Long (New York, 2001), 368–370.

2. USG, *Papers of Ulysses S. Grant,* ed. John Y. Simon et al., 28 vols. to date (Carbondale, Ill., 1967–), 10:394.

3. USG, *Personal Memoirs,* 391–398.

4. Ibid., 398–402; Robert Garth Scott, *Into the Wilderness with the Army of the Potomac* (Bloomington, Ind., 1985), 9–19; Theophilus F. Rodenbough, "War-Horses," in Francis Trevelyan Miller, ed., *The Photographic History of the Civil War,* 10 vols. (New York, 1911), 296, 298 and n. Other notable works on the Wilderness are Edward Steere, *The Wilderness Campaign* (Harrisburg, Pa., 1960), and Gordon C. Rhea, *The Battle of the Wilderness, May 5–6, 1864* (Baton Rouge, La., 1994).

5. USG, *Personal Memoirs,* 402; Joseph P. Cullen, "Battle of the Wilderness," *CWTI* 10 (April 1971): 7.

6. USG, *Personal Memoirs,* 402; *OR,* I, 36, pt. 1:18, 189, 318, 539, 906; Scott, *Into the Wilderness,* 30–35; Cullen, "Battle of the Wilderness," 8–9.

7. USG, *Personal Memoirs,* 403; *OR,* I, 36, pt. 1:189, 539–540.

8. Theodore Lyman, *Meade's Headquarters, 1863–1865: Letters of Colonel Theodore Lyman from the Wilderness to Appomattox,* ed. George R. Agassiz (Boston, 1922), 91.

9. HG interview of Horatio G. Wright, n.d., HG MSS, USC.

10. Horace Porter, *Campaigning with Grant* (New York, 1897), 64.

11. Ibid., 69–70.

12. USG, *Personal Memoirs,* 403–404; *OR,* I, 36, pt. 1:319, 676–677; Cullen, "Battle of the Wilderness," 11.

13. USG, *Personal Memoirs,* 404; Scott, *Into the Wilderness,* 98–108, 212–213.

14. USG, *Personal Memoirs,* 404–406; *OR,* I, 18, pt. 1:320–321, 540, 906; Jeffry D. Wert, *General James Longstreet, the Confederacy's Most Controversial Soldier: A Biography* (New York, 1993), 381–386.

15. USG, *Personal Memoirs,* 406; *OR,* I, 36, pt. 1:190, 322, 540; Wert, *General James Longstreet,* 386–389.

16. USG, *Personal Memoirs,* 406–407; Douglas Southall Freeman, *R. E. Lee: A Biography,* 4 vols. (New York, 1934–1935), 3:294–297.

17. USG, *Personal Memoirs,* 407–408; *OR,* I, 36, pt. 1:323–324, 907.

18. Porter, *Campaigning with Grant,* 63–64.

19. HG interview of James H. Wilson, March 1897, HG MSS, USC; James Harrison Wilson, *Under the Old Flag: Recollections of Military Operations in the War for the Union, the Spanish War, the Boxer Rebellion, etc.,* 2 vols. (New York, 1912), 1:390; John R. Bumgarner, *The Health of the Presidents: The 41 United States Presidents through 1993 from a Physician's Point of View* (Jefferson, N.C., 1994), 110.

20. Wilson, *Under the Old Flag,* 1:389.

21. USG, *Personal Memoirs,* 408.

22. Ibid., 375–376, 410; William T. Sherman, *Memoirs of General William T. Sherman, by Himself,* 2 vols. (Bloomington, Ind., 1957), 2:32–33; William F. Smith, "Butler's Attack on Drewry's Bluff," *B&L* 4: 207–208.

23. USG, *Personal Memoirs,* 410–412; Edward G. Longacre, *Lincoln's Cavalrymen: A History of the Mounted Forces of the Army of the Potomac, 1861–1865* (Mechanicsburg, Pa., 2000), 261–262.

24. Longacre, *Lincoln's Cavalrymen,* 262–263; Philip H. Sheridan, *Personal Memoirs of P. H. Sheridan,* 2 vols. (New York, 1888), 1:366–367.

25. USG, *Personal Memoirs,* 377–378, 413–414, 420; HG interview of M. H. Strong, n.d., HG MSS, USC; Sheridan, *Personal Memoirs,* 1:370.

26. USG, *Personal Memoirs,* 412–413; Wilson, *Under the Old Flag,* 1:393–394; Longacre, *Lincoln's Cavalrymen,* 262.

27. USG, *Personal Memoirs,* 416–418; *OR,* I, 36, pt. 1:191, 667–669; Bruce Catton, *A Stillness at Appomattox* (Garden City, N.Y., 1953), 111–116.

28. USG, *Personal Memoirs,* 419–423; *OR,* I, 36, pt. 1:192, 335–336; Freeman, *R. E. Lee,* 3:316–320.

29. USG, *Personal Memoirs*, 422–423; Catton, *A Stillness at Appomattox*, 123–125; Joseph P. Cullen, "Spotsylvania," *CWTI* 10 (May 1971): 46–47.

30. USG, *Personal Memoirs*, 422; *OR*, I, 36, pt. 1:909–910; Freeman, *R. E. Lee*, 3:323–324; E. B. Long and Barbara Long, *The Civil War Day by Day: An Almanac, 1861–1865* (Garden City, N.Y., 1971), 500.

31. Long and Long, *Civil War Day by Day*, 500.

32. USG to JDG, May 13, 1864, USG MSS, LC.

33. USG, *Personal Memoirs*, 376–382, 425–422; *OR*, I, 36, pt. 1:192, 337–338; Smith, "Butler's Attack on Drewry's Bluff," 209–210; Sherman, *Memoirs*, 2:33–36.

34. USG, *Personal Memoirs*, 376–377; Smith, "Butler's Attack on Drewry's Bluff," 210–212; Edward G. Longacre, *Army of Amateurs: General Benjamin F. Butler and the Army of the James, 1863–1865* (Mechanicsburg, Pa., 1997), 96–100.

35. USG, *Personal Memoirs*, 426. For more on Sigel's defeat, see William C. Davis, *The Battle of New Market* (Garden City, N.Y., 1975). The only book-length source on Banks's disastrous foray up the Red River is Ludwell Johnson, *Red River Campaign: Politics and Cotton in the Civil War* (Baltimore, 1958).

36. USG, *Personal Memoirs*, 426–431.

37. Ibid., 431; *OR*, I, 36, pt. 3:113–114, 543, 612–613; Joseph P. Cullen, "When Grant Faced Lee Across the North Anna," *CWTI* 3 (February 1965): 22.

38. USG, *Personal Memoirs*, 432–437.

39. Lyman, *Meade's Headquarters*, 130; Porter, *Campaigning with Grant*, 164–165.

40. USG, *Personal Memoirs*, 439; Longacre, *Army of Amateurs*, 113–116; William F. Smith, "The Eighteenth Corps at Cold Harbor," *B&L* 4: 222–223.

41. USG, *Personal Memoirs*, 439–442; *OR*, I, 36, pt. 1:22–23, 194, 344–346, 543–544, 913–914; Smith, "Eighteenth Corps at Cold Harbor," 222–228; HG interview of Horatio G. Wright, n.d., HG MSS, USC.

42. USG, *Personal Memoirs*, 444–445. A full-length study of Grant's generalship, devoted to proving the "butcher" label inaccurate and unfair, is Edward H. Bonekemper III, *A Victor, Not a Butcher: Ulysses S. Grant's Overlooked Military Genius* (Washington, D.C., 2004).

43. USG, *Personal Memoirs*, 445.

44. USG to JDG, June 15, 1864, USG MSS, LC.

45. *OR*, I, 36, pt. 3:598–599.

46. USG, *Personal Memoirs*, 447–448.

47. Ibid., 448, 458–459; Sheridan, *Personal Memoirs*, 1:413–425. The only book devoted to the campaign that produced the largest all-cavalry battle of the war is Eric J. Wittenberg, *Glory Enough for All: Sheridan's Second Raid and the Battle of Trevilian Station* (Washington, D.C., 2001).

48. USG, *Personal Memoirs*, 452; *OR*, I, 40, pt. 1:12, 295–300; pt. 2:19, 22–31.

49. USG, *Personal Memoirs*, 449n–50n, 451, 454; *OR*, I, 40, pt. 1:303; David M. Jordan, *Winfield Scott Hancock: A Soldier's Life* (Bloomington, Ind., 1988), 141.

50. USG, *Personal Memoirs,* 451–52; *OR,* I, 36, pt. 1: 863–884; 40, pt. 1: 444, 620; David M. Jordan, *"Happiness Is Not My Companion": The Life of General G. K. Warren* (Bloomington, Ind., 2001), 162–165.

51. USG, *Personal Memoirs,* 452, 455; *OR,* I, 40, pt. 1:303–304; pt. 2:25–30; Jordan, *Winfield Scott Hancock,* 142.

52. Lyman, *Meade's Headquarters,* 166.

53. USG, *Personal Memoirs,* 454–457; *OR,* I, 40, pt. 1:705; Longacre, *Army of Amateurs,* 143–154; Jordan, *Winfield Scott Hancock,* 142–144.

54. Frank Wilkeson, *Recollections of a Private Soldier in the Army of the Potomac* (New York, 1887), 162.

55. USG, *Personal Memoirs,* 456; Pierre G. T. Beauregard, "Four Days of Battle at Petersburg," *B&L* 4: 540–544; Freeman, *R. E. Lee,* 3:407–421.

56. USG, *Personal Memoirs,* 456; *OR,* I, 40, pt. 1:12–13, 40, 167–168, 306–307, 522–523.

57. Freeman, *R. E. Lee,* 3:422–425; USG to JDG, June 19, 1864, USG MSS, LC.

Chapter 12

1. Abraham Lincoln, *Complete Works of Abraham Lincoln,* ed. John G. Nicolay and John Hay, 12 vols. (New York, 1905), 10:126; Horace Porter, *Campaigning with Grant* (New York, 1897), 216–224.

2. *New York Times,* June 28, 1864.

3. USG, *Personal Memoirs of U. S. Grant,* ed. E. B. Long (New York, 2001), 460; *OR,* I, 40, pt. 1:620–625, 730–733; pt. 2:232, 255–257, 267; James Harrison Wilson, *Under the Old Flag: Recollections of Military Operations in the War for the Union, the Spanish War, the Boxer Rebellion, etc.,* 2 vols. (New York, 1912), 1:455–482; Edward G. Longacre, *Grant's Cavalryman: The Life and Wars of General James H. Wilson* (Mechanicsburg, Pa., 1996), 134–145.

4. USG, *Personal Memoirs,* 457–458; *OR,* I, 40, pt. 1:169, 325–327.

5. Cyrus Ballou Comstock, *The Diary of Cyrus B. Comstock,* ed. Merlin E. Sumner (Dayton, Ohio, 1987), 276.

6. *OR,* I, 40, pt. 1:284; pt. 2:299–301; William Farrar Smith, *From Chattanooga to Petersburg Under Generals Grant and Butler: A Contribution to the History of the War, and a Personal Vindication* (Boston, 1893), 158, 160–162; Edward G. Longacre, *Army of Amateurs: General Benjamin F. Butler and the Army of the James, 1863–1865* (Mechanicsburg, Pa., 1997), 166–167, 175; Edward G. Longacre, "A Perfect Ishmaelite': General 'Baldy' Smith," *CWTI* 15 (December 1976): 18.

7. Smith, *From Chattanooga to Petersburg,* 52–53, 174–179; Longacre, *Army of Amateurs,* 176–178; *OR,* I, 40, pt. 2:558–559, 598; pt. 3:32; William D. Mallam, "The Grant-Butler Relationship," *Mississippi Valley Historical Review* 41 (1954): 261–262.

8. Smith, *From Chattanooga to Petersburg,* 52–53, 174–179.

9. Ibid., 43–44, 50–56; *OR*, I, 40, pt. 2:558–559, 594; pt. 3:19–20, 113–114, 334; Porter, *Campaigning with Grant*, 245–246; Longacre, *Army of Amateurs*, 178–181.

10. USG, *Personal Memoirs*, 460; Stephen W. Sears, *Chancellorsville* (Boston, 1996), 250; T. Harry Williams, *Lincoln and His Generals* (New York, 1955), 324–325.

11. James Grant Wilson, *General Grant* (New York, 1897), 344; Comstock, *Diary*, 280.

12. Harry J. Maihafer, *The General and the Journalists: Ulysses S. Grant, Horace Greeley, and Charles Dana* (Washington, D.C., 1998), 200; Geoffrey Perret, *Ulysses S. Grant, Soldier & President* (New York, 1997), 344–345.

13. USG, *Personal Memoirs*, 460–461.

14. Kenneth P. Williams, *Lincoln Finds a General: A Military Study of the Civil War*, 5 vols. (New York, 1949–1959), 5:280–281; Williams, *Lincoln and His Generals*, 325–326; Joseph T. Glatthaar, *Partners in Command: The Relationships Between Leaders in the Civil War* (New York, 1994), 211–212.

15. USG, *Personal Memoirs*, 461; Jubal A. Early, "Early's March to Washington in 1864," *B&L* 4: 492–499.

16. Clarence E. Macartney, *Grant and His Generals* (New York, 1953), 327–328; Glatthaar, *Partners in Command*, 212–213.

17. USG, *Personal Memoirs*, 469–471; Williams, *Lincoln and His Generals*, 329–334; Philip H. Sheridan, *Personal Memoirs of P. H. Sheridan*, 2 vols. (New York, 1888), 1:346–347; *OR*, I, 37, pt. 2:558, 582; 42, pt. 2:21; 43, pt. 1:40; Theodore Lyman, *Meade's Headquarters, 1863–1865: Letters of Colonel Theodore Lyman from the Wilderness to Appomattox*, ed. George R. Agassiz (Boston, 1922), 210–111; George Meade, *The Life and Letters of George Gordon Meade, Major-General, United States Army*, 2 vols. (New York, 1913), 2:218–224, 247; Freeman Cleaves, *Meade of Gettysburg* (Norman, Okla., 1960), 285–286; USG, *General Grant's Letters to a Friend, 1861–1880* (New York, 1897), 41–42.

18. USG, *Personal Memoirs*, 462, 466; Porter, *Campaigning with Grant*, 258–259; Henry Pleasants, Jr., and George Straley, *Inferno at Petersburg* (Philadelphia, 1961), 46–51; Bruce Catton, *A Stillness at Appomattox* (Garden City, N.Y., 1953), 221–224.

19. USG, *Personal Memoirs*, 462, 465, 468; Porter, *Campaigning with Grant*, 269–261; *OR*, I, 40, pt. 1:308–310, Sheridan, *Personal Memoirs*, 1:446–449; David M. Jordan, *Winfield Scott Hancock: A Soldier's Life* (Bloomington, Ind., 1988), 152–154.

20. USG, *Personal Memoirs*, 467 and n; Cleaves, *Meade of Gettysburg*, 276–277; Ezra J. Warner, *Generals in Blue: Lives of the Union Commanders* (Baton Rouge, La., 1964), 277.

21. USG, *Personal Memoirs*, 467–468; *OR*, I, 40, pt. 1:58–74; pt. 3:637–668; Pleasants and Straley, *Inferno at Petersburg*, 104–114; Catton, *A Stillness at Appomattox*, 244–252; Daniel Ammen, *The Old Navy and the New . . . with an Appendix of Personal Letters from General Grant* (Philadelphia, 1891), 531.

22. *OR*, I, 40, pt. 1:42–163; David L. Wilson and John Y. Simon, eds., *Ulysses S. Grant: Essays and Documents* (Carbondale, Ill., 1981), 106–108; *OR*, I, 40, pt. 1:17.

23. USG, *Personal Memoirs*, 471; Porter, *Campaigning with Grant*, 276–278; *OR*, I, 42, pt. 1:216–220, 637, 639; Jordan, *Winfield Scott Hancock*, 155–158.

24. USG, *Personal Memoirs*, 472–473; Meade, *Life and Letters of Meade*, 2:222; David M. Jordan, *"Happiness Is Not My Companion": The Life of General G. K. Warren* (Bloomington, Ind., 2001), 180–185.

25. USG, *General Grant's Letters to a Friend*, 39; Lincoln, *Complete Works*, 10:203–204.

26. USG, *Personal Memoirs*, 482–483; Thomas Lawrence Connelly, *Autumn of Glory: The Army of Tennessee, 1862–65* (Baton Rouge, La., 1971), 391–455; Evan Rowland Jones, *Lincoln, Stanton and Grant: Historical Sketches* (London, 1875), 272–273; William W. Hassler, "A Sunny Temper and a Warm Heart," *CWTI* 6 (November 1967): 44; Wilson and Simon, eds., *Ulysses S. Grant: Essays and Documents*, 93–94.

27. William T. Sherman, *Memoirs of General William T. Sherman, by Himself*, 2 vols. (Bloomington, Ind., 1957), 2:105–109; Connelly, *Autumn of Glory*, 456–466.

28. Comstock, *Diary*, 287.

29. USG, *Personal Memoirs*, 476; Porter, *Campaigning with Grant*, 285; *OR*, I, 43, pt. 1:17–24, 40–46.

30. USG, *Personal Memoirs*, 474–475; *OR*, I, 43, pt. 1:46–48; Comstock, *Diary*, 289; Sheridan, *Personal Memoirs*, 2:11–40; Jeffry D. Wert, *From Winchester to Cedar Creek: The Shenandoah Campaign of 1864* (Carlisle, Pa., 1987), 47–129.

31. *OR*, I, 43, pt. 1:52–54; Sheridan, *Personal Memoirs*, 2:62–99; Wert, *From Winchester to Cedar Creek*, 168–238.

32. USG, *Personal Memoirs*, 476–477; Porter, *Campaigning with Grant*, 300–302; Longacre, *Army of Amateurs*, 211–220; *OR*, I, 42, pt. 1:679–682, 795–797. The most detailed chronicle of Butler's offensive on the Northside is Richard J. Sommers, *Richmond Redeemed: The Siege at Petersburg* (Garden City, N.Y., 1981).

33. USG, *Personal Memoirs*, 477, 481; Porter, *Campaigning with Grant*, 302–304; *OR*, I, 42, pt. 1:434–443. See Sommers, *Richmond Redeemed*, for Meade's advance on the Southside as well.

34. Douglas Southall Freeman, *R. E. Lee: A Biography*, 4 vols. (New York, 1934–1935), 3:499.

35. *OR*, I, 42, pt. 3:581.

36. USG, *Personal Memoirs*, 484; *OR*, I, 39, pt. 2:355; Sherman, *Memoirs*, 2:140, 144.

37. USG, *Personal Memoirs*, 483–486, 488–490, 493–497; Porter, *Campaigning with Grant*, 287–296, 314–320; Sherman, *Memoirs*, 2:129, 140; *OR*, I, 39, pt. 2:364–365; *ORN*, I, 21:415–424.

38. JDG, *The Personal Memoirs of Julia Dent Grant (Mrs. Ulysses S. Grant)*, ed. John Y. Simon (Carbondale, Ill., 1975), 135–136; Sylvanus Cadwallader,

Three Years with Grant, as Recalled by War Correspondent Sylvanus Cadwallader, ed. Benjamin P. Thomas (New York, 1955), 119–120.

39. Rod Gragg, *Confederate Goliath: The Battle of Fort Fisher* (New York, 1991), 3–16, 25–26, 34, 242.

40. USG, *Personal Memoirs,* 506–512; *OR,* I, 46, pt. 1:394–400; Porter, *Campaigning with Grant,* 336–339, 346, 361–363, 367–70, 373, 381; Longacre, *Army of Amateurs,* 245–267. Gragg, *Confederate Goliath,* is the most comprehensive and accurate modern-day source on the Fort Fisher expeditions.

41. USG, *Personal Memoirs,* 497–499; Sherman, *Memoirs,* 2:195–231; *OR,* I, 44:9–14.

42. USG, *Personal Memoirs,* 501–502; *OR,* I, 45, pt. 1:32–37, 339–344. The most satisfying account of the Franklin-Nashville Campaign is Wiley Sword, *Embrace An Angry Wind: The Confederacy's Last Hurrah—Spring Hill, Franklin, and Nashville* (New York, 1992).

43. USG, *Personal Memoirs,* 333–335, 343–346.

44. Ibid., 505; *OR,* I, 45, pt. 1:38–46, 344–347. The best books specific to the Battle of Nashville are Stanley F. Horn, *The Decisive Battle of Nashville* (Baton Rouge, La., 1956), and James Lee McDonough, *Nashville: The Western Confederacy's Final Gamble* (Knoxville, Tenn., 2004).

45. USG, *Personal Memoirs,* 513, 515–519; Porter, *Campaigning with Grant,* 386, 388, 401; Sherman, *Memoirs,* 2:288–306; *OR,* I, 47, pt. 1:17–28; JDG, *Personal Memoirs,* 136.

46. USG, *Personal Memoirs,* 516, 519; *OR,* I, 47, pt. 1:29; 49, pt. 1:323–326, 350–370; Edward G. Longacre, *Mounted Raids of the Civil War* (South Brunswick, N.J., 1975), 304–326.

47. USG, *Personal Memoirs,* 522–23; JDG, *Personal Memoirs,* 137–138.

48. USG, *Personal Memoirs,* 523; *OR,* I, 46, pt. 2:801–802, 823–825, 1259, 1264, 1275–1276; II, 8:315; Longacre, *Army of Amateurs,* 279–280; Jeffry D. Wert, *General James Longstreet, the Confederacy's Most Controversial Soldier: A Biography* (New York, 1993), 397–398; Bernarr Cresap, *Appomattox Commander: The Story of General E. O. Ord* (San Diego, Calif., 1981), 163–167.

49. USG, *Personal Memoirs,* 523–524.

50. Ibid., 526–527, 530–531; Porter, *Campaigning with Grant,* 395–401, 412–424; Sherman, *Memoirs,* 2:324–333.

51. USG, *Personal Memoirs,* 524, 526–527; Horace Porter, "Five Forks and the Pursuit of Lee," *B&L* 4: 708.

52. USG, *Personal Memoirs,* 528–529; *OR,* I, 46, pt. 1:316–19, 322–325; Porter, *Campaigning with Grant,* 404–406.

53. USG, *Personal Memoirs,* 531–535; Porter, *Campaigning with Grant,* 426–441; *OR,* I, 46, pt. 1:675–677, 796–837, 1100–1110; Jordan, *"Happiness Is Not My Companion,"* 210–234.

54. USG, *Personal Memoirs,* 536–538; *OR,* I, 46, pt. 1:677–680, 839, 902–905, 1160–1161; Longacre, *Army of Amateurs,* 294–296.

55. Lincoln, *Complete Works,* 11:48.

56. USG, *Personal Memoirs*, 541–542; Porter, *Campaigning with Grant*, 449–452.

57. USG, *Personal Memoirs*, 543–545; Porter, *Campaigning with Grant*, 452.

58. USG, *Personal Memoirs*, 545–547; *OR*, I, 46, pt. 1:55, 604, 681–682, 840, 1107, 1180; pt. 3:510, 582; Sheridan, *Personal Memoirs*, 2:176–179.

59. USG, *Personal Memoirs*, 547–548, 550; Porter, *Campaigning with Grant*, 458–459; *OR*, I, 46, pt. 3:619.

60. USG, *Personal Memoirs*, 550–551, 553; Porter, *Campaigning with Grant*, 460–465; *OR*, I, 46, pt. 3:619, 641.

61. USG, *Personal Memoirs*, 551–552; *OR*, I, 46, pt. 1:1109.

62. *OR*, I, 46, pt. 1:1109–1110, 1162–1163.

63. USG, *Personal Memoirs*, 552–554; Porter, *Campaigning with Grant*, 462, 464, 466–467.

Bibliography

Unpublished Materials

Badeau, Adam. Papers. Firestone Library, Princeton University, Princeton, N.J.

Comstock, Cyrus B. Diary and papers. Library of Congress.

Garland, Hamlin. Papers. Doheny Library, University of Southern California, Los Angeles.

Grant, Ulysses S. Papers. Bancroft Library, University of California, Berkeley.

_____. Papers. Century-Civil War Collection. New York Public Library, New York, N.Y.

_____. Papers. Dreer and Gratz Collections, Historical Society of Pennsylvania, Philadelphia.

_____. Papers. Gilder Lehrman Collection, New York, N.Y.

_____. Papers. Henry E. Huntington Library, San Marino, Calif.

_____. Papers. Illinois State Archives, Springfield.

_____. Papers. Illinois State Historical Library, Springfield.

_____. Papers. Library of Congress.

_____. Papers. Missouri Historical Society, St. Louis.

_____. Papers. Rutherford B. Hayes Presidential Center, Fremont, Ohio.

_____. Papers. State Historical Society of Wisconsin, Madison.

_____. Papers. United States Military Academy Library, West Point, N.Y.

Meade, George Gordon. Papers. Historical Society of Pennsylvania.

Porter, Horace. Diary and papers. Library of Congress.

Sherman, William T. Papers. Library of Congress.

_____. Papers. University of Notre Dame Library, South Bend, Ind.

Smith, William Farrar. Papers. Vermont Historical Society, Montpelier.

Wilson, James H. Diaries. Historical Society of Delaware, Wilmington.

_____. Papers. Library of Congress.

Newspapers

Dayton Daily Journal
Detroit Free Press

Galena [Ill.] *Gazette*
Illinois State Journal [Springfield]
New York Herald
New York Sun
New York Times
New York Tribune
Philadelphia Inquirer

ARTICLES AND ESSAYS

Alexander, Edward Porter. "The Movement Against Petersburg." *Scribner's Magazine* 41 (1907): 180–194.

Ambrose, Stephen E. "Fort Donelson a 'Disastrous' Blow to South." *Civil War Times Illustrated* 5 (June 1966): 4–13, 42–45.

_____. "Struggle for Vicksburg: The Battle & Siege That Decided the Civil War." *Civil War Times Illustrated* 6 (July 1967): 4–63.

Ammen, Daniel. "Recollections and Letters of Grant." *North American Review* 141 (1885): 361–373.

Badeau, Adam. "General Grant." *Century Magazine* 30 (1885): 151–163.

_____. "The Mystery of Grant." *Cosmopolitan* 20 (1896): 483–492.

Bauer, Dan. "The Big Bender." *Civil War Times Illustrated* 27 (December 1988): 35–43.

Bearss, Edwin C. "The Campaigns Culminating in the Fall of Vicksburg, March 29–July 4, 1863." *Iowa Journal of History* 59 (1961): 173–180, 238–242.

_____. "The Day at Shiloh." *Register of the Kentucky Historical Society* 63 (1965): 39–69.

_____. "The Iowans at Fort Donelson: General C. F. Smith's Attack on the Confederate Right, February 12–16, 1862." *Annals of Iowa* 36 (1961–1962): 241–268, 321–343.

_____. "Sherman's Demonstration Against Snyder's Bluff." *Journal of Mississippi History* 27 (1965): 168–186.

_____. "Unconditional Surrender: The Fall of Fort Donelson." *Tennessee Historical Quarterly* 21 (1962): 47–65, 140–161.

Beauregard, Pierre G. T., "The Battle of Petersburg." *North American Review* 145 (1887): 37–77, 506–515.

_____. "Four Days of Battle at Petersburg." In Robert Underwood Johnson and Clarence Clough Buel, eds., *Battles and Leaders of the Civil War.* 4 vols. New York: Century Co., 1887–1888, 4:540–544.

_____. "The Shiloh Campaign." *North American Review* 142 (1886): 1–24, 159–194.

Becker, Carl M. "Was Grant Drinking in Mexico?" *Bulletin of the Cincinnati Historical Society* 24 (1966): 68–71.

Bemporad, Jules R. "Individual Psychotherapy." In Ira D. Glick, ed., *Treating Depression* (San Francisco: Jossey-Bass Publishers, 1995), 95–121.

Billings, Elden E., ed. "Letters end Diaries: The St. Louis Riots." *Civil War Times Illustrated* 2 (June 1963): 39–40.

Brown, D. Alexander. "Battle at Chickasaw Bluffs." *Civil War Times Illustrated* 9 (July 1970): 4–9, 44–48.

Byers, Samuel H. "Some Recollections of Grant." In *Annals of the War, Written by Leading Participants North and South* (Philadelphia: Times Publishing Co., 1879), 342–356.

Casey, Emma Dent. "When Grant Wooed and Won Julia Dent." *Sunday Magazine* 24 (January–February 1909): 178–179.

Castel, Albert. "Victory at Corinth." *Civil War Times Illustrated* 17 (October 1978): 12–22.

Catton, Bruce. "Grant and the Politicians." *American Heritage* 19 (October 1968): 32–35, 81–87.

_____. "Grant Writes Home." *American Heritage* 24 (October 1973): 92–93.

Chase, John L. "Unconditional Surrender Reconsidered." *Political Science Quarterly* 70 (1955): 258–279.

Chetlain, Augustus L. "Reminiscences of General Grant." *Magazine of History* 5 (1907): 155–165, 198–205.

Cleveland, Henry Whitney. "Grant's Military Abilities, by a Confederate Officer." *Magazine of American History* 14 (1885): 341–350.

Coffin, Charles C. "The May Campaign in Virginia." *Atlantic Monthly* 14 (1854): 124–132.

Cooling, Benjamin F. "The Reliable First Team: Grant and Charles Ferguson Smith." In Steven E. Woodworth, ed., *Grant's Lieutenants: From Cairo to Vicksburg* (Lawrence: University Press of Kansas, 2001), 43–61.

Covington, James W. "The Camp Jackson Affair." *Missouri Historical Review* 55 (1961): 197–212.

Crane, James I. "Grant as a Colonel: Conversation between Grant and His Chaplain." *McClure's Magazine* 7 (1896): 40–45.

Crawford, T. C. "General Grant's Greatest Year." *McClure's Magazine* 2 (1894): 535–543.

Cullen, Joseph P. "Battle of the Wilderness." *Civil War Times Illustrated* 10 (April 1971): 4–11, 42–47.

_____. "Spotsylvania." *Civil War Times Illustrated* 10 (May 1971): 5–9, 46–48.

_____. "When Grant Faced Lee Across the North Anna." *Civil War Times Illustrated* 3 (February 1965): 16–23.

Current, Richard N. "Let Us Have Peace: Ulysses S. Grant and the Politics of War and Reconstruction, 1861–1868." *Hayes Historical Journal* 11 (Summer 1992): 40–42.

Curtis, David. "Early Failure of a Conquering Hero." *Pacific Historian* 19 (1975): 356–362.

Daniel, Larry J. "Bruinsburg: Missed Opportunity or Postwar Rhetoric?" *Civil War History* 32 (1986): 256–267.

Deupree, J. G. "The Capture of Holly Springs, Mississippi, Dec. 16, 1862." *Publications of the Mississippi Historical Society* 4 (1901): 49–61.

Dillon, Rodney E., Jr. "Don Carlos Buell and the Union Leadership." *Lincoln Herald* 82 (1980): 363–373.

Dodge, Grenville M. "Personal Recollections of General Grant and His Campaigns in the West." *Journal of the Military Service Institution of the United States* 36 (1905): 39–61.

Dorsett, Lyle W. "The Problem of Ulysses S. Grant's Drinking During the Civil War." *Hayes Historical Journal* 4 (Fall 1983): 37–48.

Dorsheimer, William. "Frémont's Hundred Days in Missouri." *Atlantic Monthly* 9 (1862): 115–125, 247–258, 372–384.

Early, Jubal A. "Early's March to Washington in 1864." In Robert Underwood Johnson and Clarence Clough Buel, eds., *Battles and Leaders of the Civil War.* 4 vols. New York: Century Co., 1887–1888, 4:492–499.

Edwards, Elisha Gray. "Before Grant Won His Stars." *McClure's Magazine* 5 (1895): 38–44.

Fischer, LeRoy H., ed. "Grant's Letters to His Missouri Farm Tenants." *Agricultural History* 21 (1947): 26–42.

Fry, James B. "An Acquaintance with Grant." *North American Review* 141 (1885): 540–552.

Fuller, Alfred M. "Grant's Horsemanship: An Incident." *McClure's Magazine* 8 (1897): 501–503.

Garland, Hamlin. "The Early Life of Ulysses Grant." *McClure's Magazine* 8 (1897): 125–139.

_____. "The First Meeting of Lincoln and Grant." *McClure's Magazine* 9 (1897): 892–895.

_____. "Grant at the Outbreak of the War." *McClure's Magazine* 9 (1897): 601–610.

_____. "Grant at West Point: The Story of His Cadet Days." *McClure's Magazine* 8 (1897): 195–210.

_____. "Grant in a Great Campaign: The Investment and Capture of Vicksburg." *McClure's Magazine* 9 (1897): 805–811.

_____. "Grant in the Mexican War." *McClure's Magazine* 8 (1897): 366–380.

_____. "Grant's First Great Work in the War." *McClure's Magazine* 9 (1897): 721–726.

_____. "Grant's Life in Missouri." *McClure's Magazine* 8 (1897): 514–520.

_____. "Grant's Quiet Years at Northern Posts." *McClure's Magazine* 8 (1897): 402–412.

Gertz, Elmer. "Three Galena Generals." *Journal of the Illinois State Historical Society* 50 (1957): 24–35.

Gilberson, N. S. "Captain Grant's Old Post, Fort Humboldt." *Overland Monthly* n.s. 8 (1886): 22–25.

Gordon, Lesley J. "'I Could Not Make Him Do As I Wished': The Failed Relationship of William S. Rosecrans and Grant." In Steven W. Woodworth, *Grant's Lieutenants: From Cairo to Vicksburg* (Lawrence: University Press of Kansas, 2001), 109–127.

Grant, Frederick Dent. "Halleck's Injustice to Grant." *North American Review* 141 (1885): 513–522.

_____. "With Grant at Vicksburg." *Outlook* 24 (1898): 167–176.

Grant, Ulysses S. "The Battles of Shiloh." In Robert Underwood Johnson and Clarence Clough Buel, eds., *Battles and Leaders of the Civil War.* 4 vols. New York: Century Co., 1887–1888, 1:465–486.

_____. "Chattanooga." In Robert Underwood Johnson and Clarence Clough Buel, eds., *Battles and Leaders of the Civil War.* 4 vols. New York: Century Co., 1887–1888, 3:679–711.

_____. "Preparing for the Campaigns of 1864." In Robert Underwood Johnson and Clarence Clough Buel, eds., *Battles and Leaders of the Civil War.* 4 vols. New York: Century Co., 1887–1888, 4:97–117.

_____. "The Vicksburg Campaign." In Robert Underwood Johnson and Clarence Clough Buel, eds., *Battles and Leaders of the Civil War.* 4 vols. New York: Century Co., 1887–1888, 3:493–539.

Grant, Ulysses S., III. "Civil War: Fact and Fiction." *Civil War History* 2 (1956): 29–40.

Green, Anna M. "Civil War Public Opinion of General Grant." *Journal of the Illinois State Historical Society* 22 (1929): 1–64.

Harrison, Lowell. "Jackson . . . Is a Ruined Town." *Civil War Times Illustrated* 15 (February 1977):4–7, 45–47.

Hassler, William W. "A Sunny Temper and a Warm Heart." *Civil War Times Illustrated* 6 (November 1967): 36–44.

Hay, Thomas Robson. "The Battle of Chattanooga." *Georgia Historical Quarterly* 8 (1924): 121–141.

Henry, Robert Selph. "Chattanooga and the War." *Tennessee Historical Quarterly* 19 (1960): 222–230.

Holcombe, John L., and Walter L. Buttgenbach. "Fort Henry, Tennessee." *Journal of the United States Artillery* 39 (1913): 83–90.

Holzman, Robert S. "Ben Butler in the Civil War." *New England Quarterly* 30 (1957): 330–345.

Howard, Oliver Otis. "Chattanooga." *Atlantic Monthly* 38 (1876): 203–219.

Howard, Oliver Otis, and Ely S. Parker. "Some Reminiscences of Grant." *McClure's Magazine* 2 (1894): 532–535.

Hurst, T. M. "The Battle of Shiloh." *Tennessee Historical Magazine* 5 (1919): 81–96.

Johnson, Ludwell. "Civil War Military History: A Few Revisions in Need of Revising." In John T. Hubbell, ed., *Battles Lost and Won: Essays from Civil War History* (Westport, Conn.: Greenwood Press, 1975), 3–18.

Johnston, Joseph E. "Jefferson Davis and the Mississippi Campaign." *North American Review* 143 (1886): 585–598.

Jones, George R. "Joseph Russell Jones." *Lincoln Herald* 74 (1972): 41–52.

Jones, Idwal. "A Captain at Fort Humboldt." *Westways* 43 (January 1949): 67–98.

Jones, J. William. "Appomattox: The True Story of the Surrender." *Historical Magazine* 31 (1873): 235–239.

Jordan, Thomas. "The Campaign and Battle of Shiloh." *United Service* 12 (1885): 262–280, 393–410.

Keise, Thomas J. "The St. Louis Years of Ulysses S. Grant." *Gateway Heritage* 6 (Winter 1985): 10–21.

Keller, Robert H., Jr. "Ulysses S. Grant: Reality and Mystique in the Far West." *Journal of the West* 31 (1992): 68–80.

Kelly, R. M. "Holding Kentucky for the Union." In Robert Underwood Johnson and Clarence Clough Buel, eds., *Battles and Leaders of the Civil War*. 4 vols. New York: Century Co., 1887–1888, 1:373–392.

Kirkpatrick, Arthur R. "Missouri in the Early Months of the Civil War." *Missouri Historical Review* 55 (1961): 235–266.

Kurtz, Henry I. "The Battle of Belmont." *Civil War Times Illustrated* 2 (June 1963): 19–21, 24.

Lawrence, Eugene. "Grant on the Battle-Field." *Harper's Magazine* 39 (1869): 210–225.

Leslie, Leigh. "Grant and Galena." *Midland Monthly* 4 (1895):195–215.

Long, E. B. "John A. Rawlins, Staff Officer Par Excellence." *Civil War Times Illustrated* 12 (January 1974): 4–9, 43–46.

_____, ed. "Dear Julia: Two Grant Letters." *Civil War History* 1 (1955): 61–64.

Longacre, Edward G. "'A Perfect Ishmaelite': General 'Baldy' Smith." *Civil War Times Illustrated* 15 (December 1976): 10–20.

Mallam, William D. "The Grant-Butler Relationship." *Mississippi Valley Historical Review* 41 (1954): 259–276.

Marszalek, John F. "'A Full Share of All the Credit': Sherman and Grant to the Fall of Vicksburg." In Steven E. Woodworth, ed., *Grant's Lieutenants: From Cairo to Vicksburg* (Lawrence: University Press of Kansas, 2001), 5–20.

McFeely, William. "The Personal Memoirs of Ulysses S. Grant." *History Today* 12 (December 1982): 5–10.

McGhee, James E. "The Neophyte General: U. S. Grant and the Belmont Campaign." *Missouri Historical Review* 67 (1973): 465–483.

McMurry, Richard M. "Sherman's Meridian Campaign." *Civil War Times Illustrated* 14 (May 1975): 24–32.

McWhiney, Grady. "Braxton Bragg at Shiloh." *Tennessee Historical Quarterly* 21 (1962): 19–30.

"Miracle on Missionary Ridge." *American Heritage* 20 (1969): 60–73.

Moffett, Cleveland. "Grant and Lincoln in Bronze." *McClure's Magazine* 5 (1895): 419–432.

Mullen, Jay C. "The Turning of Columbus." *Register of the Kentucky Historical Society* 44 (1966): 209–255.

Myers, James E. "Lincoln and the Jews." *Midstream* 27 (1981): 26–29.

Northrop, Jack. "Richard Yates: A Personal Glimpse of the Illinois Soldiers' Friend." *Journal of the Illinois State Historical Society* 56 (1963): 121–138.

Nye, Wilbur S. "Grant—Genius or Fortune's Child?" *Civil War Times Illustrated* 4 (June 1965): 5–15, 43–44.

Parrish, William E. "Frémont in Missouri." *Civil War Times Illustrated* 17 (April 1978): 4–10, 40–45.

Porter, Horace. "Appomattox: Grant's Last Campaign." *Century Magazine* 35 (1888): 126–152.

_____."Five Forks and the Pursuit of Lee." In Robert Underwood Johnson and Clarence Clough Buel, eds., *Battles and Leaders of the Civil War.* 4 vols. New York: Century Co., 1887–1888, 4:708–722.

_____. "Lincoln and Grant." *Century Magazine* 30 (1885): 939–947.

_____. "Personal Traits of General Grant." *McClure's Magazine* 2 (1894): 507–532.

_____. "Reminiscences of General Grant." *Harper's Magazine* 71 (1885): 587–598.

Reid, Brian H. "Another Look at Grant's Crossing of the James, 1864." *Civil War History* 39 (1993): 291–316.

Rhodes, Charles D. "The Vicksburg Campaign." *Journal of the Military Service Institution of the United States* 42 (1909): 193–209.

Rice, Allen Thorndike. "Sherman on Grant." *North American Review* 142 (1886): 111–113.

Ripley, C. Peter. "Prelude to Donelson: Grant's January 1862 March into Kentucky." *Register of the Kentucky Historical Society* 68 (1970): 311–318.

Rodenbough, Theophilus F. "War-Horses." In Francis Trevelyan Miller, ed., *The Photographic History of the Civil War.* 10 vols. New York: Review of Reviews Co., 1911, 4:292–318.

Roland, Charles P. "Albert Sidney Johnston and the Loss of Forts Henry and Donelson." *Journal of Southern History* 23 (1957): 45–69.

Ropes, John Codman. "General Sherman." *Atlantic Monthly* 68 (1891): 191–204.

Rosecrans, William Starke. "The Campaign for Chattanooga." *Century Magazine* 34 (1887): 129–135.

_____. "The Mistakes of Grant." *North American Review* 141 (1885): 580–599.

Russell, Henry M. W. "The Memoirs of Ulysses S. Grant: The Rhetoric of Judgment." *Virginia Quarterly Review* 60 (1990): 189–209.

Shanks, W. F. G. "Chattanooga and How We Held It." *Harper's New Monthly Magazine* 30 (1868): 137–149.

Sharp, Thomas. "Colonel Dent of Whitehaven: The Father-in-Law of General Grant." *McClure's Magazine* 9 (1897): 667.

Sheffield, Delia. "Reminiscences of Delia B. Sheffield." *Washington Historical Quarterly* 15 (1924): 49–62.

Sherman, William T. "The Battle of Pittsburg Landing: A Letter from General Sherman." *United States Service Magazine* 3 (1865): 1–4.

_____. "The Grand Strategy of the War of the Rebellion." *Century Magazine* 35 (1888): 582–598.

"Sherman's Estimate of Grant." *Century Magazine* 70 (1905): 316–318.

Simon, John Y. "From Galena to Appomattox: Grant and Washburne." *Journal of the Illinois State Historical Society* 58 (1965): 165–189.

_____. "Grant at Belmont." *Military Affairs* 45 (1981): 161–166.

_____. "Grant at Hardscrabble." *Missouri Historical Bulletin* 35 (1979): 191–201.

_____. "The Paradox of Ulysses S. Grant." *Register of the Kentucky Historical Society* 81 (1983): 366–382.

_____. "That Obnoxious Order." *Civil War Times Illustrated* 23 (October 1984): 13–17.

Simpson, Brooks D. "'All I Want Is to Advance': Ulysses S. Grant's Early Civil War Career." *Gateway Heritage* 15 (Summer 1994): 4–19.

_____. "The Doom of Slavery: Ulysses S. Grant, War Aims, and Emancipation, 1861–1863." *Civil War History* 36 (1990): 36–56.

Smith, R. J. "Man Proposes and God Disposes: The Religious Faith of Ulysses S. Grant." *Cavalry Journal* 26 (June 2001): 12–16, 28; and (March 2004): 4–9.

Smith, William Farrar. "Butler's Attack on Drewry's Bluff." In Robert Underwood Johnson and Clarence Clough Buel, eds., *Battles and Leaders of the Civil War.* 4 vols. New York: Century Co., 1887–1888, 4:206–212.

_____. "Chattanooga: Was It Fought as Planned?" *Century Magazine* 31 (1886): 146–147.

_____. "The Eighteenth Corps at Cold Harbor." In Robert Underwood Johnson and Clarence Clough Buel, eds., *Battles and Leaders of the Civil War.* 4 vols. New York: Century Co., 1887–1888, 4:221–230.

_____. "General W. F. Smith at Petersburg." *Century Magazine* 54 (1897): 318.

_____. "In Reply to General Grant." *Century Magazine* 32 (1886): 153–159.

_____."Operations Before Fort Donelson." *Magazine of American History* 15 (1885): 20–43.

_____. "Shiloh." *Magazine of American History* 15 (1885): 292–304, 382–390, 470–482.

Smith, William Wrenshall. "Holocaust Holiday: Vacationing at Chattanooga, 1863." *Civil War Times Illustrated* 18 (October 1979): 28–40.

_____. "St. Louis in the Civil War: Camp Jackson and General D. M. Frost, its Commander." *Magazine of Western History* 11 (1890): 267–276.

Stotsenburg, John M. "The Fort Donelson Campaign." *Journal of the United States Cavalry Association* 10 (1897): 417–428.

Temple, Wayne C. "U. S. Grant in Military Service for the State of Illinois." *Lincoln Herald* 83 (1981): 705–708.

_____, ed. "A Signal Officer with Grant: The Letters of Captain Charles L. Davis." *Civil War History* 7 (1961): 428–437.

Thayer, John M. "Grant at Pilot Knob." *McClure's Magazine* 5 (1895): 433–437.

Thompson, Joseph D. "The Battle of Shiloh." *Tennessee Historical Quarterly* 17 (1958): 345–367.

Throne, Mildred, comp. "Comments on the 'Hornet's Nest,' 1862 and 1887." *Iowa Journal of History* 55 (1957): 249–274.

Trefousse, Hans L. "Civil Warriors in Memory and Memoir: Grant and Sherman Remember." *Georgia Historical Quarterly* 75 (1991): 542–556.

Treichel, James A. "Lew Wallace at Fort Donelson." *Indiana Magazine of History* 59 (1963): 3–18.

Tucker, Glenn. "The Battles for Chattanooga!" *Civil War Times Illustrated* 10 (August 1971): 4–45.

Walker, Peter F. "Command Failure: The Fall of Forts Henry and Donelson." *Tennessee Historical Quarterly* 16 (1957): 335–360.

Wallace, Harold L. "Lew Wallace's March to Shiloh Revisited." *Indiana Magazine of History* 59 (1963): 19–30.

Watrous, A. E. "Grant as His Son Saw Him: An Interview with Colonel Frederick D. Grant About His Father." *McClure's Magazine* 2 (1894): 515–542.

Welles, Gideon. "Lincoln's Triumph in 1864." *Atlantic Monthly* 41 (1878): 90–106.

Wert, Jeffry D. "One Great Regret: Cold Harbor." *Civil War Times Illustrated* 17 (1979): 23–35.

West, Richard S., Jr. "Gunboats in the Swamps: The Yazoo Pass Expedition." *Civil War History* 9 (1963): 157–166.

Westwood, Howard C. "'Grant's Role in Beginning Black Soldiery." *Illinois Historical Journal* 79 (1980): 225–38.

_____. "Ulysses S. Grant and Benjamin Butler in the Appomattox Campaign." *Illinois Historical Journal* 84 (1991): 39–54.

_____. "The Vicksburg Campaign: The Raiment of the Gods of War, May 13–14, 1863." *Journal of Mississippi History* 44 (1982): 193–216.

_____. "The Vicksburg/Port Hudson Gap—The Pincers Never Pinched." *Military Affairs* 46 (1982): 113–119.

Whitsell, Robert D. "Military and Naval Activity between Cairo and Columbus." *Register of the Kentucky Historical Society* 61 (1963): 107–121.

Williams, T. Harry. "Beauregard at Shiloh." *Civil War History* 1 (1955): 17–34.

Wilson, James Harrison. "Reminiscences of General Grant." *Century Magazine* 30 (1885): 947–954.

_____. "A Staff-Officer's Journal of the Vicksburg Campaign, April 30 to July 4, 1863." *Journal of the Military Service Institution of the United States* 43 (1908): 93–109.

Wilson, Ronald G. "Meeting at the McLean House." *American History Illustrated* 22 (September 1987): 46–49.

Zilversmit, Arthur. "Grant and the Freedmen." In Robert H. Abzug and Stephen E. Maizlish, eds., *New Perspectives on Race and Slavery in America: Essays in Honor of Kenneth M. Stampp* (Lexington: University Press of Kentucky, 1986), 128–145.

BOOKS AND PAMPHLETS

Abbott, John S. C. *The Life of General Ulysses S. Grant, Containing a Brief but Faithful Narrative of Those Military and Diplomatic Achievements. . . .* Boston: B. B. Russell, 1868.

Adamson, Hans Christian. *Rebellion in Missouri, 1861: Nathaniel Lyon and His Army of the West.* Philadelphia: Chilton Co., 1961.

Alexander, Augustus Washington. *Grant as a Soldier.* St. Louis: privately issued, 1887.

Allen, Walter. *Ulysses S. Grant.* Boston: Houghton, Mifflin & Co., 1901.

Ambrose, Stephen E. *Halleck, Lincoln's Chief of Staff.* Baton Rouge: Louisiana State University Press, 1962.

The American Civil War Book and Grant Album. Boston: William H. Allen, 1894.

Ammen, Daniel. *The Old Navy and the New . . . with an Appendix of Personal Letters from General Grant.* Philadelphia: J. B. Lippincott Co., 1891.

Anderson, Nancy Scott, and Dwight Anderson. *The Generals: Ulysses S. Grant and Robert E. Lee.* New York: Alfred A. Knopf, 1988.

Arnold, James R. *Grant Wins the War: Decision at Vicksburg.* New York: John Wiley & Sons, Inc., 1997.

Arnold, Matthew. *General Grant, by Matthew Arnold, with a Rejoinder by Mark Twain.* Edited by John Y. Simon. Carbondale, Ill.: Southern Illinois University Press, 1966.

Atkinson, Charles F. *Grant's Campaigns of 1864 and 1865: The Wilderness and Cold Harbor.* London: Hugh Rees Ltd., 1908.

Badeau, Adam. *Military History of Ulysses S. Grant, from April, 1861, to April, 1865.* 3 vols. New York: D. Appleton & Co., 1868–1881.

Balch, William R. *Life and Public Services of General Grant: Being a Complete Life of the Great Hero.* Hartford, Conn.: Ralph H. Park & Co., 1885.

Ballard, Michael B. *U. S. Grant: The Making of a General, 1861–1863.* Lanham, Md.: Rowman & Littlefield Publishers, Inc., 2005.

Baltz, Louis J., III. *The Battle of Cold Harbor, May 27–June 13, 1864.* Lynchburg, Va.: H. E. Howard, 1994.

Barnwell, Robert Woodward. *Sherman and Grant Contrasted for Historians.* N.p.: privately issued, 19—.

Battine, Cecil W. *The Crisis of the Confederacy: A History of Gettysburg and the Wilderness.* New York: Longmans Green & Co., 1905.

Bauer, K. Jack. *The Mexican War, 1846–1848.* New York: Macmillan Publishing Co., Inc., 1974.

Bearss, Edwin C. *The Campaign for Vicksburg.* 3 vols. Dayton, Ohio: Morningside, 1985–1986.

Bearss, Edwin C., and Chris Calkins. *Battle of Five Forks.* Lynchburg, Va.: H. E. Howard, 1985.

Bearss, Edwin C., and Warren Grabau. *The Battle of Jackson, May 14, 1863.* Baltimore: Gateway Press, 1981.

Bigelow, John, Jr. *The Chancellorsville Campaign: A Strategic and Tactical Study.* New Haven, Conn.: Yale University Press, 1910.

Bill, Alfred Hoyt. *Rehearsal for Conflict.* New York: Alfred A. Knopf, 1947.

Boatner, Mark Mayo, III. *The Civil War Dictionary.* New York: David McKay Co., Inc., 1959.

Bonekemper, Edward H., III. *A Victor, Not a Butcher: Ulysses S. Grant's Overlooked Military Genius.* Washington, D.C.: Regnery Publishing Co., 2004.

Bowers, John. *Chickamauga and Chattanooga: The Battles That Doomed the Confederacy.* New York: HarperCollins, 1994.

Bowery, Charles R., Jr. *Lee & Grant: Profiles in Leadership from the Battlefields of Virginia.* New York: AMACOM, 2005.

Boyd, James P. *Military and Civil Life of Gen. Ulysses S. Grant.* Philadelphia: Standard Publishing Co., 1885.

Brisbin, James S. *The Campaign Lives of Ulysses S. Grant and Schuyler Colfax.* Cincinnati: C. F. Vent, 1868.

Brooks, Noah. *Washington in Lincoln's Time.* Edited by Herbert Mitgang. Chicago: Quadrangle Books, 1971.

Brooks, William E. *Grant of Appomattox: A Study of the Man.* Indianapolis: Bobbs-Merrill Co., 1942.

Bumgarner, John R. *The Health of the Presidents: The 41 United States Presidents through 1993 from a Physician's Point of View.* Jefferson, N.C.: McFarland & Co., Inc., 1994.

Bunting, Josiah. *Ulysses S. Grant.* New York: Times Books, 2004.

Burne, Alfred H. *Lee, Grant and Sherman: A Study of Leadership in the 1864–65 Campaign.* New York: Gale & Polden, 1939.

Burr, Frank A. *A New, Original and Authentic Record of the Life and Deeds of General U. S. Grant.* Philadelphia: National Publishing Co., 1885.

Butler, Benjamin F. *Autobiography and Personal Reminiscences of Major-General Benj. F. Butler: Butler's Book.* Boston: A. M. Thayer & Co., 1892.

_____. *Private and Official Correspondence of Gen. Benjamin F. Butler during the Period of the Civil War.* Compiled by Jessie Ames Marshall. 8 vols. Norwood, Mass.: Plimpton Press, 1917.

Butterfield, Daniel. *Major-General Joseph Hooker and the Troops from the Army of the Potomac at Wauhatchie, Lookout Mountain and Chattanooga.* New York: Exchange Printing Co., 1896.

Cadwallader, Sylvanus. *Three Years with Grant, as Recalled by War Correspondent Sylvanus Cadwallader.* Edited by Benjamin P. Thomas. New York: Alfred A. Knopf, Inc., 1955.

Calkins, Chris. *The Appomattox Campaign, March 29–April 9, 1865.* Conshohocken, Pa.: Combined Books, 1997.

_____. *The Battles of Appomattox Station and Appomattox Court House, April 8–9, 1865.* Lynchburg, Va.: H. E. Howard, 1987.

_____. *Thirty-six Hours Before Appomattox, April 6 and 7, 1865.* Farmville, Va.: Farmville Herald Press, 1980.

Carpenter, John A. *Sword and Olive Branch: Oliver Otis Howard.* Pittsburgh, Pa.: University of Pittsburgh Press, 1964.

_____. *Ulysses S. Grant.* New York: Twayne Publishers, 1970.

Carter, Samuel. *The Final Fortress: The Campaign for Vicksburg, 1862–1863.* New York: St. Martin's Press, 1980.

Castel, Albert E. *General Sterling Price and the Civil War in the West.* Baton Rouge: Louisiana State University Press, 1968.

Catton, Bruce. *Grant Moves South.* Boston: Little, Brown & Co., 1960.

_____. *Grant Takes Command.* Boston: Little, Brown & Co., 1968.

_____. *A Stillness at Appomattox.* Garden City, N. Y.: Doubleday & Co., Inc., 1953.

_____. *U. S. Grant and the American Military Tradition.* Boston: Little, Brown & Co., 1954.

Cavanaugh, Michael A. *The Petersburg Campaign: The Battle of the Crater, "The Horrid Pit," June 25–August 6, 1864.* Lynchburg, Va.: H. E. Howard, 1989.

Chamberlain, Joshua Lawrence. *The Passing of the Armies: An Account of the Final Campaign of the Army of the Potomac, Based upon Personal Reminiscences of the Fifth Army Corps.* New York: G. P. Putnam's Sons, 1915.

Chetlain, Augustus L. *Recollections of Seventy Years.* Galena, Ill.: privately issued, 1899.

Childs, George W. *Recollections of General Grant.* Philadelphia: Collins, 1885.

Church, William Conant. *Ulysses S. Grant and the Period of National Preservation and Reconstruction.* New York: Garden City Publishing Co., 1926.

Cleaves, Freeman. *Meade of Gettysburg.* Norman: University of Oklahoma Press, 1960.

Coffey, David. *Sheridan's Lieutenants: Phil Sheridan, His Generals, and the Final Year of the Civil War.* Lanham, Md.: Rowman & Littlefield, 2005.

Comstock, Cyrus Ballou. *The Diary of Cyrus B. Comstock.* Edited by Merlin E. Sumner. Dayton, Ohio: Morningside House, Inc., 1987.

Conger, Arthur L. *The Rise of U. S. Grant.* New York: Century Co., 1931.

Connelly, Thomas Lawrence. *Army of the Heartland: The Army of Tennessee, 1861–1862.* Baton Rouge: Louisiana State University Press, 1967.

_____. *Autumn of Glory: The Army of Tennessee, 1862–1865.* Baton Rouge: Louisiana State University Press, 1971.

Coolidge, Louis A. *Ulysses S. Grant.* 2 vols. Boston: Houghton Mifflin Co., 1917.

Cooling, Benjamin F. *Fort Donelson's Legacy: War and Society in Kentucky and Tennessee, 1852–1863.* Knoxville: University of Tennessee Press, 1997.

_____. *Forts Henry and Donelson: The Key to the Confederate Heartland.* Knoxville: University of Tennessee Press, 1987.

Coppée, Henry. *General Thomas.* New York: D. Appleton & Co., 1893.

_____. *Grant and His Campaigns: A Military Biography.* New York: C. B. Richardson, 1866.

_____. *Life and Services of Gen. U. S. Grant.* New York: Richardson & Co., 1868.

Cox, Jacob D. *The March to the Sea, Franklin and Nashville.* New York: Charles Scribner's Sons, 1882.

Cozzens, Peter. *The Darkest Days of the War: The Battles of Iuka & Corinth.* Chapel Hill: University of North Carolina Press, 1997.

_____. *No Better Place to Die: The Battle of Stones River.* Urbana: University of Illinois Press, 1990.

_____. *The Shipwreck of Their Hopes: The Battles for Chattanooga.* Urbana: University of Illinois Press, 1994.

_____. *This Terrible Sound: The Battle of Chickamauga.* Urbana: University of Illinois Press, 1992.

Crafts, William A. *Life of Ulysses S. Grant: His Boyhood, Campaigns, and Services, Military and Civil.* Boston: Samuel Walker & Co., 1868.

Cramer, Michael J. *Ulysses S. Grant: Conversations and Unpublished Letters.* New York: Eaton & Mains, 1897.

Cresap, Bernarr. *Appomattox Commander: The Story of General E. O. Ord.* San Diego, Calif.: A. S. Barnes & Co., Inc., 1981.

Dana, Charles A. *Recollections of the Civil War.* New York: D. Appleton & Co., 1899.

Dana, Charles A., and James Harrison Wilson. *The Life of Ulysses S. Grant, General of the Armies of the United States.* Springfield, Mass.: Gurdon Bill & Co., 1868.

Daniel, Larry J. *Shiloh: The Battle That Changed the Civil War.* New York: Simon & Schuster, 1997.

Davis, Burke. *Gray Fox: Robert E. Lee and the Civil War.* New York: Rinehart & Co., 1956.

_____. *To Appomattox: Nine April Days, 1865.* New York: Rinehart & Co., 1959.

Davis, William C. *Battle at Bull Run: A History of the First Major Campaign of the Civil War.* Garden City, N.Y.: Doubleday & Co., Inc., 1977.

_____. *The Battle of New Market.* Garden City, N. Y.: Doubleday & Co., Inc., 1975.

_____. *Breckinridge, Statesman, Soldier, Symbol.* Baton Rouge: Louisiana State University Press, 1974.

Deaderick, John B. *The Truth about Shiloh.* Memphis, Tenn.: S. C. Toof & Co., 1942.

Deming, Henry C. *The Life of Ulysses S. Grant, General United States Army.* Hartford, Conn.: S. S. Scranton & Co., 1868.

Denison, Charles W. *The Tanner-Boy and How He Became Lieutenant-General.* Boston: Roberts Brothers, 1864.

Detzer, David. *Donnybrook: The Battle of Bull Run, 1861.* New York: Harcourt, Inc., 2004.

Devens, Charles. *Two Addresses Commemorative of General Grant.* Worcester, Mass.: privately issued, 1885.

Dodge, Grenville M. *Personal Recollections of President Abraham Lincoln, General Ulysses S. Grant and General William T. Sherman.* Council Bluffs, Iowa.: Monarch Printing Co., 1914.

Dowdey, Clifford. *Lee.* Boston: Little Brown & Co., 1965.

Downey, Fairfax. *Storming of the Gateway: Chattanooga, 1863.* New York: David McKay Co., Inc., 1960.

Earle, Peter. *Robert E. Lee.* New York: Saturday Review Press, 1973.

Eaton, John, and Ethel O. Mason. *Grant, Lincoln, and the Freedmen: Reminiscences of the Civil War with Special Reference to the Work of the Contrabands and Freemen of the Mississippi Valley.* New York: Longmans, Green & Co., 1907.

Eisenschiml, Otto. *The Story of Shiloh.* Chicago: Norman Press, 1946.

Ellington, Charles G. *The Trial of U. S. Grant: The Pacific Coast Years, 1852–1854.* Glendale, Calif.: Arthur H. Clark Co., 1987.

Elliott, Charles Winslow. *Winfield Scott, the Soldier and the Man.* New York: Macmillan Co., 1937.

Engle, Stephen D. *Don Carlos Buell: "Most Promising of All."* Chapel Hill, N.C.: University of North Carolina Press, 1999.

Ewing, Thomas. *Letter of the Hon. Thomas Ewing to His Excellency Benj. Stanton, Lieut. Governor of Ohio, in Answer to His Charges Against Our Generals Who Fought the Battle of Shiloh, on the 6th of April, 1862.* Columbus, Ohio: R. Nevins, 1862.

Fellman, Michael. *Citizen Sherman: A Life of William Tecumseh Sherman.* New York: Random House, 1995.

Foote, Shelby. *The Civil War: A Narrative.* 3 vols. New York: Random House, 1958–1974.

Force, Manning F. *From Fort Henry to Corinth.* New York: Charles Scribner's Sons, 1881.

———. *General Sherman.* New York: D. Appleton & Co., 1899.

Frazer, Robert W. *Forts of the West: Military Forts . . . West of the Mississippi River to 1898.* Norman, Okla.: University of Oklahoma Press, 1965.

Freeman, Douglas Southall. *Lee's Lieutenants: A Study in Command.* 3 vols. New York: Charles Scribner's Sons, 1942–44.

———. *R. E. Lee: A Biography.* 4 vols. New York: Charles Scribner's Sons, 1934–1935.

Frost, Lawrence A. *U. S. Grant Album: A Pictorial Biography of Ulysses S. Grant from Leather Clerk to the White House.* Seattle: Superior Publishing Co., 1966.

Fuller, J. F. C. *The Generalship of Ulysses S. Grant.* London: J. Murray, 1929.

Furgurson, Ernest B. *Not War But Murder: Cold Harbor, 1864.* New York: Alfred A. Knopf, 2000.

Garland, Hamlin. *Ulysses S. Grant: His Life and Character.* New York: Doubleday & McClure Co., 1898.

Glatthaar, Joseph T. *Partners in Command: The Relationships between Leaders in the Civil War.* New York: Free Press, 1994.

Goodwin, Donald. *Is Alcoholism Hereditary?* New York: Oxford University Press, 1976.

Gragg, Rod. *Confederate Goliath: The Battle of Fort Fisher.* New York: HarperCollins, 1991.

Grant, Jesse Root. *In the Days of My Father, General Grant.* New York: Harper & Brothers, 1925.

Grant, Julia Dent. *The Personal Memoirs of Julia Dent Grant (Mrs. Ulysses S. Grant).* Edited by John Y. Simon. Carbondale, Ill.: University of Southern Illinois Press, 1975.

Grant, Ulysses S. *Battle of Shiloh and Organizations Engaged.* Washington, D.C.: Government Printing Office, 1909.

———. *General Grant's Letters to a Friend, 1861–1880.* New York: Crowell, 1897.

———. *Illustrated Life, Campaigns and Public Services of Lieut. General Grant . . . with a Full History of His Life, Campaigns, and Battles, and His Orders, Reports, and Correspondence with the War Department and the President in Relation to Them.* Philadelphia: T. B. Peterson & Brothers, ca. 1865.

_____. *Letters of Ulysses S. Grant to His Father and His Youngest Sister, 1857 to 1878.* Edited by Jesse Grant Cramer. New York: G. P. Putnam's Sons, 1912.

_____. *Official Report of Lieut.-Gen. Ulysses S. Grant, Embracing a History of the Operations of the Armies of the Union from March, 1862, to the Closing Scene of the Rebellion.* New York: Beadle, ca. 1866.

_____. *The Papers of Ulysses S. Grant.* Edited by John Y. Simon et al. 28 vols. to date. Carbondale, Ill.: Southern Illinois University Press, 1967–.

_____. *Personal Memoirs of U. S. Grant.* Edited by E. B. Long. New York: Da Capo Press, 2001.

_____. *Report of Lieutenant-General U. S. Grant, of the Armies of the United States, 1864–'65.* New York: D. Appleton & Co., 1866.

Grant, Ulysses S., III. *Ulysses S. Grant, Warrior and Statesman.* New York: William Morrow & Co., 1969.

Green, Horace. *General Grant's Last Stand: A Biography.* New York: Charles Scribner's Sons, 1936.

Greene, A. Wilson. *Breaking the Backbone of the Rebellion: The Final Battles of the Petersburg Campaign.* Mason City, Iowa.: Savas Publishing Co., 2000.

Greene, Francis V. *The Mississippi.* New York: Charles Scribner's Sons, 1882.

Hamilton, James J. *The Battle of Fort Donelson.* South Brunswick, N.J.: Thomas Yoseloff, 1968.

Hartje, Robert G. *Van Dorn: The Life and Times of a Confederate General.* Nashville, Tenn.: Vanderbilt University Press, 1967.

Hatcher, Edmund N. *The Last Four Weeks of the War.* Columbus, Ohio: Co-operative Publishing Co., 1892.

Hattaway, Herman, and Archer Jones. *How the North Won: A Military History of the Civil War.* Urbana: University of Illinois Press, 1983.

Headley, Joel Tyler. *Grant and Sherman: Their Campaigns and Generals.* New York: E. B. Treat & Co., 1865.

_____. *The Life of Ulysses S. Grant, General-in-Chief, U. S. A.* New York: E. B. Treat & Co., 1868.

Headley, Phineas C. *The Life and Campaigns of Lieut.-Gen. U. S. Grant, from His Boyhood to the Surrender of Lee.* New York: Derby & Miller, 1866.

Heitman, Francis B., comp. *Historical Register and Dictionary of the United States Army.* 2 vols. Washington D.C.: Government Printing Office, 1903.

Heth, Henry. *The Memoirs of Henry Heth.* Edited by James L. Morrison, Jr. Westport, Conn.: Greenwood Press, 1974.

Hendrickson, Robert. *The Road to Appomattox.* New York: John Wiley & Sons, 1998.

Hennessy, John. *The First Battle of Manassas: An End to Innocence, July 18–21, 1861.* Lynchburg, Va.: H. E. Howard, Inc., 1989.

Hess, Earl J. *Banners in the Breeze: The Kentucky Campaign, Corinth, and Stones River.* Lincoln, Nebr.: University of Nebraska Press, 2000.

Hesseltine, William B. *Ulysses S. Grant, Politician.* New York: Dodd, Mead & Co., 1935.

Hewett, Janet B. et al., comps. *Supplement to the Official Records of the Union and Confederate Armies*. 3 pts., 99 vols. Wilmington, N.C.: Broadfoot Publishing Co., 1994–2001.

Hirshon, Stanley P. *Grenville M. Dodge, Soldier, Politician, Railroad Pioneer*. Bloomington, Ind.: Indiana University Press, 1967.

Hitchcock, Henry. *Marching with Sherman: Passages from the Letters and Campaign Diaries of Henry Hitchcock, Major and Assistant Adjutant General of Volunteers, November 1864–May 1865*. Edited by M. A. DeWolfe Howe. New Haven, Conn.: Yale University Press, 1927.

Hoehling, A. A. *Vicksburg: 47 Days of Siege*. Englewood Cliffs, N.J.: Prentice-Hall, 1969.

Horn, John. *The Petersburg Campaign, June 1864–April 1865*. Conshohocken, Pa.: Combined Books, 1993.

Horn, Stanley F. *The Decisive Battle of Nashville*. Baton Rouge: Louisiana State University Press, 1956.

Howe, M. A. DeWolfe, ed. *Beacon Biographies of Eminent Americans*. Boston: Houghton Mifflin Co., 1911.

Howe, Thomas J. *The Petersburg Campaign: Wasted Valor, June 15–18, 1864*. Lynchburg, Va.: H. E. Howard, 1988.

Howland, Edward. *Grant as a Soldier and Statesman: Being a Succinct History of His Military and Civil Career*. Hartford, Conn.: J. B. Burr & Co., 1868.

Hughes, Nathaniel Cheairs. *The Battle of Belmont: Grant Strikes South*. Chapel Hill, N.C.: University of North Carolina Press, 1991.

Humphreys, Andrew A. *The Virginia Campaign of '64 and '65: The Army of the Potomac and the Army of the James*. New York: Charles Scribner's Sons, 1883.

Hunt, Gaillard, comp. *Israel, Elihu and Cadwallader Washburn: A Chapter in American Biography*. New York: Macmillan Co., 1925.

Johnson, Ludwell. *Red River Campaign: Politics and Cotton in the Civil War*. Baltimore: Johns Hopkins University Press, 1958.

Johnson, Richard W. *Memoir of Maj.-Gen. George H. Thomas*. Philadelphia: J. B. Lippincott & Co., 1881.

Johnston, Joseph E. *Narrative of Military Operations during the Civil War*. New York: D. Appleton & Co., 1874.

Johnston, William Preston. *The Life of Gen. Albert Sidney Johnston*. New York: D. Appleton & Co., 1878.

Jones, Archer. *Confederate Strategy from Shiloh to Vicksburg*. Baton Rouge: Louisiana State University Press, 1961.

Jones, Evan Rowland. *Lincoln, Stanton and Grant: Historical Sketches*. London: F. Warne & Co., 1875.

Jones, James Pickett. *"Black Jack": John A. Logan and Southern Illinois in the Civil War*. Tallahassee: Florida State University Press, 1967.

Jordan, David M. *"Happiness Is Not My Companion": The Life of General G. K. Warren*. Bloomington, Ind.: Indiana University Press, 2001.

_____. *Winfield Scott Hancock: A Soldier's Life*. Bloomington, Ind.: Indiana University Press, 1988.

Kaltman, Al. *Cigars, Whiskey, and Winning: Leadership Lessons from General Ulysses S. Grant.* Paramus, N.J.: Prentice-Hall, 1998.

Kennett, Lee. *Sherman: A Soldier's Life.* New York: HarperCollins, 2001.

King, Charles. *The True Ulysses S. Grant.* Philadelphia: J. B. Lippincott Co., 1914.

Kiper, Richard L. *Major General John Alexander McClernand, Politician in Uniform.* Kent, Ohio: Kent State University Press, 1999.

Korda, Michael. *Ulysses S. Grant, the Unlikely Hero.* New York: Atlas Books, 2004.

Larke, Julian K. *General Grant and His Campaigns.* New York: J. C. Derby & N. C. Miller, 1864.

_____. *The Life, Campaigns, and Battles of General Ulysses S. Grant, Comprising a Full Account of the Famous Soldier from His Earliest Boyhood to the Present Time.* New York: Ledyard Bill, 1868.

Lee, Robert E., Jr. *Recollections and Letters of General Robert E. Lee, by His Son.* Garden City, N.Y.: Garden City Publishing Co., 1924.

Lender, Mark Edward, and James Kirby Martin. *Drinking in America: A History.* New York: Free Press, 1987.

Lewis, Lloyd. *Captain Sam Grant.* Boston: Little, Brown & Co., 1950.

_____. *Letters from Lloyd Lewis, Showing Steps in the Research for His Biography of U. S. Grant.* Boston: Little, Brown & Co., 1950.

_____. *Sherman, Fighting Prophet.* New York: Harcourt, Brace & Co., 1932.

The Life and Services as a Soldier of Major-General Grant, the Hero of Fort Donelson! Vicksburg! And Chattanooga! Philadelphia: T. B. Peterson Brothers, 1864.

Lincoln, Abraham. *Complete Works of Abraham Lincoln.* Edited by John G. Nicolay and John Hay. 12 vols. New York: Lamb Publishing Co., 1905.

Long, E. B., and Barbara Long. *The Civil War Day by Day: An Almanac, 1861–1865.* Garden City, N. Y.: Doubleday & Co., Inc., 1971.

Longacre, Edward G. *Army of Amateurs: General Benjamin F. Butler and the Army of the James, 1863–1865.* Mechanicsburg, Pa.: Stackpole Books, 1997.

_____. *Grant's Cavalryman: The Life and Wars of General James H. Wilson.* Mechanicsburg, Pa.: Stackpole Books, 1996.

_____. *Lincoln's Cavalrymen: A History of the Mounted Forces of the Army of the Potomac, 1861–1865.* Mechanicsburg, Pa.: Stackpole Books, 2000.

_____. *Mounted Raids of the Civil War.* South Brunswick, N. J.: A. S. Barnes & Co., Inc., 1975.

Lyman, Theodore. *Meade's Headquarters, 1863–1865: Letters of Colonel Theodore Lyman from the Wilderness to Appomattox.* Edited by George R. Agassiz. Boston: Atlantic Monthly Press, 1922.

Macartney, Clarence E. *Grant and His Generals.* New York: McBride Co., 1953.

_____. *Lincoln and His Generals.* Freeport, N.Y.: Books for Libraries Press, 1970.

Maihafer, Harry J. *The General and the Journalists: Ulysses S. Grant, Horace Greeley, and Charles Dana.* Washington, D.C.: Brassey's, Inc., 1998.

Maney, R. Wayne. *Marching to Cold Harbor: Victory and Failure, 1864.* Shippensburg, Pa.: White Mane Publishing Co., 1995.

Mansfield, Edward D. *A Popular and Authentic Life of Ulysses S. Grant.* Cincinnati: R. W. Carroll & Co., 1868.

Marshall-Cornwall, James H. *Grant as Military Commander*. New York: Van Nostrand-Reinhold, 1970.

Marszalek, John F. *Commander of All Lincoln's Armies: A Life of General Henry W. Halleck*. Cambridge, Mass.: Harvard University Press, 2004.

_____. *Sherman: A Soldier's Passion for Order*. New York: Free Press, 1993.

Marvel, William. *Lee's Last Retreat: The Flight to Appomattox*. Chapel Hill: University of North Carolina Press, 2002.

_____. *A Place Called Appomattox*. Chapel Hill: University of North Carolina Press, 2000.

Matter, William D. *If It Takes All Summer: The Battle of Spotsylvania*. Chapel Hill: University of North Carolina Press, 1988.

McClellan, Carswell. *The Personal Memoirs and Military History of U. S. Grant versus the Record of the Army of the Potomac*. Boston: Houghton, Mifflin Co., 1887.

McClure, Alexander K. *Abraham Lincoln and Men of War-Times: Some Personal Recollections of War and Politics During the Lincoln Administration*. Philadelphia: Times Publishing Co., 1892.

McClure, James B., ed. *Stories, Sketches and Speeches of General Grant, at Home and Abroad, in Peace and in War*. N.p.: privately issued, 1879.

McCormick, Robert R. *Ulysses S. Grant, the Great Soldier*. New York: D. Appleton-Century Co., 1934.

McDonough, James Lee. *Chattanooga: A Death Grip on the Confederacy*. Knoxville: University of Tennessee Press, 1984.

_____. *Nashville: The Western Confederacy's Final Gamble*. Knoxville: University of Tennessee Press, 2004.

_____. *Schofield: Union General in the Civil War and Reconstruction*. Tallahassee: Florida State University Press, 1972.

_____. *Shiloh—In Hell Before Night*. Knoxville: University of Tennessee Press, 1977.

_____. *Stones River—Bloody Winter in Tennessee*. Knoxville: University of Tennessee Press, 1980.

_____. *War in Kentucky: From Shiloh to Perryville*. Knoxville: University of Tennessee Press, 1994.

McDonough, James Lee, and James Pickett Jones. *War So Terrible: Sherman and Atlanta*. New York: W. W. Norton & Co., 1987.

McElroy, John. *The Struggle for Missouri*. Washington, D.C.: National Tribune Co., 1909.

McFeely, William S. *Grant*. New York: W. W. Norton & Co., 1981.

_____. *Ulysses S. Grant: An Album*. New York: W. W. Norton & Co., 2004.

McKee, Irving. *"Ben-Hur" Wallace: The Life of General Lew Wallace*. Berkeley: University of California Press, 1947.

McKinney, Francis F. *Education in Violence: The Life of George H. Thomas and the History of the Army of the Cumberland*. Detroit: Wayne State University Press, 1961.

McMaster, John Bach. *The Life, Memoirs, Military Career and Death of General U. S. Grant.* Philadelphia: Barclay & Co., 1885.

McMurry, Richard M. *John Bell Hood and the War for Southern Independence.* Lexington: University Press of Kentucky, 1982.

McPherson, James M. *Ordeal by Fire: The Civil War and Reconstruction.* New York: Alfred A. Knopf, 1982.

McWhiney, Grady. *Braxton Bragg and Confederate Defeat—Volume I: Field Command.* New York: Columbia University Press, 1969.

———, ed. *Grant, Lee, Lincoln and the Radicals.* Evanston, Ill.: Northwestern University Press, 1964.

Meade, George. *The Life and Letters of George Gordon Meade, Major-General, United States Army.* 2 vols. New York: Charles Scribner's Sons, 1913.

Mendelson, Jack H., and Nancy K. Mello. *Alcohol: Use and Abuse in America.* Boston: Little, Brown & Co., 1985.

Meredith, Roy, ed. *Mr. Lincoln's General, U. S. Grant: An Illustrated Autobiography.* New York: E. P. Dutton & Co., 1959.

Miers, Earl Schenck. *The General Who Marched to Hell: William Tecumseh Sherman and His March to Fame and Infamy.* New York: Alfred A. Knopf, 1951.

———. *The Last Campaign: Grant Saves the Union.* Philadelphia: J. B. Lippincott Co., 1972.

———. *The Web of Victory: Grant at Vicksburg.* New York: Alfred A. Knopf, 1955.

Miller, J. Michael. *The North Anna Campaign: "Even to Hell Itself," May 21–26, 1864.* Lynchburg, Va.: H. E. Howard, 1989.

Monaghan, James J. *Swamp Fox of the Confederacy: The Life and Military Services of M. Jeff Thompson.* Tuscaloosa, Ala.: Confederate Publishing Co., 1956.

Moran, Philip R., ed. *Ulysses S. Grant, 1822–1885: Chronology, Documents, Bibliographical Aids.* Dobbs Ferry, N.Y.: Oceana Publications, 1968.

Morris, Roy. *Sheridan: The Life and Wars of General Phil Sheridan.* New York: Crown Publishers, 1992.

Murfin, James V. *The Gleam of Bayonets: The Battle of Antietam and the Maryland Campaign of 1862.* New York: A. S. Barnes & Co., Inc., 1965.

Nichols, George Ward. *The Story of the Great March, from the Diary of a Staff Officer.* New York: Harper & Brothers, 1865.

Noe, Kenneth W. *Perryville: This Grand Havoc of Battle.* Lexington: University Press of Kentucky, 2001.

O'Bright, Alan W., and Kristen R. Marolf. *The Farm on the Gravois: Ulysses S. Grant National Historic Site, St. Louis, Missouri.* St. Louis: U. S. Grant National Historic Site, 1999.

Odell, Samuel W. *The Lives and Campaigns of Grant and Lee: A Comparison and Contrast of the Deeds and Characters of the Two Great Leaders in the Civil War.* Chicago: Star Publishing Co., 1895.

Official Records of the Union and Confederate Navies in the War of the Rebellion. 2 series, 30 vols. Washington, D.C.: Government Printing Office, 1894–1922.

Optic, Oliver [William Taylor Adams]. *Our Standard-Bearer; or, The Life of General Ulysses S. Grant: His Youth, His Manhood, His Campaigns, and His Eminent Services in the Reconstruction of the Nation His Sword Has Redeemed.* Boston: Lee & Shepard, 1868.

O'Reilly, Francis Augustin. *The Fredericksburg Campaign: Winter War on the Rappahannock.* Baton Rouge: Louisiana State University Press, 2003.

Patrick, Marsena R. *Inside Lincoln's Army: The Diary of Marsena Rudolph Patrick, Provost Marshal General, Army of the Potomac.* Edited by David S. Sparks. New York: Thomas Yoseloff & Co., 1964.

Pemberton, John C. *Pemberton, Defender of Vicksburg.* Chapel Hill: University of North Carolina Press, 1942.

Pennypacker, Isaac R. *General Meade.* New York: D. Appleton & Co., 1901.

Perret, Geoffrey. *Ulysses S. Grant, Soldier & President.* New York: Random House, 1997.

Pfanz, Donald. *The Petersburg Campaign: Abraham Lincoln at City Point, March 20–April 9, 1865.* Lynchburg, Va.: H. E. Howard, 1989.

Phelps, Charles A. *Life and Public Services of General Ulysses S. Grant from His Boyhood to the Present Time.* Boston: Lee & Shepard, 1868.

Pleasants, Henry, Jr., and George H. Straley. *Inferno at Petersburg.* Philadelphia: Chilton Book Co., 1961.

Pond, George E. *The Shenandoah Valley in 1864.* New York: Charles Scribner's Sons, 1883.

Poore, Benjamin Perley, and O. H. Tiffany. *Life of U. S. Grant.* Philadelphia: Hubbard Brothers, 1885.

Porter, Horace. *Campaigning with Grant.* New York: Century Co., 1897.

Post, James L. *Reminiscences by Personal Friends of Gen. U. S. Grant.* St. Louis: privately issued, 1904.

Priest, John M. *Nowhere to Run: The Wilderness, May 4th & 5th, 1864.* Shippensburg, Pa.: White Mane Publishing Co., 1995.

_____. *Victory Without Triumph: The Wilderness, May 6th & 7th, 1864.* Shippensburg, Pa.: White Mane Publishing Co., 1996.

Proceedings in Congress on the Occasion of the Reception and Acceptance of the Statue of General Ulysses S. Grant, Presented by the Grand Army of the Republic, May 19, 1900. Washington, D.C.: Government Printing Office, 1901.

Quinn, Brian P. *The Depression Sourcebook.* Los Angeles: Lowell House, 2000.

Rable, George C. *Fredericksburg! Fredericksburg!* Chapel Hill: University of North Carolina Press, 2002.

Reed, Samuel R. *The Vicksburg Campaign and the Battles about Chattanooga under the Command of General U. S. Grant, in 1862–63: An Historical Review.* Cincinnati: Robert Clarke & Co., 1882.

Remlap, L. T. [Loomis T. Palmer], ed. *The Life of General U. S. Grant: His Early Life, Military Achievements, and History of His Civil Administration.* San Francisco: A. Roman, 1885.

Rhea, Gordon C. *The Battle of the Wilderness, May 5–6, 1864.* Baton Rouge: Louisiana State University Press, 1994.

_____. *The Battles for Spotsylvania Court House and the Road to Yellow Tavern, May 7–12, 1864.* Baton Rouge: Louisiana State University Press, 1997.

_____. *Cold Harbor: Grant and Lee, May 26–June 3, 1864.* Baton Rouge: Louisiana State University Press, 2002.

_____. *To the North Anna River: Grant and Lee, May 13–25, 1864.* Baton Rouge: Louisiana State University Press, 2000.

Richardson, Albert D. *A Personal History of Ulysses S. Grant.* Hartford, Conn.: American Publishing Co., 1868.

Ringwalt, John L. *Anecdotes of General Ulysses S. Grant, Illustrating His Military and Political Career and Personal Traits.* Philadelphia: J. B. Lippincott Co., 1886.

Rodenbough, Theophilus F., comp. *From Everglade to Cañyon with the Second United States Dragoons.* New York: D. Van Nostrand, 1875.

Rodenbough, Theophilus F., and William A. Haskin, eds. *The Army of the United States: Historical Sketches of Staff and Line.* New York: Merrill & Co., 1896.

Rodick, Burleigh Cushing. *Appomattox, The Last Campaign.* New York: Philosophical Library, 1965.

Roland, Charles. *Albert Sidney Johnston, Soldier of Three Republics.* Austin, Tex.: University of Texas Press, 1964.

Roman, Alfred. *The Military Operations of General Beauregard in the War between the States.* 2 vols. New York: Harper & Brothers, 1884.

Ross, Ishbel. *The General's Wife: The Life of Mrs. Ulysses S. Grant.* New York: Dodd, Meade Co., 1959.

Sanborn, Margaret. *Robert E. Lee, the Complete Man, 1861–1870.* Philadelphia: J. B. Lippincott Co., 1967.

Schaff, Morris. *The Battle of the Wilderness.* Boston: Houghton, Mifflin Co., 1910.

_____. *The Sunset of the Confederacy.* Boston: J. W. Luce & Co., 1912.

Schofield, John M. *Forty-six Years in the Army.* New York: Century Co., 1897.

Scott, William Garth. *Into the Wilderness with the Army of the Potomac.* Bloomington, Ind.: Indiana University Press, 1985.

Sears, Stephen W. *Chancellorsville.* Boston: Houghton Mifflin Co., 1996.

_____. *Landscape Turned Red: The Battle of Antietam.* New Haven, Conn.: Ticknor & Fields, 1983.

_____. *To the Gates of Richmond: The Peninsula Campaign.* New York: Ticknor & Fields, 1992.

Shalhope, Robert E. *Sterling Price: Portrait of a Southerner.* Columbia, Mo.: University of Missouri Press, 1971.

Sheridan, Philip H. *Personal Memoirs of P. H. Sheridan, General, United States Army.* 2 vols. New York: Charles L. Webster & Co., 1888.

Sherman, William T. *General Sherman's Official Account of His Great March through Georgia and the Carolinas, from His Departure from Chattanooga to the Surrender of General Joseph E. Johnston.* New York: Bruce & Huntington, 1865.

_____. *Home Letters of General Sherman.* Edited by M. A. DeWolfe Howe. New York: Charles Scribner's Sons, 1909.

_____. *Memoirs of General William T. Sherman, by Himself.* 2 vols. Bloomington, Ind.: Indiana University Press, 1957.

_____. *The Sherman Letters: Correspondence between General Sherman and Senator [John] Sherman from 1837 to 1891.* Edited by Rachel Sherman Thorndike. New York: Da Capo Press, 1969.

_____. *Sherman's Civil War: Selected Correspondence of William T. Sherman, 1860–1865.* Edited by Brooks D. Simpson and Jean V. Berlin. Chapel Hill, N.C.: University of North Carolina Press, 1999.

Simon, John Y. *Grant and Halleck: Contrasts in Command.* Milwaukee, Wisc.: Marquette University Press, 1996.

Simpson, Brooks D. *Let Us Have Peace: Ulysses S. Grant and the Politics of War and Reconstruction, 1861–1868.* Chapel Hill: University of North Carolina Press, 1991.

_____. *Ulysses S. Grant: Triumph over Adversity, 1822–1865.* Boston: Houghton Mifflin Co., 2000.

Singletary, Otis A. *The Mexican War.* Chicago: University of Chicago Press, 1960.

Sketches of the Lives and Services of Ulysses S. Grant and Schuyler Colfax, National Republican Candidates for President and Vice President of the United States. Washington, D.C.: Chronicle Printing Co., 1868.

Smith, Gene. *Lee and Grant: A Dual Biography.* New York: McGraw-Hill, 1984.

Smith, Jean Edward. *Grant.* New York: Simon & Schuster, 2001.

Smith, Nicholas. *Grant, the Man of Mystery.* Milwaukee: Young Churchman Co., 1909.

Smith, William Farrar. *Autobiography of Major General William F. Smith.* Dayton, Ohio: Morningside, 1990.

_____. *From Chattanooga to Petersburg Under Generals Grant and Butler: A Contribution to the History of the War, and a Personal Vindication.* Boston: Houghton, Mifflin & Co., 1893.

_____. *The Relief of the Army of the Cumberland, and the Opening of the Short Line of Communication Between Chattanooga, Tenn., and Bridgeport, Ala., in October 1863.* Wilmington, Del.: C. F. Thomas & Co., 1891.

_____, comp. *The Re-opening of the Tennessee River near Chattanooga, October 1863, as Related by Major General George H. Thomas and the Official Record.* Wilmington, Del.: Mercantile Printing Co., n.d.

Snead, Thomas L. *The Fight for Missouri, from the Election of Lincoln to the Death of Lyon.* New York: Charles Scribner's Sons, 1886.

Sommers, Richard J. *Richmond Redeemed: The Siege at Petersburg.* Garden City, N.Y.: Doubleday & Co., Inc., 1981.

Spruill, Matt. *Storming the Heights: A Guide to the Battle of Chattanooga.* Knoxville: University of Tennessee Press, 2003.

Stackpole, Edward J. *Sheridan in the Shenandoah: Jubal Early's Nemesis.* Harrisburg, Pa.: Stackpole Books, 1961.

Stansfield, F.W.H. *The Life of Gen'l U. S. Grant, the General in Chief of the United States Army.* New York: T. R. Dawley, 1864.

Steere, Edward. *The Wilderness Campaign.* Harrisburg, Pa.: Stackpole Books, 1960.

Stern, Philip Van Doren. *An End to Valor: The Last Days of the Civil War.* Boston: Houghton Mifflin Co., 1958.

Stickles, Arndt M. *Simon Bolivar Buckner, Borderland Knight.* Chapel Hill: University of North Carolina Press, 1940.

Swift, John Lindsay. *About Grant.* Boston: Lee & Shepard, 1880.

Sword, Wiley. *Embrace An Angry Wind: The Confederacy's Last Hurrah—Spring Hill, Franklin, and Nashville.* New York: HarperCollins, 1992.

_____. *Shiloh: Bloody April.* New York: William Morrow & Co., Inc., 1974.

Symonds, Craig L. *Joseph E. Johnston: A Civil War Biography.* New York: W. W. Norton & Co., 1992.

Thayer, William M. *From Tannery to the White House: The Life of Ulysses S. Grant, His Boyhood, Youth, Manhood and Private Life and Services.* New York: Hurst, 1885.

Thomas, Benjamin P. *Abraham Lincoln: A Biography.* New York: Alfred A. Knopf, 1952.

Thomas, Benjamin P., and Harold M. Hyman. *Stanton: The Life and Times of Lincoln's Secretary of War.* New York: Alfred A. Knopf, 1962.

Thomas, Wilbur D. *General George H. Thomas, the Indomitable Warrior: A Biography.* New York: Exposition Press, 1964.

_____. *General James "Pete" Longstreet, Lee's "Old War Horse," Scapegoat for Gettysburg.* Parsons, W.Va.: McClain Printing Co., 1979.

Todd, Helen. *A Man Named Grant.* Boston: Houghton Mifflin Co., 1940.

Trudeau, Noah Andre. *Bloody Roads South: The Wilderness to Cold Harbor, May–June 1864.* Boston: Little, Brown & Co., 1989.

_____. *The Last Citadel: Petersburg, Virginia, June 1864–April 1865.* Boston: Little, Brown & Co., 1991.

_____. *Out of the Storm: The End of the Civil War, April–June 1865.* Boston: Little, Brown & Co., 1994.

Tucker, Glenn. *Chickamauga, Bloody Battle in the West.* Indianapolis: Bobbs-Merrill Co., Inc., 1961.

Tucker, Phillip Thomas. *The Forgotten "Stonewall of the West": Major General John Stevens Bowen.* Macon, Ga.: Mercer University Press, 1997.

Van Horne, Thomas B. *The Life of Major-General George H. Thomas.* New York: Charles Scribner's Sons, 1882.

Van Orden, William H. *Life and Military Services of General U. S. Grant.* New York: Street & Smith, 1896.

Walker, Peter. *Vicksburg: A People at War, 1860–1865.* Chapel Hill: University of North Carolina Press, 1960.

Walsh, George. *"Whip the Rebellion": Ulysses S. Grant's Rise to Command.* New York: Forge Books, 2005.

Walters, John Bennett. *Merchant of Terror: General Sherman and Total War.* Indianapolis: Bobbs-Merrill Co., Inc., 1973.

Warner, Ezra J. *Generals in Blue: Lives of the Union Commanders.* Baton Rouge: Louisiana State University Press, 1964.

_____. *Generals in Gray: Lives of the Confederate Commanders.* Baton Rouge: Louisiana State University Press, 1959.

The War of the Rebellion: A Compilation of the Official Records of the Union and Confederate Armies. 4 series, 70 vols. in 128. Washington, D.C.: Government Printing Office, 1880–1901.

Welles, Gideon. *Diary of Gideon Welles.* Edited by Howard K. Beale. 3 vols. New York: W. W. Norton & Co., Inc., 1960.

Wert, Jeffry D. *From Winchester to Cedar Creek: The Shenandoah Campaign of 1864.* Carlisle, Pa.: South Mountain Press, Inc., 1987.

_____. *General James Longstreet, the Confederacy's Most Controversial Soldier: A Biography.* New York: Simon & Schuster, 1993.

Wheeler, Richard. *The Siege of Vicksburg.* New York: Thomas Y. Crowell, 1978.

Wigger, John H. *Taking Heaven by Storm: Methodism and the Rise of Popular Christianity in America.* New York: Oxford University Press, 1998.

Wilkeson, Frank. *Recollections of a Private Soldier in the Army of the Potomac.* New York: G. P. Putnam's Sons, 1887.

Williams, Kenneth P. *Lincoln Finds a General: A Military Study of the Civil War.* 5 vols. New York: Macmillan Co., 1949–1959.

Williams, T. Harry. *Lincoln and His Generals.* New York: Alfred A. Knopf, 1952.

_____. *McClellan, Sherman, and Grant.* New Brunswick, N.J.: Rutgers University Press, 1962.

Wilson, David L., and John Y. Simon, eds. *Ulysses S. Grant: Essays and Documents.* Carbondale, Ill.: Southern Illinois University Press, 1981.

Wilson, James Grant. *General Grant.* New York: D. Appleton & Co., 1897.

_____. *The Life and Campaigns of Ulysses Simpson Grant . . . Comprising a Full and Authentic Account of the Illustrious Soldier from His Earliest Boyhood to the Present Time.* New York: Robert M. DeWitt, 1868.

Wilson, James Harrison. *The Life of Charles A. Dana.* New York: Harper & Brothers, 1907.

_____. *The Life of John A. Rawlins, Lawyer, Assistant Adjutant-General, Chief of Staff, Major General of Volunteers, and Secretary of War.* New York: Neale Publishing Co., 1916.

_____. *Under the Old Flag: Recollections of Military Operations in the War for the Union, the Spanish War, the Boxer Rebellion, etc.* 2 vols. New York: D. Appleton & Co., 1912.

Winik, Jay. *April 1865: The Month That Saved America.* New York: HarperCollins, 2001.

Wister, Owen. *Ulysses S. Grant.* Boston: Small, Maynard & Co., 1900.

Wittenberg, Eric J. *Glory Enough for All: Sheridan's Second Raid and the Battle of Trevilian Station.* Washington, D.C.: Brassey's Inc., 2001.

Wolpert, Lewis. *Malignant Sadness: The Anatomy of Depression.* New York: Free Press, 1999.

Woodward, William E. *Meet General Grant.* New York: Sun Dial Press, Inc., 1939.

Woodworth, Steven E. *Six Armies in Tennessee: The Chickamauga and Chattanooga Campaigns.* Lincoln: University of Nebraska Press, 1998.

Worthington, Thomas. *Shiloh; or, The Tennessee Campaign of 1862: Written Especially for the Army of the Tennessee.* Washington, D.C.: McGill & Witherow, 1872.

Young, John Russell. *Around the World with General Grant: A Narrative of the Visit of General U. S. Grant, Ex-President of the United States, to Various Countries in Europe, Asia, and Africa, in 1877, 1878, 1879.* 2 vols. New York: American News Co., 1879.

INDEX